THE PEOPLE'S

DOCTOR

GEORGE HATEM
AND CHINA'S
REVOLUTION

Edgar A. Porter

UNIVERSITY OF HAWAI'I PRESS

HONOLULU

02 01 00 99 98 97   5 4 3 2 1

Library of Congress Cataloging-in-Publication Data
Porter, Edgar A.
  The people's doctor : George Hatem and China's revolution / Edgar
A. Porter.
    p. cm.
  Includes index.
  ISBN 0–8248–1840–7 (cloth : alk. paper). — ISBN 0–8248–1905–5
(paper : alk. paper)
  1. Hatem, George, 1910–   . 2. Physicians—China—Biography.
3. China—History—20th century.   I. Title.
R604.H37P67 1997
951.05'092—dc20
[B]   96–34018
                                                        CIP

University of Hawai'i Press books are printed on acid-free paper and meet the
guidelines for permanence and durability of the Council on Library Resources.

Book design by Paula Newcomb

This book is dedicated to my sons Ron, Patrick, and Michael

The test of a Party member's loyalty to the Party, the revolution and the cause of communism is whether or not he can subordinate his personal interests absolutely and unconditionally to the interests of the Party, whatever the circumstances.

Liu Shaoqi, *How to Be a Good Communist*

Bring quickly the best robe, and put it on him: and put a ring on his hand, and shoes on his feet; and bring the fatted calf and kill it, and let us eat and make merry; for this my son was dead, and is alive again; he was lost, and is found.

Luke 15:22–24

Writing this biography has allowed me the opportunity to meet with a rich cross-section of Americans and Chinese who knew George Hatem as a colleague, friend, or family member. After beginning to research Hatem's life it became clear that some in China were suspicious of an American wandering about, asking detailed questions of a man they universally admired. It was only after two years of research that the Chinese door opened to me, and for this I want to thank Gu Wenfu, Xiong Lei, and Zhao Hong at Xinhua News Agency. They introduced me to Ambassadors Huang Hua, Han Xu (deceased), and Ling Qing and to Madam Wang Guangmei, Chair of the Chinese People's Political Consultative Congress and widow of former President Liu Shaoqi, all old friends and comrades of George Hatem. After others discovered that government leaders of this stature met with me, interviews with them followed quickly and easily.

John Colling, a long-time friend of George Hatem, provided an important introduction to Hatem's wife, Su Fei, who welcomed me to her home, where she spent several days answering my questions and sharing stories. She also allowed me the opportunity to read through her husband's personal papers. The combination of her detailed description of Dr. Hatem's life and access to his letters and other documents proved crucial to the completion of the biography. I am indebted to Su Fei for her support and for her gracious hospitality.

On the American side, the Hatem families in Raleigh, North Carolina, and Buffalo, New York, welcomed me into their homes and kindly shared their memories and family documents. In Raleigh I am especially grateful to Greg Hatem for his support. I will never forget the day he handed me a box of letters to and from his uncle Shag dating from the 1920s through the 1980s. He also shared pictures and introduced me to family members and friends. Greg's brothers Joe Pat and Mickey and his mother, Marie, joined Greg in supporting me in my research, and to all the North Carolina Hatems I remain appreciative. In Buffalo, the families of Theresa Hatem Ode, Ernie Hatem, and Martha Hatem Hashem also provided insights and encouragement.

Several colleagues at the University of Hawai'i assisted in various stages of this book. Of special note are Willa Tanabe, Dean of the School of Hawaiian, Asian, and Pacific Studies, Roger Ames, Director of the Center for Chinese Studies, George Simson, of the Center for Biographical Research, and Frank Tang, professor in the Department of American Studies. Others at the University of Hawai'i who supported this effort are Daniel Kwok, Chair of the Freedom Forum Asian Studies Fellowship Program for Journalists and Mark Jurgensmeyer, former Dean of the School of Hawaiian, Asian, and Pacific Studies. Several people read all or part of the original manuscript, making valuable suggestions about the text. They include Dawn Anderson, Paul Rausch, Allan Awaya, Deborah Sharkey, Denise Sugiyama, Tian Chenshan, Du Xiaoya, and Robert Valliant. I am especially grateful to Joel Bradshaw for his editorial suggestions and Rikki Scollard for her early encouragement. Travel grants received from the University of Hawai'i Matsunaga Institute for Peace and the Office of Research Relations were crucial in gathering data in the early stages of research.

Outside the university several people offered suggestions on the research and writing of this book. Of special mention are Sun Yizhi, Israel Epstein, Bob Dye, Peggy Porter, Mark Shlacter, and Giovanni Murator, who discovered and shared with me materials on George Hatem's medical school experiences in Geneva. I am especially appreciative for the assistance provided by Marilyn Burlingame, Senior Achives Specialist at the University of Missouri-Kansas City responsible for the Edgar Snow Papers. To all of those in China and the United States who granted me interviews I am especially grateful.

Finally, I want to thank my wife Ran Ying and my three sons Michael, Patrick, and Ron for their encouragement and patience. It is to the boys that this book is dedicated.

During his lifetime, Shafick George Hatem would be identified as a Jew, a Muslim, a Turk, an American, a New Zealander, a Russian, a Lebanese, an Iranian, a Uighur, and a Canadian. His family called him Shafick, some friends called him Shag, others called him George, and people throughout the world called him Dr. Ma. Raised in the Maronite Catholic Church in the United States, he died surrounded by his Communist comrades in China. He changed his name, his religion, his politics, and his nationality when it suited him. Or, more to the point, when it suited China's Communist party, for this American-born son of immigrants, never rooted to any land but comfortable in many, adopted China and its Communist party in his mid twenties and showed absolute allegiance to them both for the rest of his life.

In 1934, at age twenty-four, Hatem transported underground Party members around Shanghai. In 1936, he joined the Red Army at the end of the Long March. In 1937, he became the first Westerner to join the Chinese Communist party. He entered Beijing with the People's Liberation Army in 1949 as part of the conquering Communist force and soon afterward became the first foreigner granted Chinese citizenship in the People's Republic. He led the way in China's struggle against venereal disease and leprosy and joined the political struggles of modern China up until his death in 1988.

As a youth, Hatem was recognized as an intelligent yet unruly boy. His family loved and nourished him but eventually sent him away to reform school, then to a surrogate family thousands of miles from home. Hatem studied for a medical career, not because he wanted to, but only to fulfill the wishes of his parents. As a college student, he was selfish, traveling around the world at his family's expense while misleading them with frequent hollow promises that he would return to them soon. He constantly pleaded for money. Yet after moving to China in his early twenties, this same carefree young man ultimately broke from his self-indulgent lifestyle to submerge himself in a dangerous political movement demanding uncompromising discipline and forbearance. This is the story of both men. It shows how one evolved into the other through a mix of historical circumstance, blind luck, and humanitarian ideals.

Few, if any, foreigners have come as close to seeing China as intimately as Shafick George Hatem/Ma Haide without also losing the ability to integrate back into their own culture with the ease he displayed. Few, if any, foreigners have been accepted into Chinese society as readily and appreciatively as he was. Certainly none have had such intimate access to some of the most powerful figures of twentieth-century China as Hatem did. His story stands alone in the history of modern China.

THE PEOPLE'S DOCTOR

Dr. Sun yat Sen, as the leader of the "Juokmoun Jow Foke Houn Hou," which in English means "Down with the Manchus," in a speech in the Chinese Theatre in New York last April, predicted the success of the Chinese revolution.

New York Times, October 15, 1911

Shafick George Hatem was born in America but raised in the tradition of the Maronite Catholics of Lebanon, a people isolated from their Islamic neighbors by their religious heritage and steeped in a hard life close to the soil.[1] Above Beirut lies the Shuf Mountain village of Hamana, a Maronite stronghold whose roots date to the eighth century. In 1902, a Lebanese labor contractor working for American textile manufacturers entered Hamana looking for strong young men to work the mills of Lawrence, Massachusetts. He promised free room and board in return for five years of labor. When the contract expired, the young immigrants could seek regular wages in the mill or look for other employment. One man who accepted this offer was George Hatem's father, twenty-six-year-old Nahoum Salaama Hatem.

Nahoum worked three years in the mills, then escaped the rest of his five-year contract by joining the U.S. Army in the summer of 1905. However, he did not remain a soldier for long. By September he was discharged from his regiment in Ohio for a medical disability.[2] He returned to his work in the mills and contemplated his prospects. American friends encouraged him to find an American girlfriend, but his difficulty with the English language, his cultural ties to his homeland, and family expectations in his home village all pulled him back to Lebanon. In the spring of 1909, seven years after leaving his family, Nahoum returned to his home village of Hamana to find "an Arabian wife."[3]

Because he was related to so many in his home village, Nahoum visited surrounding villages to find a suitable mate. It was not long before he met Thamam Joseph in nearby Bahannes. She was two years younger than he and without marriage prospects. Both families approved of the match, and within a few weeks the young couple married. A few days later, they sailed for America to establish their new family.[4]

After arriving in Lawrence, they moved to Buffalo, New York, where Nahoum found work in the steel mills. The family grew quickly. Their first child, Shafick George Hatem (nicknamed "Shag") was born on September 26, 1910. Shafia followed in 1912, Freda in 1914, and Joseph in 1915. The young children soon had aunts and uncles to help look after them, with the arrival from Lebanon of Thamam's two sisters and Nahoum's brother George. In 1915 George married Thamam's sister Zmurad. Two brothers had married two sisters, and for the next two generations these two families would act as one.

About the time young Hatem reached his first birthday in late 1911, Sun Yat-sen, soon to be hailed the father of modern China, was crisscrossing the United States raising money for his anti-Manchu Revolutionary Alliance. Passing through Denver, Colorado, on his way to Kansas City, Missouri, he read in the local newspaper that an uprising against the Qing dynasty was under way in China. He hurried to Europe, and from there returned to Shanghai, arriving on Christmas Day 1911. On January 1, 1912, he was named provisional president of the newly formed Chinese Republic. China had changed forever, and its new leaders called on the people of China to take their destiny into their own hands and throw off the rule of foreigners and warlords.[5]

Shag and his brother, two sisters, and cousins experienced a childhood familiar to immigrants in American industrial towns during the early years of the twentieth century. Their neighbors were from diverse backgrounds—Lebanese, Italian, African American, and others—but all were poor. Clothes were rarely new, and shoes were usually worn through. Still, there was security in the family and Church and comfort in knowing that the community would assist those in need.[6] And there was always the hope that, with education, the children could rise above poverty and bring the rest of the family along with them. Shag's father was typical: "Moderately literate in Arabic, for many years he didn't know much English. But like so many immigrant parents at that time, he was determined to give his own kids an education—as a way out of the hard workers' life."[7] In his later years Shag told his closest friend Rewi Alley that his parents "wanted their kids to have a security they had never had, and they thought we could find it in the professions. There was not much incentive to become a steel worker like my father. Apart from the wretched and often dangerous labor, in those days a steel worker on strike might be shot down in cold blood by company police! Poor parents were more than willing to tighten their belts if there could be any chance, any way that one of their boys could be a doctor, lawyer, or accountant."[8] Shag's family, he realized early in life, expected him to prepare for a medical career.

As the Hatem family was struggling to establish itself in 1913, the new graduates of Wesleyan College for Women in Macon, Georgia, were sitting for their portraits. One of the graduates was twenty-year-old Song Qingling, daughter of a reform-minded Methodist minister in China who sent his daughters to the United States for a Western Christian education. Known to her close friends in college as Suzi, this future Chinese revolutionary and mentor to many of its Western and Chinese supporters served her school as literary editor of the college newspaper and as secretary of the Literary Society. In 1911, hearing of the successful revolution led by Sun Yat-sen, she climbed on a chair to pull down the Qing dynasty dragon flag on her wall, replacing it with the new flag of the Republic that her father had sent her. In front of her surprised American classmates, she threw the old banner on the floor, kicked at it, and exclaimed, "Down with the dragon! Up with the flag of the Republic!" Within a few months she would write an essay for her school paper entitled "The Greatest Event of the Twentieth Century," extolling the "emancipation of 400 million souls" and calling the event "this wonderful revolution." Song Qingling planned from that day forward to throw herself into the revolution supported by her father and led by Sun Yat-sen, who would become her husband.[9] Over the nearly ninety years of her extraordinary life, she set an example for millions who supported China's revolution. Three-year-old Hatem would later become one of the most dedicated recruits to her lifelong struggle.

From his earliest years, Shag learned the pain and embarrassment of being poor. When Shag was four years old, the workers in his father's factory went on strike. His father joined, not out of political conviction, but because "everyone else did." Finally, after weeks of no income, he drifted away from the strike and worked for a while as a carpenter. His cousin Theresa recalled that, during the strike, "Shag knew hunger."[10]

When young Shag started school at the Maronite Catholic St. John Maron's School in 1916, his father bought him a pair of used boots. Neither father nor son realized they were for girls. After being laughed at for his ignorance, but not wanting to anger or humiliate his father, Shag took to removing the boots before entering the schoolhouse. His sister Shafia was his accomplice, hiding the boots during the day.[11]

A medical crisis threatened the family in 1918 when the great influenza epidemic swept through Buffalo. The entire family was bedridden, so no money came in for weeks. Friends from the Church and community brought in baskets of food. When this ran out, pickles that Shag's mother had put up for the winter kept them going until they all recovered. In later years, Shag spoke frequently of these childhood experiences as shaping his political consciousness and steering him toward revolutionary struggles.

Following the bout with influenza, the Hatem family moved to neighboring Lackawanna, New York, where Nahoum began a new job with Bethlehem Steel. Shag enrolled in Public School Number Three (later named Roosevelt School), but he did not take well to the move. By his own admission, he was an undisciplined child and often in trouble at school. His father was frequently called to the principal's office to discuss the boy's unruly behavior.[12] The family always put a positive slant on this, saying he misbehaved because school failed to challenge him. Nonetheless, his parents were eventually forced to consider serious disciplinary measures. When Shag was eleven years old they enrolled him in a local orphanage that also served as a reform school. This school for "special" children in the Buffalo area was run by a stern and feared Catholic priest named Father Baker. In these harsher surroundings, Shag spent mornings in the classroom and afternoons as an apprentice in the school print shop. He hated it, saying, "Kids couldn't really be kids in such a place. When you first came the older boys would start setting you up to fight the others, one by one. That made your status, who you could beat and who you couldn't. That's where I learned to fight. At the end of a year my Dad took me out after I told him, 'If you don't, I'll run away because they beat you there all the time.' "[13]

While young Hatem was dodging the blows of his classmates and schoolmaster at the Catholic reform school, a seemingly insignificant event was taking place in steamy Shanghai, halfway around the world. In July 1921, thirteen delegates from throughout China, representing about sixty members of the Chinese Communist party, met secretly on the top floor of a girls' school in the French Concession to hold the first plenary session of their fledgling Party. Spooked by strangers lurking around the building, they quickly dispersed, only to reconvene aboard a boat on a nearby lake. The delegate from Hunan Province was a young propagandist and activist named Mao Zedong. He was twenty-eight years old and not yet a major player in the Party leadership. This small, clandestine meeting was the founding congress of the Chinese Communist party.[14]

In the years following World War I, Shag's father sought to improve the family's livelihood by turning to sales. He serviced a route between Buffalo and the southeastern United States, connecting with other Maronite immigrants in that part of the country. In 1923 he sent Shag to live with J. R. Abiunis, a demanding and authoritarian Maronite shopkeeper in Greenville, North Carolina, who hailed from the same Lebanese village as the Hatems.[15] Abiunis was not offering charity. Instead, Shag remembered him as one who "undertook to send me to high school there if I worked in his general store evenings and Sundays. A stern Maronite, he had several kids like me doing cleaning, cooking, housekeeping—everything. So I never had a chance to play in my teens—basketball, baseball, football or anything. Each day was: school—store—homework. If we played about after school, we were scolded or beaten. In high school I was a good student because there was nothing else I could do, and ended up as valedictorian of my class."[16]

In 1923 membership in the Chinese Communist party increased to about 300. Though still in its formative stages, the Party found enough basic principals in common with the Nationalist party that it proposed a united front against the warlords of northern China and the armed forces of foreign governments and businesses alike. In October, at the request of Sun Yat-sen, Lenin sent his Comintern agent Mikhail Borodin to advise the Nationalists as Sun contemplated an alliance with the Communists. Both parties agreed that it was in their own interest to unite, and they established a joint military academy on the island of Huangpu, ten miles outside Guangzhou (Canton). The first commandant was Chiang Kaishek, a young follower of Sun's who had recently returned from Moscow where he had studied military organization. The director of the political department was Zhou Enlai, recently returned from a study tour of France. While abroad Zhou studied Marxism and joined both the French and the Chinese Communist parties. This was the first united front between the Nationalists and the Communists. One of those who came to Guangzhou that year to attend the Third Congress of the Communist party, where the decision was made to join in the united front, was Mao Zedong, still more than 10 years away from assuming leadership of the Communist party.[17]

Living in the South, away from the protection of an immigrant neighborhood and shared community values, Shag encountered alien political and cultural practices. In Greenville he witnessed the harsh reality of racial segregation and later admitted to participating in it. In 1963, while reflecting on his own political education there, he remembered "but not proudly—we children trying to ape the adults by insisting on our right to the sidewalk when we met Negro children on their way to their segregated, one-room school. Then there are memories of Saturday night beatings of Negroes by the cops, the usual stories of so-called rape followed by real lynchings."[18]

Even while mimicking the racist behavior of the adults in Greenville, Shag knew that, as an outsider in the community, he also was subject to a degree of segregation. "In my North Carolina boyhood I knew discrimination—racial and religious" he remembered. "Against the blacks it was open, against us more veiled. We immigrant kids were regarded as foreigners, Catholics, black-haired people or Jews—the Lebanese were lumped with the latter. Though going to school with white Protestants, we never mixed with them in society. Even when I was asked to go to some of their homes to tutor their kids, I'd leave right after the lesson."[19]

Despite the ethnic and religious discrimination, Shag managed to impress many in town as a hard-working, intelligent student. Some fifty years after graduating from high school, one of his former classmates reflected on Hatem's reputation. "I remember him very pleasantly. He was the smartest person in the class—without any question. . . . His interests were intellectual and philosophical. He was not the type to ever become bitten by the bug of materialism."[20]

A young boy's life in a small southern town also had its lighter moments. Shag joined the community festivities the day the tobacco auctioneer sold over one million pounds, enjoyed the humor of Will Rogers when he performed in Greenville, and even witnessed the old time religion of the tent revivalists who passed through.[21] He spent one summer at a youth camp in Fort Bragg, where he learned how to shoot a rifle and earned an invitation to join the National Rifle Association.

The Church provided social activities for the Lebanese families. The young people joined local and regional clubs established by their parents to reinforce their own traditions and facilitate potential marriages within the Lebanese community. The young women knew Shag as a scholar, but also as a fun-loving young man who enjoyed meeting the girls as much as the next teenager. He found his best friends, and his first girlfriend, at the Lebanese social gatherings he attended in North and South Carolina.

By his senior year, his parents and the rest of his family had joined him in Greenville. They were aided by Abiunis, who brought Nahoum into his business, and then helped him to open his own dry-goods shop named "The Liberty Store." On his business stationery Nahoum placed a logo of the Statue of Liberty standing prominently to the right of the letterhead. Just as their ancestors had adjusted to life among an Islamic majority in Lebanon, Nahoum and his Maronite family were quick to adapt to their new community in the United States. Shag learned this lesson well, as fifty years in China would show.

Cannibalism in Kansu has been verified by the China International Famine Relief Commission. Thousands have returned to nomadic, virtual savage life and are wandering over the famine regions. Winter undoubtedly will kill countless numbers. The total of those now suffering is estimated as at least 20,000,000.

The Week in China, August 3, 1929

Actualities present a black picture of conditions in China, in the politico-military field as well as the economic sphere. There is no gainsaying this: any attempt to paint a different portrait is futile where the following facts are so completely self-evident:

    1.—Only a herculean effort can stave off a new and stupendous civil war.

    2.—Soviet Russia is apparently taking full advantage, militaristically, of the government's plight.

    3.—Famine and destitution remain widespread, and winter is barely a month away.

The Week in China, October 19, 1929

After graduating from high school, Shag received scholarship offers from several colleges in the area. However, his family—reflecting the distrust of many first-generation immigrants—feared such offers might conceal usurers' traps. So, after looking at other options, Shag enrolled at the University of North Carolina (UNC) at Chapel Hill in the fall of 1927, with his family paying the bills. This uniquely liberal institution in the South provided a safe alternative, since the tuition was manageable on his father's income.[1]

By the time Hatem entered college, the Nationalist and Communist parties had worked together for four years in an uneasy alliance to rid the country of warlords and imperialists. Both claimed as their guiding figure Sun Yat-sen, who had died in 1925, and both sought the support of his widow Song Qingling. Chiang Kai-shek assumed control of the Nationalist party at Sun's death and for two years continued to lead the united front from his headquarters at the Huangpu Military Academy. He also continued to depend on Soviet advice and arms. By April 1927, however, Chiang had grown fearful of the Communist party's influence in the national move-ment and, in the early morning of April 12, ordered an attack on the Com-munist-dominated labor unions of Shanghai. A wave of arrests and executions of suspected Communists and leftists rushed through Shanghai over the next several weeks, spreading to other parts of the country in the following months. Communist party leaders fled south to Wuhan, then to Guangzhou. By December 1927 the wave of terror had crested as rebels were tied together in groups of ten or twelve and thrown into the Pearl River. The remnants of the Communist party retreated into the mountains bordering Jiangxi and Fujian provinces. Madame Song Qingling moved to Moscow for two years, from where she helped lead the resistance to Chiang's "betrayal" of the revolution her husband had led. It was during these weeks of killing and torture that an adventurous thirty year old from New Zealand named Rewi Alley landed in Shanghai seeking any thrill the city might offer. He little expected what he found. Apolitical when he first arrived, this burly, working-class sojourner would spend the rest of his life first discovering the plight of China's downtrodden, then joining in the revolution to turn that plight into hope for a more humane future. His friendship with Song Qingling and his influence on Hatem would last over 50 years, changing both their lives.[2]

Shag started college confused and torn. As he registered for his classes, he showed little enthusiasm for the medical career his father expected him to pursue. He was so sure he preferred engineering instead that he drew up plans for a company he and a friend would start after graduat-ing. One college friend, Salvitere Turchielli, remembers that Shag was passionate about engineering, following experiments in civil engineering with particular interest.[3] When word of this reached home, his father quashed any such plans and left him no alternative but to concentrate on medicine. Reluctantly, Shag obeyed, abandoning his dreams in order to placate his family.

In 1927 a student could expect to complete a pre-med program in three years. Uneasy about spending so much of his family's money, Shag tried to shorten the time by taking extra courses and attending summer school. He also tried to help out financially where he could.[4] His family's help was enough for most of his educational expenses, but social occa-sions required a bit more. So, for the first time in his life, he earned some extra spending money by waiting on tables in the Phi Alpha Beta cafe-teria on weekdays and selling shoes in a dry-goods store on Saturdays.

The check stubs from his freshman year show that he spent his money on practical daily needs related to school, the Church, room, and board.

University life provided little respite from the discrimination he felt before arriving at Chapel Hill. His memories still remained vivid decades later when, reflecting on both administrators and students, he said that "in the initial interview before you entered they'd size you up with questions which seemed quite innocent, like 'What colour of tie do you like best?' or 'Who's your favorite baseball player?' But your answers would be enough to indicate your background and values. And dormitories were assigned on the basis of your name. I was put with a roommate called Harry Schwartz, because they took me to be Jewish. And the fraternities wouldn't touch me, except for a Jewish one—they invited me though I told them I wasn't Jewish."[5]

While Shag may have felt the continuing stings of discrimination, he does not portray himself during that period as politically active in any way. He says that during those years he remained serious, studious, and hardworking, without any meaningful social life. His college grades proved adequate, but not spectacular. His strongest classes by far were in the physical sciences, where he ranked near the top of his class. In the social sciences, however, he struggled through with a C average. His classmates attest to his quick intellect and tenacity in academics. Fellow pre-med student E. B. Aycock of Greenville, who shared a floor with Shag in UNC's "F" Dorm, says that he "was a very smart man. We had a zoology course that undoubtedly was the hardest course in the undergraduate school. He'd write the lectures down just as fast as he could and then rush back and type up his notes and made a copy for me. That probably had a lot to do with my passing the course."[6] One of his roommates, Tony Libbus, remembers Shag speaking Arabic, French, and English fluently. He recalls that Shag was a "terrific" fellow. "He was the brains of this outfit of ours and he helped me a great deal."[7] His friend "Sal" Turchielli remembers Shag as one of a group of six to eight young men who came to depend on each other for company and support. Shag, he said, "was a very conscientious kind of guy, he took things seriously. He was kind of dedicated, more so than I, anyway. But even though he was serious, which includes his behavior, he had a great sense of humor. I had lots of respect for him."[8]

College life included more than study and work, however. Shag attended chapel every morning. He and a group of students started UNC's Fencing Club, and he also joined the Dialectic and Philanthropic Society.[9] Years later he would reflect on those discussions and remember the days when the world's problems seemed too simple, and he just had to wait for his chance to straighten them out.[10] In 1978, on his first return to North Carolina since his student days, he confided that the one speaker he remembered most clearly was Norman Thomas, the best-known socialist of that era. He told his hosts, "My friends say that that's where I got my socialistic leanings."

Despite his later claims to the contrary, college life was not so full of academics and debates that Shag missed out on an active social life. Far from it. He kept up with the male and female friends he made through the Lebanese clubs and developed a reputation for being as much interested in the opposite sex as in academics. His correspondence with a high-school sweetheart blossomed, playful and appropriate for their age.

> October 29, 1927
> Dear Shafick, Do you meet any new girls and go to parties? How long do you think it will be before I see you? Please try and come here the next time you spend the weekend at home because I do want to see you and also to know if you are still bashful. Write me.
> As ever, Love, Evelyn.

As the months wore on, this young girl, so smitten with the far-away Shag, grew frustrated at his too infrequent letters. She thought perhaps he was studying too hard and wrote, "Oh you fresh freshie. Too busy to do anything but study." Later she discovered that maybe he was not writing her often enough because he was writing to too many others, not because he was studying too hard. After Shag told her of other girls he was writing, she replied, writing in red ink,

> November 5, 1927
> Dear Shafick,
>   I believe you have been very busy with your girlfriends instead of your lessons. . . . As for being jealous I am a little bit, but I need not be because I can't keep you from writing to other girls and as far as knowing their names I don't give a d—>
>   You talk in your letter about being so lonesome and you wish you had a picture of me to cheer you up. How about your other girls? . . . As you have said your ownself, "If you love someone they are worth fighting over." So I am living up to it.
> Yours truly, Evelyn

By the end of his first year at UNC, Shag had many new friends, and sometimes they were not above taking "creative" shortcuts to good marks. Once, concerned about a summer-school chemistry exam, he asked a friend who had just finished taking the same course to give him the questions and answers from his exam. His friend, Danne Kaul, obliged, and Shag got through the exam all right. In September, after summer school ended, he wrote Kaul and told him that the classes had drained him, that he was just starting to relax. Kaul, who had just seen to it that he got through one of those classes, responded: "Just started to rest. Bunk!!! You've been resting all summer down at the hill. The only time you've ever labored was when you had to make a three no-trump hand. Write and tell me when classes start back."

In July 1928, just as Hatem finished his first year of college, Edgar Snow, a twenty-two-year-old journalist from Kansas City, Missouri, arrived in Shanghai after a Pacific journey through Hawai'i and Japan. He found it a city of a million and a half people living in a "tepid, steaming mist." Surprised by the pervasive foreign influence, he commented, "Strange, isn't it, that this, the most progressive, the wealthiest port in China, should be controlled by foreigners!" He heard of the armies led by Chiang Kai-shek's Nationalists heading north from Guangzhou and assumed that "the foreigners will be obliged to relinquish their claims here and return the reins of administration to the rightful rulers of the lands." But at first blush, Snow was not drawn to China. Writing home, he told his family, "I do not know how long I shall be in Shanghai. Perhaps for three weeks, possibly that many months. If I can get a job on a boat sailing south to the Philippines or India I may leave at once. . . . Like his eventual friend and fellow traveler Shag Hatem, Snow decided to stay in China a bit longer than expected.[11]

Shag's correspondence with male friends over the two years he attended UNC revolved around academics and women. Of special interest to his friends was Shag's enjoyment in "playing the field." In one letter, "Daddy," another Lebanese American friend wrote, "Shag, you old sonofagun, why don't you give the girl a break. . . . You're a heartbreaker, Shag." His friend Sal advised him to stick to one woman, that his reputation for dating several might hurt him some time. But he was forced to acknowledge that sometimes there were advantages, since it allowed more fun at the "necking parties" they both enjoyed.

At UNC, Shag also associated with many students outside the Lebanese American community. While the relationships were warm, he was never allowed to forget he was different. His friend Sal remembers, for instance, that "we used to kid him about those Persian countries like where his family came from—we would ask him how many wives could he get if he went back over there. This wasn't any kind of discrimination, though, just joking around."[12]

Growing tired of life in the South, where he was not allowed to forget he was different, Shag contemplated a change. One option was to go abroad to study medicine. If he could not arrange to study overseas, he wanted to go back to Buffalo. By early summer of his second year at UNC, he was applying to schools in France, Germany, Lebanon (then part of Syria), and Buffalo. Of the four, he was drawn most strongly to the Medical School of the American University in Beirut, close to his parents' home village. He received no response from the other programs but soon heard good news from Beirut. As soon as he received his acceptance letter, he got ready for a quick departure.

By July 1929, Shag's friends and family were aware of his plans to study in Beirut. Everyone voiced support, though some were sad or envious. A new college girlfriend, Treva, wrote after hearing of his acceptance, "Really, I am glad for you that you are getting your heart's desire —To study medicine in Syria. I do hate to think of 'Daddy' and 'Sal' returning to Carolina without you, Shag. Have a nice trip abroad but don't do anything I wouldn't, hear!" Two weeks later, just before his departure, she wrote, "Shag, I know you will have a good time during the next few years and when I next see you (19????) you will be so dignified that I will probably have to say Dr. George Shafick Hatem every time I wish to speak to you. Well, I won't mind a bit in the least for you certainly will deserve it."

Shag ended up not graduating from UNC, at least not by the time he left. According to his official transcript, he was three credits shy of graduating when he left in 1929. He had come that close to finishing a three-year degree in two years. In 1987, while honoring this now-famous alumnus, the university retroactively adjusted his three-credit discrepancy and, sixty years after he first enrolled there, awarded him his Bachelor of Science in medicine.[13]

On August 13, 1929, Shag applied for a passport, listing his status as "student." The application states that the eighteen-year-old planned to sail in September for Beirut, Syria, in order to take "medical courses" at the American University there for a period of five years. The application was approved on August 16, and within two weeks he was off to New York with his parents. He sailed for Beirut on September 2.[14]

On September 27, the day after his nineteenth birthday, Shag arrived in Beirut. While he was en route, his family opened a letter addressed to him from the medical school in Buffalo. He had been accepted into their program.[15] Would he have stayed in the United States if he had delayed his departure a few days? His family probably would have preferred that, but it is not clear what Shag would have decided. He obviously wanted to go abroad, but could he have withstood his father's insistence that he stay? There is certainly a strong possibility that, if the mail had arrived one day earlier, his own—and a bit of China's—history would have been different.

Why did Shag leave the United States and go to Beirut to study medicine? There were several explanations. First, he remained uneasy about the discrimination he felt in North Carolina and questioned how successful he might be when evaluated by the admissions offices of American medical colleges. He gravitated to the Jewish students with whom he was identified and with whom he shared the sting of prejudice. Some of them also had decided "to get past the unspoken racial quota in medical schools" and go abroad to study.[16]

Another reason to go to Beirut was the possibility of obtaining a quality education at a lower price. Shag was one of many young Americans in those years attracted for financial reasons to the Rockefeller-sponsored American University Hospital in Beirut. All students received scholarships and were assured that the curriculum was the same as any medical school in the United States.[17] Grey Dimond, an American physician who first met Hatem in the 1970s, says, "The Depression was bitter hard for the Hatems, and Shag's decision to go to Beirut to medical school was the result, at least in part, because he could not get in an American school or if he did, he was not offered scholarship equal to that coming from Lebanon.[18]

Also, there can be no doubt that the pull of his parents' homeland was a strong motivation to study in Beirut. Throughout his university years in North Carolina, Shag clung to his Lebanese roots through his family and friends. He moved more comfortably among them than among white, Protestant southerners.

Others have offered a more conspiratorial explanation for his actions. It is at this point in his story that the first shades of mystery and myth appear. Various arms of the U.S. government have painted a picture that stands in stark contrast to the socially active and academically focused young pre-med student that appears in accounts by Shag himself, his family, and former classmates. One official who got to know Shag years later insists that even as a university student he had a Marxist political agenda. Herbert Hitch, a naval intelligence officer in China in the 1940s, says that Shag joined one of the early "Communist cell groups" set up on university campuses and led by Soviet agents. Hitch says that the first three such cells were established at UNC, Johns Hopkins University, and the University of Wisconsin. (He adds that, at the time Shag was recruited, Alger Hiss was recruited at Johns Hopkins.) He insists that Shag, whose company he enjoyed in China and whom he grew to admire for his humanitarian work, was one of the founding members of the cell at UNC.[19] Hitch goes even further, stating that the Communist International helped fund Shag's education at UNC and later encouraged him to study medicine in Europe.[20]

It is difficult to prove or disprove these allegations with absolute certainty. This is due, in part, to the Central Intelligence Agency's (CIA) refusal to release documents pertaining to Hatem's political movements throughout his life.[21] Nevertheless, these allegations seem rather fanciful. First, there is no evidence of Communist activity among students in North Carolina until well into the 1930s, long after Shag had departed. Second, it is clear that his family sacrificed much to finance his education, even to the point of having his brother Joe spend summers earning money for Shag's studies. The family collectively put Shag through college. Besides, even within the family he had the reputation of being one who "loved to dance, loved to party. He wasn't sitting in his room, studying, crying about being discriminated against. Nor was he organizing the workers of the world."[22] From all appearances, Shag was not politically active until he arrived in China several years later. He admits reading *The Communist Manifesto* only after moving to Shanghai in 1933.[23] Neither Shag nor his family or friends have ever alluded to youthful political activity. Over the years there would have been no reason to hide it, since he was proud of his Communist allegiance throughout most of his adult life. But the charges remain part of the public record, even though the evidence proves elusive at best.

As young Hatem was landing in Beirut to begin his studies, fellow American Agnes Smedley, only recently arrived in China after a trip through the Soviet Union, was touring the city of Wuxi, just west of Shanghai. Already well known for her progressive and biting diatribes against fascism and corruption, she now saw Chinese youths beheaded in the streets by local landlords. When she returned to Shanghai, she met the New Zealander Rewi Alley. He had just completed an extended trip through northeast China, where he found thousands dead from starvation, their bodies raked into moats at the edge of towns. He told her that he saw little or no food coming in, but he did see the Catholic church buy property at a premium price, and he saw women and children sold cheaply to fill Shanghai factories and brothels. On a train along the way, Alley briefly and fortuitously crossed paths with the young American writer Edgar Snow, who was also touring the northeast in order to investigate the famine that no one seemed to be acknowledging in the higher circles of Beijing. Snow told Alley of trees stripped of bark for food and of children eating sawdust to fill their bellies. Worst of all, he visited what was left of the street markets and saw human flesh hung for sale. Each of these three foreigners had been transformed by what they saw. Over the next several years none of them would allow the outside world to remain ignorant of it. All three gravitated to Madame Song Qingling to find answers and to join in support of the fledgling revolution. Although none now knew it, by the fall of 1929 these experiences of Shag Hatem's future friends and mentors in Shanghai had ensured that before long he too would be taking his first steps toward revolution.[24]

When Shag left the United States in September 1929, his family had no doubts about his future. He would get his medical degree and return within a few years to set up a practice close to home. It was his family obligation, and not open for debate. When he stepped on board the ship, however, he began the first leg of a journey that would take him away from the United States for almost 50 years. Nobody who knew him would ever have believed it. Certainly Shag would not have predicted it.

Soon after he arrived in Beirut, Shag visited his father's home village of Hamana in the mountains above the city. There he was embraced as a son of the village. There and in Beirut he experienced none of the prejudice he had faced in the United States. He was no longer known as the son of immigrants who would never quite fit into a white Protestant society. The warm reception in his ancestral home showed the depth of respect given this Maronite Christian returning from abroad.[25] It was the first time he was received so freely and without suspicion.

Over the next two years in Beirut, Shag studied, traveled, visited family, searched for romance, and tried to survive economically. By all accounts, he did well in his classes. During his first year he took a total of six courses, ranging from anatomy to embryology. His highest grade was an 88 percent in anatomy; his lowest was a 79 percent in hygiene. Since 70 percent was considered a passing mark, his efforts were considered respectable, though not exceptional. During his second year he enrolled in ten courses. That year his highest mark was a 90 percent in obstetrics, but he barely passed clinical methodology at 70 percent. He also studied surgery, parasitology, pathology, and bacteriology, all subjects he would put to good use throughout his life.[26] In later years, he voiced pride in his American University education, saying that the school "was financed by the Rockefeller Foundation and known for high medical standards (another was the Peking Union Medical College, now the Beijing Capital Hospital). The Rockefellers would get first-rate professors from the USA to teach in these places in their sabbatical years, which resulted in their turning out some fine physicians and surgeons."[27]

In Beirut, Shag also continued his active social life. A favorite Hatem family story shows a humorous and ironic side of his search for romance. One day a group of young women from his family village of Hamana arrived in Beirut. He welcomed them to the university, taking special interest in one he found particularly attractive. But his advances failed to impress her, and she returned to her home village within a few days. Almost fifty years later, Shag met the same woman again during his first return visit to the United States. Now the mother of his younger brother's wife, she reminded him of their encounter in Beirut in 1930 and identified herself as the girl whose affections he had tried to win. Shag's American family was well aware of his reputation as a young flirt and social gadfly, and they were amused that after five decades he could still not escape his earlier reputation.[28]

Shag did not just alternate between studying and socializing. He joined the university basketball team and challenged friends to spirited games of ping pong. He explored the world within his reach by organizing a bicycle tour of parts of Europe and Africa during the holidays.[29] He discovered that the world held many wonders and, although he still planned to return home after finishing his medical degree, there were stirrings of further international travel.

Life in Beirut was rewarding, but money was tight. He continued to depend on his family, just as he had in North Carolina. Despite the Depression's effect on his father's business, neither his parents nor other members of his family questioned their obligation to his education. To support his brother, Joe quit school and moved to Buffalo, where his Uncle George found him a job digging ditches for twenty-five cents an hour. During the peak of the Depression, Uncle George borrowed five hundred dollars from the bank, sent it to Shag, and then he and Joe worked to pay it off. When that debt was paid, he borrowed another five hundred dollars and started the whole process again.

Because of this drain on their bank accounts, all the other Hatem children joined Joe in either postponing or downgrading their own college plans. Cousin Theresa in Buffalo intended to enroll in Syracuse University, but the money originally set aside for her went to Shag instead. She put off her plans until Shag's mother Thaman took a bus from North Carolina to Buffalo just to insist that Theresa enter college. She told Theresa that the North Carolina Hatems would furnish her with all the clothing she needed while in school. Theresa was persuaded to enroll in Buffalo State College, which was closer to home and much less expensive. She was disappointed at being unable to attend Syracuse and vented her frustration in a blistering letter to Shag, chastising him for his selfishness and pointing out the sacrifices everyone was making for him.[30] But even Theresa, like the others in the family, knew that after he attained his medical degree, he would return to the United States and establish a lucrative practice close to home. When that happened, all their sacrifices would find reward in his prestige and wealth. In the meantime, he was to study, represent the family in their homeland, and depend on them for as much help as they could offer.

In his letters home, Shag spoke of both his own and his parents' responsibilities. And in almost every letter, he reminded them that he was coming home when he finished. He was always coming home—soon.

> Beirut Syria
> Jan. 8, 1931
> Dear Folks,
>   I have just received your [letter] which was registered and contained a check for $50.00. This was very kind of you and I hope that by this time business has so improved that you don't mind it.
>   I am in quite good health and have just finished the mid term examinations. Medicine is progressing along without trouble and I hope that in a year and a half more I'll be an intern in some hospital in America. As it stands now I will not get an M.D. degree unless I spend a year in America and then come back to Syria for an exam. I'm trying to find some way out of this and If I do I'll let you know. . . .
>   About the clothes and Suits I wish you would let me know exactly [to] who[m] & when they are being sent so I can ask for the man & get them. I need them very bad and I'm waiting for them-please send them soon. . . .
>   I certainly missed you this Xmas and I hope we won't be separated from many more Xmases.
> Your loving son,
> Shafick

After two years of studying hard and playing the role of the obedient son returned to the homeland, Shag's letters home started to show a bit of youthful independence and rebelliousness. Though his enthusiasm for school remained high, his role as a returning son began to wear thin. In a letter to his sister Freda, Shag shared his frustration at the treatment he received from some of the Hamana family, especially when he was asked to pay for staying in the family-owned hotel in the village.

February 12, 1931
Beirut, Syria
Dear Freda,

I'll take this opportunity to answer your letter and the one I received from father together, so any news I tell you tell the rest of the dear folks.

If I remember correctly my last letter was written during the hard days of examinations. Now the exams are over and our second term started yesterday. The results of the examination will come today and in my next letter I'll tell you the results. I think I passed everything so there is nothing to worry about.

I want you to tell father that I won't be able to try to see Uncle Daker before Easter and also the check for $50.00 of which I was to give him $25.00. I used [it] to pay my tuition and the other check to pay my rest of the rent and food so at present I do not have $25.00 to give him (Unc. Daker). Anyway let him wait and he really doesn't need it. It was a terrible thing of him to do it after many invitations. Never again will I stay in Hamana more than one day and I'll never sleep there again. They may charge me for it.

As for the school in U.S. that I'm going to it is undecided because I spoke with some professors and they advised me not to change. They had very good reasons and I think I'll take their advice and stay here. It will take only one year more but I guess the practice will not do me harm in the extra year. . . .

Your loving Brother
Shafick

By the summer of 1931, Shag had endured enough of school, family, and Syria. He needed a break and decided with some of his classmates to take a bicycle tour of Europe. Their first stop was Geneva, where he visited former Beirut classmates who had transferred to the University of Geneva Medical School. Before returning to Beirut, the group also visited France, Italy, and Germany.

After staying a few days in Geneva, Shag had many things to tell his parents. As usual, he shared with them his daily life, then asked them for help. One wonders what he would have worn if his father had not owned a clothing store.

Geneva Switzerland
July 25, 1931
Dear Folks,

I have spent two weeks in Geneva. Here they are very nice to students &
they have many societies for students in medicine. . . . It has not cost me very
much to stay here because of this. . . . We are leaving Geneva on bicycles and
intend to go to Germany and then Paris. From Paris we are going to Italy &
then a boat to Syria. I'll be back in Syria by some time in September. . . .

There are some things I would like for you to send to Syria as soon as you
get this letter because of the time this gets to you & you send the things it
will be September. Here are the things I need.

1. My underwears—2 pieces are all finished so will you please send me one
   dozen pants & 1 doz. shirts underwear
2. Shoes—they are all worn out. I would like 2 pair 6.5 size
3. Sock—most of them & nearly all have holes. Send 2 dozen. Cheap ones
4. 1 pr. of heavy tennis shoes
5. a few neckties & few shirts

My gowns for the hospital I'll buy in Syria. I think that will be best. Will
you wash the stuff & wear the shoes so as not to have to pay duty. The
clothes before lasted two years & maybe these will last as long. Have the
underwear of the 2 piece kind please.

You must think I'm a terrible son always asking for money & clothes etc.
but I'm spending not one cent more than necessary during the year but during vacation I must enjoy myself a little after so much studying. I'm spending
even with the vacation less than what I would spend in a university in
America. . . .

Kiss ma, Freda, Joe & Shafia for me and I hope youall in very good health.
Do you realize that I've been away from home for 2 years & I haven't seen
you? At times I sit down & nearly cry for homesickness gets me. May we
hope to God we can see each other soon.
Your Loving Obedient Son
Shafick

*By the time Hatem returned to Syria from his European vacation, the Japa-
nese had established a formidable military and industrial presence in Manchuria (northeast China). What resistance they faced came from the army
of the "Young Marshal," Zhang Xueliang. Zhang, the son of warlord Zhang
Zuolin, whose assassination the Japanese had orchestrated in 1928, controlled most of Manchuria with his 400,000 troops. In a move that surprised*

many, he had recently aligned himself with his father's former enemy, Chiang Kai-shek, with the provision that he would continue to rule the northeast. This united force threatened the Japanese and nudged the two countries closer to all-out war.

On the evening of September 18, 1931, local Japanese officers in Liaoning Province, concerned at the threat of growing military resistance to their exploitation of Chinese agricultural and mineral fields, set off explosives along the railroad line outside the city of Mukden. They were attacked by Zhang Xueliang's troops, and full-scale fighting erupted between Chinese and Japanese troops. These battles set the stage for what later became known in the West as World War II and in China as the Anti-Japanese War. Chiang Kai-shek, fearful of diverting his forces to a major battleground in the north until he could finish off the Communists, refused to resist the Japanese invasion and ordered Zhang Xueliang to retreat south of the Great Wall. By the end of 1931, all of Manchuria was under Japanese control.[31]

After returning to Beirut, Shag enrolled for the fall semester. One of his courses was tropical medicine, soon to become his primary medical interest. While he continued to make progress in school, his grades dropped as he began reevaluating his goals and his current medical program. He was impatient at its slow pace, and his visit to Geneva after two years in Beirut had stirred ideas. He was looking to leave, but uncertain which direction to take. He could either return to the United States to be closer to the family he obviously missed, or he could go back to one of the places he had visited during his recent vacation in Europe. He wrote his parents:

Beirut Syria
September 13, 1931
Dear Folks,
    I've just received your letter of Aug 22 and am glad to hear that all of you are in the best of health. I'm still feeling well although for the past two weeks it has been so hot that I've felt sick. Nothing serious. School will start soon and then another year will be on its way. Maybe we will arrange it to go home for our 5th year and thus make it a 4 yr course. We are going to see the president and ask him if he can arrange to let the American students go to the U.S. for the fifth year. If he does then we have only two yrs more in Syria thank God.
    If this doesn't happen I may go to a four year school as they have in

France, Lyon, Montpelier or Geneva. I know enough French to study the last two years which will be spent in the clinic and hospital and then I'll spend my internship on the 5th yr. in the states. I'll save a year and get to be an M.D. one year sooner. The expenses will be a little more but the year saved will make it up.

 I'll close with best regards to all and love to you.

Your Son Obedient

Shafick

P.S. Please send me a size 36 belt with a buckle-wide belt. Mine is worn out.

The president of the medical college refused the American students' request to return to the United States to complete their studies. With this option closed, Shag and his American classmates looked to Europe. Shag decided to join his friends in Switzerland and applied for admission as a transfer student to the Medical College in Geneva. The American University forwarded his transcripts with the following comment from the registrar:

> Mr. Hatem was admitted into the first year of our Medical School in October 1929 after examination of the certificates coming from the State of New York and on the basis of his schooling at the University of North Carolina in the United States of America. . . . During the whole length of his stay with us, Mr. Hatem had a satisfactory behavior and, as a student, he demonstrated intellectual capacities above average.

After being accepted at Geneva, Shag left Beirut and settled in at 24 Rue des Peupliers, Chez Mme Berthalet, Geneva. His good friend Bob Levinson transferred with him. They began classes in May 1932.

The bodies of 36,704 dead Chinese were found in the streets of Shanghai, in the Whangpoo River within the city limits, or in Soochow Creek, during 1932, according to the annual report of the Public Benevolent Society. . . . All were civilians, of whom 3,088 were adults or half-grown persons, while 33,616 were the bodies of infants. It is surmised that most of the dead infants were victims of infanticide.

New York Times, March 19, 1933

Letters from Shag to his family show a man always on the go, looking for new ways to reach each new goal as soon as possible. He was an obedient son, studying hard and representing the family to scores of Hatems and other relatives he did not know. But he was not obedient enough to stay in his ancestral homeland when new horizons beckoned. Beirut could not match the romance and adventure of other places, and there was the added attraction of possibly speeding up his medical education. Shag also began to feel that Beirut offered little to prepare him medically for his work back in the United States. At least that is how he saw it in later years when he explained that "the diseases we saw in Beirut were not very common in the U.S. and one reason we went on to Switzerland to Geneva was to have more contact with "WASP" [white Anglo-Saxon Protestant] diseases."[1]

When Shag arrived in Geneva, he was welcomed by friends already studying there, some of whom were members of the Jewish community. He appreciated the welcome and found it unnecessary to disabuse them of the assumption that he too was Jewish. It was not the first time for this American-born Maronite Christian to be so identified, and it was not the last time his adopted Jewish community would serve him well.[2]

Shag wrote his family almost immediately. The move during the Christmas holidays put him in a foul mood. He was both homesick and angry with his father at the same time. This medical school business was taking too long, and he was not so sure if it was a good idea to keep pursuing a medical degree. His repressed frustration at abandoning his own interest in engineering shows in a letter to his sister Freda. He feared his brother Joe would fall into the same trap, and he shared his elder brother's wisdom in a letter to her.

> February 23, 1932
> Geneva, Suisse
> Dear Sister,
> I have just received your letter of Jan. 27, 1932 and it made me feel very homesick especially since you all missed me Xmas. . . .
> How is Shafia & Joe getting on in School. They are graduating aren't they? I wonder what Joe is going to do. I know that Shafia is going to study and teach. No one should force him to study any special thing. He should have the special right to choose his profession & unless he does he will never be a success in it. Of course he should go to college. Before he does I suggest that he talk with his Teachers & Principal and see their ideas of him as a student and see what they think his best abilities are. Such a matter of choosing a career is not a simple thing and once your started on it one cannot change easily without losing a great part of his work.
> Tell the folks to send me the money to the following address:
> S. Hatem
> c/o Bob Levinson
> 24 Rue des Peupliers
> Geneva Suisse
> Chez G. Messay

After arriving in Switzerland, Shag discovered that he needed more money than his parents could provide. With the Depression strangling his cash flow, he and a few friends started an underground publishing company. These young entrepreneurs gained access to the questions and answers on previously administered final examinations in all the major courses taken at the medical school, then mimeographed and bound them for sale. Demand was strong. These same young businessmen also composed theses for students not inclined to write their own—if they could afford the price.[3]

While Shag was studying and playing in Switzerland, his family was struggling in the small town of Greenville, North Carolina. They had to search for ways to keep their heads above water even as they sent whatever money they could to pay for Shag's tuition, books, room and board, and the boxes of clothes they sent him throughout the year.

Money they had stashed away in the local bank to pay for his education was lost in the crash, and by early 1932 the Liberty Store closed down. Shag's mother returned to Buffalo, and his father visited Roanoke Rapids, North Carolina, to look into a new dry-goods business. Despite the Depression, the J. P. Stevens Company opened a new factory in the Roanoke Rapids area, and Nahoum hoped the flow of workers into that area would create a viable demand for clothing and other goods. Shag's sisters and brother stayed in Greenville while their parents plotted their future.

While Shag studied in Beirut and Geneva, he and his family exchanged at least a letter every week. In the spring of 1932, however, letters from the United States stopped, and Shag heard nothing from home for over a month. Having no idea what was happening back home, he worried constantly as he awaited the next letter. When summer came, letters finally started flowing again. Only then did he discover the hardships his family had endured during the leanest times of the Depression. He was told not to worry, that the family once again had its feet on the ground. Although greatly relieved to find out why they had stopped writing, he was disconsolate at their predicament and eager to be of what help he could from such a distance. His first letter was his attempt to play big brother on the occasion of sister Shafia's and brother Joe's graduation from high school.

Geneva
June 8, 1932
Dear Sister and Brother,

How quickly time flies and how fast the years pass by. It has been only a few years since I left you both as small kids still fighting among each other over the silliest things. Here after a few years both have graduated and now are Man and Woman. A teacher is a very responsible position, while Joe will also be a teacher or a professor or something.

I was thrilled & happy to see that both of you have graduated with flying colors. Of course I always knew that you could do it but this came all of a sudden. I want to congratulate each one of you and I'm sorry that I could not be there to do it in person.

My pen cannot write all I wish you but one thing I ask of you — always play fair and be honest with yourself. I wish both all the luck in the world and I am sure you'll go far in your chosen fields. Bravo Sister & Brother!! I hope to see you in another year.

Your wellwishing brother,
Shag

At the same time he sent a letter to his sister Freda that took a decidedly different tone, expressing his outrage at being left out of the family discussion during their recent tribulations, as well as his deep, perhaps guilt-laden, appreciation of his parents' sacrifices.

> Dear Freda,
>   I certainly am a little mad at you for not writing sooner and telling me about it. You can't imagine how worried I was when I heard about my mother being in Buffalo, my father in Roanoke [Rapids] and I hadn't heard from any of you in ages. It was certainly something to worry about. Now that everything is explained I'm not worried but I'm not very happy about those events but I'm sure good old father did everything he could for us. He and Mother are really wonderful parents to work so hard for all of us and take the trouble to educate us and spend all their lives working for us. We don't realize it until we go to foreign countries and see how much we miss other people that have been so good to us: I want you, Shafia & Joe to be obedient to them and take care of them till I come back.
> Your Loving Brother,
> Shag

As he entered the final stage of his search for a medical degree, what plans did he have for the future? It is clear that by this time one of his goals was to concentrate on dermatology, especially as it related to the study of tropical diseases. He arranged in the summer of 1932 to be assigned to the dermatology clinic of the Cantonal Hospital in Geneva. Knowledge gained there would serve him well when he returned to the southern United States, he reasoned, where such diseases could still be found. However, he was learning more than tropical disease control. For part of his training he worked in the maternity ward of the Cantonal Hospital, and he wrote his family that during the summer of 1932 he delivered six babies. Shag's education prepared him for a variety of medical needs. He would need all of it, and then some, within a few years. But it would not be in North Carolina.

Of special interest, and later in life of special importance, was his class in the treatment of venereal disease, handled at that time by dermatologists. His instructor was Professor Charles Dubois, a physician and teacher Shag remembered with respect throughout his career. Dubois, he says, first taught him that venereal disease is a social disease that, with proper understanding and treatment, can be alleviated. Shag says that this class left him with visions of going forward into battle with tubes full of antitoxins, ready to save the world from what were once considered untreatable societal ills.[4]

With his medical education almost complete and his medical interests more focused than ever, Shag found himself dealing with new and unsettling emotions about his family. He still resented the family's unwillingness to share their hardships with him when their business folded. He lived with the guilt that he could not help the family in any way and, in fact, that he was a drain on already scarce resources. Worse yet, he found that his resentment and guilt touched his deep-seated disappointment at not pursuing an engineering degree, and these feelings translated into anger at his father.

Obvious signs of this new and distant attitude toward the family are evident in a letter to his parents in August 1932. The anger and the guilt are clearly apparent. Here for the first time Shag offers the possibility that he may not begin his medical career in the United States.

Geneva, August 16, 1932
Dear Folks,

I certainly was surprised when you did not write for over a month. I'm happy now that you wrote me now and I'm answering it. I do not write any more except as an answer to your letters. I always answer every one.

When I heard of Joe not being able to go to college I felt very, very bad and sorry. I knew that I have taken his share of money for myself in my schooling. It will be 6 years of College and Medical School spent on me. My share should only be 4 years. I took away two of his years. I wish now that I had been real strong with you and refused to take medicine and chose another field which I could finish in 4 years. There is no use crying over spilt milk. I want you to promise me one thing—that after I finish this next year you will send him to College. You can do it. By next October I hope to be finished with Medical School and have written my thesis and have it published. After that for the next two years I won't cost you any money. I will be taking a 2 year internship in some big hospital in New York City or Buffalo or somewhere. During these two years I will not earn a single penny but I'll be learning. The future after that I don't know. It is a long ways till then. I have two ideas in mind: one: try to get some government work, 2. go out of the States to some Colonies. I don't know which I'll do yet. General practice doesn't seem to appeal to me.

I'm in quite good health but as usual anxious about money. I'm not going to say anymore than that.

From the papers I see that business is starting to pick up. I really hope so because it has been bad for quite a long time.

I close now with love to all and kisses to you from

Your Loving son

Shafick

For the next several months, Shag spent little time writing his family. He sent short notes saying that his health was good and that he was focusing on his final exams and writing his thesis. He continued to ask for money to cover school expenses and clothes for the rest of the year. He may have felt guilty about asking, but he let them know their obligation continued until he was out of school. He also indicated that he might not return home as soon as everyone wanted. In a February 1933 letter, this possibility comes through more strongly than ever.

Dear Folks,

I have just received the coat, bedroom slippers & socks for which I thank you very much. . . . The coat fits very well only I have to raise the belt. It is too low.

I am quite busy these days & in 3 weeks I present the first part of my doctorate examination. The second part in July or August with my thesis.

I received all the money you sent and thank you more than ever. My thesis and diploma with document will [cost] about $200.00, Tuition for next semester (April)—60.00, Expenses for each month—50.00. . . .

To include the trip to America you must figure on $700.00, that is if I return to America. Of course I may stay abroad or get a job with some company or specialize and then return to America to take my internship after a year or two. Times are very hard in the States and are getting worse. . . .

Your Obedient Son,

Shafick

While Hatem was considering his options in February 1933, the Communist party of China was fighting for its very existence. Sending over 300,000 troops into the mountains and villages of Jiangxi, Chiang Kai-shek continued to ignore the Japanese danger to the north as he concentrated on wiping out what was left of the Chinese Communist party. He had hoped to eliminate them through his 1927 "housecleaning," in which hundreds of thousands of Communists, workers, and students were hunted down and executed by his troops. But the Communists had retreated to this southern province to regroup and reorganize. In February 1933, the fourth of what would eventually be five such campaigns failed, as Commander Zhu De's troops cap-

*tured over 20,000 Nationalist troops and threw Chiang's army into disarray.
The fifth campaign, which began in October 1933, saw Chiang mass close to
one million troops against the Communists. With such numbers, he succeeded in dislodging them from Jiangxi, only to watch them maneuver over
and around his troops for the next several months, finally breaking through
his lines in the spring of 1934 and heading north. Thus began the most
famous retreat in twentieth-century military and political history, for with
this maneuver the Chinese Communist party and its Red Army began the
legendary Long March.*[5]

To finish his medical degree in Geneva, Shag was required to enroll in
three semesters of study, pass a series of oral exams, and write a thesis.
He continued taking the prescribed courses, from gynecology and pediatrics to clinical psychiatry. He also studied clinical dermatology and
venereology. The latter course led him to his thesis topic, "The Irreducible Wassermann," which focused on the treatment of incurable syphilis,
a common problem faced by all physicians in the era before the development of penicillin. Shag distinguished between "irreducible Wassermann," a type of syphilis that for unexplained reasons does not respond
to treatment, and "resistant Wassermann," which can be combatted successfully after years of treatment.

Shag argued that whether a patient's symptoms fall into the "irreducible" or the "resistant" category, treatment of a varied nature must be
enforced in the early stages of latency. However, he reaches the somber
conclusion that

> There are no fixed rules for the treatments of an irreducible or resistant
> Wassermann. Any treatment followed with this purpose must have, as a base,
> specific drugs (mercury, arsenic, bismuth) combined to other treatments
> suitable to each particular case.[6]

His emphasis on the early detection and constant treatment of even
incurable syphilis, while not unique in medicine, shows Shag's inclina-
tion even at this early stage of his development to attack the disease with
whatever means available and as early as possible. This is the approach to
medicine that he would carry with him to China and one that would
evolve into a unique medical experiment the world health community
would watch with fascination. For it was through the treatment of venereal disease that Shag first got to know China, and his lifelong interest in
this disease made him an international figure before his death.

Shag's thesis was accepted by the Medical College of the University of Geneva on July 25, 1933. He immediately sent copies to his family, signing his letter with the inscription, "Shafick Hatem, M.D." They eagerly anticipated his return home. But by the time he finished his thesis, his mind was made up. He would not go home after graduation. In fact, it appears his mind may have been made up well before 1933, but he withheld the truth from his family until it was time to depart for Asia. He may have decided as early as 1931, when he went to Geneva, that he would travel to Asia before returning to the United States. On his application to renew his passport in Geneva in 1931, he listed three locations he wanted to visit while residing in Switzerland, two of them not surprising for the time and place he lived, but the third strikingly out of place for someone of his background and education. He looked forward to trips to Italy, France, and the "Far East."[7]

Why did traveling to the Far East intrigue him? Numerous plausible justifications have been cited. The problem is that there appear to be almost as many reasons given as there are people reporting them. Even Shag himself, in his own writing and in his words quoted by others, gives conflicting motives for his desire to visit China.

His future comrade in China, Edgar Snow, reports that Shag became interested through Asian students he met in Geneva.[8] Shag's wife, Su Fei, argues that her husband's first thoughts of going to China surfaced while interning with some fellow students in 1932. In her account, he was reading a French newspaper that ran a story about an intriguing disease found in Asia. He mentioned this to two of his colleagues and told them he might want to go to China after graduating and asked if they would want to go with him. They also were interested and began hatching plans to travel there. Hatem told one visitor in 1985 that he went, at least in part, for "youth's final fling."[9] The family was led to believe that he would work himself around the world, stopping in a few ports only long enough to make money. He was still coming home, but on a slow boat while he saw the world. At least this is what the family wanted to believe.

Yet this does not explain why Shag listed the Far East as a possible travel destination in 1931, so soon after his arrival in Geneva and even earlier than the conversation reported by his wife. Was it on a whim? Was it due to an innocent childhood interest he carried into adulthood? Was he drawn from some earlier study of dermatology to China, hearing it might be an exotic and challenging place to explore case studies of venereal disease, which at the time was treated by dermatologists? A conspiracy theory might lead one to return to former intelligence officer Hitch's allegation that Shag was under the sponsorship of the international Communist movement while in Europe. Was he possibly directed to

China through the network of Soviet agents he would have met in Europe? Otto Braun, the Comintern agent who accompanied the Red Army on the Long March, reports that, upon arriving in Yan'an, Shag confided to him that he went to China "to place himself at the disposal of the Chinese Red Army."[10]

Shag himself does not deny that he was familiar with Communist activities and literature prior to his arrival in China, nor that he was drawn to a socialist environment in which to practice medicine. "In Switzerland," he said, "we had worked all day once in our university surgery on people wounded when troops had shot up a demonstration of the unemployed. And in the lodging houses where we lived we had met 'perennial students' who were revolutionary exiles from fascist countries—Hungarians, Bulgarians, and the like. They sold us newspapers—like *Drapeau Rouge*, published by the Swiss Communist party. There one student in our group, Dr. Katz, mentioned that he had a brother in the Soviet Union and we talked for a while of trying to go there to work."[11]

Despite comments by Shag and others who knew him that he was drawn to communism before entering China, it is not at all clear that he embraced communism of any shade until well into his China experience. Certainly he gives no hint of this to his family in any of his letters home, and his constant need for money and clothing goes a long way toward disproving Hitch's allegation that his education was funded by the Communist International. It is intriguing speculation, however, and the possibility that Shag was encouraged to go to China by European Communists cannot be ignored, especially given that his friend and soon-to-be companion Lazer Katz had a brother serving the cause in the Soviet Union at the time.

Of all the reasons Shag himself proposed in later years, a careful look at his correspondence during the final year of study in Geneva leads to the conclusion that Shag's motivation was threefold. First, as he stated many times, he wanted a globetrotting adventure. This is supported by Grey Dimond, who says, "Thus, by the time he reached Shanghai, his ties to the United States were slender. He had not been there for four years; there was no family business or girl-friend to pull him home. His medical education was foreign and the Depression was at its worst. He had his medical degree, but he had no goal and Shanghai was pure adventure. He was young, educated, but adrift between cultures."[12]

Second, he wanted to study tropical diseases. In 1984, reflecting on his fifty years in Chinese medicine, Shag said, "I went to China in 1933. Many people have asked me why, and I say for two reasons: to see what was there, and to study tropical medicine. My classmates and I didn't even know if they had tropical medicine in China, but it was good enough to get a one-way ticket from our families for a year."

The third and perhaps most important reason was that Shag simply did not want to go home, no matter how often he stated his intent to do exactly that. The primary reason for his reluctance to return can be found in the expressions of frustration and guilt he shared with his family upon finding out about their financial difficulties. He was hurt at being placed outside the family circle, all the while still seeing himself as the "obedient" eldest son. That position was now tarnished, and he was bitter. He saw now that his return to the United States might not be such a triumphant one, and he no longer relished the trip home. He decided to flee his family obligations for a while rather than face such a return. In the 1970s, while visiting family in the United States, a nephew asked him why he never came home. "Shag looked around the room, leaned over to me and said he didn't come back, in fact he never intended to come home, because he just had to get away from the family."[13]

Meanwhile, as he sat in Europe preparing his move, Shag's family back in North Carolina still prepared for his return. Nahoum looked forward to a son who would bring both respect and wealth to the family. He also hoped that before Shag came home he would return to Syria to find a proper Maronite bride. The family business, while only just climbing out of the Depression, allowed them some freedom to prepare for a joyful homecoming. As the day of his expected return approached, his mother purchased his graduation and homecoming gift, a living room furniture set for the home of Roanoke Rapids' newest physician.

By all accounts Shag's family, especially his parents, were gravely disappointed when they learned of his plans. In the summer of 1933, six years after their son had begun his long and winding journey toward a medical degree, they received a letter telling them of his decision not to return home immediately after graduating, but to go first to the Far East, to Shanghai. His father wrote and told him he was a fool and demanded to know when he would return to set up practice in North Carolina. Shag answered that he expected to practice medicine in China for a short time, but he did not know exactly how long he would remain. Six years of family sacrifice would have to wait a bit longer to find reward in the triumphant return of the doctor son.[14]

The family response to Shag's decision is summed up by Theresa, who remembers that "Brother Joe left college and dug ditches to earn money to send to Shag. Aunts, uncles, all pitched in, sending Shag enough to complete his study. No sacrifice was too great, for they knew that 'this boy' was something special. To say they were disappointed when he wrote that he would be returning by way of Shanghai would be putting it mildly."[15]

It was a bitter pill to swallow for the Hatems of North Carolina and Buffalo, and they did not understand Shag's motives. But he still said he was coming home, so they waited. Little did his mother imagine that the furniture she bought to welcome her eldest son home would sit unused by him for the next 45 years, for it took that long for Shag to see his graduation gift. He used it for the first time in 1978, on his first trip back to the United States. No one had dared get rid of it, for it was his, and he was always coming home. Soon.

4 . SHANGHAI MARXISTS

In an effort to increase enthusiasm for the anti-Communist drive, Chiang Kai-shek, according to the Chinese newspapers, has increased the reward offered for the capture or killing of Communist leaders. The rewards for Chu Teh [Zhu De] and Mao Cheh-tung [Mao Zedong], taken alive, are $100,000 each, and $80,000 each if their heads are brought to General Chiang's headquarters properly certified.

New York Times, October 14, 1933

The utmost confusion prevails concerning the actual situation in the anti-Communist campaigns in Kiangsi [Jiangxi] and Szechwan [Sichuan] Provinces, the government claiming important victories, while private advices indicate the Red menace is growing.

New York Times, November 11, 1933

I am still looking around. I do not want to go home so I am staying in China.

Ma Haide, to a friend in the United States, August 1935

On August 3, 1933, Shag Hatem, now twenty-two years old and knowing little or nothing about China, received his new passport and prepared for his trip to the Far East. With colleagues Lazer Katz and Robert Levinson, Shag boarded a ship in Trieste that took him to several ports in Asia, including Singapore and Hong Kong.[1] On September 5, the three young American doctors landed in Shanghai, where they planned to establish temporary residency as they began their medical practice.[2] When he officially registered with the U.S. consulate in Shanghai soon after his arrival, Shag declared that he planned to "practice medicine on behalf of self" and return to the United States within "one year or perhaps two."

He and his friends were immediately overwhelmed by the sights and energy of Shanghai. Years later Shag remembered that first encounter.

When we got to Shanghai the first evening, we took a walk along the main street, Nanjing Road. It was a real sight, millions of people, it seemed. We'd

34

never seen that many people. There were mothers carrying their children so lovingly and so tenderly, and my classmate said, "Any people who love children as much as they do must be a good people."[3]

The day after arriving, Shag wrote home to share his first impressions of Shanghai.

> Foreign Y.M.C.A. of Shanghai
> 150 Bubbling Well Road
> P.O. Box 1647
> Sept. 6, 1933
> Dearest Folks,
> Just arrived in Shanghai where I'll stay for a short time. I will write you full particulars later but I have just landed and am taking care of my baggage and customs.
> Shanghai is nothing like you imagine it to be. It is very large and as clean and modern as Buffalo even cleaner. It has all the comforts of America.
> I'm in very good health. I have never felt so well since I remember. I hope all of you are in very good health and that we'll soon be together again.
> Write to me in c/o the American Express Co. Shanghai, China.
> I hope to hear from you very soon and will end with love to all of you & kisses from your son.
> Loving
> Shag

Excited by the familiar, Western-like impression of Shanghai, Shag in his early days viewed the city through the tunnel vision of the foreign community. As his twenty-third birthday approached, he wrote his family again.

> Foreign Y.M.C.A. of Shanghai
> The Bubbling Well Road
> P.O. Box 1647
> Sept. 24, 1933
> Dear Folks,
> As these few days pass I will have aged another year. I hope you have not forgotten my birthday is the 26th of Sept. We have not celebrated our birthdays to-gether for five years and the last time you saw me I was 18 years old. I wonder if you'll recognize me. I have quite a number of grey hairs and people think I'm 30 years old. That is as it should be. It may inspire confidence. I'm sure that you will recognize your son.

I'm feeling fine and profiting a great deal from this trip. I would like to hear from you—a letter at least. It takes more than a month to reach here. I hope you will write. . . .

We are looking over the Public Health Dept. and its means of preventing Epidemics. I will close with love & kisses to all of you from "Doc".

Despite their attraction to the city, Shag and his colleagues found Shanghai less than welcoming as they attempted to establish a medical practice. They were unfamiliar with the culture and customs of China and inexperienced in setting up a medical business. Wilfred Burchett, a Western Marxist and one of Shag's frequent visitors in post-liberation China, states that upon arriving in Shanghai, Shag was "guileless, good-hearted, apolitical."[4] Rewi Alley, the man who was to befriend, guide, and support Shag over the next half century, said, "It was not easy for him when he arrived in 1933. He was unknown, and the mere display of a medical practitioner's sign did not mean that paying patients would automatically come to him and his partners."[5]

As young Dr. Hatem struggled to establish himself, the financial difficulties faced in setting up a practice forced him yet again to ask for help from his family.

Foreign Y.M.C.A. of Shanghai
150 Bubbling Well Road
P.O. Box 1647
Oct. 9, 1933
Dear Folks,

I have received the letters where you inform me that all is well and that you would like a few Chinese things. . . . I am now studying tropical diseases here and enjoy the work very much. Here they have the same diseases that may occur at home but much more difficult and very interesting to know.

By the way, how is business with you at home and how are your future plans. What ideas do you have for me when I get home. Of course you know when I get home I will take a year & a half internship or maybe 2 years internship before starting my practice. Another thing—is Joe now going to college and how is he getting on? . . .

I would like to ask for $50.00 if you have it. If you have, send it out at once or let me know. Don't worry if you haven't got it but I sure would like to have it. I thought I wouldn't ask you for any more money but it seems like I will. Anyway please forgive me & don't worry. My love to all our folks and my uncles and aunts.

With kisses from Shafick your son.

P.S. When you send the money don't send a check. They are very hard to cash. Send money orders or Express.

Shag and his two friends knew they had to look beyond their families for support, however, so they set out to gain favor with the wealthy foreign community that lived extravagant lives apart from the Chinese. They quickly saw that their easiest access to the foreigners in Shanghai was through the local Jewish community. This was only natural, since both of Shag's colleagues were Jewish, and everyone they met assumed that Shag shared the same heritage. Rather than disabuse them, the three hatched a plan that turned this misunderstanding to their advantage. Shag's dark, Middle Eastern features helped. "The most well-off Jewish community were the Sephardi—coming from Iraq, Persia and India, not from Europe. And they looked down on the Ashkenazi—or European—Jews. So one of our bunch, Dr. Lazar Katz, said to me, "You be a Sephardic Jew, you're Middle Eastern. Result—the Sephardis started to invite and help all of us on my account."[6]

The first opportunity for the three doctors to practice medicine was in the American-run St. Luke's Hospital. Soon they were also working in the British-sponsored Lester Chinese hospital. They spent their time primarily in the charity wards of these hospitals.

While working in the two hospitals, the young American doctors also set up a private clinic on the side. Most of their business was in the profitable treatment of venereal disease, although they also had to deal with occasional epidemics, such as a mumps outbreak in early 1934. The location of their private clinic, the Continental Bank Building located on Jiajing Road in the foreign concession, placed them in the center of the expatriate community.

Shag was thrilled to have his own clinic and immediately wrote his parents with the good news.

Dr. Hatem
Dr. Katz
Dr. Levinson
Continental Bank bldg.
10 Kiukiang Road
Tel. 10501
March 27, 1934
Dear Folks,
    I have just received your last letter and I'm happy to hear that you are all well.

I am in quite good health and am working and enjoying it. My Hospital work takes most of the morning and some hours in the afternoons and then I do private practice with my firm whose name you see above and who also were with me in Syria, Geneva & Shanghai. The world does not give anyone a free living but one must work hard. Thats what I'm doing. I am trying to make you very proud of your son who you gave so much to and who you won't forget I hope. He is thinking of you all always and hopes to be soon with you. I am trying to do everything I can for the future so that I will benefit most of what you have done for me. We have a very nice office of which I'll send you pictures and we have our private patients. It is very difficult to get patients until people know us but it is better now. We have just started and I hope it goes.

Anyway, I'll be home in a year's time for my internship in New York that I'm trying to get and then we'll be together again.

I read my father's arabic very easily and it made me almost cry. I am very happy for those few sentences which encourage me and make me feel like a man. Dear father I know you have confidence in me and I know you'll back me up in my work. I am enclosing a prescription blank. I send you all my love & I wish you to be very proud of me. I am working hard for all of us—
Love from your obedient son,
Shafick

The prescription blank sent with the letter read:

Pts. Name Dearest Father & Mother
Rx I will prescribe and wish for you all the happiness in the world. I am not forgetting all you have done but I ask for your confidence and let me do what I see fit.
Kisses M.D.S.— 10,000,000. Take as directed from all my heart. That is my prescription.
Dr. S. Hatem *M.D.*

The "quickest way for young doctors to get started in Shanghai" in those days, as Edgar Snow later explained, was to treat venereal disease.[7] While his practice did not make money at first, Shag soon expanded into the more profitable business of providing medical care to prostitutes and their customers. His first big break came in June 1934, and it gave him his first look at the social ills eating away at China, ills that he had avoided for the first several months. He recalled that there "was a very high-class dermatologist and venereologist going on a three month vacation. I was hesitant to take over his practice, because I didn't know if I would earn enough to contribute to my other classmates. But the doctor told me, 'My dear young man, you have nothing to worry about.' And he outlined what my income would be. 'We have a roster of a hundred foreign prostitutes who have to come in regularly to have their passbooks signed that they are fit. And we have a roster of 200 Chinese for whom you have to examine and sign the passbooks. We have a contract with the Dutch steamship lines that their captains and first mates will get their venereal disease treatments in our office. We have the Shanghai police force on contract. And if this is not enough, we charge US 300 per abortion, and the *Round the World Cruises* have our cards.' "[8]

His interest in venereal disease, coupled with his desire to make some money at long last, persuaded Shag to take the practice. It was not pleasant to observe up close the underside of Shanghai society, but this very ugliness brought him financial comfort, and the longer he stayed, the more he found himself fighting off the lure of even more riches. He was regularly offered bribes by both prostitutes and their police protectors to provide bogus clean bills of health.[9] It was a way of life that many foreign physicians found profitable, without a tinge of guilt or concern for those they treated. Shag never let on to his family exactly what kind of medicine he practiced. Making money off Chinese prostitutes would not be easy to explain back home.[10]

Before long, the unrelenting poverty and corruption in Shanghai began to take a toll on the three young Americans. Once, news arrived in Shanghai about a flood on the banks of the Yangzi River. The three physicians volunteered their services to assist the victims, only to be told by Nationalist government officials that this was a minor flood and that no more than two million would be killed or displaced. They need not trouble themselves, they were instructed.

Soon a pivotal event pushed Shag's two colleagues over the edge. Shag recounts what happened at his clinic while he was substituting for the doctor on vacation. "Meanwhile, what was my friend doing in our practice? He was sitting in the office waiting for patients when a well-dressed gentleman with a nice briefcase came in. He said, 'We have a proposition for you. You are a young, struggling physician and we'd like to help you. I have two kilogrammes of pure heroin and you, being a doctor, can cut it and dispense it. You're in the International Settlement of Shanghai, so nobody can touch you because you have extra-territorial rights. You can make a fortune in no time.' "[11]

That evening, after rejecting the offer, the three young physicians talked of leaving China and returning home. Katz and Levinson said they were disgusted with the conditions they found and their inability to do anything about it. The plight of Shanghai's poor surrounded them, and all three doubted their ability to contribute to the overwhelming need for medical care. "You could diagnose, write prescriptions, but the people you wanted to help had no means of paying for the medicine."[12] On reflection, Shag said that "I and some of the rest of us, began to ask ourselves, why was the condition of those poor patients so awful. And why did only the terminal cases get to hospital at all. We began to think more about the social aspects—and to doubt how much good it was to be just doctors in the face of the real problems."[13]

Six months after arriving, Katz booked a ticket and left China for the United States. He had a "well off" fiancée waiting for him, and that prospect clearly outweighed Shanghai's offerings. Levinson, heeding the call of his family and disgusted with life in Shanghai, returned home six months later.[14] But the lifeline between Shag and his family proved too weak to pull him back. Su Fei says he decided to stay in China "to see what would happen to this society."[15]

It is clear that Shag had some sense of what it was he wanted to stay around to see and why he wanted to see it. He was adventurous, but not directionless. Soon after he established his medical practice in Shanghai, and before his friends left the country, he had established friendships with more than the community of Jewish merchants in Shanghai. He grew preoccupied with the suffering he saw around him and discreetly sought out those in China who might provide answers to his questions. As a first step, he accompanied a friend he had met at the YMCA to the Zeitgeist Bookshop, known to the police in Shanghai for its radical foreign visitors and Marxist literature. Only twelve by eighteen feet in size and poorly lit, this bookstore was located only a few blocks from Shag's clinic. Operated by Irene Wedemeyer, a German Marxist married to a member of the Chinese Communist party, the bookstore served as the gathering place for the small band of Western leftists in Shanghai who supported the struggles of the outlawed but determined band of Chinese Communists then isolated in south China. The government considered the bookstore to be not only a gathering place for European and Chinese leftists, but also a hub in the chain of communication with the Comintern.[16] Ruth Weiss, a young Austrian Ph.D. who met Shag shortly after she arrived in Shanghai in the mid-1930s, remembers that the bookstore enticed people off the busy street for three reasons: "There were books in several languages, more or less progressive in nature, progressives and spies."[17]

After his friends left, Shag visited the bookstore almost every day. In his early visits he only browsed the shelves and talked to no one.[18] When conversations finally began, he impressed those working there with his sensitivity to China's problems and his desire to do something about them. It was through these visits to the bookstore that Shag first learned of the work carried out by the Chinese Communist party and where he was first introduced to basic Marxist ideology. He read the works of American Communist writer Mike Gold and was impressed by Forsyth's *Redder than the Rose*.[19] Wedemeyer talked to Shag about political issues and arranged for him to meet other seasoned radicals who visited the store. So while Shag was busy treating prostitutes, assuring his family of his return home, and taking in the comforts of a foreigner's life in Shanghai with his professional friends, he also was quietly opening a path to the Chinese revolution. He took one step at a time, but the steps led in one direction only.

At this point, it is interesting to reflect once again on the suspicions of some that Shag went to China with more than medicine on his mind. For someone seeking evidence of a political motivation to go to China, it is easy to read mischief into Shag's visits to the leftist bookstore in Shanghai so soon after arriving in Shanghai. Was he told before arriving in China that he should go there to meet others involved in political struggle? Did someone meet with him upon his arrival and encourage him to visit there? Or did he just hear of this place by chance and visit it as an innocent sojourner, intrigued by its message? He insists that it was the latter, that he had no notion of joining up with the vanguard of leftists in Shanghai until he met these people through his visits to the bookstore. Whatever his initial motivation, the Zeitgeist Bookshop in Shanghai appears to have marked a fork in the road for Shag. He was clearly drawn by dynamic and persuasive personalities into a struggle to wipe away the pain he saw around him. Of these personalities, three proved most important to Shag: Agnes Smedley, Rewi Alley, and Madame Song Qingling.[20]

Agnes Smedley had come to China in May 1929. Already well known for her support for working-class struggles around the world, her arrival in Shanghai earned her immediate attention from the Special Branch of the Shanghai Municipal Police, an outfit assigned to watch political activists. She also was followed for years by the U.S. Consulate-General, who worked closely with the local police. The Chiang government accused her, correctly, of distributing Communist literature. She was protected to some degree by her close relationship with Song Qingling, a relationship that was somewhat strained in later years.

By 1930, Smedley had gravitated to the leftist literati in Shanghai, a newly burgeoning collection of writers and artists. Some of these intel-

lectuals formed the League of Left Wing Writers, and Smedley immediately set her energies to work for this organization. Among her colleagues were Lu Xun, China's leading writer of the twentieth century,
and Mao Dun, a young writer who was to play an important role in
throwing the support of progressive intellectuals toward the Communist
party. This involvement with China's leading intellectuals gave Smedley a
greater understanding of China's problems and a greater passion to recruit as many Westerners as possible to the struggle. Haranguing potential candidates day and night if needed, Smedley spent long hours at the
Zeitgeist Bookshop. "All she needed was the most casual hint that a
newly arrived foreigner had leftist political leanings and she was on to
them." The bookstore was where she first met Shag.[21]

By 1932, Smedley had met Rewi Alley, an apolitical, outgoing young
New Zealander who had arrived in China in 1927 seeking adventure and
a new life. He walked the streets of Shanghai for the first time on April 21
of that year, only a few days after Chiang Kai-shek broke the united front
he held with the Communists and began the systematic killing of anyone
suspected of Communist party membership or sympathies. Alley was not
prepared for what he witnessed: groups of young men and women
marched down the streets to the execution grounds because of their
political ties. He did not understand, but he was fascinated. He decided
to stay and learn as much as he could of the language and the people.
Beginning as a firefighter in the International Settlement, he soon grew
interested in the plight of the young mill workers around Shanghai and
used his position with the fire department to monitor their working conditions, seeking ways to help make their lives more tolerable. A British
friend and schoolteacher named Henry Baring—soon to be assassinated
by the Shanghai police—told him he first had to study Marxism. Just
before Baring's death, he not only introduced Alley to Marxist theory,
but also introduced him to the leftist community in Shanghai, led by
Agnes Smedley.[22]

Alley and Smedley had much to offer each other. Smedley had lived a
life of action for years, and she encouraged Alley's political development.
Alley, on the other hand, offered Smedley and others in the foreign community of Shanghai an in-depth look at the day-to-day problems Chinese
workers faced. Soon after they met, Alley took her on a tour of the factories he inspected regularly. The impact on Smedley, who prided herself
on her toughness, was immediate. "What you have shown me is too hor-
rible, too ghastly. I do not know how any decent person could go on
looking at it. What are you going to do about it?" she quizzed Alley. He
could only answer that he had no idea, but that he wanted to change the

structure that allowed conditions like this to exist. Gripping his wrist, she told him, "Then let us get along with the job of changing it."[23] After this visit, Smedley took Alley to visit Song Qingling, at that time the most important supporter of the progressive movement in China. And so the paths of Smedley, Alley, and Song Qingling crossed. These three were to have the greatest impact on the small but dedicated group of foreigners in China who struggled against the social and political terror they found around them. The recruitment of Shag to this Shanghai circle was, in some ways, the completion of a cadre that would represent Communist China to the Western world for the next half century.

Alley first met Shag in 1933 at the weekly social gathering of Shanghai's political left. "It was in the home of Agnes Smedley, in Shanghai," he recalled, "and I well remember him as being a stocky, breezy, wide awake young American, interested in everything around him."[24] The relationship between the tough, thirty-seven-year-old Alley, a twice wounded veteran of World War I, and twenty-three-year-old Shag Hatem, a young physician, would be one that lasted through the next fifty years of adventure, turmoil, victory, and struggle. Their special friendship never waned.

Memories differ on exactly what political affiliations Shag formed in the first months of his involvement in this new circle of friends. Both Shag and Alley report that in 1933 a political study group formed around Alley, with Shag one of his students. Su Fei says the study group also included Smedley and Ruth Weiss, along with Taletha Gerlach, an American YWCA worker who later became Song Qingling's personal secretary, and Heinz Shippe, a Marxist theoretician from Germany. According to Su Fei, they studied Marx's *Capital* and *Communist Manifesto,* as well as issues related to land distribution, the evolution of human society, and China's relationship with the West. While Su Fei says that her husband easily assimilated the principles of Marxism-Leninism because of his background as a member of the American proletariat, Shag himself later remembered that Alley "told us a little about Marxism-Leninism, but that didn't mean much to me at that time."[25]

What did make an impression on the young doctor were stories of the Red Army and his own visits to the execution grounds of Shanghai. Alley told Shag and the others, "There's an army out there fighting to change this whole thing. They're serious. And if you don't believe me, I'll take you out and show you what really happens."[26] He then took Shag and the others to the outskirts of Shanghai, in the area where the Shanghai airport now stands, to watch the systematic executions of young Chinese who opposed the Nationalist government. To some it was a tourist attraction, literally a stopping place for the world travelers passing through

Shanghai. For Shag it was a confirmation of the path he was beginning to take. "Young people were being taken out to be shot," he recalled, "some blindfolded. They were marched in a row and would yell, 'Down with the Guomindang (Nationalist party)! Down with imperialism! Long live communism! Long live the Red Army!' And then they were shot. Some weren't really Communists; they were just students or workers who had said something against the local authority or the boss. And then I realized that people who are willing to be shot and still yell slogans to liberate the people and change society must be pretty serious people."[27]

Exactly who introduced Shag to Marxism remains a mystery. Many take credit for being there when it happened. Ruth Weiss, one of Shag's comrades at the time, says she joined him, Heinz Shippe, and Shippe's wife Trudy Rosenberg in a Marxist study group. This group was led by Shippe, the only theoretician among them and rumored by some to be an important Comintern agent in China.[28] This group, which Weiss says met in 1935, studied Marxist literature very seriously under Shippe's tutelage. They read works such as "Marxism, Leninism on the Path to Social Revolution in Asia" and "Marxism: Outlook on Human Social History." Most of the time, Shippe lectured and the others listened. Weiss also remembers that there was "maybe one exam" and that the group was encouraged by Smedley, though Smedley herself did not join it.[29] They met sporadically, and changed meeting places regularly. It was an amiable group, socializing regularly in local restaurants following their serious political discussions.

Weiss says she knew of Alley's discussion group and that it was progressive, but never Marxist in nature. She also says that Shag was not a member of Alley's group. While it is difficult to be certain, it appears that Shag did indeed join more than one study group, just as he stated. After starting with Alley in 1933 and 1934, he apparently moved on to a more theoretically grounded study group led by Shippe in 1935.

Weiss stresses one understandable yet insurmountable problem that makes it difficult today to sort out all the relationships and political activities during that period. The problem is that no one wrote anything down for fear of endangering comrades, friends, and family. Alley once warned Weiss about this after she had written him during his travels outside of Shanghai. He sent word back to her through a friend, saying, "Tell Ruth to collect butterflies—do anything—but don't write letters." People disappeared quickly and without warning when their names were found in correspondence linked to those who were politically suspect.[30]

The clandestine activities of those supporting the cause of revolutionary change in China during the 1930s were not all seriousness and intrigue. There were many social activities, with frequent parties and dances. On one such occasion, at a party to celebrate the October Revolution, Shag approached a "pretty, graceful, middle-aged woman talking to guests in fluent English."[31] Not knowing who she was, he asked her to dance. Only after the dance did Smedley tell him that she was Madame Song Qingling, widow of Sun Yat-sen, matriarch of the progressive movement in China, and enemy of the reactionary Nationalist party led by her brother-in-law Chiang Kai-shek. Smedley took Shag over to Madame Song, introducing him as a friendly doctor recently arrived from Geneva, and introducing her as "Suzi," the American name used by her close foreign friends. The embarrassed Shag apologized for being so forward with her earlier but was told not to worry, since this was just a small party attended by good friends.[32] By this time Smedley and Madame Song, who had first met in Moscow in 1928, were working closely together, and Smedley was eager for her newest recruit, the young American physician, to meet the matriarch. As soon as they were introduced, Madame Song saw that he could make a contribution. She was impressed by his profession, his eagerness, and his winning charm and good humor. It was a major jump from the venereal disease clinics of Shanghai to the conspiratorial parlor of Song Qingling. Before the evening was over, Shag was another recruit to the struggle.

As he drifted closer to Marxism, Shag struggled to explain to his family his changing views of China, although not in any detail. In one letter written in early 1935, he wrote for the first time of problems he saw in China. His family had never before received such a letter from him and interpreted it to mean he was unhappy and perhaps in poor health. He wrote back to allay their concerns.

Dear Folks

. . . I am very surprised that you misread my other letter for I am not suffering and not unhappy considering that I am away from you dear folks and miss you. . . .

I intended to have left here by now but I was not thru and then I might get a wonderful job here with good work & salary as a doctor. I think that it would be wise to take this job and work for a while and make some money. Anyway I am waiting for an answer about this job and when you get this letter I will know definitely. . . .

Please don't worry about me at all. I am not feeling bad and I am not worried except about all of you and how bad you feel about my not being home. Please don't worry and give me a little time to try out my work here

and then I'll come home bigger and better than ever. I always think of you all
and hope all of you are in good health.

Again I repeat I am staying here just a little while longer to see about these
jobs. I have money so don't worry and I am in good health and love you all
and think of you all the time.

Love and kisses to Pa & Ma Freda, Joe & Shafia

Your loving son,

Shafick

Although meant in part to soothe his family's anxiety, this letter actually
led them further astray. In reality, Shag was not seeking another job and
had no plans to return home in the near future. He was beginning to
participate actively in the underground political movement of Shanghai.
The distance between the wayward son in Shanghai and his family back
in North Carolina grew as the days passed. The family he left behind was
in many ways replaced by a surrogate family of Chinese patriots and
Western Marxists.

The role Shag was to play in his remaining year in Shanghai proved
useful both to the movement he now supported and to his own political
development. At the request of his new friends, Shag used his profession
as a cover for their activities. What better place than a foreigner's medical
office to hold secret underground meetings? He sometimes watched the
door to his clinic during these meetings and served as the lookout for
meetings elsewhere. He had a car, something most foreigners in his
political circle were without, and used it to smuggle messages to and
from Madame Song, who was fearful for the safety of underground
members seen with her. At times he visited jailed revolutionaries on
behalf of Madame Song on the pretext of providing medical care to the
prisoners.[33]

By now Shag was pulled closer into the circle. Alley showed him how
to carry ammunition to Communist party members by hiding it under
the seat of a rickshaw, and he learned of a secret radio transmitter/
receiver operated out of Alley's home that allowed the underground in
Shanghai to communicate with the liberated areas of northwest China.
Shag also used his car to smuggle underground Communist party members on the first leg of their escape from Shanghai aboard ships bound
for the Soviet Union. As early as 1934 he exhibited journalistic skills as a
political propagandist for China's revolution. With a push from Smedley
he wrote articles on the Chinese Red Army for the New York *Daily
Worker.* After the arrival of Max and Grace Granich, American Communists who started the *Voice of China* in Shanghai, Shag continued to write

about the struggles in China, always under a pseudonym. Alley, already embarked on a career as a propagandist for the Communist party, continued to serve as his mentor and guide by editing all of Shag's articles and encouraging him to use the pen as well as the scalpel.[34]

Shag wrote his family sparingly now. He dared not tell his parents what he was up to, but he did not hide his satisfaction with his purposeful life. By August 1935 he would write hastily and without the warmth of earlier years. "There is not much else to say about myself except that I am very interested in my work and am very happy about it. It is indeed a pleasure to have an occupation and profession that one loves to do. This makes it very easy. . . . I love you all and you know it no matter what my actions do say sometimes. You will forgive me and I close with my love to all of you." Following a series of such letters, the family's correspondence slackened as they began to lose all hope of his return.

While keeping his family in the dark about his new direction in life, he shared his new interest with other friends in the United States who might better understand. The letters to his family, when compared to those he sent to trusted friends, show a man living two lives. On the same day that Shag sent his family the letter saying only that he was happy with his life, he wrote a letter to his recently departed medical colleague Lazar Katz, confiding that he was now indeed a supporter of China's revolutionary struggle. It was the most revealing indication yet to those outside Shanghai that the young doctor had found new meaning in life.

August 1, 1935
Dear Katzie,

I am still looking around. I do not want to go home so I am staying in China. The folks quit writing to me since I told them this and now I am free to do what I please. I cannot agree with them that I should come home and start an office. I detest private practice and I will never do it. I will always try to do something else. There are more things in the world than yourself and your family. There is the whole world in misery and your minor problems are nothing. I would like to go to Russia but that would be just like running away. I'll wait till the rest of the countries become like Russia and in the meantime I will do what I can to help. To have a practice to cure a couple of old fat people and sit on my can doesn't suit me any longer. I have energy and I have a different view toward life. I know what I want, why I want it, and how to get it. I'll work hard and be happy. I will never get to be a rich doctor and it is so futile that I ever thought so. Any small salary job as a doctor suits me and I think that I have one.

My future plans are as follows: . . . in September I start in the insane asylum that has just been built for 600 patients. I will work only half day for room and board and 100 mex dollars a month. Then there is another contract job with a company which would pay 150 a month. I can take only one and that is all. I will be O.K. In the meantime I am very interested in China and the Chinese efforts at liberation. It is very interesting and I am quite content. No I am not in love and have no girl friends but I will soon remedy that situation. I may not be so well off as you see it Katzie but I assure you that I am very well off and life means so much to me now. Life on a broad view not limited by any racial or national ties, life that offers the greatest freedom. You understand why I need it, because I was brought up in the same school that you were and I have learned the lesson of freedom as applied on a world scale.

I'm sure this sounds like preaching but it is all so true and Katzie I only wish that you were here and we could easily understand each other and talk seriously about many things. You know that for you I wish you the utmost happiness and fulfillment of all your desires. . . .

I am your friend forever, and you know it. Love to Sefma, Btesh, Fred and your family and brothers and sisters and your dear mother. Appleman is in America with Bob.

From your Shag of Shanghai[35]

By early 1935, the Long March had begun—a 6,000-mile tactical retreat to the north by 80,000 men and 35 women, headed for a destination not yet defined. Up to this point the Shanghai foreigners who supported the Red Army knew little or nothing about Mao Zedong. While he was an important member of the Communist party leadership, he was not yet the paramount leader he would become. His view that the peasants should play the central role in the revolution was not popular with the Moscow-trained leadership to whom he reported, nor to many of the leftists who supported the Party in Shanghai.

It was not until January 1935, at the Zunyi Conference of Politburo members held in Guizhou Province, that Mao moved to wrestle the leadership away from Bo Gu, a Soviet-trained Marxist, Li De (Otto Braun), the Comintern agent sent by Stalin to help lead the Party, and others. He and his supporters accused this group of leading the Party to the brink of extinction. Mao was named to the Standing Committee of the Politburo. Zhu De and Zhou Enlai were placed in charge of all military matters, with Zhou holding the final say. These decisions made, the Red Army continued its trek north. Soon Mao gained the title of Political Commissar of the Red Army, sharing leadership with Zhou and Zhu. In September 1935, the army reached northern Shaanxi Province, where the Central Committee decided to establish its new revolutionary headquarters. The Long March was coming to a triumphant end. Soon the leadership moved its new camp to the town of Baoan. "Thus," states the official history of the Chinese Communist party, "the Zunyi meeting established the correct leadership of the new Central Committee represented by Mao Zedong. . . . Saving the Party and the Red Army at an extremely critical moment, it constituted a turning point on which hinged their survival in the history of the CPC and marked the maturity of the Party from its infancy."[36]

By now Shag's letters home to his family must have seemed baffling. There is little doubt they proved unsettling. These were new ideas coming from their son. On December 9 he wrote, "I know you miss me and love [me] and I miss you all and I love you but some sacrifices must be made sometime in life because life is not so simple as we think. News about China I think you get from the papers as much as anything I can write to you. There are innumerable amount of people starving both from floods and lack of work. The people suffer terrible and the government is worse than useless, corrupt and dishonest. Of course the foreigners in China occupy a privileged position and don't bother about these things." The despair and helplessness felt by the family at Shag's obvious disinterest in returning home is reflected clearly in a letter written by his sister Freda in the fall of 1935.

Box 25
Roanoke Rapids
Dear Shafick,

We have received your letter and was very glad to hear from you. I hope you won't delay in writing to us as you have done before, because we were worried.

Joe is leaving for college September 23. He is going to Greenville College because they have a place for boys now. I think he is going to study medicine. One thing about Joe, we shall never send Joe abroad to schools as we have done you. That was the biggest mistake anyone can do, but as long as you are satisfied it ought to be ok. I wrote and asked you to tell me more about your work but you seem like you haven't any news to tell us anymore.

I guess by the time you receive this letter it is your birthday. I'm hoping you have a happy birthday and many many more to come. It is useless to tell you that we hope you were here so we could celebrate your birthday

together, but I know you will enjoy it just the same. I haven't anything to tell you so we close with best regards and lots of love to you. Everyone here hopes you a very happy birthday.
Your Sister,
Freda

For years his family had awaited his return, which almost every letter told them was imminent. But now, for the first time, they doubted that he planned to return at all. Something was going on with their son. They were losing him—to whom or what they did not know—but they would not give him up easily. Finally Nahoum, fed up with his son's refusal to come home, decided to act. A few days after Christmas 1935, Shag received a letter saying his father was coming to China to bring him home. He was shocked at such a plan and responded immediately. Although attempting to show appreciation for their concern, he let them know in clear terms that this was a terrible idea.

Dec. 30, 1935
Shanghai
Dear folks,
 . . . I really am surprised to hear that my father is coming to China. This would be very good but I am extremely sorry that he will spend so much money that he can put in the bank for Joe's education, for we never know what will happen later. I wish you would tell father that I wish he would not come out here and waste all that money and anyway I expect to be home in the near future. Just be patient a little longer and everything will be as you wish it. I really intend to be home in a short while. Even if he came out here now I could not go back until I finish my work here and I will not go back, until then. If he has that much money extra let him save it for Joe. Maybe he thinks something is wrong with me and that is why I don't come home. This is absolutely foolish and I am exceedingly all right.
 . . . Things in China are quite unsettled and many things are happening. Things in Shanghai are quiet and nothing is happening although in the northern part of China the students and the people are trying to stop Japan from coming and taking all China. Things are becoming more and more serious but Shanghai is just like the United States, very quiet and peaceful . . .
Your obedient son
Shafick
P.S. Regards to all our friends. *Tell dad I wish he would not come!*

Hoping this response would placate the family and keep his father at home, Shag awaited his family's next move as he turned again to his work with the underground. The thought of his father coming to China to take him kicking and screaming back home was unsettling, if not downright embarrassing. In retrospect, one wonders what course in life Shag would have taken had his father come to Shanghai. Would the old family ties, which the "obedient son" had vowed meant most to him, have torn him away from China and from the revolution that now dictated his almost every move? Or would he have greeted his dad respectfully and then sent him as soon as possible back to the United States, all the time hiding his new friends and activities? We can only speculate how his father's visit might have swayed Shag, for after receiving his son's letter, Nahoum canceled his trip. Shag understated the relief he felt when he wrote back in early 1936: "I am glad that father decided not to come out here, because to spend so much money that can give Joe an education and the rest of the things that you need is not very easy to make up. Furthermore my plans are to be in the States soon. I cannot say any dates but as soon as I complete my plan you can rest assured I will come home like a homing pigeon and you will never be able to get rid of me."

Most of Shag's political work for the Communist underground involved illegal and dangerous activities unrelated to his medical practice. While the adventure was exciting, he remained frustrated that his professional skills seemed of little use to the revolution. That began to change in May 1935, when Alley asked him if he knew anything about chromium plating, a trade that Alley became familiar with in his duties as factory inspector. Alley was convinced the industry caused permanent impairment to those working in it. The fact that most of the workers were children only heightened his and Madame Song's interest in commissioning research on this hazardous work. Shag said he knew nothing of any disease connected with it but would look into it. So Alley, using his contacts in the business community, arranged for Shag to carry out a study of this trade.[37]

The report appeared in April 1936 under the title *Industrial Health in Shanghai China: A Study of the Chromium Plating and Polishing Trade*. It was published by the Chinese Medical Association, with funding from the Henry Lester Institute of Medical Research in Shanghai. This is the work Shag alluded to when telling his parents that, even if his father came to China, he could not leave until important obligations were met.[38] The report chronicled his research in Shanghai factories, in which he and his medical assistants examined two hundred workers.

A simple routine was followed: a social worker gathered and recorded details on the living conditions, hours of work, etc. A medical assistant recorded the medical history and one physician carried out a physical examination causing as little loss of working time as was compatible with a proper though not overdetailed observation of each employee.[39]

Shag and his colleagues soon found that Alley's fears were justified. Of the 200 workers examined, 141 were under twenty years old, with most aged fifteen–nineteen. He found 7 workers who were only eleven years old.

An entrepreneur, who may have paid a visit to a country district, will bring back a small boy promising the parents that he will have him taught a trade. He goes from workshop to workshop, till finally he finds a master who is in need of another unpaid assistant. He hands the boy over and for this may receive a sum of some $5 for his services, and the new master may not even know his name or any facts concerning him. It is obvious that should he fall ill, or become injured, there is little sense of responsibility on the part of the manager or owner of the workshop. . . .

It is . . . known that when the boy has served an apprenticeship of three or four years and is demanding that he receive some pay, it is often found convenient to replace him by a younger unpaid boy in good health fresh from the country.[40]

The research team investigated living accommodations, sleeping accommodations at the factories, diet, air quality, and general working conditions. Their findings were alarming.

This industry in China is seen to have rhinitis, ulceration and perforation of the nasal septum, phagedenic ulcers or "chrome holes," conjunctivitis, injuries, lead poisoning and a form of pneumoconiesis or fibrosis of the lung, as its specific risks. Other diseases such as tuberculosis, trachoma, otitis, skin diseases are common to the general poorer classes in China and are intensified here under the conditions of labour found in this industry.

. . . The general conclusion which may be drawn from the evidence gathered is that the alarming health conditions of the working population in the plating and polishing industry is due more to the extra-occupational factors such as living conditions, ill ventilated lofts, long working hours, poor food, etc. than to the specific risks of the occupation.

. . . Only when industry of China can be rigidly controlled and regulated and the general economic condition of the working population elevated to a normal standard of living, can progress in public health and industrial health protection be made.[41]

With this research report and the conclusions he drew from his investigation, Shag reconciled his profession and political activism. In 1984, he reminisced about the report.

> The chapter on nutrition showed that the young workers we surveyed—average age 14—were on a starvation diet. I counted and recorded the ulcers on their hands, caused by chromium plating solutions. All this convinced me that the only people who could really put an end to such horrors were the Chinese Communists and their Red Army.[42]

After arriving in China, Shag wondered how his small contribution could ever be felt in a society so depressed and downtrodden. He studied politics with new mentors and friends to discover answers, but that study, and the occasional movement of illegal documents and underground Party members, had little to do with his chosen profession of medicine. This experience researching the chromium plating industry opened his eyes to the potential contribution his professional skills could make toward China's development. More important, however, was the fact that others saw what he could do with his medical knowledge and the passion for politics he now coupled with that knowledge.

As the report on the ill effects of chromium plating approached publication, Shag took time to write two letters to his family. One he sent to his brother Joe. For the first time he shared in detail his new interests. He also tried to get Joe to join him, at least in spirit. He told Joe that he should work with the United States Communist party and help in the worldwide revolution. He also told him that he planned to send Joe a subscription to the *Daily Worker.* Joe wrote back immediately, telling his brother to forget sending the newspaper, as it could ruin his chances for making a living in the South. Shag wrote back an angry letter asking Joe if he planned to be a slave for the rest of his life.[43]

He sent to his parents another, softer letter in January 1936. This time, he sounded tired and evasive.

> Dear Folks,
>   I have not written to you for some time because it was not so easy to express myself in a few words and explain everything. I am enclosing you a clipping from a newspaper on the work that I am doing. I have been so busy that I did not have time to explain it all but soon it will be published and

then I am able to send you a copy. If you read this clipping it will explain what I have done and what I am doing. This is very good and very useful work and I will continue it till I leave. . . .

Spring is here and I remember dear Carolina and the nice springs we have there—the garden and chickens and digging and so forth makes me home-sick and the nice quiet evenings and the crickets—it is wonderful. Please be patient with me. I want to be with you and happy but some things must be done.
Your loving son
Shafick

"It is not so easy to express myself in such a few words and explain every-thing" and "some things must be done." One can only guess at how these words were interpreted by the Hatem family in North Carolina, but in hindsight they are clear. Shag's life now revolved completely around a world of political conspiracy and intrigue, and he had proven his worth. If he had indeed entered China fully aware of his goal, as statements by Hitch and various bits of circumstantial evidence seem to indicate, he had achieved it. He was now caught up in the struggle. If he entered China naive but sensitive to the plight of those living under pov-erty and oppression, as most accounts indicate, he gravitated naturally to the left, finding purpose in the ideas of Communist theoreticians and political activists. By 1936 it no longer mattered when or where he decided to join the struggle, for now he was totally committed to the revolution as he saw it playing out in Shanghai. Every day that pulled him deeper into that struggle drew him an equal distance away from the comfortable, privileged lives of his former classmates. More important, his commitment distanced him even further from his family in the United States, whom he had not seen for over six years.

After the letters he wrote in February 1936, only one piece of mail reached his family over the next eight years: his report on chromium plating. But this piece of mail left the family confused, for the return address was not their son's; in fact, he told them he would not have a fixed address for the near future. In order to shield them, he fabricated a story that he was on his way to the interior of Tibet to engage in some medical research funded by the Rockefeller Institute. His cousin Theresa remembers the day this news reached the family. "Little did we know that word from him or his whereabouts would be nil. From 1936 until sometime during World War II there was no word from him. The family prayed, cried, sang ballads, and had heavy hearts. To help his mother through those sad times my brother Ernest (age 10), was sent to

North Carolina to live with the Hatems. This would help Mrs. Hatem, we hoped, divert some of her waking hours to take care of an active 10 year old."[44]

His family was now far from Shag's mind as he devoted his medical skills to aiding the core of the movement to change China—the Chinese Communist party. As he had told his friend Katz, he now knew what he wanted, why he wanted it, and how to get it.

The record of Chiang Kai-shek as head of the Nanking (Nanjing) government since 1927, marked for the most part by compliance to Japanese demands, gives no certain indication of his future policy.

New York Times Editorial, July 22, 1936

Then the Red Army in the northwest sent down a message that they wanted an honest foreign journalist and a doctor. The foreign journalist picked out was Edgar Snow. They didn't ask for an honest doctor, so they took me.[1]

Ma Haide, 1984

Shafick George Hatem's passport issued in Shanghai on his arrival in 1933 stated his intention to return to the United States within one, "perhaps two" years. On August 2, 1935, Hatem appeared before James B. Pilcher, U.S. Vice Consul in Shanghai, to renew his passport. Hatem listed his profession as physician and his residence as 260 Yu Yuan Road, Apartment 4, in Shanghai. He was told that this passport would serve him for two years. In the space allowed to inform the government of his expected return to the United States, he wrote "unknown." It would be twelve years before he visited a U.S. consular official again to renew his long-expired passport.

By early 1936 Hatem knew that his future, at least in the short term, lay in the northeast area of China. He wanted to see for himself the new world of communism in China. He was encouraged by many in Shanghai to venture there, to offer his services, and to learn firsthand what this Communist movement was really all about. Several people encouraged him, and several have taken retrospective credit for his eventual move. Max Granich, in an interview in 1984, recalled that he was initially responsible for persuading the young doctor to venture to the Red Army base. During a discussion in which Hatem bemoaned the difficulties of making a living as a physician in China, Granich pointed out that the Red Army and the areas controlled by it were in great need of medical help. Granich said that Hatem responded enthusiastically to the idea of leaving Shanghai to join the guerrillas, and asked Granich to assist him in arranging the trip.[2]

In a discussion with his friend Wilfred Burchett, Rewi Alley explained that it was he who first told Hatem of the opportunity to join the Communists in their military camp. Alley says that at that time Hatem was looking for an opportunity to use his medical skills for political ends and was contemplating a move to Spain in support of the Republican cause if he failed to connect with the Red Army.[3]

Agnes Smedley also took credit for encouraging Hatem to go to Shaanxi. She insisted that he discover the truth about what was happening in China firsthand by joining the Red Army.[4] Edgar Snow reports that Smedley introduced Hatem to Liu Ding, an engineer and underground Communist party member in Shanghai. Liu told Hatem tales of egalitarian life in the Communist-controlled areas of China and the need for doctors there. Snow says that this discussion was a turning point in Hatem's life, as he was at the point of deciding whether to stay in China or to return to the United States. The encouragement to stay, the fact that he was made to feel needed, and the hope that he could make a mark in China all combined to cement his decision to remain in China.[5] In an interview in 1973, Hatem confirmed this, saying that Liu Ding pleaded with him to use his medical knowledge to aid the Communist struggle.[6] Years later Hatem explained, "I wanted to take part in the revolution in its front lines. I had a new aim."[7]

Ruth Weiss supports the view that Smedley first introduced Hatem to the idea, explaining that in 1936 she knew that Hatem was going to Shaanxi, and she asked Smedley to help her arrange a similar trip. Smedley, in her usual blunt manner, told Weiss that she had nothing to offer the Red Army and could not go.[8] Hatem, on the other hand, had much to offer in his medical skills. There is no question that Smedley's connections were impressive enough to allow her to know the needs of the Red Army and to make the arrangements for Hatem to venture to its base. Her close relationship with Song Qingling guaranteed this.

No matter who first encouraged him to go to Shaanxi, it is clear that Song and Smedley were the two Hatem credits with securing his invitation to the Communist base camp and working out the details of the trip. Hatem admitted that he was eager to go and could think of little else in late 1935 and early 1936. He told Madame Song, who by now he addressed as "Suzi," that he wanted to join the Communists while they were still on the Long March in Jiangxi. He told her he wanted to be a "revolutionary doctor." However, no arrangements could be made when he first showed such an interest. Finally, when the Red Army reached the northwest, he made his first effort to join them. In March 1936, with the help of Madame Song, he headed for Xi'an to meet with the Communist underground. He remembers that he "hung around the missionaries and the British-American Tobacco Company people as though I was an idle traveler." However, after waiting the prescribed twenty days in Xi'an with no contact from the underground, he returned to Shanghai dejected but determined to try again. Back in Shanghai, Hatem sought out Agnes Smedley. She told him she would use her contacts to help make new arrangements for another attempt. Song Qingling also continued to work on his passage to the guerrilla base area.[9]

In casual conversation with Alley years later in the comfort of his home in post-liberation Beijing, Hatem reflected on his determination as a young, naive rebel to join the Red Army. "It was quite a decision to take. . . . I spoke no Chinese, except a few words of Shanghai dialect, and I had really only that Shanghai perspective of China, knowledge of not much more than the casual bystander. . . . I thought I knew that the Red Army might be China's hope, but very few other people in my world thought so. . . . And so I went to Xi'an, but arrangements could not be made for me to go beyond there and I had to return to Shanghai, despondent and miserable, wondering whether the whole effort might not fail."[10]

Finally, a second chance came, this time in the form of a message from Mao Zedong to Song Qingling in June 1936. Hatem, showing the winning and self-effacing humor that won him friends throughout his life, says, "Then the Red Army in the northwest sent down a message that they wanted an honest foreign journalist and a doctor. The foreign journalist picked out was Edgar Snow. They didn't ask for an honest doctor, so they took me."[11]

After receiving Mao's message, Madame Song summoned Hatem to her house. When he arrived he found her alone. She informed him of the invitation from Mao and told him to prepare for the journey. She told him about the choice of Snow as the journalist and told him to travel to Xi'an as a tourist after first meeting Snow in Zhengzhou. She then gave Hatem one half of a torn five-pound note. In Xi'an he would be approached by someone with the other half. He would know then that he and Snow were in safe hands and on their way to Baoan. When he reached the liberated area in the northwest, he was to report to her regularly on the medical situation there, for she wanted to provide any

needed medical supplies. Hatem returned home immediately and prepared to depart. He packed his medical bag, camera, flashlight, coffee,
sugar, and cigarettes and prepared to leave the next day.[12]

Aside from these personal and medical needs, he carried political
information hidden in a secret compartment in his bag. "Actually," he
said, "I had become both doctor and messenger. In my luggage, I had all
kinds of documents, put in the bottom of tin cases of medicine and sol-
dered up. There were documents on [the] United Front, the 7th Congress of the Communist International and George Dimitrov's anti-fascist
united [front] speech, none of which I believe, had reached the Red
Army in full text up to that time."[13]

The next morning, after gathering personal and political materials, he
left for Zhengzhou. His commitment to Song Qingling was uppermost
in his mind. "At the time of my departure, Madame Song earnestly
engaged me as her representative stationed in Yanan, requesting that I
report with as much detail as possible on the medicine and hygiene of
the northwest in order to get more aid for the base."[14]

Approaching Zhengzhou, Hatem felt tense and suspicious. Although
he had lived in China for three years, he could not speak the language.
He had never met Edgar Snow, who lived in Beijing, and did not even
know what he looked like. He suspected spies all around him. As his
train pulled into the city, Hatem looked out his window and saw a well-
dressed man with a gauze mask covering his face and a camera dangling
from his neck. He leaned out the window, a foreign face obvious to
anyone looking, and saw the man study him carefully. The man then
shouted, "Shag, Shag, you're here at last." Helped by this stranger, he
then climbed out through the train window and met Edgar Snow for the
first time. Their foreign faces, especially their large noses, attracted
throngs of curious Chinese, and the two tried to carry on a conversation
above the commotion they started. Boarding the train for Xi'an, they
talked of their mutual friends Madame Song, Agnes Smedley, and Rewi
Alley, but stayed clear of politics. At Snow's urging, they played the part
of typical foreigners concerned only with special treatment and separa-
tion from common Chinese.[15] Years later, Hatem reflected on this first
leg of the journey with his new friend, remembering that "Snow was
brave and helpful in our travels together. He told me, 'If you look like an
arrogant, well-to-do foreigner, you might as well act like one in a good
cause. Just carry a visiting card in your pocket and if anyone tries to stop
you, flip it out and go right past them, don't stop or look back—they'll
let you through because that's what they expect of anyone important.'

That's the way we got all the stuff, medicines, documents and all, past the Kuomintang officials and guards."[16]

Snow, like Hatem, had tried more than once to visit the Red Army. As early as 1932, he had wanted to write the first Western account of this band of rebels. These early attempts failed, however, and in 1936 Snow traveled to Shanghai to seek the help of Madame Song. "I sought her help, so that at least I should be received by the Reds as a neutral, not a spy."[17] Joining Madame Song in the discussion were Agnes Smedley and China's leading progressive writer, Lu Xun. Snow explained to them what he wanted to do, and they gave him a sympathetic hearing, with the exception of Smedley, who seems to have coveted the chance to be the first foreign journalist to enter the Communist camp in the northwest. They were especially impressed after hearing that Random House publishers had given him an advance on a possible book coming out of such a journey.[18] His timing was perfect, for Mao's call for a journalist came only days later.

Within a few weeks of his return to Beijing, Snow was visited by Xu Ping, a university professor and acquaintance. He reports that Xu presented him with a letter written in invisible ink instructing him to travel to Xi'an. In fact, the letter was addressed to Mao Zedong and would serve as both safe passage and a letter of introduction. There was no note from Madame Song, but he suspected it was through her intervention that he was allowed entry into the Red-held area.[19] Years later, in an interview with American journalist John Roderick, Liu Shaoqi, then head of the Communist underground in China's northeast and later president of China, confided that it was he who gave final authorization for Snow's and Hatem's trip.[20]

Snow and Hatem give quite different accounts of the role each played in this fascinating journey. In Snow's account of his meeting with Hatem, he says that they met for the first time in Xi'an rather than in Zhengzhou.[21] Huang Hua, who joined the two Americans in Xi'an soon after their arrival there, supports Hatem, insisting that it was in Zhengzhou that they met.[22] Helen Foster Snow says she remains unclear on where the two first met, but she believes that Hatem has it right on this point. She also insists that until he embarked on the trip, Snow had never heard of Hatem.[23] In his book *Red China Today,* Snow says that not only did he not know of Hatem prior to the trip, he was not aware Hatem was making the same journey until he arrived in Xi'an.

> I . . . was given a letter to Mao Tse-tung, written in invisible ink. Armed with
> that, I went to Sian [Xi'an] and put up at the Guest House, where I was told

to expect a call from a certain 'Pastor Wang.' He would arrange to have me smuggled through the Nationalist lines into the Red districts, a hundred miles to the north. Soon after my arrival George Hatem introduced himself to me and told me that he was aware of my mission; he was also waiting for a call from Pastor Wang.[24]

It is not surprising that Snow would know nothing of Hatem, given the secretive nature of the underground movement in Shanghai and Beijing at that time. There is no reason Madame Song or Smedley would have told Snow of the young doctor and his role in supporting the political movement in which they were so deeply involved.

Other disagreements arose in the years following the journey. Hatem insisted that before leaving Shanghai he had already committed himself to the Communist party and that the torn five-pound note was the ticket for both him and Snow to Mao Zedong's headquarters. He argued that Snow never held a letter written in invisible ink, as he avowed in his writings. Furthermore, said Hatem, because Snow was not affiliated with the Communist party in any way, only someone close to the Party, like himself, could have been entrusted to make official contact with the underground. Helen Foster Snow counters that Snow did indeed have the contacts to make his own arrangements and that the invisible-ink letter did exist.[25]

In attempting to smooth over these differences, Hatem said that "Ed occasionally upgraded a story in order to make it better, and this is one of those examples. Ed was not always accurate, but we always forgave him because he meant well."[26] Rewi Alley agrees, saying, "Ed sometimes dressed up the truth to make a better story." He went on to say that Snow "sometimes would dress little parts of the story to give it more character, but never altered the accuracy of the reporting."[27]

It is possible—and in fact likely—that Snow and Hatem each held documents allowing them entry into the Communist-held areas, and that because of the secretive nature of their trip neither knew of the other's arrangement. Perhaps after so many years, one or both of them forgot some details. Whatever the actual circumstances, Snow and Hatem embarked together on a perilous, history-making adventure. Despite the different stories that came out decades after the fact, they no doubt enjoyed each other's company and depended on each other for survival while aiming for their respective goals. The scribe and the doctor that the Communists in Baoan had requested were on their way. All three parties gained much from the experience.

6. TWO BANDITS IN SEARCH OF CHAIRMAN MAO

Plundering Communist invaders laid siege today to the important provincial city of Titao, fifty miles south of Lanchow. Chinese officials estimated that 70,000 Red troops had concentrated in Southern Kansu Province.

New York Times, September 12, 1936

I was after a story. Dr. Hatem was a missionary in search of a mission.

Edgar Snow, 1961

In Xi'an the adventures shared by Hatem and Snow began in earnest. From that point on through the next quarter century, however, the world would be kept in the dark about the role Shafick George Hatem played in this saga. For all but a few, the young doctor vanished from the world he had known prior to 1936. Edgar Snow played a key role in Hatem's disappearance, for in his chronicle of this journey, *Red Star Over China,* there appears not one word about Snow's traveling companion. In Snow's autobiography published in 1958, Hatem still proves invisible. While his name appears occasionally in documents and remarks about China's revolution made by foreign visitors to Communist-held areas in the northwest, it was not until Snow's *Red China Today,* published in 1961, that Hatem makes a public appearance. Until then only a few people outside China knew of Hatem's trek to the northwest and his life with the Red Army. While the reasons for this—and for the mystery that surrounded him after his disappearing act—will be explored in more detail later, the original intent to keep his presence a secret was explained by Hatem in 1984. "Ed, in the first edition of his *Red Star Over China,* and for many years afterwards, didn't write about me being his companion. He had been asked not to because the people who had helped us in Shanghai might suffer if, after having left, I was reported as having turned up in the Northwest. This helped my incognito. The only related rumor that came out was that 'a Turkish doctor' was helping popularize the Red Army's work among Moslems (the Hui nationality) in China's northwest."[1]

As Hatem moves toward adventure and away from his past, we pick him up entering Xi'an with Snow, hoping to meet their guerrilla-base contact. Both on the train and at the station they found themselves followed by Nationalist agents at every turn. After taking three rickshaws, one each for them and one for their luggage, they arrived at a three-story guest house run by the Capital West Travel Agency, the only guest house for foreigners in Xi'an with modern furniture and bathroom facilities. Snow, the interpreter and lead man of the journey, played the demanding foreigner to the hilt. Hatem, lacking both language skills and experience outside Shanghai, willingly followed Snow's lead. With the arrogance expected of foreigners, Snow registered them at the desk and had their luggage taken to their room.[2]

After arriving, Snow cabled a prearranged coded message to his wife in Beijing. He told her to make arrangements with Wang Rumei, a friend and one of the leaders of the progressive student movement in Beijing, to come to Xi'an as soon as possible to assist Snow in his coming interviews. While his Chinese was passable, it was not fluent enough for the important conversations he hoped lay ahead. The young student, later to rise to the highest levels of Communist party and Chinese foreign ministry leadership under his underground Party name Huang Hua, had only recently been freed from jail for his role in the December 9 antigovernment student demonstrations in Beijing.[3] He was aware of Snow's trip and told him before he left Beijing that he would like to join the trek to Baoan.

As soon as Wang Rumei (Huang Hua) got Snow's message, he left for Xi'an. When he arrived one week later, he was surprised to find another American with Snow who was introduced as "Shag." He knew nothing about this man, nor would he learn much during the stay in Xi'an. Huang Hua, in recalling his initial meeting with Hatem, says, "In Xian he did not tell me anything about himself, and I did not inquire. My first impressions were that this was a man who was joyful and prudent."[4] While the first few weeks of this relationship between Hatem and Huang Hua proved distant, the two were just beginning a lifelong friendship.

The guest house where Snow and Hatem stayed was controlled by the Nationalist government, so they assumed that the rooms were bugged and that the waiters, waitresses, and other staff were spies. Soon after their arrival they were visited by a military officer who checked their passports and asked their business. The officer informed Snow he could

not report on the situation in the military zone surrounding Xi'an without explicit approval from Generalissimo Chiang Kai-shek. Snow said he
had no plans to spy, and that his companion would not be writing anything, since he was a physician, not a journalist. They came to Xi'an, he
said, to see the sights. After leaving the room, they were told there were
more than a dozen men in the hotel assigned to watch and protect them,
for Xi'an was now a dangerous place to visit.[5] When Huang Hua joined
them, the police were told that he was a student from Beijing researching
the banking industry in that area.[6]

Any serious conversation in the room was out of the question, so they
spent the next two weeks in the hotel engaged in mundane conversation
and playing gin rummy. As their tourist cover began to lose credibility,
Snow added a further reason for their stay in Xi'an. "To satisfy the hotel
manager's curiosity we told him we were going on a scientific expedition
in Chinghai [Qinghai] as soon as the rest of our party arrived."[7]

To cover up their true plans, Hatem and Snow visited old acquaintances of Snow's, mostly military and government leaders in the Nationalist party. They used this cover to contact underground Communist
party members. One such contact was made soon after their arrival when
they attended a dinner with General Yang Hucheng. Yang was Chiang
Kai-shek's pacification commissioner of Shaanxi Province, and the two
young Americans were eager to hear his report on the Reds now holding
the area north of Xi'an. Though he offered nothing, the evening was not
a total waste, because Wang Bingnan also attended. Recently returned
from studying in Germany, Wang was a family friend and protegé of
General Yang who now acted as Yang's personal secretary. More important, he was an underground Communist party member spying on Yang.
In later years he became an important political official in China's foreign
ministry and a personal acquaintance of Hatem's.[8]

They also visited Zhang Xueliang, the young general who was soon
to lead a revolt against the generalissimo in an attempt to force him to
negotiate with the Communists. But the Young Marshal, as he was
known, did not share this plan with Hatem and Snow, and their cover
remained intact as they paid social calls on the leaders of the Nationalist
government.

The two sojourners, now joined by Huang Hua, grew impatient
while waiting for the underground to arrange their trip to Baoan. They
did chance one meeting with a Party contact, but it was to no avail.
Hatem recalled, "In Xian we met Dr. Wunsch, a dentist, a refugee from
Nazi Germany. He was a very timid person, but eager to do what the
Party wanted. They had asked him to set up his dental office in the city,

to be a centre for underground work there. And a Party member had been detailed as his nurse. But when we met him, he was alone, and had not delivered the documents and books he brought because the guards and the killings in the city had scared him. They were still in the luggage deposit place in the Railway Station where he had left them and when he saw me and Ed Snow he said, 'It's dangerous, what shall I do?' Later in the Xian Incident, Dr. Wunsch was one of those killed accidently."[9]

On one occasion while they waited, four Nationalist officials came to Huang Hua's room to question him about his and his American friends' intentions in Xi'an. After initially refusing them entrance into his room, he decided to take a different tack and engaged them in enthusiastic conversation about the "Young Marshal" Zhang Xueliang. They softened at this, and he then turned the conversation to personal topics, asking them about their families, friends, and hometowns. When he discovered one of them was from the same town as one of his closest friends, he played on this relationship and eventually broke down their suspicions. They gave him no further trouble and the trio settled back, still waiting for their contact to arrive.[10]

Late one morning, as they fought heat and boredom, someone approached their door and asked to enter. Hatem opened the door and found before him a strong, heavyset gentleman wearing a long gray silk gown. He was carrying an umbrella in one hand and a large package in the other. He introduced himself in clearly spoken English as Mr. Wang, a Christian minister. He told them that the manager of the hotel informed him that the two Americans enjoyed antiques. As he traded in valuable antiques, he explained, he would like to show them his collection of Tang dynasty horses and camels. The Nationalist spies hovered outside the door, but they seemed to know the gentleman and showed no interest in his visit. The Americans invited him in. Only years later did Hatem discover that Wang was in fact Dong Jianwu, a Protestant minister and underground Party member that Song Qingling had secretly sent to Xi'an to make contact with Mao Zedong and Zhou Enlai.[11]

For several minutes the three discussed antiques, with Snow asking how much Wang wanted for two horses. According to Su Fei, the discussion and consequences developed in the following manner.

Snow: Well, . . . we want the two horses. How much?
Preacher Wang: The price is negotiable, but I want cash. And foreign currency is most welcome.
Snow: Foreign currency? American dollars or Francs?
Preacher Wang: I want British pounds only.[12]

Following this disclosure, Hatem took Snow into the bedroom and showed him his half of the five-pound note. This was the first Snow knew of the secret code sent by Madame Song. Snow quizzed the antique dealer once more, making sure he wanted only British pounds. When satisfied, Hatem gave Pastor Wang his half of the note, and Wang produced the other half. He told them to stay in the hotel and that he would visit them again soon. They had made their contact with the Party underground. Only a few more steps to go and they were on their way to Baoan.[13]

Within days, the next step was taken. One morning Hatem and Snow received two visitors to their room. Pastor Wang, accompanied by a young Nationalist officer wearing sunglasses, offered to take the two foreigners on a sight-seeing excursion. The four of them took an official car to an ancient Han city that had served as the capital of China over two thousand years before. After arriving at the site and getting out of the car, the officer, who for the duration of the trip had said nothing, removed his sunglasses and asked with a large and proud grin on his face if Snow and Hatem recognized him. Hatem, because he could not speak Chinese, had no idea what was going on. Snow, reflecting on this unexpected and bizarre meeting, remembers thinking:

> Recognize him? I had never met a Chinese like him in my life! I shook my head apologetically. He released a hand from my arm and pointed a finger at his chest. "I thought maybe you had seen my picture somewhere," he said. "Well, I am Teng Fa" [Deng Fa] he offered—*"Teng Fa!"* He pulled back his head and gazed at me to see the effect of the bombshell. Teng Fa? Teng Fa . . . why, Teng Fa was chief of the Chinese Red Army's Security Police. And something else, there was $50,000.00 on his head![14]

Snow quickly explained to Hatem who their host was. Deng Fa took each by the arm, and they walked around the old city, talking about the political situation in Xi'an and how the Communist party viewed the struggle against the Japanese and the Nationalists. As Snow interpreted for Hatem, they received instructions on how they were to be smuggled out of Xi'an and into areas held by the Red Army. They were to leave early the next morning.[15] Huang Hua was to follow a week later along the same route.[16] As they left for the hotel, Deng Fa delighted in telling them he was actually living with the Young Marshal right under Chiang Kai-shek's nose. With connections like these, they knew they were on their way to Baoan.

The men returned to their room in Xi'an and prepared to leave. The first thing Hatem did was inoculate Snow against smallpox, typhoid, cholera, and malaria, all deadly diseases they would encounter on their trip north. Following this, Snow crafted a cable to send to a friend in Beijing telling him that he would begin his return to Beijing the following day. The cable was picked up by the secret police, as Snow intended; as a result, their shadows in Xi'an relaxed and looked forward to the departure of the two troublesome Americans.[17]

That evening at midnight Snow and Hatem peered outside their window. They were looking for a prearranged signal, the lighting of a joss stick stuck in the wall that surrounded the guest house. When it came, Hatem first climbed out the window and jumped to the ground. Following him came their luggage, handed down by Snow, then Snow himself. They ran toward the signal and climbed the wall with their luggage, finding Pastor Wang on the other side riding a bicycle. The two of them then jumped on a cart and were whisked down the dark streets to an army base controlled by Zhang Xueliang. After stealing onto the base, Hatem and Snow fit into the back of a six-ton Dodge army truck loaded with supplies, primarily uniforms and cotton padded jackets, and waited for the next move. Snow reports that it came at dawn, when the gates of the ancient city were open "noisily dragging their chains before the magic of our military pass." As they passed through the gate, they burrowed themselves as deeply as they could under the clothing.

The truck headed out on a narrow dirt road, reaching the Wei River within an hour. There they boarded a ferry. After arriving on the other side, an officer in Zhang Xueliang's army climbed on top of the clothing and yelled into the pile for the two to come out, that they were now clear. They refused to move, fearful it was a trick. After several more enticements, however, they decided to take the chance and climbed out. After stretching and getting their bearings straight, Hatem and Snow climbed on top of the clothing and took the scenic route from there, ever watchful for bandits who might attack them. They most feared bandits of no particular political persuasion—highwaymen after anything they could get.[18]

As night fell, they found themselves in Lochuan, the largest county seat between Xi'an and Yan'an. The officer accompanying them found a room in a local inn, complete with an assortment of available singing girls if they desired (they politely refused) and an uninvited crowd of rats, mice, and lice as guests. Pigs and donkeys were lodged in the next room. Snow, who had traveled extensively in China and other parts of Asia, was uncomfortable but not surprised at the accommodations. The same cannot be said for Hatem, who for the first time was away from the comforts of the foreigners who lived in China. Snow chastised him for his timidity. "Shag," Snow told him, "forget your medical principles. This is Northwest China, not the United States." Hatem followed Snow's lead and pulled a rope down from the ceiling, where he tied into a bundle all of his clothing and what food he carried on him. Snow said they should sleep without any clothing to keep the lice off them during the night. For the next several hours they fought off mice and rat attacks, with Snow sleeping some and Hatem not at all.[19]

The next morning Hatem and Snow began another day's journey into the rebel area. As they traveled north, they saw few people, but they marveled at the sharply defined mountains and cave dwellings dug into the hillside. The land looked desolate to Hatem. The view from the truck showed that many of the caves were vacant, since the intense fighting in the area had driven the peasants from their homes. Soon they arrived at their next destination, Yan'an. Not yet the revered cradle of the rejuvenated Communist party after its Long March, it was at this time the headquarters for Zhang Xueliang's Northeast Army, which had concluded a truce at the time with the Red Army divisions on the outskirts of the town.

Yan'an was an ancient city, a military outpost through which countless nomadic armies had passed on their incursions into China. It was a city surrounded by mountain walls, with ideal natural defensive fortifications seemingly made for machine guns and lookouts.[20] Although he had no way of knowing it at the time, it was a place that Hatem would return to soon after this first entry into Red Army territory. The empty caves he now gazed upon would soon turn into his own living quarters and the hospital he would direct for over a decade.

On the second morning, Hatem and Snow were introduced to another Nationalist officer, who presented them with a donkey and a muleteer. The first officer carried their luggage; the second served as their guide to the Red-controlled area. They asked few questions and did not even know if their guide was a White or a Red (a Nationalist or a Communist). They headed out of Yan'an open eyed and apprehensive, and before long entered a barren stretch of no-man's-land, for the area between the Reds and Whites was controlled by neither but was overrun with bandits loosely aligned with the Whites.

After four hours, the two approached a village, hoping it was controlled by the Reds. Before entering, they spied a swimming hole and decided to wash off the dust accumulated during their journey. As they relaxed in the water, they looked up to find themselves surrounded by a small group of twelve- and thirteen-year-old boys, each with a redtassled spear in his hand. Escorted to the village in their underwear, the two foreigners found themselves prisoners of the young rebels and under the guns of the village leaders. Their captors locked them in a cave, where they anxiously awaited their fate. Every time they heard sounds outside, they peered out the broken window in the door to the cave. Hatem, not understanding Chinese, had no idea what was going on and feared their trip would be over before it began. Years later, reflecting on this episode, Hatem confided to Snow that "I don't think I ever shook inside more than I did in that first Chinese village when we crossed to the Red side. . . . No one knew who we were or what we were doing there. Huddled up on that k'ang in a cave, surrounded by a bunch of strange peasants. They kept looking at your cameras and our watches. I told you they looked like bandits to me. . . . I was really low then. I realized for the first time we'd put our lives in the hands of people we knew nothing about. Maybe we would end up in a couple of cannibal pies."[21]

Snow eased his mind by saying they were still in a Red-dominated area and that he had heard of the "little red devils" in the liberated zones. He showed little concern for their safety, easing Hatem's anxiety. By the middle of the afternoon they were brought eggs and steamed bread. Both waited for the next act to unfold.

In less than an hour they were visited by the village chief, who told them he had made arrangements for the next leg of their trip. In the morning they were awakened and escorted quickly out of the village. They left in haste because there were "White bandits" in the area. Snow remembers thinking at the time, "I got up without further persuasion. I did not want anything to happen to me so ridiculous as being kidnapped by White bandits in Soviet China."[22]

They headed for a nearby town where, they had been told, Mao Zedong was headquartered. When they arrived, escorted by the first Red Army soldier they had met along the way, they found that Mao was deeper in the Red-held area. They immediately headed out with a larger escort of Red Army men who were stationed in that area to suppress White bandits. Soon they arrived in Baizhaoping, another small town controlled by the Reds. When they arrived, they learned that the story had spread that White bandits led by two foreigners were in the area. They also learned from a newly introduced Red Army commander that they had been followed by bandits over the previous few days, but that the Red forces watching out for them had discovered the small band less than a mile from Hatem and Snow and routed them.[23]

The journey was proving somewhat unnerving for the two sojourners, and at this latest stop they feared they were still considered White bandits. What an irony that would prove, if they had been through so much to reach the Red Army, only to be held as Whites! But they were much nearer their goal at that moment than they realized, for within minutes their luck changed. Snow explains: "But presently a slender young officer appeared, ornamented with a black beard unusually heavy for a Chinese. He came and addressed me in a soft, cultured voice. 'Hello,' he said, 'are you looking for somebody?' He had spoken in *English!* And in a moment I learned that he was the notorious Chou En-Lai (Zhou Enlai)."[24]

Zhou Enlai was not looking for Snow and Hatem. He was on other business for the Communist party when he stumbled upon them. He knew, however, that these two foreigners were expected, and when he called them by name, they relaxed for the first time in days. For the next few hours they talked with Zhou, the two foreigners recalling how foolish they felt being captured by twelve-year-old children, and with Zhou telling them that they had been looking for them for days, and were pleased just to have them safely in their camp at last. He went on to show a Nationalist newspaper account of Snow's death at the hands of the Communists. There was no word of Hatem in the story.[25]

It was decided during this initial meeting with Zhou that Hatem's identity would remain hidden. Li Keneng, an aide to Zhou, commented that if Chiang Kai-shek knew Hatem was in the Red area, he would put a price on his head and begin investigating his connections in Shanghai. Zhou then told Snow that he should never mention Hatem when he recounted the details of his trip. He was free to write about anything else but that. All agreed, and Snow joked that in his recounting of the trip he would identify Hatem only as "one of my grooms."

In conversations over dinner that evening, Hatem quizzed Zhou on the medical situation in the Red-held area. He found out little, since most of the discussion centered on their remaining journey. But he did discover that his arrival had doubled the number of Western-trained physicians in the Red Army. The only other one was a Chinese doctor trained in the United States. Hatem showed little surprise, but in fact he was taken aback. He had no idea the Red Army was so short of doctors.[26]

During dinner Hatem and Snow sensed a China different from what they had seen before. One of their lessons came from an unlikely source. Parched and thirsting for cold water, both refused the hot boiled water ever-present in China, and Snow told a young boy-soldier to fetch them cold water. He was ignored. He called to another boy with the same order. Again he was ignored. "Then I saw that Li K'e-nung [Li Keneng, head of the communication section] was laughing at me behind his thick-lensed goggles. He plucked my sleeve. 'You can call him "little devil," ' he advised, 'or you can call him "comrade" *(t'ung-chih)*—but you cannot call him *wei!* (hey!). In here everybody is a comrade. These lads are Young Vanguards, and they are here because they are revolutionaries and volunteer to help us. They are not servants. They are future Red warriors.' "[27]

This introduction to life in the Red-held area in China was both dismaying and affirming to Hatem. There was something going on here, something that might hold promise for a new China. The children Hatem saw in the streets of Shanghai, some sold, some working as prostitutes, struggled through a life as far removed from this scene as could be imagined. Explaining what each of them witnessed, Snow said, "I had never before seen so much personal dignity in any Chinese youngsters. This first encounter was only the beginning of a series of surprises that the Young Vanguards were to give me, for as I penetrated deeper into the soviet districts I was to discover in these red-cheeked 'little Red devils'—cheerful, gay, energetic and loyal—the living spirit of an astonishing crusade of youth."[28]

The next morning Hatem and Snow were accompanied by one of these "little red devils" to Zhou Enlai's cave. They were surprised to find only one guard at the door, with farmers and soldiers milling about the village at ease. As they entered his quarters, they found Zhou bent over a desk reading telegrams. He told them that he was in contact with the Red commanders at every front, as well as the Soviet areas held by the Reds. These Reds, who had been labeled only "remnants" by Nationalist officials in Xi'an, were obviously stronger and much more organized than even their supporters in Shanghai and Beijing realized.[29]

Zhou soon put aside the telegrams, pulled out a map of the Soviet area, and proceeded to work out an itinerary for the two foreigners. With a red pencil he marked the areas they should visit. First they would travel to Baoan, a three-day ride, where they would find Chairman Mao and other leaders of the Party. After staying there for several days they would journey to the military fronts at Wuqizhen, Yuwangbao, and Qingyang. They would then return to Baoan. He outlined a ninety-two-day trip, half of which would be spent on foot or horseback in transit. It was more than they expected, for neither anticipated the Soviet-held area to be so widespread. Zhou told them that they would leave the following day with a detachment from the communication corps that was returning to the provincial capital. Zhou told them he would wire Mao and inform him of their expected arrival in three days. He reminded them that Snow was invited because, even though not a Communist, he was

trusted by the Party to tell the truth of what he saw. Zhou told Hatem
that he was expected to investigate the medical facilities in the area, but
that he had to stay close to Snow during the three months because he
did not speak Chinese.[30]

For much of that day and evening Hatem and Snow visited with
Zhou. Snow, mindful at all times of his extraordinary opportunity, took
out his Kodak movie camera and gave it to Hatem, directing him on how
to shoot it. Snow asked Zhou to mount his horse and move toward him
as Hatem photographed the action. That evening Snow and Hatem listened as Zhou, somewhat reluctantly, recounted highlights of his life.[31]
During the talk Zhou also lectured the two on current Chinese politics.
He referred to the map, showing how a united front against the Japanese
could be won, if only Chiang Kai-shek would agree to it. He also predicted that if Chiang did unite with the Communists, this would speed
the victory of the revolution, because Chiang knew nothing about organizing and arming a peasant army. Zhou went on to analyze Chiang as a
politician and a soldier, knowing him well from the Huangpu Military
Academy days. It was Hatem's first in-depth reading of the revolution as
presented by one of its prime architects.[32]

Early the following morning, Zhou saw the two Americans off as they
headed off to Baoan on fresh horses and in their new Red Army uniforms. Comfortable in their new uniforms, they were less so with their
horses. Hatem had no experience with horses and was so frightened of
falling off—especially along the narrow mountain paths they encountered—that his breathing became labored. The second day, he gave up
on the horse and walked the rest of the way.

The walk proved an important step for Hatem in his journey to a new
life, for along the way he visited with the soldiers. Most of them were in
their teens and already battle hardened. Along the way he heard testimo-
nials from the boys about their lives as peasants before and after they
joined the Red Army. A common sentiment was expressed by one young
soldier named Local Cousin. "Here everybody is the same," he told
Snow and Hatem. "It is not like the White districts, where poor people
are slaves of the landlords and the Kuomintang [Guomindang]. Here
everybody fights to help the poor, and to save China. The Red Army
fights the landlords and the White bandits and the Red Army is anti-
Japanese. Why should anyone not like such an army as this?" Another, a
seventeen-year-old called Old Dog by his friends, said, "The Red Army
has taught me to read and to write. . . . Here I have learned to operate a
radio, and how to aim a rifle straight. The Red Army helps the poor."[33]

Hatem and Snow also learned something about the spirit of the Red

Army. Some of this they learned by hearing the seemingly endless number of revolutionary songs these young soldiers would burst out singing at every opportunity. Once, when stopped in a village for the night, the curious villagers gathered around the two foreigners, and Snow and Hatem took the opportunity to draw them into a dialogue, with Snow interpreting for Hatem. Comments from the villagers were similar to those they heard from the soldiers. The Red Army fights landlords, it fights the bandits, and it fights the Japanese. All of these run away, they said, from "our" Red Army. It was the possessive nature of the relationship with the Red Army that struck Hatem and Snow. This identification with the army, any army, was a new thing in China, and the two foreigners looked forward even more to their time with this peasant army.[34]

As Hatem moved through the villages and around the mountains of Shaanxi on the third day of his journey to Baoan, he began to grapple in earnest with the Chinese language. He was envious of Snow's language ability, and the motivation to learn Chinese grew with every step he took. There was so much to understand. How could he contribute if he did not know how to communicate with the common soldier? The young boys delighted in teaching him the common words of their vocabulary: Communist party, masses, comrade, cave, and river were a few of the first words he learned. It was just the beginning of a new lifestyle and new worldview, for his language ability would soon blossom, as would his understanding of China's revolution and the role the Communist party would play in bringing about that revolution.[35]

Generalissimo Chiang Kai-shek has been seized by General Chang Hsueh-liang in Shensi [Shaanxi] Province in an effort to force the Nanking [Nanjing] Government to declare war against Japan. . . . Following the mutiny General Chang . . . advocated cooperation with the Communists and formal approval of a policy of armed resistance to Japan.

New York Times, December 13, 1936

When, unable to digest the food, I grew thinner and thinner, the old Long Marchers began to offer me the bits of rock candy each carried, wrapped in several layers of paper. What a precious and selfless gift—their final, carefully husbanded source of energy and life! To them I wasn't a foreigner, but a comrade in a common cause in which each helps the other. Internationalism came to them so easily, so naturally. My memory of them was to help me stick to the revolution through many crises in later years—in the firm belief that whatever zigzags might occur would always be overcome.

Ma Haide

Winding around the hills of Shaanxi after a dusty three-day journey, Hatem and Snow finally reached the crest of the hill overlooking their destination. Stretched below them, green with cultivation and active with purposeful movement, lay Baoan, "Defended Peace." Encircled by its ancient walls, this fortress used in previous centuries by armies of the Qin and Tang dynasties against the northern invaders from Mongolia now protected China's Communist party.

As they descended the hill, bugles blew to announce their arrival and people waved banners of welcome written in English and Chinese: "Welcome to the American journalists investigating Soviet China," "Down with Japanese imperialism!" "Long live the Chinese revolution!" At the end of the street-long welcoming procession stood most of the members of the Chinese Communist party's Central Committee and Politburo. Mao Zedong was not there, but later that evening he stopped by the dining hall briefly to welcome them.[1]

Hatem's first impression of Chairman Mao focused on his physical characteristics. He found the forty-three-year-old chairman tall for a Chinese, thin, and in need of a haircut. Unlike Zhou Enlai, Mao cared little for his personal appearance and walked with slightly bent shoulders. Hatem was equally impressed by his bright and quick eyes and enjoyed his easy nature and wit. At their first meeting, for example, Mao joked that the Politburo was expecting two American friends, but instead he found before him two soldiers dressed in Red Army uniforms. However, Hatem and Snow soon discovered that Mao was a complex man and sometimes found conversation with him unsettling, since Mao "had a way of gazing sidelong at you, waiting for the effect of his words and their logic to be understood, and challenged. Seemingly relaxed to the point of carelessness, he masked an ever-alert and imaginative mind."[2]

Mao's first question to Hatem highlights this impression. He asked, "Have you studied philosophy?" Hatem, not sure how to respond, remarked that his field was medicine, that philosophy was only a hobby. Chairman Mao responded that it was good he knew at least some, because to be a rebel one needed to understand philosophy.[3]

The two foreigners, especially Snow, were eager to spend time with Mao, but he told them that they should first get settled in their quarters, then explore Baoan. When they had been there a while, he would invite them to his cave for discussion. Snow and Hatem settled down in the "foreign office hostel," a compound of four one-room huts made of mud brick. Over the next few weeks the two foreigners, soon joined by Huang Hua, fell quickly into a relaxed relationship with their Red hosts. They shared meals with Politburo members and their wives, with Snow particularly proud of his efforts teaching poker to this illustrious lot.

In the evenings the three men retreated to their quarters to share their impressions of Baoan and talk of their lives. Huang Hua recalls that it was during these evening discussions that he first learned of Hatem's life in Shanghai, Europe, and the United States. The discussions forged a friendship that would continue throughout Hatem's lifetime.[4]

While quickly impressed with the relaxed confidence of the people in Baoan, especially when compared to Xi'an and other Nationalist-held cities, they found themselves equally impressed with the presence of a strong political and military infrastructure. In the huts, caves, and streets of Baoan they found ministries of foreign affairs, finance, agriculture, public health, defense, education, and planning. The young commander Lin Biao headed a military academy with eight hundred students. Publishing houses producing textbooks, newspapers, and magazines sprang forth from mouths of caves.[5]

On July 16, Hatem accompanied Snow to Chairman Mao's cave for the first of many interviews that later appeared in Shanghai newspapers and in *Red Star Over China*. For the next two weeks Hatem sat while Mao told Snow about the China he knew and the China he wanted for the future. He discussed ancient and modern history, the Long March, and the revolutionary ideas of the Communist party. The interpreter for these talks, who was important for Snow as well as Hatem because of Mao's thick Hunan accent, was Wu Liangping, Mao's personal secretary and a former student in the Soviet Union and Europe. Huang Hua joined them for some of the later sessions. As Hatem listened, he picked up sketchy insight into Marxism.[6] "Crucial to my own Marxist education," he said, "was sitting in on the talks that Mao Zedong gave to Edgar Snow about China. . . . This took a couple of weeks. Then we went to interview other leaders and would sit and listen to them. It was the best kind of university. And that's why I then came to a bit of understanding of the Chinese revolution rather quickly, before that I had hardly any."[7]

The atmosphere in Mao's cave was relaxed and, like all proper Chinese homes welcoming guests, well supplied with food. Not all discussion was serious. Mao, a Hunan native, offered them hot peppers throughout their visits. He told them that he had discovered the "scientific" rule that those who enjoyed hot peppers made the best revolutionaries, and this was why so many revolutionaries came from Hunan Province. Without hot pepper, he said, he could not eat, and without eating he could not make revolution. "To me," he quipped, "no peppers means no revolution." He Zizhen, Mao's wife and one of the few women to complete the Long March, constantly reinforced Mao's revolutionary diet and encouraged the two foreigners in their education by baking hot-pepper bread made from local sour plums. On one occasion she brought with it a tray of apricots, which Snow and Hatem took eagerly. However, they were so bitter that Hatem "shook all over" when eating them. For the rest of his life, Su Fei remembers, he could not think of He Zizhen without thinking of the bitter apricots she served him.[8]

At times Mao's relaxed nature took the two by surprise. Once, while discussing Party policies with Snow, the chairman casually turned down his trousers to look for "some guests," as Snow describes it. Another time, while visiting with Snow and Hatem in Lin Biao's cave, Mao cursed the heat and pulled off his pants. He continued the visit in his underwear, casually interjecting comments and studying a map on the wall until the evening drew to a close.

During one interview session Snow asked to take pictures of Mao.

One picture had Mao reviewing troops alongside Lin Biao, presenting "the feeblest imitation of a salute I ever saw," in Snow's words. Another photo, this one the classic picture of Mao in Yan'an still found in homes and office buildings throughout China forty years later, was taken by Snow, but with little cooperation from Mao. Standing before his one-room cave to have his picture taken, the chairman made a halfhearted attempt to straighten his uniform and his long hair. Snow told him that his hair was too long for the effect he wanted, and asked him to put on a cap. He Zizhen went into the cave to find the chairman's cap, but Mao told her it was lost. Exasperated, she told Snow that her husband was always bare headed and that he should just photograph him like that. Snow insisted, at which time a bemused Hatem walked up to Snow, removed his Red Army cap, and unceremoniously placed it on Mao's head. Years later, gravely ill in Geneva, Snow joked about Hatem being the only person in the world to "put a cap" on Chairman Mao.[9] The ease with which Hatem took this action indicates how comfortably he moved throughout Baoan and the confidence he felt in his growing relationship with Mao Zedong.

Once, Mao invited Hatem and Snow to attend a mass meeting of the Red Army taking place in a village just outside the city walls of Baoan. When they arrived they were surprised to find themselves on the speakers' rostrum. The slogan for the meeting was in their honor. Banners exclaimed, "We are not isolated. We have the support of international friends." It was the first such political rally Hatem attended, but it was far from the last. While Snow interpreted, Hatem followed the rally: "They set up a podium and a big stage with some logs and trees and a few branches to camouflage it," Hatem recalled years later. "And they said, 'We're going to bring all of the armies together and we want you to talk to them.' It would be very encouraging. The meeting was on a field about the size of an American football field. The seated soldiers in the front rows had machine guns, the ones in the second row had a couple of mortars and rifles, and in three or four more rows they had bayonets on the tops of their rifles. And then, as I looked off into the distance, I could see all the agricultural tools that China had invented in 2,000 years. They had no arms. The chief speaker made a very fiery speech. He said, 'We're going to liberate China. All the oppressed people of the world will support us. We're going to get rid of imperialism. We're going to get rid of the Kuomintang. Down with all of them! Victory is in front of us!' And Edgar Snow seated on the stage turned to me and said, 'They're mighty brave people if they think they're going to do it with that army.' "[10]

Snow was then introduced, and he made brief comments on behalf of himself and Hatem, telling the soldiers in an unprepared and awkward speech of their common support for the struggle against imperialism. This was followed by noodles at the dining hall, with questions to the two unprepared Americans on issues ranging from "Why has the League of Nations failed?" to "Why is it that, although the Communist Party is legal in both Great Britain and America, there is no workers' government in either country?"[11]

During the two weeks spent interviewing Chairman Mao, Hatem provided his first medical service to the Red Army: He gave Mao a physical. This exercise proved far more important than merely presenting the chairman and the Party with a reading on his health. Mao was regularly reported throughout China to be either dead or almost dead from any number of illnesses. In Xi'an they heard he was down with tuberculosis. Hatem's affirmation of Mao's excellent health was soon reported to the world by Snow in newspapers and in *Red Star Over China*. The political impact of this news cannot be overemphasized, for it told enemies and friends alike that the movement was led by a healthy chairman and that all the Nationalist attempts to convince the country of his demise or poor health had failed. While Snow kept Hatem's presence in Baoan concealed, he did allude to his friend in *Red Star Over China* when he wrote, "I happened to be in Mao's house one evening when he was given a complete physical examination by a Red surgeon—a man who had studied in Europe and who knew his business—and pronounced in excellent health."[12]

Hatem was finally beginning to practice medicine for the Red Army. It was just the beginning, for within days he, Snow, and Huang Hua made arrangements to tour the military front under the direction of General Peng Dehuai. The evening before their departure, the chairman strolled down to the dirt road in front of the guest house and met informally with all three. He wished Snow well on his fact-finding journey and asked the journalist to send him his impressions of the front. He then turned to the other two with instructions. He told Huang Hua that he should not only pay attention to his role as interpreter for the two Americans, but should also represent the progressive students in Beijing to the soldiers at the front. He instructed Hatem to make a careful study of the medical conditions he found at the front, analyze the work of each field hospital, and suggest ways to improve the medical service in the Red areas. Mao informed him that there were plans to begin a medical college, and that his report should include suggestions about how this school should be set up.[13]

The three left Baoan, each with a horse, an automatic rifle, and a cotton uniform. They first stopped in the village of Wuqi, where they toured Red factories placed in the countryside. Hatem's education grew by the day, as did his language skills. Snow remarked, "At the start Shag couldn't ask for a bowl of water without my help, but in an amazingly short time he began speaking some Chinese."[14]

Not all their time was spent in the saddle or viewing Red factories. They were delighted to find that they could bring excitement and levity to the soldiers they met along the way. As they traveled to the front, for instance, all three were amused to find that Hatem, now sporting a black beard, was mistaken several times for Zhou Enlai, who was one of the few Chinese in the area known for his beard.[15] At one stop they visited with army commander Li Fuchun and his wife, both returned students from France. This gave Hatem the opportunity to impress his new friends and his host with his command of French, which he and Li spoke through the night while eating a welcome French meal his hosts had prepared.[16]

In addition to political discussions and formal meetings, Hatem, Huang Hua, and Snow also attended Red theater and athletic competitions. Recounting their participation in the latter, Snow again alludes to Hatem, as well as to young Huang Hua: "I took part in a basketball game on one of Wu Ch'i's [Wuqi's] three courts. We made up a scratch team composed of the Foreign Office emissary, Fu Chin-kuei [Fu Qing-gei]; a young English speaking college student working in the political department; a Red doctor; a soldier; and myself. The arsenal basketball team accepted our challenge and beat us to a pulp."[17]

For two weeks the two foreigners and Huang Hua soaked up the remarkably varied life of their Red Army hosts as they traveled over the barren hills and plains of Gansu and Ningxia until they reached the walled town of Yuwangbao, headquarters of the First Front Red Army. It was here they met commander-in-chief Peng Dehuai. Peng was awaiting the Second and Fourth Front armies of Zhu De, which were coming out of the harsh winter of eastern Tibet in the last leg of the Long March. The arrival of Snow and Hatem was not lost on the common soldier. Decades later Dai Zhengqi, a young veteran of the Long March and a nurse in the Red Army, remembered that the army "held a welcome meeting for the two foreigners, all of us wearing camouflage—dressed like bushes—because of airplane attacks from the Japanese. Dr. Ma spoke to us, and I cannot express how excited his presence made us. We had heard, and were constantly told, that there was international support for our struggle. Here, for the first time, was proof of this. It gave us all great encouragement that our struggle would be successful."[18]

While Snow chronicled military tactics and political ideology, Hatem reviewed the health of the soldiers. He discovered that the diet of the Red Army was primarily millet and cabbage, with an occasional piece of mutton or pork. No fresh vegetables were to be found, and the staple drink was boiled hot water. When not in battle he saw the soldiers rise every morning for an hour of exercise, followed later in the afternoon by two hours of sports activities such as broad jumping, running, wall scaling, and grenade throwing.[19]

As a physician, Hatem found the attention paid to physical exercise encouraging. On visits to the medical units at the front, however, he was appalled by what he found. The conditions, he said, were "very, very poor. We had nothing." The only other Red Army doctor trained in a medical school was Nelson Fu, who had attended a Methodist missionary school in Jiangxi. There was no anesthesia available for most operations, and many battles, he found, were fought to capture basic medical supplies from the enemy. To treat wounds he was shocked to find that gauze was in such short supply that it was used, washed, and reused until it turned gray and weak. It was during this time that he encountered traditional Chinese medicine for the first time. He found many of the soldiers coming up from the south fighting malaria. There was no medicine to cure them, not even common quinine. "I saw traditional doctors take a soldier sitting at the side of the road with malaria chills and give him three acupuncture needles along the last cervical and first thoracic vertebra. Within a half hour he could get up and continue marching with the rest of the troops. The relief would last about two weeks, though it was not a cure. . . . I wouldn't believe it if anybody had told me of such a result."[20]

Huang Hua tells the story of Hatem's introduction to the treatment of battle wounds. Soon after they met up with Peng Dehuai's troops, a wounded officer was brought to the commander's camp. He had been wounded in the groin area by cannon fire, and infection had set in. Hatem rushed to treat him. With little medicine or equipment, he fashioned an instrument to probe his internal organs through the penis, hoping to lessen the spread of infection. The crude procedure failed, and Hatem confronted the harsh reality facing a frontline physician serving with this dedicated but grossly ill-equipped Red Army. Discouraged but still eager, Huang Hua says Hatem met with Peng Dehuai and Dr. Fu to discuss how he might assist them. Through their encouragement he committed himself to the work of a battlefield surgeon, with responsibilities requiring skills not taught in medical school. Not withstanding his inexperience, Huang Hua says, "He moved easily into army surgery."[21]

Hatem made notes on the medical problems and practices he discovered in preparation for his medical report for Chairman Mao. He already knew the army needed more access to Western medicine. And he knew that Western medicine had to work in tandem with the more popular traditional Chinese herbs. Later he would discuss these ideas with Mao and others. For now, he just tried to keep up with this fast-moving army.

As he encountered one new adventure after another, Hatem made yet another important decision that would dictate events for the rest of his life. When Snow prepared to return to Baoan after two months in the field, Hatem informed him that he would remain at the front. He wanted to see more, and there was further investigation to do on his medical report. He also felt needed there. He and his companions had been under attack from Japanese bombers while visiting Peng Dehuai's camp, and he helped carry the dead and wounded from the battlefield, bandaging those he could save. He drew inspiration from the young peasant soldiers and saw a place for himself in supporting them. "How our men fought, and particularly how they reacted to wounds, taught me more than any words could," he said. "One boy, his brains oozing from his shattered head, would not let us take off his rifle and ammunition belt. Only to his unit's political instructor would he relinquish the weapons entrusted to him by the revolution."[22]

He told Snow of his decision to continue at the front to assist in the relief of Zhu De's army and return to Baoan later. Snow, anxious to complete his interviews and return to Beijing with what he expected to be the story of the year from China, returned north to Baoan to interview other Red Army leaders. Hatem turned farther south with the army of General Nie Rongzhen, who was off to welcome the last of the Long Marchers to liberated China. By this move, Hatem could rightfully claim that he was part of the legendary Chinese Red Army's Long March.[23]

It was shortly after Snow left the front that Hatem acquired his Chinese name. Accompanied by Huang Hua, Hatem joined with the First Front Army as it marched to Lanzhou to join up with the Second and Fourth Front armies, completing their trek out of the grasslands. On the way, they met Zhou Enlai, who was going to meet the armies on behalf of the Party Central Committee. Marching through this recently liberated, though desolate, part of China, Hatem and his fellow travelers found it increasingly difficult to find food. In one village populated by followers of Islam, they headed for the local mosque, hoping they would find something to eat there. Most of the soldiers had no experience with Muslims, and no one felt comfortable approaching the mosque. How would the imam welcome these strangers in unfamiliar uniforms? To find out, it was decided that Hatem, this Maronite Christian with Arab features, should venture forth and present himself as a fellow believer. Zhou Enlai asked him if he knew the habits and language of these people. The young doctor, eager to impress his new comrades, said that of course he knew, then entered the mosque.

He greeted the imam with a few words of Arabic he remembered from his childhood and his time in Beirut. He also wrote a few words of the language, further endearing himself to the local village elder. After that, and after looking outside at Zhou's beard (only believers in that area wore beards), the imam was pleased to welcome two of his faith to the mosque. The soldiers were invited to eat. During conversation over the meal, the imam asked Hatem his name. Not wanting to dispel the image already created, Hatem immediately identified himself as Ma, the most common name found among Islamic believers in China. Thinking fast, he added the personal name "Hande," simply because it sounded like Hatem to him. He would soon change it to Ma Haide. Leaving the village, Zhou and others laughed at his newly acquired name, especially at how quickly the foreign doctor created it. When this group finally met up with the Second and Fourth armies, Zhou introduced the foreigner as Dr. Ma.

It is not clear exactly when Ma changed his personal name from Hande, which holds no special meaning in Chinese, to Haide, which translates loosely as "virtue from overseas" and which stayed with him the rest of his life. It appears the change came in the coming months, however, since he was still calling himself Ma Hande in correspondence to friends in 1936 and early 1937. Huang Hua insists he thought of the name Haide and that it came after some conversation with Ma. He thought the image of "virtue from overseas" was appropriate. When explaining the evolution of the name, Huang laughed and said, "The name was a 'joint production' between Ma, Zhou, and me."[24] For the next fifty years he would be known by his Chinese name to the rest of the world, while the names Shag and Shafick George Hatem would fade into the background, to be used only with some foreigners, old friends, and family members in the later years of his life.[25] Ma sought invisibility outside the Red area, and his new name assisted the effort. "This helped my incognito," he said. "The only related rumor that came out was that 'a Turkish doctor' was helping popularize the Red Army's work among Moslems (the Hui Nationality) in China's northwest."[26]

Ma was now for the first time on his own without Snow. He no longer needed him. He had a new Chinese name, a new confidence, and a calling. He was welcomed wherever he went. In the midst of this

immersion into the Chinese revolution, he came to terms with his aban-
donment of his native culture and his family. "Did I think about the
United States and my early life there at that time? No. I had done so in
my Shanghai period, then I first encountered Marxism and the Communist Manifesto [and it] hit me as a stroke of lightening. Then all my past
experience with discrimination and poverty had swum up—and it all
checked. Then I thought back on the States, Beirut, Europe. But after I
went to China's Red areas I didn't think much about anything except
the struggle in front of me."[27]

Ma was personally and politically committed. But just surviving each
day at the front proved more difficult than he ever imagined. Though he
was learning the language rapidly, his Chinese was still crude, and he
depended on Huang Hua as his interpreter during the journey to meet
the Second and Fourth Front armies as they completed the Long March.
Just as the language barrier proved difficult, so did the physical hardships
and the diet he was forced to endure. The course grain that constituted
the staple for the soldiers became his diet too, and his stomach, used to
the delicacies of Shanghai, suffered. "We fought, marched and counter
marched. I ate millet, which I'd never seen before and it gave me bad
stomach trouble. At the front we ate twice a day, and it was hardly anything, just millet gruel made with water from the river's edge which was
bitter, full of sodium and magnesium salts. The peasants avoided it and
drank only rainwater, but we had no choice. I myself was getting thinner
and thinner. I couldn't eat that food, my stomach wouldn't have it."[28]
"They had been on the move under hardship conditions for nearly two
years, right through from Jiangxi, meeting with all manner of difficulties,
covering unbelievably tough country, while I had gone soft in Shanghai,
with muscles unused and an over developed taste for coffee and apple pie
a la mode! Physically hardened I was not!"[29]

But the payoff was never in material comforts; he had accepted that
earlier. The payoff was in the spirit of those he accompanied and in their
goals, which each day grew clearer to him until they became his own.
"When, unable to digest the food, I grew thinner and thinner, the old
Long Marchers began to offer me the bits of rock candy each carried,
wrapped in several layers of paper. What a precious and selfless gift—their
final, carefully husbanded source of energy and life! To them I wasn't a
foreigner, but a comrade in a common cause in which each helps the
other."[30]

It was not only the spirit of the common soldier that inspired him; he
was enormously impressed with the leaders of the Red Army. On first
eyeing General Zhu De as he brought in the last remnants of the Long

March, Ma found him "thin as a ghost, but strong and tough, with a growth of beard and clad in a lousy skin coat. . . . The most striking thing about Chu Teh [Zhu De] is that he does not look like a military commander at all. He looks like a father of the Red Army. He has the most piercing eyes, he is slow to speak, quiet, and with a wonderful smile. He carries an automatic, and is a sharpshooter and a heavy smoker. He is fifty, but looks much older, and his face is deeply lined; yet his movements are vigorous and his health excellent. His headquarters is a bustling beehive with messengers and commanders coming and going, the phone ringing all the time and radiograms being sent and received."

With the arrival of Zhu De's troops, the Red Army that had begun the Long March in south China two years before was finally whole again. Ma was there to chronicle this historic occasion. "Chu Teh had just stepped into his headquarters in Huishien when Chen Keng [Chen Geng], divisional commander in the fourth Front Red Army, telephoned him. Chu Teh became very excited. The reunion of the Red troops in the region was held in the late afternoon on the following day—to avoid bombings, which were daily. . . . What a reunion! Men threw their arms around each other, laughing and weeping at the same time, or walking arm-in-arm and pouring out questions about other comrades. Chu Teh was completely swallowed up."[31]

Not only was Ma there to tell the story to those outside the liberated area, he joined the leaders of the army on the podium as they led the victory celebration at the end of the Long March. Sitting alongside Zhu De, Lin Biao, Peng Dehuai, Nie Rongzhen, and Zhang Guotao, his identity set off a buzz from the common soldiers in the audience. Who was this foreigner sitting with their leaders? Because everyone knew that the Comintern had played a role in the Long March and in the planning of this reunion, word quickly spread that Ma was the Comintern representative invited to join in the celebration.[32] This was not the first time, and certainly not the last, that Ma's true identity escaped those who saw him. It was to be a lifelong phenomenon, one he appears to have rather enjoyed.

Of all the officers he met during this period, Ma was most taken with He Long, whose name meant, appropriately, "dragon." Ma requested and was granted the opportunity to accompany He's Second Front Army on the return journey to Baoan. After meeting him, Ma likened him to an "enormous dragon" who was afraid of nothing. His free-spirited reputation had preceded him, and the young foreign doctor found the gregarious He exactly as he had been described. The general also enjoyed Ma's company. At one point he learned that Ma was afraid to ride a horse. To test the young doctor, He challenged him to ride one of the army horses known for its bad temper. Not wanting to show his fear, Ma accepted the challenge, climbed on the horse, grabbed the saddle with all his might, and held on for as long as he could. He Long had a good laugh and, in turn, gave the young foreign doctor the horse as a gift.[33]

Living with He Long, Ma learned of his temper and of his penchant for being close to the battle. He also learned how to prepare for a quick escape from enemy attack. One night, Huang Hua recounts, he and Ma were asleep in a tent next to He Long when they were awakened by He berating his chief of staff. It seems that a large force of Nationalist soldiers was approaching He's smaller force, but the chief of staff had decided to let the troops sleep a bit longer before rousing them for an escape. He Long woke up the whole command structure with his tirade, including the guests in the tent next door, had everyone mobilized within a short time, and led his army away in a state of some confusion. As they hurried to leave, Ma and Huang gave their horses to wounded soldiers and escaped on foot. That evening their horses were returned to them "with blood all over the blankets," remembers Huang. No sooner had they recovered their horses than they found themselves separated from the army, lost in the countryside. They sought shelter with a peasant family until the army found them.[34]

Ma found many of the men ill, with exhaustion showing on their faces and their clothing in tatters. But their spirit was infectious. He sat around charcoal stoves in village huts, listening to the stories of these hardened, mostly peasant, veterans of the eight-thousand-mile Long March. They told him tales of the journey, often laced with humor. He saw Red Army officers giving up their horses to the wounded and sick, carrying their own gear as they marched toward the now united headquarters. "You could have assembled the whole Red Army on an area no larger than a football field," he said, "but they were so confident and optimistic they caused me to believe in them altogether."[35]

Ma's political education reached a new level. In Shanghai he had been introduced to the theoretical tenets of Marxism and to stories of the Chinese Communist party. Now he found himself in the very heart of the movement he had studied. Bad food, dirty lodgings, and even the language barrier could not overcome the excitement and purpose in life he now felt. "A better course of revolutionary study one could not imagine," he recalled years later. "But one thing I had already been sure of when I came—I wanted to join China's revolution. And each day in the Red areas increased that desire."[36]

While moving with the Red Army, Ma wrote back to Snow in Baoan to tell of his decision to stay longer at the front. He would not see Snow before he returned to Beijing, and there were important matters to discuss. The letter shows his newfound identity with the Communists of the Red Army and his desire to be put to the fullest use.

Dear Comrade Ed—
   We still are at Tiao Paotze & The report covers our Trip Later on I want to send out more news to Ag. & Grace & Manny in Shanghai. I can mail it to an address in Shanghai that they know. Tell them to call for mail at the place where I used to eat Friday night dinner, the Solomons. It will be enclosed in a envelope & marked—"For Shag or his friends." I wont write before another month, Another route for material sent out might be thru the Doc in S. Tell them to also contact him for I don't know which way I can send out things. Also ask them & A[37] what material she wants for her book that I can collect here for her.
   Also leave me some way or address to reach you by in Peiping [Beijing]. Leave with someone for me in Poan [Baoan]. I will code my writing by speaking of C.P etc R.A as Chinese missionaries priests etc. in my letters. Leave behind any medical stuff you don't need. Send in to me, if you can and be so kind to, book &literature as New Masses, Imprecar, American left literature Marxist books, Voice of China, China W. Review—anything on Public hygiene & and army surgery, etc. Anything readable.
   I hope you will give them A, G, M my warmest comradely greetings. I am working in 1st Corp hosp. We have about 30 wounded in both 1st and 15 corps. No serious fighting as yet.
   Warm greetings to peg and yourself and friends in Paon. I will return after 1 month as I want to work here a little more. Greetings from Wang Peng & others to you.
   Bolshevik greetings,
   Ma Han De Shag
Let me know if you get this.
P.S. how do you like my Moslem writing on those papers I sent to you?[38]

In addition to a report accompanying this letter, Ma also sent Snow a detailed list of supplies and literature he wanted sent to him. It is an intriguing list, focusing on the medical work he knew was before him. He slips in some supplies for leisure activities as well. At the end of the list he mentions some personal items he wanted Snow to send to his family in North Carolina. He may have disappeared from view to most of the world, but he had no thought of breaking entirely with his family. The list reads:

Abortion Instruments
Abortion Literature in Chinese
Agomensine Tablets
Conc. on Stomach and Intenst. Medicines as:
    Biomuth, Subnitrate, Santonin, Epsoms Salts.
Trachoma medicine—cupras citras 2%
Medicine for Scabies—Sulfur Flower, Potassium Carbonate:
    Tonics: Iron Strychinime etc.
Silver Nitrate Sticks or Pencils
Ping Pong Balls, Basket Ball
Records of Workers Songs
Salt-Sodium Chloride for Intravenous Solution
Leica films [*scratched out by either Snow or Ma*]
Books on Army Hygiene and Surgery; Public Hygiene
Biblical books
Letter home
Mail Diploma in Trunks

At the end of the list Ma wrote, "The Bargain Store, Roanoke Rapids."[39] It was in this small North Carolina town that his family could be found.

On December 3, after marching with the united Red armies for four months, Ma arrived back in Baoan exhausted yet invigorated with new responsibilities. While at the front he kept a diary, but it was not so much for his own satisfaction as it was a way for him to share what he saw with his friends in Beijing and Shanghai. The day he arrived back in Baoan he sent the diary to Snow, telling him it was the best report he could give at the time. Snow passed it on to others. Agnes Smedley found in it information for much of her reporting, including material for her posthumously published biography of Zhu De, *The Great Road*. Others, including Snow, found added material for their stories of China published in the Western press. Some of Ma's observations, such as remarks on the commanders Zhu De and He Long, were incorporated into the first edition of *Red Star Over China*. This diary shows a man consumed by the passion of the movement, careful in his descriptions of the events and hell-bent on letting his former mentors know how close to the movement he now lived. He was no longer the novice student, sitting at the feet of more experienced Marxists and revolutionaries. Now he was at the center, and he taught them through his experiences. This initial attempt at a diary was a unique, firsthand account of one of the most important episodes of the twentieth century, as it gives insight into a crucial time in the struggle of the Red Army and the Chinese Communist party.[40] The report begins with an introduction:

Arrived from 4 months at front yesterday, I hurry to send this to you as past information and lots more. I had a part talk with Chu Teh [Zhu De], Ho Lung [He Long], etc. material to be sent a little later after this material is written and I read the hundreds (?) of maps and papers, etc.—anyway you have still enough to go on till the next letter.

The 2nd Front Army arrived at Tai Pin Tien & moved to Ping Fen Jen. Here were Hdq. of 2nd with Ho Lung there. Went to meet Ho Lung with 1st Corp Hdq. Travelled 100 li in day and went out of Pin Feng Jen to receive Ho Lung and Staff. They came trotting their Horses around a corner of the mountain path. Ho Lung mounted on a beautiful Red Loke (Hupeh) Charger, a beautiful horse. Ho Lung is an expert on horses and a beautiful rider. He brought several chargers with him which resemble the Arabian horses but smaller & and are very fast. On seeing us they immediately dismounted and ran towards the group. Were they just bursting with joy and eyes glistening for they all were old comrades in Armys from Nanchang uprising and had not seen each other for nearly 10 years. They embraced, hugged, walked arm in arm all asking questions & talking at once. Ho Lung is a big man, larger than average and well filled. He has the kindest eyes and faces you have ever seen while he is very conversational & the most interesting story teller.

Oct. 29. News received from White Army at night that 4 divisions of Hu Tsung-nan [Hu Zhongnan] were going to surround us that we should move faster giving the exact position of the enemy and their plans. One cavalry regiment was favorable & sympathetic with the R.A. would take up a part on mountain along our way but would not attack—sort of protect us. They would attack at 11 a.m. and we were to pass at 6 a.m. They had to attack because their movements were watched by commanding officers by plane. This is a vivid example of United Front work and the reluctance of white troops to fight anyone but the Japanese.

Nov. 7. Victory for USSR Oct. Revolution. Special food increase for delicacies for warriors today. Feasts all over, songs, drama peasant & soldiers meetings, etc. News from USSR on their celebrations. Happy day in spite of all day bombing. 1 mule killed (In Yuan Pao 72 bombs were dropped killing one donkey. It was such a laugh that the news of this spread among the peasants for 100 li.)

Nov. 9, 10, 11. All R.A. 1st 2nd 4th in this region & moving to Yuan Hsin Yuan Poa & Ho Lian Wan. War preparation in full swing because after this the R.A. will not give up anymore territory. Peng, Hsu Hai-tung, Ho chian, Chu Teh, Hsiao, Ho Lung all in daily meetings. It is momentous days before the battle. Many meetings are held with R.A. warriors giving them the reason for so big a retreat and the coming war. Are they anxious for fight? All day they clean rifles bayonets & prepare. They are ready.

Sending this diary off to Snow and others completed only one of Ma's responsibilities. The next responsibility, somewhat more sensitive and difficult, shows a new dimension to the man. When sending the diary, Ma wrote a personal cover letter to Snow with added comments written on the instruction of the Party. On the one hand, it was a letter filled with the warmth and personality so familiar to his friends. This part of the man had not changed. On the other hand, the letter displays a new-found identity as official defender and spokesperson for Communist party policies and positions. In the cover letter to Snow, a more self-confident, politically driven Ma Haide emerges. The eager, searching Shag Hatem fades even further into the background. It is a historic turning point for Ma, for beginning with these remarks, no criticism or questioning of the Chinese Communist party, other than those approved by the Party itself, would ever be attributed to Ma Haide throughout the rest of his life.

Dated December 3, 1936, Ma's cover letter began:

Just returned in 4 days from front with Wang I-che with one blanket and all alone. Hard days for us. Had a very exciting time, were nearly captured by whites, bombed to hell and back—safe and sound.

Writing out med report for medical work and 3 front A. reorg. of med depart. Received also your letter at front and I agree with you about Red China. Its the only one. I spent four months travelling with 1st, 2nd and 4th Front armies and this is the only way to see revolution in action. It was too bad you did not make the trip for it was a real life's experience and tons of material that I had not covered, have no ability to cover and use. You must come again. I arrived so overwhelmed with news that I can't write a letter—and too much work. I am too up in the air and too moved to write coherently except that brief report enclosed.

Your material collected is only one side—passive quiet at rest—my trip, and if you had made it it would make your material live, more active and you would have a complete conception of the whole. We thought at Yuan Bao that we saw the whole—wrong. There is much more! The mass work, the wars etc. come again.

I missed you for awhile but must admit not for long. People don't exist as persons but as a whole collective and I'm so thoroughly into the spirit of the thing that I can't write. I eat three bowls of Shiao Mei & like it. Yes.

Received the edibles but had no time to eat them. They are still at the front & will come in a day or two then I'll tend to them. By the way if its possible by hook or Crook to send in a portable with some ribbons, can increase my reports to make them more regular. Its too cold to write by pen now. As for other things all O.K. Food problem is settled. I eat everything. You can still send coco & tinned milk. I ask no more than that.

Your a famous character here and at the front. I've raised a beard & many mistake me for you. No harm! I've just seen first part of Mao's interviews in C.W.R. and saw him when he saw it and his picture. Its good but some part of your notes he asked me to write to you about. he says this:

"We are extremely glad *(all this not for publication)* that your interview with Mao has been published in C.W.R." On the whole we agree and think that its quite well written. But something we want to explain on your notes attached to interview.

(1) You write in your note that "universal suffrage would not be insisted upon." To our opinion we are insisting on universal suffrage which is fundamental condition of Dem. Govt.

(2) You write that according to Mao's opinion "The Communists would be willing to agree not to organize mass movements opposed to the principle of national salvation, United Front and not 'to promote' class struggle." This is an important question & must be explained as follows:

(a) We communists will not abandon our fundamental principle of class struggle (just don't bring up for emphasis that question—is his diplomatic opinion right now. G.H)

(b) In the United Front we shall do everything in our power to protect the vital fundamental interests of workers & peasants and the toiling people which is one of the most important conditions of mobilizing the people to fight Japan victoriously. (He verbally said the C's never organized mass movements opposed to above.)

(c) Nowaday the central problem is United Front against Japan so we must lead class struggle in such a way as will be most profitable to the Anti-Japanese movements. Anti-Jap. movement & class struggle in China must be made homogeneous of course. In propaganda need to speak of class struggle in such a form as before.

(d) We ask you to correct these points and leave off last paragraph in these notes and correct these already published when you reprint in other places."

I think it is more diplomatic to leave the question of class struggle quiet at this point. This does not mean the end of class struggle but its diversion into the best way to fight the Jap. imperialists. Your work is great on the English side in the publication and it certainly is very timely.

Please send on these news etc. to *friends* in Shanghai as I wont carry out early communication scheme for this is better. [This refers to Ma's letter written from the front where he outlines secret mail locations and codes used in describing activities in the Red Area.]

The stuff you borrowed is not necessary to return and as a matter of fact some more than that has already arrived in form of clothes and edibles—thanks.

Paon is a big city now, more than 1,000 people arrived in 3 days from front to work in rear. You should be here—come back old boy for this is the place to be.

Thanks for your letter received by Soviet Post & the package. More stuff I'll send out later including sketches of army life made by soviet artist and biography & interview with Chu Teh, Ho Lung & Liu Peh Chun, general R.A. chief of staff and former most famous Szechuen militarists and of the three leading chief staffs in China.

If you send in some leica films I'll send more pictures of Arm. etc. how did your pictures come out?

In ending I'm so much at home that I don't think I'll ever leave this place if I want to stay in China. Its too big for me yet to get my bearings but long live Red China.

greetings

Ma Han Teh

P.S. Enclosed also white airplane circular dropped in Red Regions, perhaps to reach you later. Hearty greetings from Mason Wu, and also from Mao and all your friends.

You, your wife.[41]

While Ma was preoccupied with his role as go-between for the Communist party and foreign friends of the Party, he still found time to write up the report Chairman Mao had requested on the medical conditions he found at the front. He completed this assignment, presenting Mao with "A Report on Medical and Health Work Inspection," in which he analyzed the medical care given at the front. After reviewing it, the Central Committee began implementing the suggestions.

The report suggested ways to improve the organization and training of medical personnel and how to better provide services to the soldiers. Of particular concern to Ma was the inability to break the Nationalist blockade against medical supplies coming into the area. He suggested ways to get around this, remembering the role Song Qingling wanted to play in improving medical care in the Red Army. Soon Madame Song, other friends, and missionaries friendly to the army were recruited to send medical supplies to the northwest. Underground routes to Beijing and Shanghai were established to buy medicine on the pretext it was for missions in the countryside. Following Ma's suggestions, it also was decided to have soldiers run the blockade and enter cities outside the liberated area just to purchase anesthesia. It proved a dangerous undertaking, but one born of desperation, and many were killed in the attempt.

Ma discovered that the lack of Western medicine made the modern doctor almost useless. The entire army seemed to depend on traditional Chinese medicines. As he discovered and grew dependent on Chinese medicines, he recommended labeling the traditional medicines by what they cured rather than by their ingredients. In this way, he and the Western-trained medical workers who joined him later could dispense them with confidence, as the names of the herbs meant nothing to them.

To make these medicines more available, Ma suggested that factories be expanded to mass produce them. "We had medical factories making traditional Chinese medicine. We had already started the idea that modern and traditional doctors can and must work together. During this period we decided on a number of prescriptions which the traditional practitioners recommended as useful and valuable. In our factories we made the herbs and plants and things into infusions or syrups or pills and powders, so that they could be carried around."[42]

On Chairman Mao's instruction, Ma also presented ideas that led to the development of the Red Army medical school. The school recruited out of the ranks of common medical workers and emphasized the importance of hands-on experience. The path to becoming a doctor was up through the ranks, culminating in a nine-month school experience. Those accepted into the school must first have served as an orderly, nurse's aide, nurse, first-aid corps member, or pharmacy worker. After serving in one or more of these capacities, one could enter the medical college. This enterprising system of education for medical doctors in China, born of the unique needs and practical conditions in the countryside, was revolutionary and set the stage for major changes in medical care in China for decades to come. Out of this practice would come the famous "barefoot doctors" of post-liberation China. As Ma said, "The millions of people in the areas behind the enemy lines were treated by nine-month trained doctors. Until practically 1949, we never had many fully trained doctors working in our medical system. But we had set up all the policies, principles and methods of working with very little and taking care not only of the army, but of all the civilians where the army was."[43]

After presenting his medical report to Chairman Mao, Ma informed him that he wanted to stay with the army and help implement his recommendations. Mao assured him the request would be considered, and after reviewing the report, he told Ma that the Central Committee had discussed and approved his request. He could stay in the capacity of advisor to the Red Army's Ministry of Health.

Now serving the Red Army in an official capacity, Ma took on its material trappings as well. He was given cotton-padded shoes and a gray army cap, the same worn by others in Baoan. The supply-unit commander made one special presentation to him, awarding him a warm cotton-padded coat recently confiscated from a landlord. Ma was embarrassed to wear such a fine coat while regular soldiers made do with less, but he decided to take it. Whenever quizzed on his newfound apparel, he joked that the coat was evidence of a Red Army victory and that his wearing it would symbolize that victory. Therefore, he would wear it gladly. By now, Ma was integrated fully into the life of the Red Army. His big nose, the curse of all foreigners who prefer to walk unnoticed in China, was the only thing that kept him from melting into the sea of soldiers in the Red areas.[44]

Events affecting China, especially the Red Army and the Communist party, occurred rapidly during those months. The most important became known as the Xi'an Incident. On December 7, only days after Ma returned to Baoan with the Red Army, Chiang Kai-shek flew to his headquarters in Xi'an to conduct a series of meetings with his top military officers. Foremost among these was Zhang Xueliang, the Young Marshal from the northeast. Chiang did this against the recommendations of his most trusted advisors, who knew of discontent with his policies even among his strongest generals. Chiang was determined, however, to test the loyalty of his troops. He told them that the army was to finish off the Communist "bandits" in Baoan within two weeks—one month at the most.

Convinced now that Chiang was not going to fight the Japanese until he defeated the Communists (a scenario he thought impossible at the time), the Young Marshal, whose father had been killed in a railway explosion engineered by the Japanese, held a secret meeting on December 11 with his own officers. The decision was made to force Chiang to form a united front with the Communist Red Army. On the morning of December 12, Zhang's army attacked Chiang Kai-shek's headquarters, killing most of his bodyguards and capturing the generalissimo in his nightclothes as he hid in the crack of a mountainside behind his bedroom.[45]

When word reached Baoan that Chiang was under arrest by his own army, jubilation reigned. Huang Hua remembers Ma's reaction on hearing the news. He "failed to get a wink of sleep, being overexcited at the 12 December Xian Incident."[46] Ma waited with everyone else to see what response would come from the Party. At first there was no unified response, as individual Party leaders had different opinions about how to respond. A rally was held to celebrate the arrest, and the first emotional reaction from the speakers, including Mao Zedong, was to put on trial and punish their old enemy. Wanting to get out word of this, Ma sent a hastily written card to Snow telling him of the rally.[47] Within days, however, cooler heads prevailed, and a policy of support for a united front was presented to the world. No mention was made of punishing Chiang in this call, though his "crimes" against China were spelled out.

Included in this statement was an eight-point plan for a constructive united front effort. Ma was called upon to play his role as propagandist to the outside world, sending a translation of the official Communist response to the English-language press. Ma oversaw the translation and dissemination of a telegram that was to be broadcast to the world. The resulting "Circular Telegram Issued by the Central Soviet Government and the Central Committee of the Chinese Communist Party Proposing the Convention of a Peace Conference" was a call for support of the Communist position during this strategically important period. As usual, Ma relied on his contacts with Edgar Snow, Agnes Smedley, and others. As before, he wrote personal comments to Snow in a cover letter attached to the more important official response formulated by the Party Central Committee. The response was written on December 19. Ma's translation of the document and the telegram that accompanied his letter was written in his own handwriting and sent on December 23.

The letter to Snow accompanying the Party document gives insight into the wit of the young doctor and the elation he felt at the news arriving from Xi'an. In a departure from his usual style, he did not address Snow as "Dear Comrade Ed." Instead, he began with the salutation "Dear Chiang Kai-Shek"! The equally intriguing signature shows Ma's giddy mood at the time. He signed with the name of "He Ying Ching" [He Yingqing], one of the most hated of all Chiang's generals, who after this incident attempted to take command of the Nationalist army in order to continue the fight against the Communists. Even among loyal

Nationalists he was considered an untrustworthy opportunist who sided with the Japanese when it suited him. In fact, General He was the primary target of the Communists' eight-point plan.[48] Ma's use of the names of the two men most hated by his comrades would not have been understood by his Chinese friends. In fact, it would have offended them. But here we have one American writing to another, displaying a type of humor easily understood by both. Ma may have blended well into a Chinese community, but there was still plenty of the American left in him. The letter to Snow reads:

> Dear Chiang Kai-Shek:—
>
> Enclosed a new proposal–telegram–statement from here clarifying the stand and putting forth sincere reasons for saving the country. Give it all the publicity possible (as we know you will) both here and abroad.
>
> (The gov't. here and its forces will back the Chang–Yang demands to the end as long as they remain revolutionary and beneficial to the country. This is so in the present state and will continue if Chang–Yang follow out this line.) Anti-Jap war is the prime demand and absolute opposition to carry on civil war. This is the attitude here. (No need for publishing statement in parenthesis as official statement.)
>
> Greetings from all including your gambling club etc. to you & Shanghai. Send coco and books & typewriter.
>
> Fraternally Typewritten,
>
> He Ying Ching

When this correspondence reached Snow he immediately sent it on to Shanghai, where it was broadcast to the world. Agnes Smedley was one of the first to receive the news. *The New York Times* on January 8, 1937, blamed Smedley for conducting "radio propaganda to unite large disaffected military units in Shensi and Kansu Provinces, under the Red Banner."[49] From his hideout in Baoan, the young foreign doctor was again furnishing the outside world with information vital to understanding the Communist position in China, and again he was the first to get the word out to the world.

However, Snow, Smedley, and others received the credit for reporting the information he sent. For Ma, there was no credit outside his new-found home. He desired none at the time and gladly devoted his efforts to the Party without expectation of any reward beyond a place in the Red Army. This submersion of self-interest did not go unnoticed by the Party leadership. In a few quick months, extraordinary months that tested the commitment and character of the man, this foreigner accomplished what few if any foreigners had ever achieved, or would achieve in the future. He took giant steps toward genuine membership in a Chinese community. He remained a foreigner. That would never change. But he was no longer an outsider. Few, if any foreigners, can make that claim, no matter what age of history they represent.

A quarter-million armed men were reported to have joined in a movement to create a great Communist State in Northwest China, with an American woman playing a spectacular role in the uprising. Agnes Smedley, a former Colorado schoolteacher, who has long been associated with radical movements in Asia, was described as conducting radio propaganda to unite large disaffected military units in Shensi [Shanxi] and Kansu [Gansu] Provinces under the Red banner in defiance of the Nanking [Nanjing] government.

New York Times, January 8, 1937

Apart from his private war with Agnes Smedley, Dr. Hatem was normal, charming, witty, and likable, with a sense of humor. He always stayed out of messes, a good rule for foreigners in China.

Helen Foster Snow, after visiting Yan'an for several months in 1937

Within days of the Xi'an Incident, the Party Central Committee and its Revolutionary government dismantled its headquarters in Baoan and relocated to the more favorably positioned city of Yan'an. The cease-fire brought about by the arrest of Chiang allowed the move to Yan'an to proceed without fear of attack. All were in good spirits as they settled into this lightly populated town of only a few thousand people. Among those in the procession were two foreigners. One was the young Dr. Ma, who had been continually on the move since his arrival in the northwest.[1] This was not unfamiliar territory to Ma, as he and Edgar Snow had come through the city on their way to Baoan some six months earlier. The other foreigner was Otto Braun, known then by his Chinese name Li De. The only foreigner to take part in the Long March from its beginning, Braun was a Comintern representative who had actually helped shape Chinese Communist policies and military moves, including the Long March. At the time of the move to Yan'an, however, he found himself isolated from the Party leadership and distrusted by Mao. Braun and other Moscow-educated officials who led the Party prior to the Long March were held responsible for the policies that led to the retreat north. It was in opposition to this faction that Mao emerged as supreme leader of the Party and army following the pivotal Zunyi conference during the Long March. However, as the Comintern representative, Braun was afforded certain privileges and access to information.

Ma and Braun did not have time to get to know each other in Baoan, but Yan'an gave them the opportunity. In his memoirs from those years, Braun recalls that "Within the fortified wall, which extended over a chain of hills far above the city on the north side, were hundreds of really decent-looking houses and farms. This was also true of the immediate vicinity. Many of them, the largest and most beautiful in fact, stood empty. Their inhabitants—big landowners, KMT [Nationalist] officials, usurers, and merchants—had preferred to make a timely escape with their families. This provided a simple solution to the problem of quarters. I was assigned a small house with a neat front garden together with Dr Hatem, who by this time had acquired the name Ma Hai-te. He remained my dwelling companion until my departure for Moscow over two and a half years later."[2]

The arrogant Braun found Ma intriguing, but, like many others, discovered little about his life prior to joining the Red Army. He did develop impressions of Ma, however. "Ma Hai-te, then in his mid-twenties, did not speak Chinese at his arrival, had no practical experience as a physician, describing himself as a Communist by intention, but was disorganized and astonishingly naive politically. Only over time was I able to impart to him the rudiments of Marxism. Yet he possessed qualities which stood him in good stead in every situation: rapid comprehension, great adaptability, and youthful nonchalance. He learned to speak, but not to read or write, Chinese very quickly, . . . established himself as a general practitioner for the people, and in time qualified as a specialist for the control of epidemics—which plagued northern China. He got along well with everyone, was never in anyone's way, and made himself useful where he could."[3]

Ma's personality could break the ice of even the most rigid ideologue, and he soon established a relaxed friendship with Braun, cemented in conversation over dinner and around the card table. By September 1937 Japanese bombing hammered Yan'an almost daily, and the decision was made to abandon the town, with its easily visible houses, and move to the hillside caves where the peasants lived. Ma and Braun were assigned two caves halfway up the hillside, with their bodyguards and horse attendants sharing another one. The original occupants, who had inhabited a cluster of five caves, moved their possessions into the other two caves.[4]

During this period Ma and Braun shared a courtyard and a cook.

Both quickly grew tired of the food prepared by their Red Army cook, however, and took turns cooking each evening. Each did his best to produce a variety of European and American fare, although the local ingredients often failed to produce the desired effect.[5] Visitors, especially young people coming to Yan'an from the cities, often dropped by in the evening for a taste of Western-style meals and the liveliest social events in the town. Braun credits Ma for much of the social activity. He recalls, "At weekends, for example, our courtyard was host to artists of all genres, . . . and young people brought in by the very congenial Ma hai-te."[6] On occasion, Ma acted as Braun's interpreter, though Braun says that Ma's skills with the language were barely adequate in 1937 when, on one important occasion, they both found themselves without an interpreter during one of Mao's speeches. When not visiting or talking politics, they spent great sums of energy fighting off sandfleas and rats, two unwelcome yet constant guests in their caves.[7]

On February 7, 1937, soon after settling in Yan'an, Ma joined the Communist party. This was not a step the Party easily allowed. Membership was difficult to attain, and many well-meaning people were rejected. The decision to apply had been made prior to leaving Baoan when, one night shortly before the move to Yan'an, he tossed around in his bed, trying to imagine the best way to approach the Party about his decision. He stewed on it a while, worrying that foreigners might not be allowed to join. After all, there were as yet no foreign members. He decided that the best way to gain membership would be to become a Chinese citizen first. After that, he reasoned, he would become eligible. At midnight he bolted out of bed and headed straight for Zhou Enlai's headquarters, which he knew operated well into the early morning. Brimming with excitement, he blurted out to Zhou that he wanted to become a Chinese citizen. Zhou told Ma that this was neither the time nor the place for such an act, but that following the liberation of the country, Zhou would see to it that Ma became the first foreign citizen of New China.

Brought back down to earth, Ma left Zhou, saying he would look forward to that day. Once outside Zhou's quarters, however, he remembered that he had not raised the primary question of Party membership. He hurried to see Wu Liangping, an official of the Party's Propaganda Ministry and personal secretary to Mao, to test his chances of joining the Party. Wu, an intellectual who had studied in Moscow and Europe and who spoke fluent English, said that he would support Ma's application to join the Party after more chance for discussion. Ma also approached Zhang Hao, leader of the effort to reeducate the captured White soldiers, to ask for his support. Years later Ma remembered the discussions with his two sponsors: "My sponsors, Zhang Hao and Wu Liangping, sounded me out on my views. How did I see the role of the Communist Party in China and internationally? Why did I want to enter it? And so on."[8] Ma engaged in political study arranged by his sponsors, and finally, satisfied with his understanding and commitment, Wu told him, "Write out your application and I will sponsor you." Shortly after that, he was admitted.

Not only did Ma pass a rigorous test, he also broke new ground by becoming the first foreigner to join. On being accepted, he was overcome with emotion. Fighting back tears, he told his friends in Yan'an that membership in the Party meant, "From now on in the fighting for Chinese liberation I will not be a guest. I'll be a host." Ma speculated on why he gained acceptance: "Before admitting me, they not only listened to my words but observed my actions. I served at the front against the attacking Kuomintang General Hu Zongnan, treated the wounded, shouldered the stretchers—so they must have thought I was ok."[9]

After joining the Party, Ma opened up to his friend Huang Hua about his earlier life. In the evening, sharing a room and a kang, a heated brick bed popular in China's northern provinces, Ma told Huang of his days in Shanghai, of his friends there, and of his underground work for the Communist party. He talked of his days in Lebanon, Europe, and the United States, of his family and his education. Decades later, Huang Hua marveled at the ability of this foreigner to blend into the Chinese Communist party and the culture out of which it grew. He said, "I would say there are several reasons Ma was so successful in China. First, as a doctor he had a special skill to offer. Second, he possessed a kind, fresh and enthusiastic personality. He treated everyone the same—big or small. He showed great sympathy for people who needed his help, and finally, he never tried to put himself above others."[10]

As Ma shared his life and goals during those evenings in Yan'an, Huang Hua, like Otto Braun, was struck by his ignorance of, and even lack of interest in, political ideology. Through his evening conversations with Ma, Huang Hua says it was clear that politics was not what motivated Ma to help the Red Army. "He was committed to China's cause through a humanitarian spirit and not a Marxist ideology."[11]

Ma displayed a character and an ability that in some ways transcended the need for political understanding. He brought to China a unique heritage. If we look carefully, we can see that Ma *never* lived in a culture he could call his own. As a child he was expected to survive with Middle Eastern values in the American South, and then as a young Lebanese American he was thrown into a familiar yet foreign Middle Eastern culture. He then wended his way with ease through Switzerland and later Shanghai. Now he found himself in the most foreign of all cultures, with an agrarian revolutionary army living in the caves of northwest China. Never since his birth had he been in a place he could call his own in the way those who now surrounded him could. Not in one instance could he ever say, "Yes, this is my native home, this is exactly where I belong, where I hold the same values and deep cultural roots as those around me." He did not need that. He had never had it, and it would have been impossible to find anyway, for such a place never existed for him. Ma could only thrive where he could contribute. For him, the place, the culture, and the people with whom he lived were all secondary to his drive to make a difference. He now had Yan'an. He was at home now, not in the language, the food, the arts, or even in common, everyday activities, but in the fulfillment of his deepest need to give, and to be appreciated for that giving. He would be prepared to make whatever sacrifices it took to protect the position he now held. He would maintain whatever silence was required in the face of confusing Party orders or actions. He would be tested throughout the rest of his life. In the eyes of most Party members, he never let his comrades down.

The year 1937 was just the beginning of his new life, and it required him to watch and maneuver carefully to stay clear of trouble. In part he succeeded because of his good-natured, self-deprecating manner recognized by all who knew him. But more important than his manner was one absolute rule Ma followed that held him in good stead politically for the rest of his life: He supported Mao Zedong and never questioned an order or assignment from the Party. The fact that he pursued this policy with good humor proved a plus, but the important factor was his absolute and unqualified allegiance to the Party central leadership. This allegiance in part stemmed from his early training in an authoritarian Church and from a well-learned instinct for survival rather than from ideology or theory.

Not that there were no attempts to teach Ma greater appreciation for political theory. He may have studied some with Rewi Alley and others in Shanghai, and Otto Braun may have tried his best to instill basic Marxist theory in the politically naive young doctor, but those informal sessions proved an elementary beginning to his Party education. Ma had proved to the Party that he was faithful. Now he had to prove he was educable. He was assigned to a Party unit comprised of mostly young English-speaking members, including Huang Hua and Liao Chengzhi, the group's leader (and a member of Ma's Yan'an basketball team).[12] In this group, Ma studied the tenets of Marxism-Leninism and learned the importance of following Party discipline. Over the next several decades acquaintances would question, usually in jest, just how successful the Party was in instilling in him an understanding of theory. Most agreed, however, that he had no problem understanding the importance of Party discipline.

For the next decade, during which time many foreigners entered Yan'an as observers and diplomats, Ma's Party membership was kept quiet. It had already been decided by Zhou Enlai, Mao Zedong, and others that Ma would play an important role as the Party's face to the West. Just as there was no need to inform visitors of his personal history, including his name, he was instructed that there was no need to tell people of his Party affiliation. As with other orders, he followed this one without question.

Now that his political direction was clear, Ma focused on the medical work at hand. When the Red Army first moved to Yan'an, there were no hospitals, clinics, or health facilities of any kind. To reach the sick and wounded, who were spread about in caves or small houses, he took to the saddle with Huang Hua, carrying medicines from patient to patient, all the time figuring out how to set up the best possible medical care in the region. During this time Ma worked diligently on his language skills. Rewi Alley says that it was from his travels and conversations with Huang Hua and his motivation to speak directly to the patients that Ma quickly picked up his Chinese.[13]

After settling into Yan'an, the Red Army found itself host to several foreigners eager to see this band of Long Marchers and guerrilla fighters. The cease-fire eased the way for them to come, although it was still a tortuous journey that Chiang Kai-shek's government discouraged anyone from making. During the first year in Yan'an, the Communist party welcomed Agnes Smedley, Helen Foster Snow (Edgar Snow's first wife, who writes under the name Nym Wales), and Evans Carlson, an American military officer intrigued by the battle tactics of the Red Army.

The first new foreigner to arrive in Yan'an was Smedley. Arriving in early February 1937 after an extended stay in Xi'an, she would stay through December, bringing eleven months of creative enthusiasm to the cause and personal discomfort and trouble to the Yan'an community. Ma welcomed his old mentor, especially since she had brought along some canned food from Shanghai—the millet gruel was wearing thin. He also welcomed Smedley's young and attractive interpreter Wu Guang-wei, known to the foreigners as Lily Wu.

Smedley entered Yan'an with a chip on her shoulder, thinking Edgar Snow had stolen some of her thunder by beating her to interviews with

Mao and others. However, Ma convinced her that there was a great story to tell in the life of General Zhu De. "The fighters love him. He is their father and mother," he told her. He took her to meet Zhu, and as soon as he saw the general, threw his arms around him and kissed him "resoundingly, then stood back to observe his handiwork." Not to be outdone, Smedley also threw her arms around Zhu, causing all three to laugh at this strikingly foreign behavior. When Smedley mentioned the $25,000 price that Chiang Kai-shek had put on Zhu's head, Ma reached out and rubbed the general's scalp, murmuring "hm, hm." Smedley agreed immediately that this was the man to write about, and by April she had developed a close relationship with Zhu, spending hours at a time interviewing him for the biography she planned to write. Ma, whose Chinese was improving rapidly, joined Lily Wu and Huang Hua in translating for Zhu and Smedley, thus continuing to assist her in her research, as he had done through his earlier letters and diaries.[14]

In addition to her writing, Smedley sought to assist Ma and the army in improving health conditions at Yan'an. While in Shanghai she depended on Ma to tell her what was needed. She then purchased the medicine and sent it through secret couriers to Yan'an. In Shanghai and in the northwest she sent out international appeals for physicians and medical supplies. These appeals, in concert with Ma's suggestions, proved fruitful over the next few years, bringing such doctors as Norman Bethune, who was to become a household name throughout China.

Smedley threw herself into her work in Yan'an. She was so overwhelmed by the progress toward democratic revolution that she also applied for membership to the Chinese Communist party, not long after Ma was admitted. It is unclear whether Smedley knew of Ma's Party affiliation, but it can be assumed that, if any foreigner knew of it, it would be her. It is unlikely she would have considered applying without the precedent set by Ma. She certainly considered herself more revolutionary than Ma, and expected to be admitted. The negative response she received from the Party was totally unexpected. Her biographer describes what followed:

> When she received the rejection she burst into tears and, to the amazement of those on hand, became nearly hysterical. Party propaganda chief Lu Dingyi tried to soften the refusal by explaining that she would be of greater use as a journalist outside the party. But although she continued to devote her life to the cause of the Chinese peasant, the rejection in Yan'an was a devastating blow from which Smedley would never fully recover.[15]

Following this rejection, Smedley's relationship with Ma and almost everyone else in Yan'an deteriorated. By early summer, when Helen Foster Snow arrived, Smedley and Ma were not speaking. Ma welcomed Mrs. Snow warmly, especially since she brought with her cans of Western food, a welcome respite from the daily fare of rice, steamed bread, and dysentery pills. Helen Foster Snow, at the same time, found Ma helpful and full of good humor. He was "thin to blueness" when she first met him, but every morning he awakened her with his own rendition of the Communist International, "Arise, ye prisoners of starvation. . . ." On the other hand, she found him dead serious when discussing Smedley. Mrs. Snow says that when she entered Yan'an, Ma told her to be careful around Smedley, who had told Ma and Otto Braun that the young and attractive Mrs. Snow was merely a bourgeois writer looking for a story and could not be trusted with their confidences. She recalls, "I was surprised by the attitude of the three foreigners living in Yanan. Always, in China, isolated Westerners were desperate for new acquaintances, even for a few hours of talk. But though Dr. Hatem tried to be nice to me and Li Teh [Otto Braun], neither man was even on speaking terms with Miss Smedley. They said she had 'told lies' about them, which she may have done during one of her occasional periods of psychiatric difficulty, but they were totally unforgiving."[16]

What was the reason for the strain between these two staunch defenders of the Chinese Communist party? It is likely that Smedley was jealous of Ma's Party membership and the trust he obviously enjoyed from the leadership and the common soldier, especially after her own application was rejected. It is also clear that Smedley grew increasingly irritated with Ma and envious of his stature in Yan'an. Their relative roles were the reverse of what they used to be in Shangahi. Now he was telling her what to do. Writing to Edgar Snow in April, she said of Ma, whom she called "Han" in her correspondence:

> Of course you curse because you get so little information from here. Well, there are reasons, so far as I am concerned. Han can speak for himself. His last letter to you saying I would henceforth be in charge of sending you news, was not entirely right. He was merely getting out of work and preparing to spend the hot summer months on a nice camp bed.[17]

Problems also arose from Smedley's relationship with the men of Yan'an and the behavior of her young interpreter, Lily Wu. These revolutionaries had not seen anyone like Lily Wu in years, if ever. Lily was a carefree spirit who seemed to delight in the attention she received from those drawn to her beauty, intellect, and charm. Helen Foster Snow says she was a problem waiting to happen.

I first saw Lily Wu at the theater when she took the lead in Maxim Gorky's *The Mother*. She was the star actress in Yanan. She was not only talented but she carried herself with authority on the stage. She was well-bred, quiet, gracious, feminine, and charming, age twenty-six and already married but separated from her husband, at least geographically. Lily looked healthy and strong, with high color and clear, fair skin. She was quite beautiful. Her hair curled luxuriantly around her trim shoulders in the long bob of the 1930s. Other women in Yanan wore their hair cut short in a straight boyish bob, and you could hardly tell the sexes apart. Lily and I were the only two persons in Yanan who had curled hair and wore lipstick, though both very discreetly—not too red. This was contrary to the Yanan code. Lily looked frivolous on the exterior, but she had no sense of humor and she was deadly earnest. She spent her spare time studying and was a student at the university where she listened to lectures by Chang Kuo-t'ao and his arch-enemy Mao Tse-tung. She had been brought up a Christian and had been a student leader.[18]

Soon after Smedley and Wu arrived in Yan'an they attracted not only the fascination of the men, but the scorn of the few women who had made the Long March. The two female newcomers, one divorced and the other separated from her husband, delighted in flouting tradition. Eager to enrich the lives of those around her with her own brand of leisure activity, Smedley had a phonograph and records sent in from Shanghai. She held dance parties for the army leaders, with He Long, Zhu De, and others joining in. The affable and still Western Ma Haide enjoyed these social gatherings as much as anyone and delighted in showing his new comrades the latest steps. He was especially drawn to Lily. The women of Yan'an, however, little appreciated this Western intrusion into their lives. Zhu De's wife, already unhappy at the time her husband spent with the female reporter, "laid down the law against our dancing here," Smedley wrote in a letter to Edgar Snow. She told him that the women in Yan'an considered dancing "a kind of public sexual intercourse. So there's a big scandal, so far as I can see I've a reputation for corrupting the Army." She did not back off, however, and berated the Red Army men for bowing to their wives in a feudal fashion.[19]

Ma used the social gatherings and his friendship with Smedley to pursue a relationship with Lily Wu. In this he failed. Smedley found Ma's romantic notions about Lily amusing and discussed his interests and adventures with mutual friends. It is doubtful that Ma intended to amuse her or to offer her fodder for gossip. On one occasion, Smedley wrote to Edgar Snow, telling him that Ma had fallen for Lily Wu, but that the affection was not returned. She also told Snow that this was not the first woman Ma was attracted to in Yan'an, adding unkind details of another attempt at love. "While I'm about it, I'll give you more gossip and finish. Han went in for romance with a beautiful girl from Peiping way, but she backed out for another fellow more attractive, gentler and interesting. I was sorry for Han because he was hopeful and in a bad way about this business. I helped all I could. I think this is the reason Han moved out of our compound and moved in with Li Teh. . . . This beautiful girl lives in this compound."[20]

While it is not known exactly why his romance with the Beijing beauty failed, the reason for the brevity of Ma's infatuation with Lily Wu is much clearer. He had a rival, and that rival was Mao Zedong. Ma backed off while Smedley acted as go-between for the chairman and Lily. But Ma could hardly avoid being caught up in the scandal that exploded after Smedley alienated the women of Yan'an and encouraged Mao's relationship with Lily Wu. Soon it landed right on his doorstep, for as Mao's relationship with Lily grew, so did his need for a secret place to meet her. Ma's cave was free during the days. Edgar Snow relates some of the saga of tangled affections and controversy that followed.

> When the women of Yan'an noticed an atmosphere of defiance among the men of the town, they suspected Agnes as the primary cause. For instance, they thought it strange that a foreign woman should spend so much time talking with their husbands in her cave. . . . It was said that General Zhu De's wife—a combat veteran in her own right—did not like the fact that her husband was being interviewed alone for long periods of time by Agnes, and she told him so. . . .
>
> It was Mao's wife, He Zizhen, who appreciated Smedley the least. In return, Agnes made it plain she thought Zizhen led a colorless, cloistered existence and did not have the necessary qualifications to be a revolutionary leader's wife. She made this clear by ignoring Zizhen. As a result, although there had been no specific quarrel between the two women, there was much mutual animosity.
>
> Agnes had the habit of reprimanding young communist officials for being afraid of their wives. She told them half-jokingly that if they could not free themselves from women's oppression, they probably could not liberate

China.... Agnes' introduction of square dancing to Yan'an was the last straw. It galvanized the wives into open opposition.

Lily Wu was the star of the "social dances" that were taking place in the evenings. She also was a leading player in the "contemporary theater" troupe of Yan'an. Her specialty was leading roles in Western plays. From the beginning, Lily seemed a brilliant fairy-tale princess in contrast to the dull women of Yan'an. To the men of Yan'an, who had lived a long time among only peasants, Lily was more than a pretty face. She was comparable to Yang Guifei, the most beautiful woman in Chinese history....

The Red Army was enjoying a few months' interlude of peace between wars. And it was spring, with young rice plants coloring the red earth with green, and apple blossoms coming into full bloom. Mao, finally freed from battles which had lasted years, read many books and wrote essays on politics and philosophy. What is not well known is that Mao was also writing a large number of poems to instruct and guide Lily Wu....

Lily appeared to be reviving within him youthful fancies about delicate and refined sentiment. She always acted as mediator in conversations between Mao and Agnes, and we may assume that certain questions Mao asked Smedley were directed at Lily. She was fresh and sensitive as well as elegant. Thus, when Agnes discussed romantic love with Mao, she thought the conversation was aimed at Lily Wu. During their discussions, Mao wrote poems. Naturally Lily was able to appreciate them better than Agnes. Lily would respond poetically herself, using the same rhythm as Mao had in his poetry, and this pleased him. They discussed at length man–woman relationships in the new post-revolutionary liberated society where men and women would be equals.[21]

Smedley, in her 1943 book *Battle Hymn of China,* also writes of these encounters.

Mao often came to the "cave" where I lived with my girl secretary, and the three of us would have a simple dinner and spend hours in conversation. Since he had never been out of China, he asked a thousand questions. We spoke of India; of literature; and once he asked me if I had ever loved any man, and why, and what love meant to me. Sometimes he quoted from old Chinese poets or recited some of his own poems. One of his poems was in memory of his first wife, who had been slain by the Kuomintang because she was his wife.

His humor was often sardonic and grim, as if it sprang from deep caverns of spiritual seclusion. I had the impression that there was a door to his being that had never been opened to anyone.[22]

Otto Braun is the one who informs us that not all of the visits between Mao and Lily Wu took place in Smedley's cave. There were times, he says, that Ma made his own dwelling available for the chairman's trysts. By September, Ma and Braun had moved to the cluster of hillside caves that protected them from the incessant Japanese bombing. Braun says that Smedley made the arrangements for Lily Wu and Mao to use Ma's cave when he was not around.[23]

This placed Ma in an unenviable position, since rumors were rampant about Smedley and her interpreter's corruption of Mao and other men at Yan'an. But Ma had little room to maneuver out of this one. It was hard enough to get Smedley to take no for an answer, but there was no way he could tell Mao that the chairman's personal behavior made him uncomfortable. Mao found the foreign doctor's cave a convenient place to meet, and that was good enough for Ma and Smedley. When Ma discovered the chairman's interests in Lily Wu, he relinquished any further interest himself. As in all other instances, he supported Mao Zedong.

These entanglements soon exploded in the face of them all. Snow's account of the events that July continues:

> Late one evening after Agnes had already gone to bed there was the sound of cloth shoes outside her cave and she heard the sound of Mao's soft southern accent. The chairman was in Lily's cave next door and the light was still on. Smedley had heard him knock, then the door opening and closing. She tried to go back to sleep and just when she finally was drifting off, she heard the sound of footsteps rushing excitedly up the hill. Then the door of Lily's cave was pushed open and a woman's shrill voice broke the silence. "You idiot! How dare you fool me and sneak into the home of this little bourgeois dance hall strumpet." Smedley leapt out of bed, threw on her coat, and ran next door. There was Mao's wife standing beside the seated Mao beating him with a long-handled flashlight. He was sitting on a stool by the table, still wearing his cotton hat and military coat. He did not try to stop his wife. His guard was standing at attention at the door looking perplexed. Mao's wife, crying in anger, kept hitting him and shouting until she was out of breath. . . .
>
> Suddenly Mao's wife turned on Lily, who was standing with her back against the wall like a terrified kitten before a tiger. She railed at Lily, saying "Dance-hall bitch! You'd probably take up with any man. You've even fooled the Chairman. Then she drew close to Lily and while brandishing the flashlight she held in one hand, she scratched Lily's face with the other hand and pulled her hair. Blood flowing from her head, Lily ran to Agnes and hid behind her. Mao's wife now directed her anger against Agnes.

"Imperialist!" she shouted. "You're the cause of all this. Get back to your own cave." Then she struck the "foreign devil" with her flashlight. Not one to turn the other cheek, Smedley flattened Mrs. Mao with a single punch. . . .

The next morning the whole town was talking of nothing else. It got to the point where Mao had to regard the problem as important, so he assembled the Central Executive Committee, explained his actions, and left the final decision to them. The committee decided to treat the case as a "secret matter" and they issued a command that forbade speaking more about it. But no one could keep Mao's wife quiet. She got the other women together and asked for their support in banishing Smedley, Lily, and Mao's guard—she believed that he also had a part in this 'intrigue'—from Yan'an. And she tried to put a stop to the dancing.[24]

One account of this incident claims that this encounter took place not in Lily Wu's cave, but in Ma's.[25] Again contradictions abound, and it is possible that Smedley and Snow did not report the actual location to protect Ma. Wherever it happened, the inner circles of the Party were hemorrhaging, and Ma was close to the center, watching intensely.

He Zizhen's actions caused Mao to ask the Party Central Committee to grant him a divorce, which was approved. These events were taking place just as the Japanese were attacking Beijing at the "Marco Polo" bridge, thus beginning open warfare in China. The Central Committee acted swiftly. Mao's wife was reprimanded for her transgressions against Party discipline and sent to a village outside Yan'an, then on to the Soviet Union for "political education." Lily Wu was banished from Yan'an and sent to the front with a theater troupe. Before leaving, she burned the poetry Mao wrote for her, according to Snow. Smedley was told to cease working on her biography of Zhu De, under the pretense that she should report more on the war effort now that Japan had marched into Beijing. Much to the relief of many, including Ma, she was forced to leave Yan'an a month later.[26]

What happened to Lily Wu? In 1972, Helen Foster Snow visited China, where she visited old friends and asked about past acquaintances. When she asked Ma Haide about the fate of Lily Wu, he responded crisply and without elaboration. "She went to Xi'an," he said, "and we never heard of her again."[27]

Whatever sparked the tension between Smedley and Ma, by August their relationship had deteriorated to such a degree that Ma took little interest in treating a serious back injury Smedley received after being thrown from a pony. Helen Foster Snow says she chastised Ma for allowing his emotions to take precedence over his professional calling. She says that she "cried and cried till, to shut me up, Dr. Hatem was finally forced to climb up to Agnes' cave with me to look at her injured back." However, once there the two spoke not one word to each other except for a few medical questions and responses. Ma felt up and down Smedley's spine, declared her back not broken, and left.[28]

Helen Foster Snow, when asked what particular incident caused the rift between Ma and Smedley, said that she never knew and never inquired. "One simply did not ask questions like that in Yan'an. All of them were in a very dangerous position and it was best not to ask too many questions."[29] Life in Yan'an was full of purpose and direction for Ma. But it was, as he was learning, also full of intrigue and fraught with danger. He weathered this storm well, however, and Helen Foster Snow's summation of him in Yan'an helps us understand why: "Apart from his private war with Agnes Smedley, Dr. Hatem was normal, charming, witty, and likable, with a sense of humor. He always 'stayed out of messes', a good rule for foreigners in China."[30] This characterization supports Otto Braun's remark that Ma "was never in anyone's way, and made himself useful where he could." Ma just skirted trouble with the Lily Wu "mess," staying far enough from it to proceed with his work. He would have many opportunities over the next half century to show his uncanny ability to tread a careful path while political and personal storms swirled around him.

As in so many other instances where differences of perception, opinion, or memory occur, some of those closest to Ma himself give a different account of the story of Ma and Smedley in Yan'an. In response to a direct question about it, Huang Hua said he knew nothing of the rift between the two, even though "the three of us slept in the same room for several nights."[31] In the 1980s, while visiting in Beijing with his uncle, Greg Hatem asked Ma about the Helen Foster Snow account of his relationship with Smedley in Yan'an. "Uncle Shag said he doesn't know why she said those things. He said she misunderstood their relationship. And besides, he didn't think much of her anyway. He never felt like she treated Ed Snow well."[32] It is clear that Helen Foster Snow harbors resentment toward Smedley, in part because of the latter's disdain for her "bourgeois" lifestyle and, more seriously, for the perception that Smedley played a role in the Snows' divorce in 1944. Smedley made no secret of her belief that Edgar Snow could do better.[33] Mrs. Snow also resented the global reputation that Ma enjoyed later in life and argues that his account of the trip to Baoan with her former husband was a blatant attempt to overshadow Snow's contribution in that history-making journey. Is it possible that she later fabricated this story in an attempt to strike back at the enemies who did not afford her the respect she deserved, and at those whom she perceived to have denigrated Edgar Snow's contribution? While one can question her motives, there is no reason to believe she fabricated the story. Su Fei acknowledges that Smedley and Ma did not always enjoy each other's company, primarily, she says, due to their differences in personality. "Dr. Ma and Smedley did not spend much time together in Yan'an. Smedley was with Zhu De and Dr. Ma was engaged in his medical work. Also, they were so different in how they related to people, with Dr. Ma enjoying the company of every-one from Chairman Mao down to the lowest young soldier, and Smedley wanting to keep company with the leaders. Dr. Ma was always happy, easy to please, while Smedley was very, very difficult to please."[34] Finally, Su Fei says that, while she enjoyed Smedley's books, especially her biog-raphy of Zhu De, "I did not like her personally."[35] Because Su Fei never met Smedley, this impression could have come only from friends in Yan'an and from the man who later became her husband, Ma Haide.

There is no question that Smedley and Ma did in fact have grave dif-ferences in Yan'an, and it is likely that Lily Wu's presence was in part responsible for the rift. This should come as no surprise, since Smedley was feuding with just about everyone else there, and Ma was by then without question aligned with the Yan'an veterans on sensitive issues and policies. If common sense did not dictate such an alignment, then Party discipline certainly did. It is not likely that he would have warmly sup-ported this other foreigner, no matter how good a friend, who was alien-ating his newfound comrades just as he was attempting to prove that a foreigner could be trusted to work closely and in confidence with the Chinese Communist party. Smedley's behavior in Yan'an easily could have jeopardized his own position. Moreover, there seems no reason to dispute Smedley's comments to Edgar Snow that Ma was enamored of Lily Wu, nor Otto Braun's account of how the chairman used Ma's cave for trysts with Lily Wu. In fact, Braun liked Ma and had nothing inju-rious to say about him.

No matter how serious the differences, it is clear that over the next decade they eventually took a back seat to the larger issue of mutually and publically supporting China's Communist party. Unlike comments and insinuations found in her personal letters to Snow, in none of her books or reports did Smedley ever criticize Ma. Nor did she give away his identity in the stories of the Red Army that she published after her Yan'an trip, in which she identified him only as "the American doctor who had adopted the Mohammedan name of Ma Hai-teh."[36]

After leaving Yan'an, Smedley continued to send Ma personal supplies and to support his medical work for the remainder of her life. Just before her death in 1950, she sent him books and records for his home in liberated China.[37] Ma, for his part, was one of the more prominent speakers at Smedley's memorial service on May 6, 1951, and never spoke ill of her in any forum outside of his discussions with Mrs. Snow in 1937 and with close friends and family. It would have served no purpose to do so, since the Chinese Communist party never publicly questioned her reputation as its friend. As a loyal Party member, Ma could not oppose this evaluation of Smedley, and in fact there is no reason to believe he would want to. He continued throughout his life to praise her for bringing him into the fold of the progressive movement in China and for her contributions to the revolution.

Hankow, China. Captain Evans Carlson, a United States Marine Corp intelligence officer, returned here today from Shansi, where during the past three months he had marched the length and breadth of that province with units of the formerly Communist Eighth Route Army. . . . Everywhere Captain Carlson was warmly welcomed, after being greeted with demonstrations in which slogans were shouted and posters displayed stressing Chinese American Unity.

New York Times, March 1, 1937

Hankow, China. Dr. Norman Bethune, a Canadian doctor, Charles Parsons, an American, and Miss Jean Ewen, a Canadian, who came to China recently for medical work financed by Canadian and American peace organizations, have left here for Yenan, administrative headquarters of the former Soviet districts. They plan to set up a medical center for civilian and soldier wounded in cooperation with Chinese medical authorities.

New York Times, February 21, 1938

In the midst of dealing with Smedley, Lily Wu, and Helen Foster Snow, Ma received orders to visit the front. Under the agreement between the Communists and Nationalists that followed the Xi'an Incident, the Red Army was reorganized into three divisions, calling itself now the Eighth Route Army. In August 1937, Ma traveled with the new 129th Division to Wutai, headquarters of the army commanded by Zhu De and Peng Dehuai. He was sent to the front to receive medical supplies promised by the Nationalists in this new era of a united front; what he found was three small boxes of iodine and bandages. By the end of the year he was called back to Yan'an to help set up a hospital and organize the reception and distribution of medical aid arriving from Western allies encouraged by the efforts against the Japanese. He also was delighted to welcome to Yan'an a growing number of foreigners who supported the Communist efforts.

In December 1937, Evans Carlson, an American military officer, arrived in Yan'an to investigate the Red Army's military strength. He had heard of this new type of Chinese army from Edgar Snow during a discussion in Shanghai after Snow's visit in 1936. The Communist leadership and its Eighth Route Army welcomed Carlson to their command center. He would use what he learned there after the outbreak of World War II, when he organized American-led guerrilla units, called Carlson's Raiders.

When he arrived, Carlson was struck by the presence of the two foreigners among the Communists. The entire time he was there he knew them only by their Chinese names. Of Li De and Ma, he says, "Li Teh [Li De] was about forty, of medium height and clean shaven. He wore thick glasses, and was inclined to be irritable at times. His past was shrouded in mystery, but he obviously had had a military background, and it was said he had fled his native land because of the unpopularity of his communist leanings. [After the introduction] he promptly and bluntly accused me of being a spy. I assured him that I was not, and pointed to the fact that the army in Shansi had suffered no harm as a result of my presence. . . . Eventually we became good friends. . . . In the cave next to Li Teh lived Doctor Ma Hai-teh, who advised on medical affairs. His past too was unrevealed. I made no attempt to pry into the private affairs of either man. Ma was short, of dark complexion, and sort of an eternal optimist. His cheerful, hearty way, and the fact that he had learned to speak Chinese with amazing facility, made him extremely popular in the army. Over in Shansi men had asked me eagerly: 'Do you know Ma Hai-teh: He speaks Chinese almost as well as we do.' "

Ma's gregarious nature delighted Carlson, and in one instance cost him a good bit of money. But it was all in fun. "I met Ma late one afternoon down in the village, and invited him to have dinner with me. He agreed and we started for a restaurant famous for its Pa Pao Fan (the sweetened rice concoction). As we walked along Ma was hailed almost at every step by students and shop keepers, men and women alike. To each he would reply: 'Come on down and have dinner with us.' I was amused by the generosity with which he dispensed my hospitality, for I realized that he knew I was not pressed for money. By the time we reached the restaurant I felt like the Pied Piper of Hamlin, for in our wake were a dozen or more of young men and women, laughing, joking and thoroughly in the spirit of the occasion. It was great fun, and wholly informal. Individuals ordered what they wanted and then got up and left, or sat around and told stories of past experiences, without any sense of obligation or restraint."[1]

Of all the foreign visitors to Yan'an during this period, none was more welcome than Dr. Norman Bethune. To this day the name of Bethune resounds throughout China, and Ma ranks second only to him as the most famous foreign doctor in China. While acknowledging this, it must also be said that without Ma, there is some question whether Bethune could have accomplished what he did for the Red Army and for China.

The turbulent and volatile life of Norman Bethune paved the way for his final adventure in China. Born to a socially conscious Presbyterian minister in Canada, Bethune grew to adulthood with the desire to practice medicine, but not in a passive way. When World War I began, he volunteered as a stretcher-bearer for a division in the Canadian Field Ambulance Corps. Struck by the horror of war rather than the glory of it, he questioned its worth. He saw mostly its waste. Before the end of the war, he was wounded by shrapnel and spent six months in French and British hospitals.

After returning home to Canada, he completed his medical studies and in 1924 moved to Detroit to establish himself as a world-class surgeon, a status he never doubted would come his way. However, what he found at first was only an office in the red-light district, with few patients able to pay his fees. Like George Hatem a few years later in Shanghai, Bethune found out a lot about the problems of getting medical care to the poor as he treated prostitutes and other members of the underclass. He learned that those with the greatest need are the ones with the least access. Once, in words that could have been written by Hatem, he exclaimed to his wife, "This isn't medicine. It's like putting mustard plaster on a wooden leg. When they need treatment they either don't know it or are afraid they can't pay for it. When they finally do come, it's often too late, or their health has become completely undermined. And what can I do for a prostitute, when her problem is not really that she is diseased, but that she is a prostitute?"[2]

By 1935 Bethune's reputation as a leading surgeon was assured. He held patents on surgical tools, he had all the money he needed, and other physicians sought his advice and support. But something was not quite right. He voiced anger at his own profession, saying, "We set ourselves up in practice, all smug and satisfied—like tailor shops. We patch an arm, a leg, the way a tailor patches an old coat. We're not practicing medicine, really—we're carrying on a cash-and-carry trade. I'll tell you what's needed: a new medical concept, a new concept of universal health protection, a new concept of the functions of the doctor. . . . We go to the people! *We go to the people!*[3]

In 1936 Bethune had a chance to put his words into actions when he was asked by supporters of the Spanish Republic to lead a Canadian medical team in the struggle against fascism in Spain. At the precise moment Bethune arrived in Madrid, George Hatem, now calling himself Ma Haide, was on the march with the Red Army in China.

While in Spain, Bethune found a way to take medical services to the people rather than force the people to come to the doctor. He did it by bringing the one thing most needed by dying soldiers: blood. And he did it at the front, not in some faraway hospital that most soldiers never reached because they bled to death. "For the first time since humans learned to kill their brothers a man had appeared on the battlefield to reverse history—*to give blood, not to shed it.*"[4] On his first night at the front he saved twelve soldiers from certain death—and began a revolution in wartime medical service.

In the summer of 1937 Bethune returned to Canada on a speaking tour to raise both money and consciousness for the cause in Spain. However, he spoke about more than Spain; he challenged people to see the threat to China. "In Spain fascism has attacked 24,000,000 people, with the United States, Britain and France embargoing the Loyalists. Now, in China, the attack has spread against nearly one quarter of the total population of the earth. If the same treacherous policy of blockading the victims and making arrangements with the aggressors is continued, we may well wonder whether any man, woman or child is safe anywhere in the world."[5]

Hearing of Bethune's interest in their struggle, the China Aid Council, affiliated with Song Qingling's China Defense League, asked to meet with him in New York. Ma had sent out the call to Madame Song, Smedley, and others to recruit medical teams to northern China to aid the guerrillas in their fight against the Japanese. His call to Madame Song had reached a friendly, and enormously qualified, respondent. Bethune would go to China.

On January 2, 1938, Bethune departed for Hong Kong. He took with him equipment and surgical supplies for several medical teams. He was accompanied by Jean Ewen, a Canadian nurse who had been a missionary in China, and Dr. Charles H. Parsons. From Hong Kong he wrote his family,

I refuse to live in a world that spawns murder and corruption without raising my hand against them. I refuse to condone, by passivity, or by default, the wars which greedy men make against others. . . . Spain and China are part of the same battle. I am going to China because I feel that is where the need is greatest, that is where I can be most useful.[6]

After arriving in Hong Kong, the three flew to Hankou (now Wuhan), where they were met by Agnes Smedley. Smedley and Bethune, both quick-tempered and rarely wrong, disliked each other instantly. Neither Bethune, Ewen, nor Smedley cared for Parsons, who had exhibited only a carelessness with their funds and a knack for staying drunk. He was eventually dropped from the team. In a letter to Edgar Snow in which he relayed Smedley's impressions of the medical team, Jim Bertram, a correspondent in Hong Kong, said,

> About the C-A [Canadian-American Medical Unit]—you may hear more of this later; but it does seem that the personnel of this unit wasn't very carefully considered in the US. One man was a drunk, and never got further than Hankow. Bethune is temperamental, and rather unnecessarily extravagant. In fact, Jean Ewen seems to be the best man in the bunch. So A [Agnes Smedley] is at present in revolt against the foreign doctors. This is all very unfortunate, but mustn't be allowed to block future action.[7]

Smedley, while not at all pleased with the results of her hard work, resigned herself to Bethune's presence and arranged the group's passage to Yan'an, where they would hook up with the Eighth Route Army and the China Aid Council's representative, Ma Haide.[8] On February 22 they left for Yan'an, arriving in late March. Ewen describes their arrival.

> We passed through the gates of Yanan and were surprised, almost amazed, at its smallness. The dingy streets were lined with dingier stores and restaurants. The whole town had been waiting for Dr. Bethune since early morning with flags and drums. We were greeted by a kind-faced, gentle person, Dr. Mah Hai Teh [Ma Haide], a Lebanese American from Yonkers who had come to the Red Army in Civil War days. In fact he had joined the Long March in Kansu, many miles from here.
>
> Comrade Mah took us to supper at the newest co-operative restaurant whose speciality was coarse noodles, big fat ones. . . . After eating our fill we were invited to Dr. Mah's cave for coffee. It was, he assured us, American coffee, a gift of the Japanese emperor. . . .
>
> While we sat around talking Li Teh swaggered in. . . . We talked with Li Teh and Dr. Mah until well after eleven.[9]

Bethune had heard of Ma before entering Yan'an, no doubt from Smedley, and he grew to depend on him for his introduction to the Red Army and its medical needs. Ma, for his part, shared none of Smedley's concerns about Bethune. It was clear from the beginning that Ma, only a few years out of medical school and still in his twenties, looked on the older and internationally recognized Bethune with awe. After greeting him with a vigorous handshake and sharing with him coffee and noodles, Ma took him on a tour of the army. While walking, Ma told Bethune, "You can't realize how much everyone here has been looking forward to your coming. A surgeon with your background! And your experience in Spain! . . . By God, how we need you!"[10]

As the official representative of Song Qingling's China Defense League, which had invited Bethune to China, Ma's assignment from the Party was to improve medical services for the army and to interact with Westerners coming to Yan'an. Bethune's visit provided the opportunity to show his value in both roles. Thanks to Ma, Bethune's first glance around Yan'an was a favorable one. In his diary entry after spending hours the first night with Ma, he wrote,

> In Yanan there is a sense of confidence and purpose in administrative circles. In the towns and cities I passed through on my way here I became accustomed to the sights of semi-feudalism—filthy dwellings, polluted streets, people in rags. Here, among the ancient structures, the streets are clean, teeming with people who seem to know where they're going. . . . There is a newly created Medical Training School designed to furnish the army with medical personnel. There is a growing hospital, and though medical facilities are primitive, the government here has introduced free medical treatment for all.[11]

Over the next several days Bethune met often with Ma, who explained to him that medical services readily available in the West were practically nonexistent both in Yan'an and at the front due to lack of supplies, equipment, and staff. In response to a question about injuries treated in Yan'an, Ma told him that he had not seen one case of abdominal wounds in the base hospital. Bethune knew this was because such wounds could not be treated at the front, so that patients with abdominal wounds all died before they could get to the hospital. Following this depressing briefing, Bethune met with Chairman Mao to discuss how best he could contribute to the war effort. Mao admitted that most soldiers wounded at the front died due to lack of immediate medical attention. Bethune said he wanted to establish mobile units like the ones he had in Spain. Mao agreed, and Bethune, with Ma's assistance, began setting up a mobile medical unit for the front. He was not in Spain, however, and the problems he encountered tested his skill and patience. Without refrigeration, for instance, how could they store blood? They decided to try storing it in cool streams, a method he had experimented with in Spain. What of the lack of basic hygiene, of cleanliness in medical care? Gauze was being reused to treat wounds, something he had not seen anywhere, even in Spain. Bethune would adjust to some backwardness, but at times his infamous quick temper masked his good intentions. It was up to Ma to show him the way around some of the obstacles he found.

Once Bethune was asked to assist in surgery at the base hospital in Yan'an. The hospital was in fact a series of caves covering one side of a steep hill. The caves were in tiers, one above the other. There were four beds to a cave, with water delivered each day by donkeys. The caps, gowns, and sheets were more gray than white. Bethune, whose medical work had been housed in a grand hotel in Madrid, was ill prepared for what he found when Ma took him to the hospital. When he entered the first cave, Ewen reports that Bethune exploded at his hosts and informed them that "he damned well wouldn't work in a place like that. He declared himself on strike. He was appalled at the primitive facilities and what he considered lack of any comforts whatever. Doctors Mah and Chiang asked if he expected things to be better at [the front] but he would not change his mind."[12]

With this unexpected and unwelcome criticism of the medical work he helped lead, Ma took Bethune aside and changed from the junior, star-struck young physician to the experienced China hand. He was now the teacher, and he told Bethune there were some things about China he had to learn if he was to survive in this arena. Most important, he said, was that this hospital belonged to the people themselves. These people had never before experienced such self-reliance, such ownership. No matter how primitive Bethune found the hospital, it was a hospital run by the Chinese themselves, and the fact that people survived at all was enough for them right now. Bethune should be careful not to denigrate that effort. After the revolution was completed, China could build sophisticated hospitals for all its people. For now, they would be self-reliant and get along as well as they could.[13]

After three weeks in Yan'an, Bethune prepared to head for the front. Ma suggested that he join in the journey. Bethune agreed, and Ma approached the leadership with his request. He was denied. The Party wanted Ma close to the center, both as a representative of the China Defense League and as a valued face to the West. He was told that he would support Bethune as liaison between his work at the front and the leadership in Yan'an.[14]

What Bethune found at the front was appalling. He could not keep up with the demands. Lice crawled over open wounds, there was no extra clothing for the wounded who needed clean uniforms, and the diet consisted only of millet. Besides having to dispense constant medical care, Bethune was responsible for sending regular reports to Yan'an. In his diary he wrote, "it seems I can hardly find time to write my reports to Ma and Mao Tse-tung. But I must find the time!"[15] These reports were meant not only for the forces in Yan'an, but as messages to the rest of the world calling for greater support. When he received the reports, Ma would have them translated for Mao, then would send them to Western friends like Edgar Snow. Snow, now supporting Madame Song's efforts with the China Defense League, acted at times as Ma's conduit to that organization. In late 1939 Ma wrote Snow, "I am enclosing a report on the work of Dr. Bethune from February to July lst, 1939. . . . The report of Dr. Bethune is on his mobile operating work."[16]

Bethune's reports were filled with graphic descriptions of life at the front, and with cries for more help. In this July report he sent first to Ma, then to Snow, and then finally to the China Defense League, Bethune alerts the world to the horrors of China's struggle.

Dear Comrades,

This report will be a survey of the work of the Canadian American Mobile Medical Unit for the period from Feb. 21/39 to July 1/39—a little over 4 months spent working in the central Hobei under very active conditions of guerrilla warfare. . . .

(1) During the 4 months period, our Unit was in 4 battles at Liu Han and on March 14 to 19th; at Ta Tuan Ting on April 15; at Chi Huei on April 26 to 28th and Sung Chai Chun on May 18th. In none of these engagements was the Unit ever farther than 8 li from the firing line and at times even closer.

(2) The total number of operations performed in the field were 315—not including first aid dressings.

(3) The total distances travelled in Mid Hopei were 1504 li.

(4) The number of operating rooms and dressing stations set up was 13.

(5) The number of new Mobile operating Units organized was 2, one for the troops of General Liu and the other for the troops of Ho Lung. . . .

2. The Unit was very nearly captured at the village of Yang Chai Chueng about 40 li north east of Ho Chien. With ten minutes warning at 5 am we left one end of the village as the 400 of the enemy entered. All the staff and equipment were saved owing to the smart work of our capable manager Com. W. Long and owing to the fact that the entire staff were mounted and carried all equipment in saddle bags. If we had been carrying our equipment in the ordinary way it would have had to be abandoned with the mules. The patients were either hidden in the straw or carried on the backs of civilians. No patients were captures. . . .

3. Two wounded Japanese prisoners were operated on one with an ampu-

tation of the thigh and ten days later both returned to the enemy at Ho
Chien.

4. Fifteen operations were performed without anaesthetic as we ran out of
Chloroform. We also ran short of antiseptics and gauze but a small quantity
was obtained later. . . .

10. Personal expenditure (food, etc.) as I cook my own meals and only use
this funds, others being put into medical work.—April, $30.30; May, $21.68;
June, $18.62. These accounts are certified by the manager of the Unit,
(W. Long).
With Comradely greeting,
Dr. N. Bethune.

Additional Comments,

I believe that everyone was satisfied that operations can be successfully
performed in the field only one or two miles from the front. . . . As an example of this I will mention the two cases of perforation of the intestines by rifle
bullets operated on. The first case was operated on 18 hours after wounded
and the second 8 hours after being wounded. Both cases had almost identical
wounds—the bullet entering the abdomen at the level of the umbilicus. Both
had ten perforations and tears of the small and large intestines with escape of
intestinal contents into the abdominal cavity (including round
worms.) . . . Both were operated on at night in a dirty Buddhist temple by
the light of candles and flash lights. The first case died the following day but
the second made an uneventful recovery, in spite of being transported 60 li
every night for the following week on a rough stretcher. The difference
between life and death was the difference between 8 hours and 18
hours. . . . The remarkable number of wounded who were able to return to
duty in one month after receiving debridement of wounds early and so
escaping infection, was commented on by all commanders. Of course the
great obstacles to such treatment are two—lack of enough trained doctors,
and no surgical instruments to give surgeons to do the work even if there
were enough. . . . Why, oh why are we not receiving more help from both
China and abroad? Think of it! 2,500 wounded always in hospitals, over 1,000
battles fought in the past year and only 5 Chinese graduate doctors, 50 semi-
trained doctors and one foreigner to do all this work.[17]

A prolific writer, both in letters and in his diary, Bethune bombarded Ma
with correspondence. He used Ma as his link to the world he left behind.
During the summer of 1939 he wrote Ma proudly that he had just been
given the official title of Medical Advisor to the "Chin-Cha-Chi Military
District" under the direction of General Nieh Jungchen [Nie Rong-

zhen]. He added, "Do you think the New York people are getting any cables? Perhaps you should forward them to Madame Sun Yat-sen. She may be able to get some action. I need help. Haven't seen a newspaper or magazine (American or English) for three months. Have any arrived? What's happening in the world? What's happening in Spain? Have you received any news? I did eight operations today. . . . I am tired but enormously content. . . . I need an assistant! So much for now. We are traveling a road watered with tears and blood."[18]

For the next six months Bethune marched over north China with the Eighth Route Army, insisting that his medical staff pay more attention to cleanliness and detail in their work. His temper dogged him, but he tried to cope, perhaps remembering Ma's admonition to understand China on its own terms.

> The hospital "staffs" here consist of "doctors" of 19 to 22, not one of whom has had a college education or been in a modern hospital or medical school. The nurses are peasant boys of 14 to 18. Yet this is the only material we possess and we must make the best of it. They are very eager to learn and improve themselves. They constantly ask for criticism of their work. Although I am often irritable at their ineptitude and lack of medical knowledge, their simplicity, their eagerness to learn, their true spirit of comradeship and selflessness disarm me in the end.[19]

Bethune's own health was deteriorating, so much so that General Nieh called him to his quarters to criticize him for taking such poor care of himself. In his infrequent rests after eighteen- to twenty-hour days, he longed for Western contact. In a letter to friends in the United States and Canada, he allowed himself a moment of nostalgia.

> The mails are irregular. It takes at least five months for letters to reach me *after* they have arrived in China. I calculate that I get only one out of every 25 letters. . . . I sometimes dream of coffee, rare roast beef, of apple pie and ice cream. Mirages of heavenly food! Books . . . Are books still being written? Is music still being played? Do you dance, drink beer, look at pictures? What do clean sheets feel like in a soft bed? Do women still love to be loved?[20]

Bethune appreciated, but was never satisfied with, Ma's correspondence, which proved much too infrequent. On December 9, he wrote Ma,

> Dear Ma: I'm getting used to not hearing from you! By god, I've got to! Two months now. The Yanan Medical Unit arrived on November 25. I had

been looking forward to this arrival, not only because it will be helpful medically, but also I expected some books, magazines and papers—and some news of the outside world.

What they brought was an X-ray without a dynamo or the upright [iron], so it won't work. They also brought me Canadian cigarettes, chocolate bars, a tin of cocoa and a tube of shaving soap. Since I wear a beard I won't need the shaving soap. The other things were welcome, but I would have exchanged them all for a single newspaper or magazine book. . . .

Will you do this for me—just one thing? Send me three books a month, some newspapers and magazines. I would like to know a few facts . . . Is Roosevelt still president of the United States? Who is Prime Minister of England? Is the Popular Front government still in power in France? What's happening in Spain? Have you been in touch with Madame Sun Yat-sen's China Defense League? Is Canada or the USA sending more doctors or technicians? What has happened to Dr. Kisch? To Dr. Kotnis? Have they been stopped? Is the blockade that effective? . . .

Well, I will leave you now. Let me confess that as the Christmas holidays approach I am seized with an attack of homesickness! Memories of New York, Toronto, Montreal! If I were not so busy I could find reasons enough for a holiday.

Am preparing for another tour to get a few more Mobile Units ready, in anticipation of the expected heavy fighting. Don't forget to send me some books and to answer my questions!

Bethune[21]

As the months passed, Bethune's reputation in northwest China spread. It was said in the villages and at the front that he never grew weary, and slept only when all the work was completed. Requests to Yan'an from armies all along the front asked that Bethune be sent to their area. He was seen riding over the mountains, leading his mobile surgery unit consisting of a Chinese physician, one nurse, two assistants, and two grooms. They carried with them the only portable operating room in China. It contained "a collapsible operating table, a full set of surgical instruments, anesthetics, antiseptics, leg and arm splints, sterile gauze, and other necessities."[22]

Life at the front took a toll on Bethune. He was forty-nine but admitted that he looked seventy. He developed a persistent cough, grew deaf in his right ear, and his teeth began to rot as his gums deteriorated. He assessed his role in China and decided he would take a trip home. He missed his friends and, at the same time, wanted to raise money for his work. It was now October 1939, and he planned to leave in November, or as soon as the fighters in the area had secured a new base. During the first week of November, Bethune set up a clinic in a small village, on the stage of a small theater. Before long he was treating over a score of wounded in his makeshift clinic, operating on one patient after another. Suddenly his unit was under attack, and the nurses around him began gathering up supplies to leave. Bethune told them sternly that he would leave when he finished operating on the wounded. He worked swiftly. Suddenly a curse split from his lips, and everyone turned to look at him. He had cut his finger, which he said at the time was of no consequence. He plunged it into iodine and finished his work.

By the next day Bethune's finger was swollen and growing more painful as the hours passed. The next morning he could not get out of bed. For a few days he gathered enough strength to move with the army, though fever racked his body and mind. His Chinese colleagues reluctantly suggested amputation of the arm, for now the whole limb was discolored. Bethune refused. He had septicemia and knew that it was too late to save him.

In one of his lucid moments during the remaining few days of his life, he asked for paper and wrote out his will. He died on November 13, 1939, surrounded by grieving Chinese who had been with him every moment of the ordeal.[23] Writing almost forty years later, Ma Haide wrote that Bethune died "a martyr at his post, for lack of a few grams of penicillin that now China produces by the ton."

Word of Bethune's death reached Yan'an, and the sense of loss was incalculable. In a letter to Snow in early December, Ma recorded his immediate impressions. He clearly understood the important propaganda benefits this story held for bringing international attention to the cause. He wrote,

We have at hand a telegram from the front headquarters in Wutaishan informing us of the death of Dr. Bethune. The telegram which arrived on Nov. 15 stated that "due to an unfortunate injury while operating in a septic case Dr. Norman Bethune passed away after being infected thru a cut from the scalpel while operating, on Nov. 13. This is an irredeemable political and medical loss for the whole Eighth Route Army."

A telegram as follows has been sent to the China Aid Council America: "Unfortunate injury while operating and resultant septicemia caused death of Dr. Norman Bethune in Wutaishan November 13 *stop* Eighth Route Army mourns medical hero and conveys deepest condolences to family and friends *stop* details follow. Signed Chu Teh and Peng Tehhui.

The death of Dr. Bethune has been a terrible blow to all here and I did not and could not find enough courage on how to put such a thing in this letter. It still feels so detached from reality. I am enclosing also a copy of the article which I wrote for all the papers here. We are preparing a small booklet on the life and work of Dr. Bethune to be issued in Chinese and English. The Chinese version goes to press in ten days. There has been held in Yanan a memorial meeting for Dr. Bethune which the Comrades of the Central Committee, the Army and Government organized. A number of CC members spoke at the 4 hour meeting. Clippings in the press about the meeting will be sent to you. Please give this matter as much publicity as possible and send copies to the China Aid Council.

Here they are waiting for more details to further send to America. Dr. Bethune has left a will and other things and these are being carried out according to his wishes but as yet the details are not received here from the front. The telegrams have been sent to Wutaishan requesting further so that the family and the China Aid Council can be given details. In the meantime give as much material as there is some publicity. Copies of telegrams in Chinese which were sent abroad I enclose for I cannot get them adequately translated. The Chinese script is too literary and the translations I have don't make much heads or tail.[24]

The young American doctor idolized Bethune until his own death a half century later. Bethune's determination and expertise would continue to inspire him, and he never tired of reminding others of the example set by the Canadian. In 1983, when he was seventy-three years old, Ma sent a birthday present to the son of an American friend. It was a cloth embroidered likeness of Bethune. The message to the boy, written on Ma's professional card, read, "Thought you would like this picture of my hero, Dr. Norman Bethune."[25]

Even though he himself also made exceptional contributions, Ma could never escape Bethune's giant shadow. In part this was due to the near-icon status the latter attained after Chairman Mao published his well-known article *In Memory of Dr. Norman Bethune*, an essay many people in China can today recite word for word. In part it was because Ma never strove for the limelight. He was happy to live in the shadow of the other famous Western doctor. And in 1978 he said, "Today when I travel to various parts of the country with our medical teams I am automatically taken as a fellow countryman of Bethune. The people inquire about my family in Canada and want me to send 'greetings to the Canadian people' on their behalf. My denials that I am not Canadian do not register. How could a Western doctor working among the people of China not be one from Canada. I gracefully accept the reflected glory."[26]

It has become fashionable in the post–Cold War period to denigrate and ridicule the efforts and idealism of those Communists and internationalists who, while staring fascism and terror in the face, joined with millions of people around the world in the 1930s to strive toward the ideal of improving individuals and society by resisting evil. Neither Ma nor Bethune were initially drawn to the struggle through an attraction to Communist ideology, though both eventually embraced that ideology. These men were drawn by an idealism, a humanitarianism, an optimism that allowed them to sense victory over the poverty, disease, infection, neglect, and terror they witnessed. It was this optimism that drove them to share their medical skills with those who would lay their lives on the line. It was another era, a time of hope in struggle rather than sarcasm in avoidance. It truly was a struggle of light against darkness. Without understanding this, the life of Ma Haide can be neither understood nor appreciated.

Ten thousand young men and girls, in a university whose fees are only a penny a day for food [are] holding their classes mostly in caves [in] Yenan, the Eighth Route Army's headquarters in Shensi. . . . Their life is hard, no chairs, tables, or beds, they usually carry little boards to sit on; books are scarce; food is spartan. But their enthusiasm is enormous.

The China Critic, May 23, 1940

The first time I saw Su Fei I dropped whatever I was doing, yelled, "there goes my wife," and got on my horse to follow her. She was training theatrical troops and hardly noticed me. I kept after her for weeks and made no headway. Every bachelor in Yanan had the same idea and I was an ugly American.

George Hatem to Edgar Snow, 1960

By 1939 the struggle to unite China against Japanese invaders and Nationalist appeasers entered a new era. An increasing number of people, both Chinese and foreign, looked to Yan'an as the hope of China in its fight against Japanese aggression and feudal corruption. Support from outside arrived more frequently through united-front operations based in China, Hong Kong, and abroad.

In January 1939, Madame Song's China Defense League welcomed the Indian National Congress Medical Mission to China. This team of doctors was sent by Jawaharlal Nehru and other leaders of India's Congress party to support the medical effort at the front. Led by Dr. Dwarkanath Kotnis, their mission was to continue the work begun by Bethune with the International Peace Hospital.[1] Kotnis, like his predecessor, would eventually die at the front.

Arriving in Chongqing on their way to Yan'an, the medical team was joined by Ma's old friend Rewi Alley, also heading for the Communist-held northwest. Since Ma's departure for the Red Army camp over two years before, Alley drove himself and others to create a grass roots, democratic movement called the Chinese Industrial Cooperatives. His energy and contacts led such international figures as Eleanor Roosevelt and

Henry Luce to support his cause, which became known as the Gung Ho movement. In China, Edgar Snow helped, as did influential Hong Kong businessmen. Alley had come to Chongqing to garner support for the Gung Ho program, only to find "backbiting—squabbling—all the little bureaucrats in China." He met with Zhou Enlai at the Communist head-quarters in that city and received permission to spread the cooperative movement to the border regions controlled by the Communists. With the arrival of the Indian medical team, he now had his passage to Yan'an.[2]

Traveling in an ambulance the Indians were donating, the medical team and Alley arrived in Yan'an within a few days. They were met by a formal reception committee, which included Alley's old student and friend, Shag. Ma was not expecting Alley, who greeted him from behind with "a little kick in the pants." Dispensing with formal greetings, the two headed for Ma's cave to catch up on the latest news and to down the coffee Alley brought to a grateful Ma. Accepting Ma's invitation to move in with him during his visit, Alley found a man very different from the young physician he last saw in Shanghai in 1936. He found a man immersed in both a political and personal odyssey. "I listened to him talk, knowing how close people feel when they have been together through a great endeavor."[3]

Alley's visit, while utterly enjoyable for Ma, bewildered Otto Braun. He had no idea who Alley was, for in Ma's caution about revealing his past and his comrades in Shanghai, he had never mentioned Alley. And in Yan'an he did not introduce him. The Comintern agent thought the two were strangers who immediately took to one another. In his memoirs he says, "I only recall a red-haired New Zealander who devoted himself to the organization of production co-operatives. He had already dealt with this matter in Nationalist China and spoke fluent Chinese. He became closely acquainted with Ma Hai-te and banged away furiously on a travel typewriter in Ma's cave dwelling."[4]

Alley stayed in the northwest for several months, traveling through-out the region to set up cooperatives. He and Ma spent what few relaxed hours they could muster hunting in the mountains and discussing the current problems facing China. Shag was no longer the student, how-ever. Now he was the expert in areas Alley wanted to know more about. Alley would make frequent visits to Yan'an, and their friendship would solidify through the years.

It was not only foreign supporters who managed to get through the Nationalist lines. Increasingly, young patriots from China's cities started to make their way across battle lines and hillsides so they might experience the thrill of fighting firsthand against their enemy. For Ma Haide and the veterans of the Long March, the new support from China's young people gave them much needed hope and pleasure. Especially appreciated were the newly arrived *yang xuesheng* ("students from the outside"), who brought a breath of fresh air and a more lively social life to Yan'an. Due to the united front, residents in Yan'an for the first time found time to concentrate on efforts against the Japanese. And, for the first time in over a decade, they found time to relax a bit and enjoy the fruits of their sacrifices. Over the next several years, Ma alternately thrived and despaired in this environment.

It was during this period that Yan'an gained its international reputation as the leading center of anti-Japanese and agrarian democratic reform in China. But this era in the history of the Chinese Communist party was filled not only with agrarian reform and military action; it also was a period filled with personal agendas and rife with scandal, not just of a political nature, but also in the sensitive area of personal lives and relationships.

In July 1937, two women of the stage, Lan Ping, a beautiful actress from Shanghai, and Li Lilian, a singer from Guangzhou, arrived in Yan'an, where they were soon assigned to the newly formed Lu Xun Art Academy. They arrived just as the Lily Wu affair reached a climax.[5] Soon another young woman, a graduate of the Shanghai Physical Education University named Wu Wang, arrived in Yan'an with another group of young people. For men hardened by the rigors of war and Party struggle, the presence of newly arrived young women stirred thoughts and longings long repressed. Mao's infatuation with Lily Wu had signaled this movement. Now he and others institutionalized it. Romance, politics, and sex mingled together in Yan'an as the revolution tried to cope with the influx of politically innocent and culturally polished city women.

Su Fei, who arrived in Yan'an later in 1939, describes the environment as ripe for romance and conflict. "In Yanan at that time," she confides, "many of the old cadre were attracted to the 'yang xuesheng', even though many of them, both cadre and young people, were already married. The old cadre in Yanan saw these beautiful young girls and wanted them for their wives. The wives of these men, mostly peasant women who cared primarily for their children and knew they could not keep their men anyway, gave up their marriage without a fight. It was not so easy for many of the old unmarried cadre, however, as many of the girls looked down on these revolutionaries from the villages. The 'yang xuesheng' gravitated to those leaders with education and power. A common joke heard around the living quarters of the young girls told of one of these men taking a newly arrived girl for a walk by the river. The young girl looked at the full moon and commented on its poetic beauty. The cadre glanced up and said he saw nothing beautiful there. It just looked like a pancake to him. Many of those old men had feudal ways, and in some cases they actually kidnapped a girl they wanted and kept her locked up in a room until she agreed to marry him. All of this behavior was part of everyday life for a while in Yanan."[6]

Ma Haide was as pleased as anyone with the unexpected social benefits of the united front. Once, while walking along the road in Yan'an with Jack Chen, a newly arrived journalist, they passed a group of young women recently arrived. Ma winked at Chen and told him that the united front was certainly a wonderful thing. "And he wasn't talking politics," laughed Chen when remembering this occasion fifty years later.[7] Ma and Braun turned their cave's courtyard into the social center of Yan'an. They invited the young artists and the Party leaders who wanted to socialize, dance, play ping pong, and engage in friendly discussions around dinner.[8]

Soon both Braun and Ma locked in on recent arrivals. Ma found himself attracted to the athletic Wang Ping soon after she arrived. He watched her play basketball and other sports and joined her whenever he could. She was invited to his courtyard. At a certain point he allowed his affections to be known, but she turned him down—without explanation. Again he had been spurned. Only later did he learn that the reason for her rejection was revulsion at the thought of marriage with a foreigner, the outcome of which would be racially mixed children. Ma may have blended into the culture up to a certain point, but with some he still was an obvious outsider. He had failed in love twice already. It would be another year before he tried again. Meanwhile, he watched as others sought their new mates. The two most notorious relationships involved his friend Otto Braun's pursuit of Li Lilian and Mao's relationship with Lan Ping, later known as Jiang Qing.

By the summer of 1938, Jiang Qing and Li Lilian were regular students in Yan'an's Lu Xun Art Academy. Jiang, twenty-four years old, first met Mao when he came to the academy to give a lecture. By August she had transferred to the position of secretary of the military commission archives, a post close to Mao. Within a short period, she had moved in with Mao, causing scandal and outrage within the ranks of the Party leadership, especially among friends of his recently exiled wife, He Zizhen. Mao insisted on maintaining the relationship and on securing a divorce from his wife. Reluctantly, the Central Committee agreed, and in 1939 Jiang Qing and Mao were married. She was instructed not to engage in political activity for thirty years. One of Jiang's biographers insists the crisis came to a head when it was learned she was pregnant.[9] Whatever his reason for marriage, Mao continued to set the stage for others to follow his actions, and they did.

The second scandal to hit Yan'an struck closer to home for Ma. In fact, it took place right next door. As Jiang Qing angled toward Mao, Li Lilian found herself the target of Otto Braun, Ma's housemate, fellow foreigner, and culinary expert. Even though she had been joined by her husband, Braun would not be dissuaded from pursuing her, and she allowed herself to be caught. She was often invited to the Braun-Ma evening meal. No matter whose turn to cook it should have been, Ma was coerced into cooking for the three of them on those evenings. One evening after dinner Li Lilian and Braun withdrew to his cave, leaving Ma to himself. She stayed the night. The following morning Li Lilian's husband stormed to the mouth of the cave and demanded that his wife come out. What he found, however, was Braun storming out of his cave, brandishing a pistol in his hand and pointing it at the young man. Braun threatened to shoot him if he did not leave. Ma, hearing the excitement outside his cave, bolted out the door in time to see the spurned husband head down the hill. Ma rebuked his German friend for this behavior and told him that nothing good would come of it. Word spread quickly, and Li Lilian's reputation was tarnished forever.

The young singer stayed with Braun for the next year, living with him as his common-law wife. But it all ended suddenly one day, when Braun left without warning on a plane bound for the Soviet Union. He left Li Lilian behind, distraught and forced to fend for herself. By then her husband would have nothing to do with her, and most people treated her as damaged goods. Ma was one of the few to offer comfort and support, causing more rumors to fly suggesting that Ma now had his eyes on Li Lilian. After all, what Chinese man would now take her as his wife? If the other foreigner would take her, it was all to the good.[10]

While the rumors about Ma and Li Lilian swirled around, another group of young patriots prepared to enter Yan'an from the south. One was Zhou Sufei, a beautiful actress originally from Shenjiamen (Shen family fishing village) in Dinghai County, Zhejiang Province. For most of her adult life she has been known simply as Su Fei. Her father, a civil engineer who had studied abroad, had allowed her to attend school as a young girl. Her family owned a shipyard and was prosperous by local standards. While encouraging her to study and read, the family still held to feudal ways and arranged for her, at age fifteen, to marry a young man from another well-off family. Objecting to this, and to the unwelcome demands of her stepmother, she fled on a steamer to nearby Shanghai. There, she met Zhang Tianyi, a left-wing writer who introduced her to the theatrical community then dominated by progressive artists. For several months she performed in factories and schools with a troupe headed by Nie Er, a young composer and underground Communist party member who would later write the national anthem of the People's Republic. Once, when performing in a street play, her striking beauty attracted Wang Bin, a director for the Tianyi Film Studio. Soon, sixteen-year-old Su Fei would appear in several of his films.[11]

The next few years of Su Fei's life are shrouded in some mystery, but certain facts are clear. She left Shanghai when she was seventeen because, she says, "I and other progressive friends refused to live as a conquered people, so we left Shanghai for Yunnan Province which was out of reach from the Japanese invaders. There I joined resistance activities organized by the Communist Party and it was at that time that I became aware of how much Chinese women had suffered."[12]

At the time she reports herself engaged in the resistance movement; others report that she was struggling to disengage herself from another unfortunate relationship, this time a marriage to the son of a landlord she never loved. Out of this arranged and unhappy union a daughter was born.[13] It is not at all surprising that Su Fei shares nothing of this time in her life, and it is likely that her personal distress led her to realize "how much Chinese women had suffered." Whatever path, or convergence of paths, led Su Fei to join the Communist movement, she arrived in Yunnan Province in August 1939, with daughter in tow, preparing for the long journey to Yan'an.

She recalls, "Accompanied by my friend Ms. Lu—I called her Big Sister—I first went to Chongqing in Sichuan Province by truck. There we gathered with 40 others, mostly men, who also wanted to go to Yanan. In eight trucks we all went to Xi'an. On the way I took off my qipao [traditional Chinese formal dress] and put on the quilted clothing worn by most people in the Northwest. Due to interference from the Nationalists and constant breakdown of the trucks, it took us one month to travel from Chongqing to Xi'an. When we arrived we stayed in the Xinhua News Agency's headquarters. The men were in one room, and the women in another."[14]

When Su Fei arrived in Xi'an, she and Lu shared their room and a common bed with two other women, Wang and Zhu, who had recently arrived from Yan'an. It was from conversations with these women that Su Fei first heard of Ma. They knew quite a bit about him, for this Wang was the same Wang Ping whom Ma had only recently fallen for, and been rejected by. "Wang Ping was plain-looking with short hair. She was from Sichuan. Her friend Zhu was very pretty. One day the two of them were playing in our room, when Zhu sat on top of Wang Ping and told her she would not let her up until she told us about her relationship to Ma and why she refused to marry him. Wang struggled, but finally saw she had no way out, and said that she could not marry that foreigner because she did not want to be the mother to mongrels. [She used the commonly pejorative term *zazhong*.] This was the first I heard of Dr. Ma. Later, after we were married, I confronted him about Wang Ping and he told me indeed he had wanted to marry her. He said he found her beautiful in her athletic movements and her youthful and healthy features. I told him that I found it hard to understand how he could ever have loved some-one like her. She is not pretty at all, I told him."[15]

From Xi'an the group of young people made their way to Yan'an, arriving in October 1939. Any arrival of young people, especially women, caused a stir, and Su Fei's presence caused quite a stir. Her beauty rivaled that of an earlier arrival, fellow actress Jiang Qing. In fact, the two had known each other in Shanghai, and Jiang Qing was in the welcoming party to greet Su Fei. People saw the two together, and within days word spread that Jiang Qing's little sister had come to Yan'an. Su Fei did not mind the attention, and her perceived relationship with Jiang Qing smoothed her entry into the political and artistic communities.

After they arrived, the young people were divided up by interests and professions. Su Fei was assigned to the Lu Xun Art Academy as an instructor and performer. She and her daughter moved to the academy, which was located about three miles from the Party headquarters where Ma lived. The strenuous journey to Yan'an had taken a toll on Su Fei, and she fell ill almost immediately. The onset of winter and the new diet of millet combined to hinder her recovery. Two people came to her side, however. One was Li Lilian, the former common-law wife of Otto Braun, who stayed with Su Fei and nursed her back to health. The other was Ma, the foreign doctor she had heard about from her roommates in Xi'an. Ma was the attending physician at the Lu Xun Art Academy and, like most other men in Yan'an, took note of Su Fei's arrival. Years later Ma confided to Edgar Snow, "The minute I saw Su Fei I dropped what-ever I was doing, yelled 'There goes my wife', and got on my horse to follow her. She was training theatrical troupes and hardly noticed me. I kept after her for weeks and made no headway. Every bachelor in Yanan had the same idea and I was an ugly American."[16]

Ma's breakthrough came when Li Lilian suggested that Su Fei go see the art academy's physician. After that first encounter, Ma took advantage of every opportunity to pay her a visit. Su Fei remembers, "He came every day to visit me, to give me medicine. There wasn't much medicine at that time, and he mixed it himself. He started mixing it with something that turned it a pink color. Then he started to write my prescriptions on pink paper. Pink was the color of love. I had petty bourgeoisie sentiments then, and I liked the attention."[17]

After presenting her with the colorful medicine and prescription, Ma wrote a note on the paper, something Su Fei found strange and unexpected. Describing the events in the third person, she recalls, "In this letter he described Su Fei's disease and the name, usage and dosage of the medicine. In addition he wrote, 'I sincerely hope that you take the medicine on schedule and get well soon!' "[18]

Ma was relentless—and jealous. On the horse that He Long had given him at the front, he made a daily excursion to check on Su Fei's health, whether she needed it or not. Once, while on the road to visit her at the art academy, he took up with one of the old cadre from the army. The cadre asked Ma if he knew the beautiful new arrival named Su Fei, the one people said was Jiang Qing's sister. Ma, growing suspicious, said he had met her, but did not know her well. The old cadre then asked Ma to introduce him to her when they arrived. That was too much. Ma not only refused to introduce him, he told him he could go to hell if he had a problem with that.[19]

Ma did not hide his interest, and after a while he thought he was getting somewhere. But he was mistaken. Even though friends and Party officials tried to intercede on Ma's behalf, telling Su Fei that Ma was not only a good man, but also a good comrade in need of a wife, she was not interested in this big-nosed foreigner.[20] "Even with the attention he gave me, love did not come to mind. He was a kind doctor, he treated me well and was attentive to me. At that time he was not even a close friend. Love came later, during the 1940 Spring Festival celebration."[21]

The growing art community in Yan'an enjoyed their parties. Almost every weekend during this period, the Lu Xun Art Academy held evening dances and social gatherings frequented by old and new residents of Yan'an. By far the most anticipated celebration of the year, however, was Spring Festival, also known as Chinese New Year. Spring Festival in 1940 was especially meaningful. The base area in and around Yan'an pulsated with a growing energy that raised not only the confidence of the Party leaders in their movement, but also the confidence of new arrivals in the Party's leadership. These reinforced each other, with everyone dedicated to building a new China. Spring Festival was a time for the artists to show off their talents and for the old hands in Yan'an to enjoy Chinese song, drama, and humor as they had not been able to for years. It was an evening that many remembered fondly for decades to follow. Ma Haide was one of those to hold fond memories, for on Chinese New Year he took to the stage in the evening and won the heart of Su Fei by the following morning.

During the early afternoon on the eve of the Spring Festival, Ma rode his horse to the art academy with a purpose only few could imagine. He came not as a physician, nor as a Red Army soldier or news correspondent. He came, of all things, as a Beijing Opera performer. He had arranged with Jiang Qing and other members of the Beijing Opera troupe at the Academy to take the stage that evening in Beijing Opera attire. His goal was a modest one, to offer everyone good wishes for a happy new year and then to introduce the evening's opera. Members of the troupe spent hours putting the heavy, colorful make-up on him and dressing him in the long, flowing robe required of the performer. The audience, which included Mao Zedong and the other Party leaders, was just settling in to watch Jiang Qing perform in the traditional opera "Three Attacks on the Zu Family Village" when this foreigner strolled out on stage in traditional opera attire. He was recognized immediately under the paint, and laughter at this ridiculous-looking foreigner spread throughout the hall. Struggling to stand straight in the thick-soled opera boots, he greeted the audience with the traditional *zuoyi,* in which the greeter clasps both hands together and shakes them gently toward those he respects. He then announced in the local Yan'an dialect, "Comrades and brothers, I wish everybody here a happy new year." Finished with his greeting, Ma headed off the stage only to hear the audience clap and yell for him to stay and sing a song. He needed little prompting and returned to center stage to launch into a rendition of "The Beautiful Women of Peach River Village," an earthy, risqué folk song that sent the audience into convulsions.[22] Su Fei arrived at the hall in the middle of Ma's performance. She was struck by the comic sight before her, commenting years later, "I looked at the stage and saw Ma's huge eyes behind the makeup, singing this song that had everyone laughing. He had a terrible voice, but he surely was active. In the back of the room Chairman Mao was laughing so hard he couldn't sit up straight."[23]

Following this performance, Ma continued the revelry and tried his hand at *jiaguan,* a Beijing Opera piece traditionally performed only during Spring Festival that wishes everyone success in the coming year. This was even worse than his folk singing, but it was just as entertaining to the audience, and he left the stage to enthusiastic applause and raucous laughter. This foreigner had gotten the Spring Festival off to a joyous start.

The stage now belonged to Jiang Qing and her opera troupe. Su Fei was no fan of Beijing Opera and soon left the performance to check on one of her roommates, the pregnant widow of a soldier recently killed at the front. Ma changed back to his old self and joined the audience. By eleven o'clock that night the opera was finished, and everyone moved to a large meeting room in the old Catholic church where they continued the evening with a dance. Su Fei and the other residents at the Academy lived in the former nuns' quarters of the church, and when she heard the music she ventured out of her room to the dance floor. She saw Ma dancing and marveled at the gracefulness of his moves. He had been waiting for her to return to the festivities and nodded toward her when their eyes met. When the music for the next dance began, he greeted Su Fei and asked her to dance. She confessed that she could not dance, but Ma assured her he was a good teacher, and the two of them took to the dance floor. Ma held her hands, commenting on their ivory-like quality. They danced several times over the next two hours until the party ended about 1:00 A.M.[24]

After the party Ma showed no interest in traveling the two miles back to his cave, especially given the presence of wolves in the region. He readily accepted the offer to stay the night with the poet Xiao San, a friend who lived on the hillside overlooking the Art Academy. Before leaving the dance, he told Su Fei where he would be spending the night. He hoped this would induce her to visit him the next day. Su Fei, however, had no such plans. She and her roommates retreated to their quarters for what she expected to be a short night's sleep. Lying in bed, exhausted but stirred by Ma's attentions, she was roused by her roommate's cries that the baby was coming. Excited and looking for a way to help, Su Fei and Ling Lan, another roommate, grabbed a flashlight and quickly headed out of the old church and up the hillside. They needed a doctor, and the only one they knew of was the foreigner staying the night with Xiao San. They wandered about the hillside looking for the right cave—they had never visited Xiao San and did not know where he lived. All the dwellings looked the same at two o'clock in the morning. It was cold and they both began to cry and yell for Dr. Ma, who finally heard them when they chanced to pass in front of Xiao San's cave. When he came to the door of the cave to see Su Fei calling his name, he was momentarily elated, thinking she had come to visit him. His suggestion must have worked! He was quickly disappointed, however, when they told him to follow them down the hill to their room so he could deliver a baby. He told them he was not the type of doctor who delivers babies and that they should find someone else. "No," they said, "you are a doctor, and that's what we need." He hurried into his winter clothing and headed down the hill with them. By the time they reached the woman in labor, a crowd of Art Academy students and instructors had converged on the room, all anxious to help but none qualified. Ma asked for the father to come help and was told he had died. So he asked Su Fei and Ling Lan to assist him. About 5:00 A.M. they delivered a baby girl, with Ma giving her the name "Collective" because of the group effort that helped bring her into the world.

After the mother and baby were pronounced healthy, Su Fei told Ma he should wash his face and brush his teeth. "Naively, I offered him my own toothbrush," she recalls. He thanked her but told her he would use his finger instead. "Who taught you that," she asked. "My father," he answered. She then told him he should go back to the hillside cave and get some sleep, but Ma was in no mood for that. He had just delivered a baby and had now opened a new chapter in his relationship with the most beautiful girl in Yan'an. To leave her at this moment was the last thing on his mind, so he asked her to walk with him down to the Yan River to watch the sun rise. They both knew that the Yan was known more popularly as the "Love River" because it afforded many couples a few moments of privacy and intimacy. Su Fei glanced at her friend Ling Lan, who signaled her approval, and they left for their walk.

As they walked, he told her of his life, of the United States, of his family and his friends. She told him of her days in Shanghai and her family in Zhejiang. He talked of his feelings for her and of his past failures at love in China. "He told me he had failed twice in love and it was all because he was a foreigner. I told him about the debate that went through my mind." Finally, Ma told her that he wanted to marry her, and Su Fei consented.[25]

Ma was dumbstruck. Twice before, such conversations had ended badly for him. Now the most beautiful girl in Yan'an had said yes to him. "Really? Really?" he shouted. Then "we hugged and kissed," remembers Su Fei. Ma took her back to the art academy stable, where he mounted his horse and told her he would immediately report their plans to Party officials in Wangjinping, where the political department headed by Wang Jiaxiang was located. He arrived at Wang's office before breakfast and told him he was there to receive permission to marry. Wang and others just coming into the office asked Ma whom he planned to marry. Ma told them, "You guess." They all said it must be Li Lilian. Enjoying the guessing game, Ma finally told them it was Su Fei. He then told them of her family background, her work at the Lu Xun Art Academy, and her agreement to the plan. Wang said he would allow the marriage, and "for the next few days Ma was so excited he acted crazy."[26]

After gaining official permission, they both sought the support of their friends. Ma immediately sent a telegram to Rewi Alley, now in Chongqing. He not only wanted to share the news, he needed money to finance a proper wedding. "Getting married *stop* send money *stop* George," the message read. Alley, who now was the surrogate family member Ma relied on for money (much as he had relied on his real family earlier in life) sent him two hundred yuan, the equivalent then of about fifty dollars, a sizeable sum for that time and place. This would buy the food and drink needed to entertain all those coming to this first wedding of its kind between a foreigner and a Chinese in Yan'an.[27] While happy to assist his young friend, Alley paid dearly for his graciousness. He was interrogated by the Nationalist police, asked why he was sending money to the Reds, and eventually lost that government's support for his Indusco rural development work. He claimed the loss was due in part to the two hundred yuan he had sent to Yan'an.[28]

Su Fei's excitement over the decision aroused a great deal less enthusiasm among her friends than among Ma's. She knew her decision would prove controversial, but she did not expect it to alienate her from her closest comrades. She counted among her best friends Tian Fu, Xu Keli, and Yang Lie, all of whom had traveled with her from Chongqing to Yan'an months before. While she was assigned to the Lu Xun Art Academy, they enrolled in the Yan'an Women's University. Every Sunday the four of them got together to climb a nearby hill, where they shared their experiences and their hopes. The week following Su Fei's decision to marry Ma proved no different. She could not wait to share the news with her close friends. But this special day for her was doomed from the start, for halfway up the hill they were forced to seek cover from a Japanese air raid. After the planes left, the four young women got up and knocked the dirt and debris off their clothing and out of their hair. Taking advantage of the sudden quiet as they watched the planes depart, Su Fei announced, "I'm going to be married." Stunned by the news, for they knew nothing of her precipitous courtship with Ma, they asked whom she planned to marry. Her answer was met with furtive glances and a long silence. Then the words tumbled out: "Ma Haide is already in his thirties. How can you know that he does not already have a wife back in America? Like Li De, he will probably leave his Chinese wife later on and go away. What about you then?" Tian, her closest friend, scolded her. "He's an American and he's from a capitalist country. How can you marry a capitalist?" Another said, "Now he is perfect in your eyes. One day when he cannot stand the hard life here any more, then runs away and leaves behind mongrel children, what will happen to you then?"[29]

Su Fei buried her head in her hands, letting her friends bombard her with these stinging attacks. She tried to retaliate. "He and Li De are not the same, he loves China and the Chinese people." "He is not a capitalist. His father is a worker." "He left his home country and came to China. He gives no thought to personal gains or losses." She may as well have remained silent, for her friends not only insisted she change her mind, they rallied others to their support. One such was a cousin of Su Fei's who also was studying at the Women's University. When they met, her cousin derided her. "Aren't you ashamed to get married in such a short time since you came to Yanan? Even if it was proper to get married in so short a time, why do you marry a foreigner when there are so many Chinese around?" The two argued for hours, with Su Fei's cousin finally breaking it off. "Alright! Alright! Go ahead and marry this foreigner. But I'll tell Tian Fu and others that none of us will go to your wedding."[30]

While Su Fei agonized over this estrangement from her friends, Ma scurried around Yan'an preparing for the wedding. Although he was given permission to marry Su Fei, he was not satisfied with only a verbal agreement. His Western need for legal documents took precedence over the less formal Chinese procedures. He insisted on submitting a written report on his marriage plans, and a week later he received a formal response granting permission to marry. He wanted to speed up the process as much as possible, but he wanted it done properly. Marriages in Yan'an were not usually registered, but Ma insisted that his would be. Accompanied by Li Lilian, Su Fei's only supporter, they went to the border region government registration office to have the marriage documented. Su Fei recounts the scene: "I still remember that in the marriage registration office there was only a table and two benches. A Youth, 16 or 17, who was there dared not give us a certificate when he saw it was a foreigner who wanted to register but neither did he dare to refuse. He ran out and we sat for a while. After a long minute, he came in, smiling and said we could register. So we wrote on the marriage certificate: Ma Haide, 30: Sufei, 21, registering to get married on March 3, 1940. . . . Witness, Li Lilian. . . . And the certificate was sealed with the red stamp of the Border Region government."[31]

Ma now had his marriage certificate. Su Fei found the whole exercise unnecessary but slightly amusing and even a bit moving. The final symbolic act to legalize the marriage came when the young man presenting the marriage certificate started to cut the document down the middle, intending to give one portion to each of them. Ma quickly stopped him, saying that the certificate should never be cut in half, for the two of them would never separate. This marriage certificate was the only one of its kind ever issued in Yan'an.[32]

The wedding party that followed the registration was colored by both joy and sadness. First, Ma insisted that a wedding picture be taken. Although this too was not a common practice in Yan'an at the time, Su Fei agreed to it, providing Ma further documentation of the event. Using the money sent by Rewi Alley, Ma arranged for a feast of several tables. Held at the Yan'an Shengli cooperative restaurant, the party was attended by representatives from the public health and foreign affairs offices and from the Lu Xun Art Academy. Huang Hua remembers the event as being festive and filled with the rough and off-color humor often associated with such occasions, especially those held in the countryside. It was presided over by Wang Jiaxiang, head of the political department of the Party Central Committee's Military Commission.[33] Ma showed his solidarity with the Red Army by inviting Wang Deniu, a veteran soldier who had been assigned to assist the young foreign doctor in his daily needs, to sit between Ma and Su Fei as the guest of honor. He toasted the veteran Wang as if he were a parent, telling everyone that Wang was part of his new family.[34]

For Su Fei, the party only reinforced her sense of isolation from her friends. She had hoped they would change their minds and join in her wedding celebration. Time and again she asked Ma to delay the start of the feast for a few more moments, hoping her cousin and friends would join them. Soon it appeared that all who were coming had arrived, and Ma felt they could wait no longer. The party began, with Su Fei watching the door moment by moment, knowing that the Women's University was only a few steps away from the Shengli cooperative. Her friends never came.[35]

After toasts and good wishes signaled the end of the banquet, the two newlyweds retired to Ma's cave. They took with them a gift presented by the supply department—a new quilt with a red silk cover, courtesy of a landlord whose property had been confiscated by the Red Army. They lit candles, a rare treat since most nights they used the cheaper lampwick, and sat down to talk. Ma, hardly able to contain his happiness, was immediately brought back to earth and forced to deal once more with his foreignness, for his wife suddenly broke into tears, crying uncontrollably. She then told him in detail of what her friends thought about their marriage, of their comments about his leaving her, and of their ideas about his foreign background and intentions. Ma told her that he understood their view of foreigners, and that only their actions could win her friends over. He offered her a chance to escape from the relationship that night if she felt she could not tolerate the pressure from her friends. Having twice before lost in love, he must have found this bitterly difficult to say. But he need not have worried. Su Fei had come too far to back out now. She was distraught, but she was not about to call it off. "I felt isolated from my friends," she said, "but this gave me time to sort out the problem. What was behind their attitude? Mainly, it was overall resentment against the imperialist invasion of China. For decades, the Chinese nation had lived in humiliation under foreign powers. Therefore it was felt that marrying a foreigner was degrading. However, this idea was incompatible with the concept of world revolution to which we were dedicated. How could you explain Ma Haide's coming to China and leading an austere life in China's revolutionary center, Yan'an, leaving behind his well-paid job and comfortable life? The more I thought, the more excited I got. Why shouldn't I love him? He gave the Chinese people all he had! He rescued from the snow-covered fields a pregnant woman who was about to give birth; he sucked the blood from the leg of a peasant who was bitten by a snake. His nose was bigger than ours, and that was the only difference between him and the fine fighters of my country. Gathering up my courage and strength, I confidently took up my challange and decided to ignore the well-intentioned advice from my comrades."[36]

Eventually Ma proved himself to Su Fei's friends, and over the years they changed their view of this marriage and sought to rekindle their friendship with Su Fei. "Later," she commented, "when these people came to our house, Ma Haide received them like old friends."[37]

Chunking Belief that the government of Generalissimo Chiang Kai-shek is opposed to further expansion of the Chinese Communists and is prepared to use force against them as a last resort if they prove recalcitrant was expressed here yesterday by reliable sources.

New York Times, April 7, 1940

. . . it was soon obvious that Ma was under suspicion from Kang Sheng.
  Su Fei, reflecting on the Rectification Campaign of the early 1940s in Yan'an

Following his marriage to Su Fei in early March, Ma concentrated on his duties as a physician, propagandist, Party member, foreign affairs expert, and husband. In Yan'an at that time each newlywed couple enjoyed a one-week vacation. Su Fei says Ma refused to take advantage of this luxury. As a Party member and as a physician on call at all times, he decided to go back to work the day after their marriage. By this time he functioned as chief physician to the Party Central Committee, a post he would hold for several years. Each time Peng Dehuai, Chen Yi, Ye Jiangying, or other leaders arrived in Yan'an from the front, it was Ma's responsibility to check them out and look after their medical needs. Just before Su Fei arrived, Ma was concerned primarily with the health of Zhou Enlai. Zhou had arrived in Yan'an from Chongqing during the summer for meetings and lectures at the Party school. Ma gave him a physical when he arrived, although it proved difficult to get him to sit still long enough to complete it. Zhou passed the physical with no cause for concern. Within days, however, the American doctor called on him again, this time in response to an urgent call from Zhou's staff. On July 10, while traveling to Party headquarters with Mao Zedong's new wife Jiang Qing, he had been thrown from his horse. It seems that at one point in the journey Jiang Qing had wanted to impress Zhou with her skill on horseback, and took her mount flying past him. As she raced by, her horse tangled hoofs with Zhou's horse, which reared and threw him to the ground, breaking his right arm.

Ma and two recently arrived Indian doctors examined Zhou after he returned to Party headquarters. They wrapped his arm, though they failed to set it properly because of the crude medical supplies in Yan'an. Ma told Zhou to rest and ordered a daily massage to the arm. Zhou's response was to begin writing with his left hand. Although Ma checked him regularly, by mid-August the arm was permanently disfigured. For the rest of his life, Ma blamed himself for the disfigurement.[1]

While popular with his Chinese comrades, some of his foreign friends grew impatient with Ma in his role as correspondent and chronicler of the revolution and its needs. Israel Epstein, publicity coordinator for the China Defense League newsletter in Hong Kong during this period, remembers that he and his colleagues constantly pushed Ma to send more information on the medical situation in and around Yan'an.[2] In late 1939, Edgar Snow journeyed to Yan'an to continue his investigation into the Communist party and the Eighth Route Army. As a supporter of Madame Song's efforts in Hong Kong, he agreed to investigate the medical needs of the liberated areas. He expected his old traveling companion Shag to feed him most of what he needed, but the results proved disappointing. In a letter to Jim Bertram in Hong Kong written soon after leaving Yan'an, Snow explains, "I did not go to the front but stayed in Yanan and vicinity where little more was known, in detail, of IPH [International Peace Hospital] than we already knew. I had no time to make an investigation on my own. Haiteh [Ma] was not very helpful. However, I brought back a meager report in Chinese."

While disappointed in Ma, Snow acknowledged that his old friend had other matters to worry about in this war-torn area. He told Jim Bertram, "Your friend Muller came up to Yanan without any difficulty—still carrying my sleeping bag which I never used. I gave it to him. He has the best wardrobe in the city but I supposed Haiteh will remedy that before long. HT [Ma] had just lost everything he owned when I arrived in Y[enan]. A bomb struck just outside his cave, killed his horse, and knocked him out. Luckily he was tween-caves passageway and did not get any shrapnel direct. Y[enan] is utterly destroyed now, the most completely demolished town I've ever seen, and not a soul lives inside the walls. . . . 40 people were killed in one cave while I was there."[3]

Attacks on the city by Japanese bombers were not the only distraction from Ma's work. The continued blockade by Chiang Kai-shek frustrated Ma and his colleagues at the recently opened Bethune International

Peace Hospital as they tried to make do with the limited supplies available to them. Somehow he had to juggle the day-to-day demands on his time with those of Madame Song and her staff in Hong Kong, who were awaiting word on just how they could support this effort. On the rare occasions that he found the time and energy to write, he presented a bleak picture. He told them he stored the entire supply of Western medicines in one drawer, dispensing sulfa pills only in case of emergency. Medical slides used in the single microscope were made from broken windows. Eye droppers were made from pieces of rubber hose, and cultures were incubated in a container placed next to a stove. Medical cotton was made from locally grown cotton; gauze was made from thread handspun by doctors and nurses. Most of the modern instruments available came from captured Japanese storehouses.[4]

On December 5, 1939, Ma sent a report outlining various aspects of the medical situation to Snow, who had just left Yan'an. He knew the frustration of these foreign friends, but in this hurriedly written response to their constant requests he asked them to understand the constraints he faced.

> To date I have on hand your two letters . . . with requests and with which I will try my best to comply for I feel the need of this thing as strongly as you do but you must also be patient with me so that a period of impressing upon people here the necessity of such work and to get the necessary cooperation to send the necessary reports, etc. with factual material. The main trouble is that reports in the usual form are largely generalities and I cannot get my hands on them easily. They more or less understand the need of sending out reports so that more support can be obtained from abroad but no one seems to be responsible for it.
>
> My idea is something like this, and I think I can do this much . . . I will send you a report of some kind every two weeks to a month and a more or less "gossip letter" with odd material in it that I can't very well make into a report and you can use this material in addition to the report, to give to the CDL. This will make it easier for me.[5]

The letter then proceeds to report on the medical situation in the liberated area.

> The Indian Medical Unit consisting of Dr. Atal, Dr. Bgassu, and Dr. Kotnis have been sent to the front to reinforce the staff of the IPH and Dr. Mueller has left with them.
> . . . in three months the 13th class of the Medical Training School will

graduate and will be sent to the front in its entirety. There will be, I think, about 40 some odd students who will graduate ...

... Entrance Examination regulations for the 8th RA Med. Training School for senior class candidates:

1. Aim of the School—To train medical cadres of unwavering anti-Japanese political principles, high technical principles, efficiency and administrative ability to meet wartime requirements.

2. Qualifications—...

3. Date and places of registration: ...

All these points which seem obvious to you and me, and anybody familiar with the conditioning factors of a guerrilla war in China, are new ideas to some of our friends, and it has taken a lot of time for them to comprehend.

Ma did not limit himself to medical issues. He spoke of political concerns and of the efforts of the international community to assist China. He knew more could be achieved if the Western community was approached in an indirect manner. Learning from the experience of a united front in the struggle against Japan, he called on his friends in Hong Kong to use the same tactic in gathering money for the medical units in China. His old friend Rewi Alley's Chinese Industrial Cooperatives, Indusco, paved the way here, Ma argued.

Another fact, which perhaps was not fully appreciated in China by people unfamiliar with foreign opinion, was the great opportunity offered by a United Front organization like Indusco in mobilizing new sources of help for mass resistance, in broadening the basis of support for CDL ... and in organizing pressure to push the government along to make greater contributions to help in the guerrilla areas, and in subsidizing mass organization.

You know there are very definite limits to the money which can be secured for direct aid to the guerrillas, which most people overseas think (whether true or not) are nearly all Xians [Ma and his friends used the code name Christians when referring to Communists]. Many ... people will not give a cent to help the Xians; many humanitarian sympathizers who are also pacifists will not give at all to help any military organization, particularly a X. one. But Industrial Cooperatives can appeal to all these groups for support ... [6]

He wanted to do more himself, he told them, but his responsibilities in Yan'an were wide ranging and his time limited. If anyone doubted this, he wanted to set them straight.

I can't leave the desk before January for indusco field picture. There is tons of work, the years report, Supply dept. work, medical work, meetings, conferences and piles of stuff on which I am already behind. I only sleep six hours and do nothing else but work.[7]

Soon after they married, Su Fei returned to her work, and her old residence, at the Lu Xun Art Academy. For the next several months they lived apart and saw each other on weekends only. As the weekend arrived, Ma mounted his horse and rode over to the Academy to pick her up. Each day he arrived to fetch her, the male students, still jealous that he "robbed" them of their prettiest resident, teased and harassed him when they saw him approach. On one of his first trips to retrieve her, some young men hid close to the entrance of the Academy and jumped out in his path. They "demanded" that he pay admission through the gate if he wanted to get Su Fei. They then rushed his horse, some holding it by the head and others rummaging though Ma's pockets for loose change and cigarettes. Then, after payment, they allowed him to pass. From then on, each time he headed for Su Fei's dwelling he made sure to carry money and cigarettes to appease his wife's "guards."[8]

Ma and Su Fei tried to catch what personal life they could on the weekends, having visitors come by after dinner to chat or attending the frequent dance parties held on Saturday nights. The weekends together were not relaxing, however, as late-night calls to deliver babies and take care of emergency illnesses took precedence over all other interests. They still had to put up with criticism of their marriage, with some saying the only reason Su Fei married Ma was to gain the extra privileges given the foreign doctor. And Su Fei's friends still refused to visit. Su Fei continued to fret over this, and when she discovered she was pregnant shortly after they married, she worried about the impression this would give to those already doubting her commitment to the work ahead in the revolution. She did not want a baby, at least not yet. Ma, although thirty years old and eager for fatherhood, agreed with his wife that the time was not right. He told her they could wait, and she should have an abortion. She aborted the pregnancy, but again they were under fire. Both, especially Ma, were criticized for jeopardizing Su Fei's health in this way. How could a physician allow such a thing to happen? What kind of person was this foreigner?[9]

Conversations between the two of them and their friends were dominated by politics, as was life throughout Yan'an. As a Party member, Ma could not avoid the discussions, and he and Su Fei tried to stay in touch with the debates and issues discussed by the leaders.

Discussion centered on the effectiveness of the United Front campaign. There was opposition within the Party about how much emphasis to put on the United Front, a position Mao Zedong characterized as "leftist" thinking.[10] Ma, involved directly in the United Front work through his connection with Madame Song and the China Defense League, was heartened by this discussion and followed the debate with keen interest.

During this period of the United Front, Ma stepped up his work with the China Defense League. As much as he found writing reports and letters a drain on his time and energy, he knew that the league's newsletter was a window to those outside who might support the liberated area's medical work. This was true now more than ever, because of the Nationalist party's increasing reluctance to abide by the spirit of the United Front, thus keeping much needed supplies from reaching the guerrilla areas. The August 15, 1940, edition of the China Defense League newsletter found his byline once again, this time identifying him as "Dr. Ma Hai-teh, Representative of the China Defense League with the International Peace Hospital." This report, taken from a letter Ma wrote, gives an update on the medical work at the front and on the needs of the army.

> I have just received a letter from the International Red Cross, Kweiyang, informing us that they have sent cod liver oil two drums, a case of quinine tablets and 50 thousand doses of typhoid-cholera vaccine for us. We have not received the stuff but I am told it is on the way.
>
> Dr. Atal has left the front. He has been ill and has to return to India. Below I quote from letters sent from the front by the unit. The letters describe the journey and their work on arrival.[11]

Ma's relationship with the China Defense League was his only concession to acknowledging the importance of the outside world. He focused totally on his new life and "thought about my home and early life in America . . . hardly at all. . . . I didn't think much about anything besides tasks and struggles facing us."[12]

While Ma may have blocked his American past and family out of the picture, they certainly had not forgotten him. In early 1940, about the time he was performing Beijing Opera for his colleagues during Spring Festival, his family, through an intermediary, made inquiries with the American Embassy in China into his whereabouts. The response gave little comfort. Written only two days after Ma's marriage to Su Fei, the American Consulate office in Shanghai responded:

March 5, 1940

Mr. Clattenburg:

   Reference is made to your inquiry concerning Shafick George Hatem, now believed lost in Tibet.

   The passport records of this Division show that Shafick George Hatem was born in Buffalo, New York, on September 26, 1910. He was last registered on December 4, 1935, at Shanghai, China, at which time he gave his address as 200 Yuen Road, Apartment 4, Shanghai. There is no subsequent record on this individual. Ruth Shipley[13]

But the family did not give up. They looked for any clues that would tell them of his fate. Finally they were guided to the China Defense League newsletter. It appears the newsletter was more than a window to the world for Ma and his medical work. Unbeknown to him, it was also the only glimpse of his life that his family in North Carolina found to verify he still existed. While he remained submerged in Yan'an with a new name, out of touch with his family, word leaked out about him. Books and articles about the Chinese resistance to Japan appeared, mentioning him by his new name. Finally, his family caught sight of these references and learned that in fact this strange doctor named Ma was their very own Shafick. They did not know how to get in touch with him, but they found that they could follow his life at least marginally through the newsletter. Thus, the only subscriber to the China Defense League newsletter in Roanoke Rapids, North Carolina, was his sister Freda Hatem, who had not seen her brother Shafick for over a decade. She awaited each edition eagerly and reported on her brother's dismaying new life by gleaning from it the few mentions of him, or contributions by him.[14]

   In the fall of 1940 Su Fei graduated from the Lu Xun Art Academy. Ma wanted her with him, and they decided she should enroll in the Women's University to engage in political study. There she met her old friends again and, for the first time since her marriage to the foreigner, they greeted her warmly. After completing her course of study, she was reassigned as an instructor to the art academy, where she once again lived each week, returning to Ma's cave at the hospital on weekends.

   During the upcoming year, 1941, each kept busy with assigned duties. Even though the United Front continued, supplies came less and less frequently from areas controlled by the Nationalists. In March the Central Committee issued a set of directives encouraging people in the liberated areas to practice economy and to produce goods for self-support. It was not really necessary for Ma and Su Fei to do this in order to maintain a decent standard of living in Yan'an. Because of his status as a foreigner, and as the personal physician of the leaders, Ma enjoyed larger living quarters than most people in the area, and his allotment of meat, eggs, and wheat were at the level of the highest Party leaders.[15] But, following the example set by Chairman Mao and other leaders, Ma and Su Fei felt it was their duty to contribute.

They opened a small garden behind their home, planting tomatoes and other vegetables on Saturdays when she returned from the Lu Xun Art Academy. On Sunday mornings they spread manure and watered the plot. Ma joined his colleagues from the hospital as they opened larger plots of "wasteland" near the hospital. For some of the peasants in the area, the sight of a foreigner carrying a hoe and transporting manure to the fields was evidence that something different was going on in China. The only foreigners they knew were missionaries who stayed inside during the winter and expected others to work in the fields for them in the summer. This foreigner worked outside in both winter and summer. Comments on this were welcome to Su Fei, who watched her husband held up as a model citizen, countering some of the anti-foreign comments of her friends.

Ma even tried his hand at carpentry, making crude stools, splints, walking sticks, and other simple creations for use in the hospital. At this he had some success, remembering long unused skills from his childhood. He also tried his hand at spinning cotton and knitting socks for soldiers at the front, but he was less successful in this. No matter how hard he tried, his needles could master only the leg portion of a sock. He could not finish a whole sock, so he would set aside several sets of half-finished ones each week, waiting for Su Fei to complete the heels and tops when she returned each Saturday. Life settled into a routine, with Ma and Su Fei tending their garden and joining in other self-support activities for the next few years.[16]

The year 1942 began well for Ma, especially after the United States entered the war against Japan. Now his two homelands were united against their common enemy. But his happiness was short lived. From a period of relative stability and optimism, life in Yan'an quickly entered a stage of frantic political activity. This time the disruption came neither from the Nationalists nor from the Japanese, but from their own leader. Mao was concerned about what he saw as growing softness and misguided policies affecting the revolution. Even Ma could not avoid the whirlwind that engulfed everyone in Yan'an from early 1942 through the middle of 1943.

The Party's first mass political movement to cleanse itself, a forerunner to many such movements over the next half century, was launched on February 1, 1942, when Mao Zedong delivered a speech at the inauguration of the Central Party School entitled "Rectify the Party's Style of Work." This speech initiated what came to be known as the Rectification Campaign.[17] As with later movements, it proved a difficult time for foreigners tied to the Chinese revolution.

The Rectification Campaign had its roots in the early days of the United Front with the Nationalists. Following the rallying cry of the Communists to oppose the Japanese, thousands of people came to Yan'an to follow the leadership of the Party in this patriotic movement. They came as intellectuals, artists, students, bourgeoisie Nationalists, and even anarchists and Trotskyites. They had little in common with the hardened veterans of the Long March. They were not tempered by the battles and struggles forged in the mountains of Hunan or the grasslands of Qinghai. Most had little knowledge of Marxism-Leninism, and some opposed what little they did know. Many resisted orders from the peasant cadre and even looked down upon many of these hardened leaders. Some of the young women students ridiculed the peasant military men who sought their affection.

The forty thousand member Party of 1937 had a staggering eight hundred thousand members just three years later. Mao worried that the new members, who far outnumbered him and his old comrades, were taking the revolution down a wrong path, one that deemphasized class struggle and encouraged "extreme democratization." He knew that most of the new members had questionable class backgrounds. Some came from landed gentry or capitalist families. But Mao also believed that anyone could be changed for the better. This movement aimed to bring about that change, no matter how some might resist.

Overcoming reluctance to change proved one of Mao's biggest concerns, for the Party leadership no longer acted as the same revolutionary organization that led the Long March. In part this was due to the United Front policy that abandoned hard-won victories, such as land reform and the establishment of regional Soviets, in an attempt to appease the Nationalists and unite the country against Japan. These new arrivals knew only the United Front policies, policies that Mao and other hardened revolutionaries knew were only temporary.[18] How could they be won over to the true principles of the revolution if this was all they knew? And how could the Party keep its own older members from straying into this abyss of ideological confusion?

Mao therefore saw three needs to address. Orthodoxy among the old comrades must be held to its traditional standards, sound ideological training must be given to the thousands of new members, and the Party must maintain the discipline that had brought it this far.[19] While addressing these three issues, Mao also insisted that Marxism-Leninism be applied in a fashion that would ring true to Chinese culture and history. This was in marked contrast to the orthodox position that Marxism-Leninism should be approached in a universal manner, as defined by Moscow and defended in Yan'an by Mao's chief rival, Wang Ming.[20] In other words, the Chinese revolution would be guided by Marxisim-Leninism, but it would be a national movement, focusing on national issues, and learning from Chinese experiences. In Mao's words:

> If a Chinese Communist who is part of the great Chinese people, bound to his people by his very flesh and blood, talks of Marxism apart from Chinese peculiarities, this Marxism is merely an empty abstraction. The Sinification of Marxism—that is to say, making certain that in all of its manifestations it is imbued with Chinese peculiarities, using it according to these peculiarities— becomes a problem that must be understood by the whole Party without delay.[21]

While not a direct attack on the foreign influence and support given the Chinese revolution, the nationalization of the movement left little room for the foreigner, Soviet or Western, to have much of an impact on its direction. How about a foreigner who cared little about ideology, but a great deal about the Chinese Communist party? In this movement, the distinction between foreign friends and foreign meddlers blurred, as Ma Haide soon discovered.

Mao's method of carrying out a complete educational overhaul of Party thinking was one that would characterize the revolution until his death forty-five years later. To overcome weaknesses in ideology and class background, everyone should engage in "intensive education, small group study, criticism and self-criticism, and thought reform."[22] To correct poor work styles and incorrect political thinking, Party members were expected not only to follow orders, but to use their judgment and energy to convey the word and work of the Party to others. Everyone should be a propagandist. Everyone should constantly study Marxism-Leninism, both alone and in their small-unit study groups, and should share what they learned with those who could make revolution. This was especially important for intellectuals who had just joined the Party. Finally, Party members should always be ready to "learn from the masses" and remain open to criticism and self criticism. Only when confronted in this way could they truly change their ways of thinking.

It was during the Rectification Campaign that the political ideology of Mao first gained wide circulation. It also set Mao on the road to becoming a leading Communist theoretician, in the company of Marx and Lenin. The mechanism for guiding the movement was in place by late May 1942 when the Political Bureau set up the General Study Committee of the Central Committee. The members of this committee were Mao Zedong, Kai Feng, Kang Sheng, Li Fuchun, and Chen Yun. Mao served as chair and Kang Sheng as vice chair. The campaign got fully under way on June 8, when the Propaganda Department of the Party Central Committee issued a formal directive launching a Party-wide study movement to rectify the Party's work and leadership.[23]

To those working on behalf of the revolution outside Yan'an, the seriousness of the Rectification Campaign was not immediately apparent. Han Xu, later ambassador to the United States, recalls, "We read the documents, and carried on discussion, but it had little impact on those of us not in Yanan."[24] Su Fei first heard of it when Mao addressed the students and staff at the Lu Xun Art Academy in what became one of his most famous and controversial political pronouncements. In this talk before the Forum on Literature and Art on May 2, 1942, Mao fired one of the first shots at intellectuals joining the revolution, telling them they should go among the people to learn what they wanted from the art world and that their art and literature should represent the lives of those for whom the revolution was most important, the workers and peasants. There is no such thing as classless art, he stressed. As the official Chinese Communist party history states,

> Mao Zedong's talks at the forum not only served to promote the rectification movement in literary and art circles but also enhanced the awareness on the part of Party members and cadres of the need to study dialectical materialism and historical materialism and to mould their world outlook.[25]

Su Fei says that at the time she and others had no idea such a speech would lead to a mass movement. "Chairman Mao did not originally plan to make it into such a big thing. The movement spread slowly, and did not reach the medical units for some time. Kang Sheng is the one who tried to spread it."[26] Kang Sheng is one of the great shadowy figures of twentieth-century China, staying by Mao's side throughout his career. By the time he died in 1975, he was one of the most feared and secretly vilified officials in the Communist party.

Kang Sheng served as head of intelligence for the Party in Yan'an, having been trained by the Soviet secret police force in the 1930s. He rose in importance not only because of his attention to Party ideological issues, but also because Mao depended on his understanding of Soviet policies and ideology.[27] Su Fei says that Kang's primary goal was to ferret out spies sent by the Nationalists and to force formerly loyal Party members to turn on their comrades. While she blames Kang Sheng for the excesses, Mao was the one who encouraged the movement that eventually got out of hand. In November 1942, Mao announced that the Rectification Campaign was necessary "not only to distinguish between the proletarian ideology (half-heartedness) but also between the revolutionary and counter-revolutionary (not of one mind). Beginning in December, all the departments and commissions of the CPC Central Committee and a number of government bodies and schools in Yan'an set about examining the cadres."[28]

But the movement got out of hand, and by April 1943 it reached new heights. The Central Committee issued "The Decision on Carrying on the Rectification Campaign," a document that said Nationalist spies "are extremely cunning and the number of spies infiltrated is astonishing." It was decided that attention would now turn "into a mass struggle against secret agents in all departments, schools and army units."[29]

Su Fei remembers how this affected her school. "It got to the point where people were creating stories. Many told lies just to get the pressure off themselves, saying they were sent by the Nationalists, lying and pointing to others as spies. The campaign split the old cadre from the younger arrivals, even though not all old revolutionaries supported Kang Sheng's methods. As a Party member Ma was expected to attend these meetings, where it soon became obvious that he was one of those under suspicion by Kang Sheng."[30]

For Ma Haide, the Rectification Campaign proved a turning point in his life as a Communist. Kang Sheng was suspicious of anyone, it seems, who did not fit his notion of a pure Communist. He was especially suspicious of foreigners. Why, he asked, was Ma so concerned with reporting their medical difficulties to friends in Hong Kong? And why did Ma find it necessary to go out late at night so often? Who was he visiting and what did he discuss at this late hour? And anyway, why would a foreigner give up his life in the comfortable West to live in caves and remain poor in China? These were serious questions Kang Sheng threw out to cast doubt on this foreigner who had grown so close to Party leaders.

Soon he took direct aim, accusing Ma of both criminal and negligent behavior in his medical work. He accused Ma of providing incompetent medical attention to Wang Ming, an ideologically discredited but still important leader of the Party at the time. Kang Sheng secretly entered these charges into Ma's official Party records, an action that placed a political shadow over Ma for the next three and a half decades.[31]

During the Rectification Campaign, political investigations were run by the Party Committee of each individual unit. In Ma's case, therefore, the charges leveled against him were first discussed in the Ministry of Public Health. But Kang Sheng found this foreign doctor especially important and insisted that all matters related to Ma be handed over to his office for his personal attention.

Kang Sheng ruled that Ma's requests for medical assistance from Song Qingling's China Defense League were an attempt to "expose the dark side of the border regions to foreigners." Sharing such information with foreigners outside Yan'an constituted spying, and this serious charge was logged in Ma's Party file.[32] It did not matter that his work was supported enthusiastically by Mao, Zhou, and other high leaders. Ma was now officially labeled a possible spy, one who had to be watched closely.

The other charge alleging Ma's incompetence in treating Wang Ming was even more bizarre. Not only did Kang Sheng enter the charge in Ma's Party file, he spread the word that Ma was either an unskilled or intentionally negligent physician bent on hurting the Party. The beginning of the story dates from before the Rectification Campaign, to a time when Mao and others criticized Wang Ming for his poor political leadership and slavish subordination to the Soviet leaders. It seems that while under attack Wang fell ill, lapsing into a state of unconsciousness. Some thought he feigned illness in order to escape direct confrontation with his attackers. The Central Committee sent Ma to check up on Wang and report back. Ma could find no medical explanation for the ailment. However, he did notice a bottle of sleeping pills beside the bed and, guessing that Wang had probably taken too many, said he would need a while longer to wake up. As Ma predicted, Wang did eventually awake from his stupor. He was groggy but well. So Ma made his report to the Central Committee, stating the facts as he saw them. The report did not sit well with Wang, who insisted he was indeed ill. He accused Ma of trying to frame him by questioning his integrity. Soon the Central Committee once again asked Ma by to check on Wang. Wang again said he was ill, this time with stomach troubles, and insisted that he had accidentally swallowed mercury from a broken thermometer placed in his mouth. He wanted to go to the Soviet Union for medical treatment. Ma gave him a physical and discovered no traces of mercury in his body. When he reported this to the Central Committee, they refused Wang the opportunity to "escape" his current difficulties. Wang Ming grew even angrier with Ma, accusing the American doctor of trying to poison him. Kang Sheng placed these charges in Ma's file, along with the charge that he had "framed Wang Ming."[33]

So Ma's political and medical career was threatened in two ways. First, unbeknown to him, his Party file now contained damning accusations questioning his loyalty and calling him a possible spy. While he was never forced to answer such charges, the files could be called up at any time. Second, his reputation as a doctor was called into question both in the official files and by word of mouth. Richard Frey, the medic who had escaped Nazi occupation of his native Austria and joined the Red Army in China, remembers General Nie Rongzhen telling him in 1944 that Ma had administered an incorrect prescription to Wang Ming and that his medical abilities were now suspect.[34] Sydney Rittenberg, who arrived in Yan'an a few years after the Rectification Campaign, said some people called Ma *mungoo daifu*, a derogatory term more biting than the English term "quack."[35] No matter how dedicated his service had been up to this point, the rumor mill of Yan'an, both official and unofficial, worked to discredit this loyal foreigner.

What Ma feared most during this time was being expelled from the Party. Despite the difficult times he faced, however, he never lost faith in the correctness of the Communist party, nor in his allegiance to it. In part this was due to the support of many high leaders. What saved him was the confidence in his loyalty held by Chairman Mao and others of the old-line leaders. There is no indication that Mao, Zhu De, He Long, or others found Kang Sheng's charges serious enough to question Ma's dedication to their cause. Su Jikan, Minister of Public Health and Ma's immediate supervisor, rallied to his support, saying he would stand by Ma no matter what the charge. Ma's position also was helped somewhat because he had joined the Party before these new and untested members had arrived in Yan'an. He could not be accused of the same naiveté they displayed. Surely, Ma thought, that stood for something. But many were behaving irrationally, and the emphasis on China's revolution following its own path without the need of foreign assistance, including this young American, forced Ma to take careful pains not to draw attention to himself.[36]

By July 1943, Mao assessed the movement swirling around him and decided his point had been made. In fact, perhaps it had gone too far. He wrote a letter to Kang Sheng, published at the time as "Experience in Guarding Against Traitors." In it he said the movement had begun "for the purpose of winning over those who have made mistakes, training the cadres and educating the rank and file." He admitted that the Central

Committee had overestimated the number of enemy spies in camp, and "it failed to set right in time the wrong practice of obtaining confessions by compulsion and giving them credence in the work of cadre examination." Kang Sheng had one final salvo to unleash, however. He issued his own report, entitled "Rescue the Ones Who Have Made Mistakes," in which he insisted the most urgent task facing them all was to "weed out hidden traitors" and to find those who had not yet confessed their sinister aims to the Party. The official Communist party history written in 1991 argues, "an excessive struggle was waged to obtain confessions by compulsion and give them credence. . . . Many comrades were taken as enemies, being wronged or framed up." Finally, on July 30, 1943, Mao ordered a halt. He acknowledged that excesses had occurred when in October he said, "Killing none and arresting few is a policy to be adhered to in this struggle against secret agents." In the spring of 1944 the Central Committee initiated an investigation into the cases of those who had been falsely accused.[37]

By the end of the Rectification Campaign, Ma's reputation remained fundamentally intact in the eyes of those who mattered most, the Party leaders he had worked with since the end of the Long March. He was lucky, because large numbers were expelled from the Party, and an undetermined number were even executed. But in some ways his life would never be the same. Even though Mao and the Party leadership tried to correct the excesses of the movement, Kang Sheng saw to it that Ma's files remained intact and available for future reference, with comments that questioned his loyalty and his medical skills.[38]

As the Rectification Campaign drew to a close, Ma and Su Fei found themselves preoccupied with new developments. Su Fei was once again pregnant. This time they decided to proceed with the pregnancy. The timing was right, since she had proven her worth to the revolution through her work at the Lu Xun Art Academy, and enough time had elapsed since their marriage to make the occasion one in which everyone could rejoice. Su Fei moved into Ma's cave at the Bethune International Peace Hospital, and the two of them prepared for their firstborn.

Ma was busy with his round-the-clock work in the hospital and, as a Party member, with the winding down of the Rectification Campaign. Su Fei found comfort in the efforts of others when he was not around. Wang Deniu, Ma's assistant who took care of his daily needs and who had been honored at the wedding, was especially attentive. Wang kept Su Fei well supplied with chicken and eggs, usually having to barter their rations of millet for such items.

Su Fei also found help from other women in Yan'an during the first few difficult months of the pregnancy. Once, early in her pregnancy, she had a craving for Sichuan hot pickled mustard vegetables. She asked Ma to ask a friend then working in Xi'an with the United Front to buy some and ship them to her. Ma, just coming out from under suspicion in the Rectification Campaign, chided his wife for requesting such special treatment, telling her it was out of the question. He, in turn, was chided by Su Fei's friends, who told him he knew nothing of "women's business" and that they would arrange to bring in the pickled vegetables. Within a few weeks the delicacy arrived.

On November 22, 1943, Su Fei gave birth to a son. They had decided before he was born that the child would carry Su Fei's family name, Zhou, and the personal name Ma. The boy was named Zhou Youma. Ma decided that his son also should have an English name, James. One never knew what the future held, and besides, at some point he hoped to introduce his son to his American family. The first few weeks of the child's life were precarious, since he weighed just over five pounds. The attending physician feared for Youma's life, especially as winter set in, and decided to have him stay in the hospital rather than in Ma's cave dwelling. Since no incubator was available, Youma was placed on a heated *kang* with cotton-padded cushions under him. Then the doctor took heated bricks, wrapped them in cloth, and lined them around the baby.

Finally, after a month in the hospital, Ma brought his son home for the first time. Su Fei, following Chinese tradition, had not left her room during the period, and this was the first time she had seen her son since giving birth. She remembers that first reunion: "Youma looked pretty good when he was brought back from the hospital. He was the very image of Ma Haide for he had big, dark and bright eyes, a high-bridge nose, a little mouth with smiles at the corner, and dark curly hair."[39]

With the Rectification Campaign over and the struggle against the Japanese at full force, Ma's work continued unhampered. As one of the few trained physicians in Yan'an, he practiced almost every type of medicine imaginable, from surgery to pediatrics to dermatology to obstetrics. Trusted once again by most of his comrades, from the lowest ranking soldier to the chairman, some of his duties during this period proved more social and educational than medical. He was approached in the streets with requests to fix everything from sore throats to fountain pens, flashlights, pens, and watches. He spent many nights patching things together, telling one friend in the Ministry of Public Health, "When they find out you are a doctor, they think you can fix anything."[40]

Once, a young soldier, a personal bodyguard to the Central Committee known by many to be a good-hearted but lazy boy, stopped Ma in the street to ask for a medical excuse from his classroom assignment that day. The boy could not read and constantly tried this ploy with the doctors in Yan'an to get out of studying. Ma decided to teach him a lesson. He listened to his heart and lungs, feigned concern, and gave him a prescription to get filled at the pharmacy. The boy, now frightened that he might really be sick, rushed to get the medicine. When he handed the prescription to the pharmacist he was told the medicine was not there. The soldier asked him what the prescription said. When told to read it himself, the boy said he could not read. The pharmacist, laughing with his colleagues, then read, "Go to the supply department to pick up a wife!" The young soldier ran to find Ma and ask why he would play such a trick on him. Ma spoke sternly, chastising him because he had bothered the doctor just so he could avoid his responsibilities. "You can't read so you're made a fool out of."[41]

Ma also served the local community, giving his own type-O blood to patients and operating on villagers in the Bethune International Peace Hospital when the need arose. Once he and one of his Indian colleagues discovered a boy nearby who had an unsightly harelip. Ma approached the family and told them he could fix the boy's face, thus making it possible for him to some day find a wife. At that time, cosmetic surgery was a luxury unknown to most people in Yan'an. Scores of nurses, doctors, students, and aides showed up at the hospital on the day of the surgery, which proved successful.[42]

It was during this period that Ma showed a growing interest in public health. He initiated education programs and instituted preventive health measures. He also returned to his first love in medicine, dermatology. As with many advances in medicine, China's improvements in public health came about during wartime. In late 1943, for instance, skin diseases were rampant among soldiers at the front. Sores spread over the bodies of many of them, diminishing and even disabling their fighting ability. As Ma and his colleagues treated these men, they discovered the problem was simply a lack of attention to basic hygiene. So he and his public health ministry colleagues undertook a campaign to educate soldiers and leaders on the importance of bathing. Leaders in the army, led by Commander Zhu De, joined in the educational movement, assuring its success.[43]

Of paramount concern to Ma during this period was his responsibility as physician to the Central Committee, a job that continued even during the disruptions of the previous year. He worried constantly about the lack of medicine and, to compensate for this shortage, he encouraged the leaders to watch their diet and to get more rest. Of particular concern to

Ma was the health of Mao Zedong, who kept awkward hours, working all night and sleeping only part of the day. Mao constantly found himself roused from his day sleeps to attend meetings and hear reports from the front. To encourage him to relax during his waking hours, Ma enticed Mao to play ping pong and mah-jongg with him, keeping him away from all other distractions at least for the duration of the games.

Ma knew Mao's habits well. Mao approached mah-jongg like a battle commander. He hated Ma's weak, defensive style of play. Once Ma held a tile that Mao needed to win. Maintaining his defensive style and not wanting to risk losing it, Ma refused to play the tile. Mao lost his temper, telling Ma that his play was "not intelligent. Play the tile so we can get the game going. We can't keep playing like this." The two of them then argued like schoolboys, finally compromising by changing the rules to speed up the game. When the game was over Ma looked at Mao and told him the arguing had been good for the chairman, for it released stress built up due to lack of sleep and the pressure of his responsibilities. Mao, never one to pay doctors much of a compliment, responded, "Only a doctor would think of this."

In addition to his concern for Mao's rest, Ma looked after the chairman's worsening arthritis. To ensure he exercised his joints, Ma would take Su Fei and their young son to Mao's cave in the evenings to have him join them for leisurely walks. They were often joined by Jiang Qing, whose company Su Fei enjoyed. The talk was usually light, since the goal was exercise and relaxation. If anyone approached Mao to engage in serious dialogue, Ma often would try to distract them with Youma's antics and lead Mao away on their walk. If several days went by without meeting the chairman, Su Fei and Ma would invite Mao and Jiang Qing to their home for dinner. Su Fei remembers those evenings as enjoyable, but not necessarily relaxing for her. "He spent a lot of time asking my opinion on politics and art," she remembers.[44]

The early 1940s put Ma through enormous highs and lows. He married the most beautiful woman in Yan'an, was under suspicion as a spy, became a father, and began a heightened interest in public health, a field that would dominate most of his professional career for the next several decades. He grew closer to Mao Zedong and other important Party leaders and looked forward to deepening these relationships and supporting the revolution. His chance came soon, but not through medicine.

The first group of foreign correspondents to visit Yanan, the directing center of the Chinese Communist areas, found a hatred of the Japanese and a determination to defend their achievements against all interference.

New York Times, July 1, 1944

America and Americans returned to my world only years later, in 1944 towards the end of World War II, when U.S. Army Observer Group (Dixie Mission) came to Yan'an.

Ma Haide

During the early 1940s Ma concentrated on his new family and his medical work. The foreigners he saw in Yan'an during this period were infrequent visitors who broke through the Nationalist lines and a few refugees from the European theater like Dr. Mueller and the recently arrived Austrian medic Richard Frey. There also were those residing in the small Soviet community Stalin had sent both to monitor and support the actions of their Chinese comrades. This group consisted of four Tass reporters, Dr. Andrei Orlov, a surgeon who worked with Ma in the Peace Hospital, and Petr Vladimirov, the official Comintern representative to Yan'an who introduced himself as a member of the Tass staff. Orlov would prove a good friend and expert surgeon whose skills Ma admired, despite Orlov's widely recognized infatuation with Su Fei. This group of Soviets would stay in Yan'an through the end of World War II, leaving in late November 1945 for Moscow.[1] All of the foreigners who visited Yan'an during this period, whether for long or short stays, developed an opinion about the Western doctor who lived and worked with the Red Army. One of the most curious was Vladimirov.

While Ma took little notice of him, Vladimirov was—like Otto Braun, Evans Carlson, and others before him—intrigued by this likable but perplexing young Western doctor who hid his identity. However, while Braun appreciated the politically naive but fun-loving doctor, Vladimirov

distrusted him. Vladimirov recorded his comments on Ma in his memoirs, published in 1974. It should be noted that these memoirs were published at the height of the Sino-Soviet conflict, leading many to discount
them on the assumption that they were heavily edited to portray the Chinese leadership in the worst light. No matter how discredited the text
may be, however, it is revealing that Vladimirov found Ma an important
character worth examining. Like others who met Ma during these years,
Vladimirov got most of the story wrong. Still enjoying his secret life, Ma
had fooled yet another. Vladimirov writes,

> May 27
> I have met Ma Hai-te several times, sometimes at Kang Sheng's office,
> sometimes in the company of Jen Pi-shih [Ren Bishi, member of the Party
> Central Committee].
> He is always seen together with the ranking officials of the Special Area.
> My Soviet colleagues say that he loves to entertain guests, throw parties, and
> always sees to it that alcohol will have its desired effect on his guests,
> although he himself drinks moderately and very cautiously.
> I asked Kang Sheng about this man and was told that Ma Hai-te is a skilled
> physician, has been working in the Pelyanshui hospital for a long time and is
> a loyal comrade. Ma Hai-te came to the Special area in 1937, although some
> name an earlier date.
> According to Kang Sheng, Ma Hai-te came to the Special Area because of
> internationalist convictions. As a medical man, he renders disinterested assis-
> tance to the Chinese Communists, he added. Being Jewish by nationality he
> is a citizen of New Zealand. He was born in the Near East, and his name is
> Mahmud. In China it was modified Ma Hai-te. I wondered where he has
> received his medical education. "He has a very fundamental education," said
> Kang Sheng. "He took his studies in the United States of America."
> My colleagues in the press bureau are sure that this New Zealand citizen
> receives good wage which goes to his fat bank account in the United States,
> and believe he is a professional intelligence officer.[2]

Later in his diary Vladimirov charges that Ma "poses as a friend of the
Communists, flaunting his progressive ideas while his real intention is to
'worm' his way into the people's confidence." Vladimirov even takes aim
at Su Fei, saying that she seems a bit too "frivolous" and interested in
passing off her charms on the Soviet Tass agents. Vladimirov suggests
that Su Fei's flirting may have been at the direction of Ma himself, as the
two of them conspired to gather information for Kang Sheng and his
intelligence arm of the Party.[3]

Other short-term visitors to Yan'an also observed Ma. Like Vladimirov, they were impressed with his close relationship to the leadership and
his simple lifestyle. Jack Chen, a writer who visited there in 1938 and
again in 1944, comments that "Ma was like a fish in water in Yan'an.
Once I went to a dinner with Mao, Zhu De and Ma. Ma was one of the
group—simple—talking informally just like friends talk. He was one of
the family, and they trusted him implicitly. I believe the reason he was so
trusted was because of his approach to his work. We knew from other
sources that he was the health man for the leadership. But he never said
that. He never did any name dropping, not like some other foreigners
the leadership knew, like those that came only to write a book."[4]

By intent and by natural acculturation, Ma integrated well into
Yan'an life. By the time more foreigners arrived in the mid-1940s, his
language skills, though still not perfect, had improved greatly. He never
asked for favors inappropriate to his rank. Huang Hua affirms this view
of his friend, saying that Ma integrated fully into a Chinese lifestyle
because of his personality and his approach to medical work. "First, he
was a doctor who treated everyone the same, big or small. He never tried
to put himself above others."[5]

The events of World War II ended Ma's isolation from the Western
world and put him once more into regular contact with Americans. It
began with the arrival of a small band of Western journalists in early
summer of 1944. These included Brooks Atkinson of *The New York
Times,* Harrison Foreman from *Reader's Digest,* and Israel Epstein,
recently of the China Defense League but now covering the war effort
for *Time-Life.* When they arrived in Yan'an they met Ma and, according
to Foreman, found him to be "of boyish good humor and enthusiasm,
and will unhesitatingly drop everything to act as interpreter. He is an
enthusiastic supporter of the Chinese Communists." But beyond this
limited profile, Foreman and his colleagues found out nothing about
Ma. "He has taken the Chinese name of Ma Hai-teh (he refuses to dis-
close his American name) so that he may more completely submerge
himself in the medical service of the Chinese Communist armies."[6]

But these few journalists were of less consequence to Ma than the
next group of Americans to arrive, who were official representatives of
the American military. Anticipating their arrival, the Party ordered Ma to
bridge the cultural and political gap between the two sides as its representative. As he remembers that time, he says, "America and Americans
returned to my world . . . in 1944 towards the end of World War II,
when the U.S. Army Observer Group (Dixie Mission) came to Yan'an."[7]

The trust that he had worked so hard to maintain, even during the Rectification Campaign, was about to be put to the test.

The story of the Dixie Mission is one of the most captivating chapters in the history of U.S.–China relations. It had a critical impact on Ma Haide, who developed lifelong friendships with many members of the mission. It also had a critical impact on them, since most would be devastated, both personally and professionally, by the anticommunist hysteria of the 1950s. But in 1944, the Korean War, McCarthyism, and the Cold War were not on anyone's horizon. For the moment, they each had a part to play in helping win a war against a common enemy. The only oddity was that one of the Americans involved was a spokesman for the Chinese.

Although the United Front against Japanese aggression had been in place since 1937, the war effort moved sluggishly. After the United States entered the war against Japan, Roosevelt looked to Chiang Kai-shek to tie down Japan's forces in China, thus weakening its power in the rest of the Pacific. But Chiang appeared uninterested in committing the bulk of his troops to this effort. Instead, he threw obstacles in the way of the Communists as they fought the invaders. One former Dixie Mission member remembers the problem this way.

> Despite the fact that the Nationalists had ostensibly agreed to forge a "United Front" with the Communists against the Japanese in 1937, Nationalist leader Chiang Kaishek would allow no supplies to reach Yanan's Red armies. Chiang wanted to play brinkman for the Allied cause in China by controlling the guns and money being sent through the US "lend lease" aid program to American-trained, Chinese warlord armies. His aim in doing so was to save his own troops to contain Communists, and as the old Chinese proverb says "let barbarians fight barbarians," he would let Europeans, Americans and warlords he did not trust fight the Japanese.[8]

Gen. Joe Stilwell, commander of the China-Burma-India Theater, grew increasingly frustrated with Chiang and let Washington know of his concern. He sent reports on the widespread corruption found in Chiang's army and sought out China experts for their advice on how to proceed. Meanwhile, the American campaign in the Pacific proceeded steadily but at tremendous cost. To aid the Allied effort, the Americans wanted to cut Japan's access to food and raw materials in China. There was a plan to send American troops into China's Shandong peninsula to help isolate the Japanese troops on the Asian mainland. Stilwell knew that only a hard-fighting and united Chinese effort could ensure success in this plan.

Two experts Stilwell depended on for advice and to articulate the problem to Washington were State Department representatives John Davies and John Service. They argued that the United States should investigate the fighting power of the Communists, which many thought to be substantial. Both men knew China well, having grown up there, and they believed that the Communists would eventually win any civil war against Chiang Kai-shek. Support only for Chiang would thus prove a costly mistake and embitter the Communists, who they recognized foremost as national patriots. They also knew the importance of carrying on intelligence work in the Red-held area, which was well behind enemy lines. With the help of these two State Department officials, Stilwell recommended that a team of observers be sent to Yan'an to investigate the fighting potential there. He forwarded this request to President Roosevelt, who, after consulting with Gen. George Marshall and the Joint Chiefs of Staff, approved the plan.

In February 1944, Roosevelt thus sent Chiang a message saying he wanted to send a team of observers to Yan'an to investigate the efforts of the Communists and to open a new avenue of intelligence operations behind the enemy's line. He would give no direct military aid to Mao Zedong, but Roosevelt hoped this mission could bring about more cooperation between the vying Chinese forces. He asked for Generalissimo Chiang's assistance. Chiang balked at the request and only approved movement within territory held by his own troops.

Washington grew impatient and proceeded to staff the mission while waiting for more cooperation from the generalissimo. Stilwell was in overall command of the mission, although he would not personally lead it to Yan'an. For that he chose Col. David D. Barrett, who had served in the American military in China for over twenty years and spoke the language fluently. The mission waited while the wrangling and positioning continued. Finally, during the third week of June, Vice President Henry Wallace arrived in Chongqing to discuss the joint war effort with Chiang. During these sessions Wallace stressed the importance of sending the team to Yan'an. Under this direct confrontation, Chiang finally yielded and approved the mission.

On July 4, Barrett met with Service, and the two of them began planning the trip to Yan'an. They quickly gathered a small group that included Maj. Melvin Casberg, a physician, Capt. John Colling, an intelligence officer and infantry expert, Capt. Paul Domke from the Signal Corps, Maj. Wilber J. Peterkin, Lt. S. Herbert Hitch, a naval intelligence officer, and a handful of enlisted men sent as mechanics, radio operators, and weapons experts. Many of these men would wander in and out of Ma's life over the next five decades.

Before leaving, the men tried to find out as much as they could about Yan'an. Peterkin and Service dined with Wang Bingnan, Zhou Enlai's personal secretary, at the Communist party headquarters in Chongqing. Colling and Hitch were invited to meet with Madame Song Qingling, who warned them to keep an open mind when visiting Yan'an and not believe everything the Nationalists had fed them. She also mentioned the need for them to take additional medical supplies to the Bethune International Peace Hospital. She told them that an American doctor worked there, and he would be waiting to receive the supplies. Finally, on July 22 the first contingent of Dixie Mission personnel left Chongqing for Yan'an in a military transport plane. A second group would depart in three weeks. Replacements and additional staff would move in and out of Yan'an through the spring of 1946.[9]

As the C-47 transport plane left Chongqing, it crossed over Japanese territory, skirted around an enemy airfield, and headed north to Yan'an. The city was well protected by the hills surrounding it, and the only landmark available to the pilot was an ancient yellow pagoda standing atop one of the hills. It took several passes up and down the valleys before the pagoda was finally sighted. But the adventure had only begun for this band of Americans, for the airstrip in Yan'an had not been used since the Soviets landed there years before to whisk away Otto Braun. It was full of holes and too short for a plane of this size, but they landed anyway.

The plane taxied down the dirt landing strip, only to have its left landing wheel sink into an old grave. The propeller hit the ground, then flew into the fuselage, breaking into a section of the cockpit. Only luck and the pilot's skill prevented serious injury. Watching this inauspicious beginning was a welcoming committee composed of the highest leaders in Yan'an. They were joined by Ma Haide, who one Dixie Mission officer described as "short and very dark," thirty-four years old but looking closer to fifty.[10] Ma wasted no time showing his American colors. He had studied the list of those coming to Yan'an, and greeted fellow North Carolinian Hitch with an enthusiastic "Hello, tarheel."[11]

The Dixie Mission contingent exchanged greetings with their hosts, then were officially welcomed with military music and short speeches. The airstrip was full of soldiers and peasants. Also attending was the Soviet contingent, headed by the distrustful Vladimirov taking pictures with his Leica. Following the ceremony, everyone returned to the wounded plane and used ropes to pull it out of the grave and back onto the landing strip. Then the Americans climbed into the ambulance that had been donated to the Bethune International Peace Hospital by the efforts of Madame Song and the China Defense League. It doubled as the official transport for the leadership on special occasions.[12]

The Americans were taken to their quarters, which despite their special arrangements for foreign guests were representative of the homes common to Yan'an residents at the time. Barrett describes what awaited them. "We were housed in some of the Yanan 'caves', which were really not caves at all, but short tunnels, about 15 feet in length, cut into the steep hillside and lined with beautifully fitted blocks of hewn stone. The single room of each cave ended in the blank face of the tunnel. In front, a door and window, set in wooden frames, provided an entrance and admitted some light. In lieu of window panes, white paper was pasted over frames, which prevented anyone from seeing anything from inside or outside. The caves were floored with grey bricks, with sand in the spaces between them. Furnishings of the room were of Spartan simplicity; a rough table, one or two plain wooden chairs, a trestle bed (planks set on saw horses) for each occupant, a stand for an enameled wash basin, and a rack for towels. There was no floor covering. Everything was clean, and ample for the requirements of anyone not expecting soft living. At night, light was supplied by tallow candles. There was no running water anywhere on the premises. The latrine, undoubtedly built with special care for the accommodation of fastidious foreigners, was located at an inconvenient distance from the living quarters, but otherwise provided entirely satisfactory sanitary facilities."[13]

The Dixie Mission found their needs looked after by a series of people. The three most directly involved in this duty were Ma, his old friend and traveling companion Huang Hua, and Chen Jiakiang. They reported to Ye Jianying, Chief of Staff of the Eighth Route Army and the official host of the American military mission, and Yang Shangkun, Ye's assistant. The assignments of the three were carefully spelled out: Huang Hua and Chen Jiakiang associated most directly and formally with head of mission Barrett while Ma became something of a free floater, enjoying the company of the rank-and-file members on a more informal basis. One of his duties was to arrange the food, lodging, and basic medical needs of the Americans.[14] Those on the Chinese side, including Ma, who were assigned to work with the Dixie Mission were divided into four sections handling liaison, research, translation, and logistical support. The heads of each of these sections reported directly to Yang Shangkun. Ma and Huang Hua worked in all four. They also met periodically for political study with their comrades in the other sections.[15]

Ma seemed especially to enjoy his time with the young enlisted men, most of whom were from working-class backgrounds like himself. All the Americans immediately labeled him "Doc Ma." When the Dixie Mission first arrived, Ma was living at the Bethune International Peace Hospital across the river from the compound. Later he moved to a free-standing building in the foreigners' compound just a few yards away from the cave dwellings. Ma and Huang Hua stayed there for most of the Dixie Mission's visit. They were joined at one point by Ling Qing, who would in coming decades serve as China's ambassador to the United Nations. Su Fei and Youma remained in the hospital quarters, but visited the compound often and even stayed there occasionally.[16]

Barrett had only a casual interest in Ma, but an interest nonetheless. The first time he mentions the young doctor is in the context of a typically American activity, softball. "On our own, members of our group sought amusement and exercise in playing softball. We were joined in this by 'Doctor Ma', an American who had been in Yanan for some years. He performed brilliantly in the outfield."[17] Like everyone else, he enjoyed Ma's company but could only guess at his heritage. He later identified him as an American doctor and sometime interpreter "who seemed much less at ease in translating from English into Chinese than when the talk was the other way around."[18] He admitted having no idea why Ma threw in his lot with the Communists, but found him "a well-spoken, pleasant, friendly man, who as far as I ever heard, did not talk politics. He had an attractive wife." At one point Barrett insists that Ma told him "he had never completed studies for a medical degree."[19] It is difficult to believe that Ma ever told anyone this, since his European degree was of great pride to him. While it is possible Ma said this to throw the Americans off the track when they probed into his past, it is more likely that Barrett just got it wrong, confusing Ma with Richard Frey, the Austrian medic who had begun medical school in Europe but left when Hitler invaded his homeland.

While Barrett noticed Ma only casually, Comintern agent Vladimirov could not keep his eyes off this suspicious American who so eagerly attached himself to fellow Americans. Since he considered Ma a spy from the beginning, he never appreciated the level of trust the Chinese placed in him. Vladimirov accompanied the Dixie Mission on their initial tours of Yan'an, and at the Bethune International Peace Hospital he saw that "Ma Hai-te is like one of their own men." He hints that Ma used his medical training to position himself close to the Party leaders so that he could gather secret information, possibly passing the information off to his fellow countrymen. "Ma Hai-te persistently tries to become doctor of E Chian-ying [Ye Jianying]. Chief of Staff E Chian-ying is informed of all plans of the CPC leadership. Ma Hai-te does his utmost (and succeeds) to accompany E Chian-ying when the latter goes hunting. . . . Ma Hai-te spends evenings in the company of his American colleagues."[20] Later, toward the end of the Dixie Mission, Vladimirov worried, "Ma Hai-te has become a 'contact' between the CPC and the Americans. Each side treasures him. Ma Hai-te has developed friendship with many workers of the General Staff."[21]

While Barrett spent much of his time with the Yan'an leadership, the rank-and-file members of the Dixie Mission found themselves gravitating toward fellow American Ma. This pleased him just fine, as he thoroughly enjoyed dining, talking, and socializing with Americans for the first time in almost a decade. He had been assigned to engage in just such activities and to be available for special interpreting assignments when needed. The job had other rewards, as he for the first time in years had access to fondly remembered Camel cigarettes, chocolate, and butter. "He was always glad to share in our goodies," one member of the Dixie Mission remembered years after first meeting Ma. The Americans enjoyed his company so much that they sometimes requested special items for him and his family when writing to the United States. Peterkin once had his wife send him baby food "for Dr. Ma's baby."[22]

Just what kind of person did these Americans find in Doc Ma? Was he more American or Chinese in their eyes? Peterkin says that for all practical purposes Ma was Chinese.[23] Service recalls that Ma "was one of them. He had completely sinofied himself. George certainly never demanded he be seen as anything else. He completely made himself Chinese, joined them and become one of them. The Chinese had experience with foreigners. They always pushed themselves as experts. He was willing to be trained and told what to do."[24]

No matter what his allegiance, Ma was unquestionably popular with the Americans, and they were impressed with his insight into the workings of Yan'an. Service called on Ma to help him gather statistical information on economic conditions in the Communist-held areas. Ma's data convinced Service that the overall standard of living had improved since the Communists had taken over.[25]

Colling remembers his first impression of Ma. "All of us had a similar impression, that it made things kind of easier for us. We could talk to someone, and we did. We questioned Ma thoroughly as to why he was there, what the conditions were and was this all put on, was it true, is it this, is it that. We found that there was very true communism there and everybody had an equal share of nothing." Colling had a different take on Ma's adoption of Chinese ways. "We found the man Ma an American, that we had common ground and that he was very pro-American. I mean very, very pro-American. This was very important to him. He really didn't talk much of his politics, but the necessity of China and America getting together, the importance of a coalition. So he became quite a catalyst for us."[26]

While he may have been American, there was never any doubt about Ma's immediate allegiance. They knew he reported to the Chinese, although they were unaware of exactly how deeply he was committed to the Communists. Most viewed him as acting out of humanitarian rather than political interests, and assumed he was not a Communist party member. Many looked upon him as a new kind of medical missionary who had devoted his life to China.[27] The only political issue he discussed centered on the importance of healthy China–U.S. relations. "He never discussed politics, but kept things vague and indefinite," remembers Service. "He hung around our headquarters, and dropped by often to eat with us. He was interested in the conversations at the mess, especially on American public opinion. Was he there to find out what we were thinking? There was a little concern about this. Maybe he reported these things. I wouldn't be surprised."[28]

Colling, Peterkin, and Service agree that Ma's presence was not a threatening one, and that his personality and his familiarity with the surroundings made him one of the most popular personalities in Yan'an. Asked if any of the Dixie Mission personnel stayed away from Ma because they distrusted him, Colling responds, "There wouldn't be any reason to. We had everything to gain by talking with Ma. I mean, that was our purpose there."[29] "In all the time I was there I never heard anything said against him," Peterkin remembers.[30]

But Ma's visits were certainly not just social. He had been a Party member for seven years, and while he may have quizzed his guests about the winners of recent World Series games and about changes in American lifestyles, he listened to their radio broadcasts and read recent editions of *Time* magazine with special purpose. Huang Hua says that following their meals with the Dixie Mission, which sometimes coincided with radio broadcasts, Ma and Huang would return to Ye Jianying's headquarters to write down the information gleaned from the broadcasts and discussions. These translations would be sent directly to Chairman Mao and other Party leaders. Periodically Communist leaders such as Mao,

Zhou Enlai, Ye, and Zhu De would brief the Americans on military and diplomatic questions. Ma and Huang Hua organized these briefings, with Ma proving invaluable to both sides because of his understanding of the two cultures. He spent much of his time analyzing and explaining the issues to his Chinese comrades.[31]

The Dixie Mission observers took note of Ma's abilities, and one, Koji Ariyoshi, insists that the principal benefactor of Ma's cross-cultural explanations was Huang Hua, who in later years became China's ambassador to the United Nations and its foreign minister. "Dr. Ma's impact on Huang Hua during our Yanan days was obviously tremendous," Ariyoshi says. "Dr. Ma helped the Chinese liaison officer because he was familiar with the American lifestyle, attitudes, and ideological bent. Every day Dr. Ma and Huang Hua came to the mess together. They spent their free time together. It seemed that in their association, an osmotic process was taking place with Dr. Ma's knowledge being absorbed by Huang Hua. . . . On some nights we had bull sessions with Huang Hua, Dr. Ma and other interpreters. This was basic education for Huang Hua to learn about Americans. Always Dr. Ma was the person trying to explain what Mao was endeavoring to accomplish for China."[32]

During their first several months in Yan'an, the Americans spent many evenings in relaxed social settings with their Chinese hosts. Ma and Su Fei frequently invited individual members of the mission to their home at the hospital for dinner and conversation. At times Mao, Zhou, Zhu, and other leaders hosted dinners. These were almost always followed by dances in the "pear orchard" during which Jiang Qing, Su Fei, and other women in Yan'an took turns dancing with the Americans. Ma loved to dance and was happy to attend these functions in his official capacity as liaison officer and interpreter. One of the most memorable occasions was after the fall of Berlin in May 1945, when Chairman Mao held a victory celebration. At his table were the then head of the Dixie Mission, Peterkin, along with Vladimirov, a few Chinese officials, Ma, and Su Fei. Ma interpreted for Peterkin, while Su Fei, "the prettiest woman in the area," sat next to him. She was everyone's favorite partner in the dance that followed.[33]

Even though Ma was temporarily released from his medical duties, he practiced medicine whenever asked. He often took visitors to visit the Bethune International Peace Hospital, which to their amazement was merely a series of about one hundred caves spread out over four levels on a hillside. He talked to them about the use of herbal cures and acupuncture in the treatment of illnesses. He impressed upon them the need for improvisation and the need of more medical support from outside.

American reporter John Roderick of the Associated Press, whose visit coincided with the Dixie Mission, accompanied Ma once to a little-known and out-of-the-way clinic up the hill. "He took me outside the hospital grounds to a small leper clinic, which he ran. He seemed especially concerned with hygiene."[34] As Ma's later work would show, this early interest in leprosy would lead to a passionate concern to rid China of the disease and would gain him eventual worldwide recognition for his efforts.

The Americans were well aware of Ma's tendency to make use of traditional Chinese cures or, as one of them called it, "home grown medicine." They were periodically struck by his informal, and not always successful, remedies, and were startled by his prescriptions. Once, when a member of the mission came down with a serious but unexplained fever, Ma was asked to treat him. After examining him, Ma said he had no medicine to prescribe, but ordered the window open to get rid of the heat in the room. That was his prescription.

Once in 1945 an epidemic of spinal meningitis broke out, and the head of the mission asked Ma to help take preventive measures. Ma's own hospital had nothing to offer, so he looked through the mission's medical chest. He suggested they take the sulfa tablets they had brought with them, a limited remedy at best.

Other serious injuries and illnesses he treated in a more conventional, and successful, manner. In the spring of 1945, Shoso Nomura, an American of Japanese ancestry who had recently arrived to interrogate Japanese prisoners, suffered from a ruptured appendix. Ma decided to operate. Nomura recovered fully, and Ma won a friend for life. In 1990, Nomura remembered "Meeting such historical figures in Yanan as Mao Tse-tung, Chou En-lai, Chu Teh, Huang Hua, Lin Pio [Biao], Peng Te-huei, et. al, was a rare opportunity and experience for a young GI, such as I. And yet the most cherished memories are those of Doc Ma. I don't think I have ever met anyone who was so down to earth and approachable. He was a man of rare talents and unique experiences. Plus, being a regular guy!"[35]

On another occasion a new member of the Dixie Mission arrived in Yan'an directly from Beijing. It seems the young man had recently visited one of Beijing's many brothels and brought along a fresh case of syphilis as a souvenir. He immediately sought out Ma, whose years in Shanghai had made him an expert on this disease. Ma treated the grateful soldier with conventional medicines and suppressed the illness long enough for the soldier to get more intensive treatment when he returned to better facilities.[36]

In July 1945, Ma, Huang Hua, and Yang Shangkun took Peterkin, Ariyoshi, and other Americans to the front at the request of Ye Jianying, who wanted them to investigate the use of American firepower by the Nationalists against the Communists. They traveled much of the way on mules, since the land was too rough for the military jeeps the Americans had brought. The weather was hot, and the mules constantly fought the horseflies swarming about. At one point Peterkin's mule bolted down a path out of control. The saddle broke, and Peterkin was thrown to the ground, rendering him unconscious. Ma found that Peterkin's ribs were broken and taped his side as best he could until they could get him to a hospital at the front.[37]

The most friendly and relaxed period for the Dixie Mission was from their arrival in July 1944 until November that year. Mao put great stock in gaining U.S. support for his war effort, and he went to extraordinary lengths to convince the Americans that Communist China posed no threat to their country. He told Service that "America does not need to fear we will not cooperate. We must cooperate and we must have American help. This is why it is important to us Communists to know what you Americans are thinking and planning. We cannot risk crossing you—cannot risk conflict with you."

For a while, the Communists found cause for optimism. They heard that Stilwell planned to send military aid for their fight against the Japanese, and Dixie Mission officers instructed Communist troops in American weaponry. The Americans also seemed genuinely impressed with both the military and economic achievements of their hosts. But the support never materialized, and in a rehearsal for the Red scare of the 1950s, all those calling for closer ties with the Chinese Communists found themselves isolated. Led by Patrick Hurley, Roosevelt's special emissary to China, opponents of the Communists rallied behind Chiang Kai-shek in his attempt to force Mao's forces out of the equation in China's future. In October, Hurley convinced Roosevelt that the original advocate of the Dixie Mission, Gen. Joseph Stilwell, should be removed from his post because of Chiang Kai-shek's antipathy toward him. Stilwell was replaced by Gen. Albert Wedemeyer, a contemptible man in the eyes of Stilwell, who labeled his successor "the world's most pompous prick." Hurley then made a bumbling surprise visit to Yan'an, ostensibly to encourage the Communists to cooperate more closely with the Nationalists. Instead, Chairman Mao gave him an earful on how the Nationalists were attempting to split the country. Mao insisted that the Nationalists mounted no significant opposition against the Japanese, while the Communists put the bulk of their forces into this effort. Hurley reacted strongly to Mao's lecture, becoming an even more staunch backer of Chiang.

Despite the tension between them, Mao and Hurley finally agreed on a plan to have the two Chinese sides work together more closely. Hurley wanted Mao to fly to Chongqing with him to meet with Chiang. Mao refused, but the Party sent Zhou Enlai back with Hurley to negotiate what they had ironed out in Yan'an. When he arrived in Chongqing, however, Chiang insisted the Communists disband their army and accept a minor role in the Nationalist government. Hurley supported the new Chiang proposal, and Zhou returned to Yan'an in late November 1944, embittered at Hurley's scheme and wondering if the potential alliance with the United States would now prove impossible.

Hurley responded to Zhou's angry return to Yan'an by opening an attack on those Americans he thought too sympathetic to the Communists. He immediately arranged to have them recalled, replacing them with military and government officials he knew supported Chiang. In December 1944, Barrett was recalled from Yan'an and replaced by Col. Morris B. Depass,[38] who was later succeeded by Peterkin.

With the dismissal first of Stillwell, then of Barrett, the atmosphere in Yan'an changed. The Americans who had been there since the summer saw this, and fought the change. But they had little or no clout, and could only watch as both their own superiors and the Communists used them less and less. Peterkin recalls, "General Stilwell, who not only was an able commander and who knew China and the Chinese and whose consuming desire was to win the war using all available means, was succeeded by General Wedemeyer, a man with no command experience, and no expertise in China and the problems of dealing with the Chinese. General Wedemeyer was a career officer, who's specialty, planning, was not prepared to cope with the intricate machinations of Chiang Kaishek and his cohorts. The unfortunate choice of General Hurley, first as personal representative of the President and later as Ambassador, brought an egocentric, senile old man into a position for which he had no qualifications whatsoever. With the relief of General Stilwell, the importance of the Dixie Mission became limited to: (1) the dissemination of weather reports; (2) the collection of Order of Battle information; (3) liaison with the Communist headquarters; and (4) the forwarding of 25 rescued flyers brought in by the Communists."[39]

As the Americans began maneuvering in earnest to isolate the Communists, so too did Mao and his colleagues act to block this move. They were in a desperate position, so they decided to take a desperate step. They would circumvent the new American leadership in China, which they distrusted completely, and go directly to Roosevelt. They looked to their relationship with the rank-and-file members of the Dixie Mission for assistance and called upon Ma to initiate the move.

One evening in late December, just after Barrett had been reassigned, Ma visited the cave of Hitch, the naval intelligence officer. Ma told him that Chairman Mao wanted to meet with him immediately. They both went to Mao's quarters, where the chairman told them that the Communists, despite the recent setbacks in negotiations, still held out hope that Washington would remain flexible and not bend to Chiang's wishes. They asked Hitch to deliver directly to Roosevelt the message that they would support a U.S. invasion of north China and would commit troops to support this effort. In return, they requested arms to assist in this invasion and to continue their fight against the Japanese. To top it off, Mao told Hitch that both he and Zhou Enlai would travel to Washington to meet with Roosevelt and his generals to work out the plans.

Hitch delivered the message to Washington, but the results proved disappointing to the Communists and devastating to those who had advocated closer ties with them. When Hurley learned of this secret message, he contacted Roosevelt and advised him to distrust the Communists. He told Roosevelt the problems in China stemmed from the Communists, who could not be trusted. Further, he said, he blamed disloyal American observers in China for encouraging them and conspiring with them against both Chiang and Roosevelt. Roosevelt, preoccupied with ending the war in Europe, supported Hurley in removing from China any American representatives the latter deemed dangerous to American interests. Those who refused to swear allegiance to Chiang, a sign of disloyalty to Hurley, found themselves threatened with criminal action and sent packing.[40] This proved no idle threat. In mid-1945, Service, one of the most knowledgeable of the State Department's China experts and the member of the Dixie Mission most respected by the Communists, was arrested in Washington and charged with espionage for passing classified documents to the magazine *Amerasia*. The Chinese Communists took Service's arrest as a direct attack on them. To Mao and his comrades in Yan'an, it was a continuation of the plot to undermine their efforts. In a radio broadcast relayed to the United States, they charged "American imperialists" with interfering in Chinese affairs and said that if they did not "withdraw their hands ... then the Chinese people would teach them a lesson they deserve."[41]

The work of Ma Haide and Huang Hua, so promising in the summer of 1944, now reflected the changing relationship. The new Dixie Mission representatives who came to Yan'an found Ma easy to talk with but more reserved than he was with earlier arrivals. He rarely acted as interpreter with the later group. "Dr. Ma would not participate as interpreter in talks that dealt with policy. He was very correct in his conduct."[42] One member who arrived in 1945 commented, "The relations between the Communists and the U.S. Army was guarded. It was proper and formal. There were a few social occasions where the atmosphere was more relaxed, but even then one did not cross certain lines. You did not talk about your personal lives, military or ideological issues."[43]

As the Party struggled to maintain relations with the Americans, Mao struggled to keep his liaison team focused. He called Ma, Huang Hua, and Chen Jiakang to his cave one night to discuss how to approach their work. Ma remembers it as a classic lesson in Marxism-Leninism. "The policy of the Liberated Areas was internationalist. I remember, when American policy veered to all-out support for the KMT . . . Chairman Mao . . . said there was a difference between the course of action taken by the U.S. government and the sympathies of the American people, and between policy makers in the U.S. government and the U.S. Army leaders [and] rank and file U.S. officials and and soldiers. You must remember all these distinctions, he said, and never blur them."[44]

As U.S. policy shifted, Mao ordered his liaison team to be more active in explaining Communist positions to the Dixie Mission leadership. In May 1945, Huang Hua and Ma met separately with various Dixie Mission members, each voicing displeasure at the changes in U.S. policy. One such meeting with Capt. Paul Domke of the Signal Corps was held in Ma's home on the evening of May 21. It lasted several hours. Domke's report of that discussion shows Ma's authority in dealing with the details of relations between the two sides. It also shows Ma's access to the leadership in Yan'an and his authority to speak for Ye Jianying, his immediate commander during this period, as well as for Chairman Mao and the Party leadership. Domke wrote,

> The real issue now, according to Dr. Ma, was what was going to happen in post-war China. The Chinese as a race had suffered untold hardships after many long years of civil strife, not to mention the present Sino-Japanese war, and it seemed to him that any further continuation of hostilities, internally, would only continue to drag China down farther into the "Slough of Chaos" from which she might never rise again. Strictly from a humanitarian viewpoint, he reflected, the people of China did not deserve it. Just how they could prevent it, or should prevent it, he did not say. . . .[45]

The undersigned [Domke] then changed the subject by observing that since coming back from the front that there seemed to be a definite cold and abrupt attitude on the part of the liaison officers as well as AMOS [Dixie Mission]. Dr. Ma answered by saying that that was probably true to a certain extent, but that it wasn't meant to be personal. The attitude of the Chief of Staff [Ye Jianying] followed the line of thinking that if the American Military had been going to do anything at all militarily in a big way in North China they would have done it a long time ago. . . . If there had been any definite plan for an over-all large scale military operation which entailed the complete cooperation of the entire 8th RA [Route Army] and new 4th A[rmy] they would have been immediately ready to cooperate one hundred percent. But, he went on to say, since the very beginning of the mission; and more espe- cially after the recall of General Stilwell from the CBI [China-Burma-India] Theatre and then later when Colonel Barrett was relieved from command of the AMOS there was never any definite statement of policy on the part of the American Headquarters in Chungking as to just what they wanted or just what they would or would not do. . . .

So far as AMOS is concerned, he stated, they will continue to cooperate on more or less friendly terms, but that it will never be with the same enthu- siasm that they'd initially showed. . . . It was noteworthy that the Chinese Headquarters, he thought, are now taking the attitude that, "Well, we're not so dumb ourselves. We know what is going on and we aren't going to have the wool pulled over our eyes."[46]

While official relations cooled, Ma continued to enjoy at least the social aspects of the Americans' presence. As he told Domke, the tension should not be taken personally. On the basis of the trust forged earlier between him and individual members of the Dixie Mission, Ma decided to call on some of them to ask a personal favor. For the first time in years, Ma found himself thinking again of his family in the United States. It had been eight years since he wrote his family with the misleading news that he was headed for Tibet. He had heard nothing from them during those years, and he had made no attempt to contact them. These Ameri- can soldiers now provided an opportunity to reconnect. He had a wife and a child they knew nothing about, and the time now seemed right to let them know something of his life.

When John Service returned to Washington, D.C., in October 1944 for debriefing, Ma gave him a letter and pictures of himself, Su Fei, and Youma. He asked Service to contact his brother Joe, but all he had was the Roanoke Rapids address. Once back in Washington, Service finally located Joe in Richmond, Virginia, where he was serving as a corporal in the army. Joe went up to Washington to visit Service in his State Depart- ment office. Gazing at the pictures and reading the letter, Joe asked Service what he knew of his brother. He told him the family had no idea about his wayward brother's whereabouts, but the correspondence he had received in 1936, just before Shag disappeared, had led Joe to think he might be working with the Communists. Now it was verified.[47]

Later, when Hitch went to Washington to deliver the secret message to Roosevelt, he carried more messages for the Hatem family. Joe was again the contact. Hitch told Joe that Ma was likely to be a Communist, or at least a sympathizer of Communism in China. Joe was visibly upset by this, remarking that he could not believe his brother was actually a Communist. He told Hitch such news would devastate his parents. Hitch argued long and hard on behalf of the long-lost brother, however, telling Joe that the family should be proud of him as a wonderful humanitarian doing meaningful work. That is the message to remember, Hitch said, and the family should not dwell too much on the political aspects.[48]

Ma's parents in North Carolina were thrilled to find out that their son was alive. When she heard the news, his mother looked to the day she would see her son again. And now she had a grandson to welcome. To prepare for her son's eventual homecoming and the arrival of Youma, she purchased a large ceramic piggy bank. When she brought it home she placed it in the kitchen, and from that day until her death she put loose change in it to pay for the gifts and clothing she would buy her grandson when he came to the United States.

The family's hopes for Shag's eventual return revived, but in the meantime they depended on the mail to unite them. They sent correspondence through the American military and through Song Qingling's office in Hong Kong. When correspondence started up once again, they saw how little their son had changed from his Beirut, Geneva, and Shanghai days, for along with the informative letters introducing his new family, he sent lists of things he needed. His needs had changed little. He requested such things as belts and clothing for him and Su Fei, but he also wanted toys for his son. The family immediately prepared a box of requested items, including a new children's bicycle to be shipped to Yan'an. Returned Dixie Mission members arranged for the gifts to be sent by military transport. Their arrival caused much excitement, since the stark life in Yan'an offered few playful diversions for the children. The bicycle was immediately assembled—all except the handlebars, which had been left out of the box. After the handlebars of another bike were added, this became one of Youma's prized possessions, making him a popular figure with the other children who rode it.[49]

Even though Ma initiated contact with his family, he gave no indication of wanting to return to the United States or to change his adopted lifestyle. He continued to talk freely with visiting Americans about the needs of daily life and the importance of U.S.–Chinese cooperation. But he refused to talk in detail with anyone about his own politics or his American family.

This is confirmed by Associated Press reporter John Roderick, who arrived in Yan'an in 1945 for what turned out to be a seven-month stay. Roderick says that he had no way of knowing if Ma was a Party member, as Ma never discussed it. It took several weeks before Roderick even found out Ma's American name. "He seemed to have shut out his past, and was totally fulfilled in his work. He was very discreet." Like previous visitors, he was impressed with how easily Ma fit into the Communist setting, especially with the familiar relations he enjoyed with Mao and other leaders. Roderick noted that at formal ceremonies Ma sat in the second row with dignitaries, just behind the central Party leadership.[50]

By the summer of 1945, formal relations between the U.S. military command in China and the Communists in Yan'an had deteriorated further. Roosevelt died in April, and Truman now commanded the war effort. Inexperienced in international affairs, he depended heavily on Roosevelt's advisors. These advisors, including Hurley in China and Averell Harriman in the Soviet Union, convinced Truman that the Communist threat was an international conspiracy under Moscow's direction. As far as Washington was concerned, the Yan'an Communists had lost any independent identity, and Dixie Mission personnel changes mirrored this. The most striking signal of this was the assignment in July 1945 of Col. Ivan D. Yeaton to replace Peterkin as mission chief. If Ma was worried about relations between the two sides during his discussions in May with Domke and Peterkin, he had even more cause for concern now. Peterkin genuinely admired and appreciated the leadership of the Communist party, and, despite the problems arising from Chongqing, hoped for closer relations. Yeaton arrived from Moscow, where he had served as a military attaché. On finding himself relieved, Peterkin tried to educate Yeaton about the situation in China, and in Yan'an specifically. Yeaton rebuffed him. "He [Yeaton] had no background on China or the Chinese but styled himself as an expert on communism. . . . When I suggested we get together for a briefing he told me that there was nothing I could tell him that he did not already know. . . . He said he wanted me to leave immediately. I refused and told him I was going to call on the top CCP officials and make my formal farewells."[51]

While members of both sides despaired at the breakdown in relations, personal friendships weathered the storm. The Party leadership held a banquet for Peterkin before he left, following it with the now customary dance. When Peterkin danced with Su Fei, he was pleased to note she was wearing perfume that he had earlier given to Ma. Before he left for Chongqing, he gave Ma and other friends in the Chinese liaison office cigarettes, soap, powdered milk, and an alarm clock.[52]

While the Dixie Mission struggled on for another seven months, its relationship with its Chinese hosts steadily deteriorated. When the Japanese surrendered in August and Truman ordered that the defeated troops surrender only to Nationalist forces in China, the Communists braced for new civil war. The Nationalists rearmed the surrendering Japanese troops to aid them in their fight to keep the Communists isolated. The United States had armed the Nationalists well, and the Communists found their own position precarious. The former seized major cities, while the latter consolidated their power in the countryside and tried to expand it. Mao saw that he needed time to prepare for the civil war, so in August he agreed to begin peace talks with Chiang Kai-shek. However, these talks failed, and in December the United States sent Gen. George C. Marshall to mediate peace between the two forces.[53]

In November, Clifford Young arrived in a tense Yan'an to serve as executive officer to Yeaton. There were only ten Americans now assigned there. When Young arrived, Yeaton told him to be careful in his movements and to keep a low profile in his relations with the Chinese. For a month, he initiated neither friendly nor informal contact with the Chinese, nor welcomed any. He looked upon Ma as one of the Chinese, and even though Ma lived in the compound at the time, it was not until Christmas 1945 that Young got to know him, when Ma, Chairman Mao, Ye Jianying, Yang Shangkun, and others joined in the Christmas party at the Dixie Mission compound, each receiving gifts from the Americans. But such relaxed times proved rare now. The civil war heated up again, and the Dixie Mission wound down its operation. In mid-April 1946 it closed for good. A small group stayed on for a few more months, operating now under the name "Yan'an Liaison Group."[54]

During the last months of the American mission's presence in Yan'an, Ma's life followed closely the changes in diplomatic movements. The negotiations Marshall headed in Chongqing established truce teams made up of Americans, Communists, and Nationalists, to operate in various locations around the country. The main negotiations would continue in Beijing, under what became known as the Executive Headquarters. The Communist party chose Chief of Staff Ye Jianying to represent its interests in Beijing. So Ma, Huang Hua, and other members of Ye's liaison team packed their bags and flew to Beijing in January 1946. Ma had yet another chance to bring Americans a better understanding of China. The Party continued to appreciate and depend on this special diplomat in their midst.

Chinese Communists accepted with some reservations today Generalissimo Chiang Kai-shek's plan to use General George Marshall as a mediator but charged that the Generalissimo had unleashed a large scale invasion of Jehol Province even as he talked of peace.

New York Times, January 4, 1946

As a result of developments in Manchuria, where Chinese Government troops have suffered a crushing defeat, the United States Consulates in Peiping and Tientsin were scheduled to send letters tomorrow to all American residents in the two North China cities suggesting that those with unessential duties leave while transportation facilities still were available.

New York Times, November 1, 1948

When Ye Jianying, Huang Hua, Ma, and others arrived in Beijing, they moved to their headquarters at the old Rockefeller hospital just off the main shopping district of Wangfujing Street. This hospital would be known after liberation by various names, most popularly Capital Hospital. Ma was assigned two principal duties. First, he represented the medical needs of the liberated area, contacting international agencies on the needs of those left in Shaanxi. Second, he continued in his role as diplomat without portfolio. As in Yan'an, he represented the Party in informal settings when foreigners were present, interpreting for Ye Jianying and other leaders, explaining Party policies, and advocating its positions. Han Xu, at that time a young Party member assigned to the Executive Headquarters, and later Chinese ambassador to the United States, recalled that Ma acted as an advisor to Ye Jianying on foreign affairs, read and explained English-language documents to the Communist negotiating team, and engaged in public relations work with foreign correspondents and military personnel. Again, as in Yan'an, Ma rarely sat in on formal negotiations among the three teams.[1]

On the medical front, Ma represented the Chinese Liberated Areas Relief Administration (CLARA). In this capacity he worked with the

United Nations Relief and Rehabilitation Administration (UNRRA) and
other international agencies. He played a unique role, because the Nationalists had no counterpart representing China's medical needs, and he
found a ready audience of relief workers anxious to hear his reports.[2] As
usual, his Western background and winning personality helped the cause,
despite the roadblocks set up by the Nationalists and the skepticism
found in official American circles. In later years Ma reflected on those
days, "The KMT [Nationalists], then in control of the city, tried to keep
us from getting any supplies. But some good Americans helped us. For
instance, Bob Drummond, responsible for American Red Cross grants in
North China, would tell me when allocation meetings were scheduled
and what was available. 'Write a report of what you need with examples
of what you're doing with it and where,' he would suggest. So at the
meeting, we'd often be the only ones with a complete and trustworthy
report, as the KMT was too lazy and corrupt. Result: the needed supplies would go by the next U.S. Army plane to Zhangjiakou (Kalgan) in
our area. In UNRRA . . . the top crust was instructed to hand everything
over to the Kuomintang-run receiving agency, and later much of it
would turn up on the black market, sold by Chiang Kai-shek's officials.
Our requests, however, were apt to be rejected or blocked. When our
liberated areas had a plague epidemic, we asked for some of UNRRA's
ample stock of sulfa drugs specific for the disease. I applied . . . They
gave us only 3,000 pills and wanted a receipt pledging to return—when
we could find another source—any pills that we had not used! But many
Americans lower down in UNRRA were fair and friendly, especially after
they had seen for themselves what was then happening in China."[3]

Ma circulated widely while representing the Party in Beijing. He met
with representatives of the United Nations Children's Emergency Fund
(UNICEF), the Rockefeller Foundation, U.S. Army personnel, and U.S.
embassy officials, among others, all with the same purpose. He told them
of the achievements in the liberated areas and the medical needs of the
people there. He especially enjoyed his visit with the Rockefeller Foundation, as he was one of their very own products from the American
University in Beirut. He forged lifelong friendships with several of the
relief and medical workers, especially those who shared a keen interest in
public health issues. These included James Grant, who later became
executive director of UNICEF, and Dr. Michael Sachs, who eventually
headed the World Health Organization (WHO).

In addition to his medical duties, Ma was assigned to discuss with as
many people as possible the overall achievements of the Communist
party and its army in the liberated areas. He did this both in private

meetings with those already sympathetic to the Communists, such as the recently arrived American writer and radical Anna Louise Strong, and in friendly and informal dinners with American members of the negotiating team. He also participated in public presentations. During breaks in the formal negotiations, he and Huang Hua established themselves in the foreign community as the primary spokesmen for the liberated area, and they found audiences hungry for their news. The impact on their listeners proved life changing for some and served to reaffirm already accepted beliefs in others.

One of those who sought out Ma and Huang Hua was a recent graduate of the master of arts program at Furen University in Beijing named Wang Guangmei. While she was tutoring undergraduates and assisting the dean of her university, she had already joined the Communist underground. Within a few years, she would marry Liu Shaoqi, who would later serve as China's first president after liberation. But in 1946 she was merely an impressionable young English interpreter whom the Party was about to assign to its Executive Headquarters. She recalls her first impression of Ma Haide. "In February 1946, I read in an English-language newspaper called the *Chronicle* that two people would make a presentation on the position of the Communist Party in the talks that had just begun. I had already been assigned to work at the Executive Headquarters, and I wanted to know more about how the Party worked before I started. This was held at a meeting house outside the Headquarters offices close to the old Beijing Hotel. When I arrived I saw Huang Hua and Ma Haide. Huang Hua, head of the Information Department, gave a talk on the Long March. The other talk, by Ma Haide, was very interesting. He talked about how they had solved medical issues at the front, especially issues related to food and clothing and the treatment of eye diseases. Ma also talked of the democratic nature of the liberated areas, and he explained how people there led a simple, often uneducated, life. Most of those who came to hear them were foreigners. I was one of the few Chinese."[4]

After she began work at the Executive Headquarters in March, Wang Guangmei often saw Ma, usually at receptions and informal gatherings. "His Chinese was very good at this time," she says. "He could even use it to tell jokes and make fun with people. He was very popular with everyone, especially the foreigners, and he took every opportunity to educate those coming to Beijing from the White areas about the achievements found in the liberated areas."[5]

Huang Hua and Ma did not confine their presentations to Beijing. They also visited other cities, including Tianjin and Shanghai. Betty

Chandler, an American then working in Tianjin, recalls the first time she met Ma. It proved a life-changing encounter. "When I was in Tianjin a group of U.S. Marines who were especially interested in China got together and formed a group called 'Views Behind the News'. One week they invited a Guomintang [Nationalist] official to present that side, and the next week they invited the communists to present their side. I was friends with some of these men, and attended their sessions. The Communist representatives were Huang Hua and Ma Haide. Ma spoke, but not Huang Hua. The Guomintang presentation was weak, but Ma inspired me with his talk about medical work and democracy in Yanan and the other areas under communist control. The Marines were also impressed. This talk was very important to me, and I thought about it in 1948 when the American consulate office told me to leave the country. I did not leave, in part because of this talk."[6]

Robbins Strong, Anna Louise Strong's nephew who was working with the YMCA at the time, often saw Ma during this time. He says that Ma never pushed himself on audiences, but was in great demand as a speaker. "He told stories," Strong recounts. "He never tried to sell you on anything, but merely through his telling of personal experiences he got his message across. Marxism was never mentioned. Nor was politics. I remember he talked to the Presbyterian church and other missions about his medical work, especially how they mobilized their work during the anti-Japanese war."[7]

Ma did not spend all his time in Beijing doing the Party's work. The war with Japan and his renewed acquaintance with Americans had stirred memories of his past. His long-submerged sense of responsibility as the eldest son now began to reassert itself. He had a son, and he wanted that son to know his American family. Relations between the Chinese Communists and America were strained, but officially open. No one on the American side knew of his well-hidden Party affiliation, and he met almost daily with Americans, both officials and common citizens. He thought the time might now be right to go home, at least for a visit. So, on April 29, 1946, he visited the U.S. Consulate in Beijing.

He had to fill out several forms.[8] First, there was the application to renew his long-expired passport. He filled out the application for both himself and his son, identified as "James Hatem, born at Yanan, Shensi, China on Nov. 22, 1943." He also signed an oath of allegiance to the United States and completed an affidavit to explain his protracted absence from the United States. In these documents, Ma explains his role as that of a medical doctor doing humanitarian work. His narrative in the affidavit reads:

I, Shafick George Hatem, a native American citizen, born at Buffalo, New York, U.S.A. do solemnly swear that I ceased to reside in the United States on or about September, 1929; that I have since resided at Syria, Switzerland and China; and that I arrived in Peiping, China, where I am now temporarily residing, on January 16, 1946, . . . my reason for such foreign residence being as follows: Completion of my medical education from 1929 to 1933. Since then I have been engaged in medical work in China, having carried on a medical practice in Shanghai from 1933–1936 and then going into the interior in connection with my medical work. Then I became connected with the International Peace Hospitals since 1939 till the present time. These hospitals were in Free China and in guerrilla area behind the line during the anti-Japanese war. Throughout the war I worked in Yanan Branch of the International Peace Hospitals. My reasons for prolonged stay in China are that there is such a great need for medical men and that I have already put in so much effort into this work in these thirteen years. Furthermore, during the war years—1937–1945—I did not have any opportunity for returning to America. I believe my efforts have contributed in a very small way to American-Chinese friendship.

He further explained that he maintained contact with his parents in North Carolina and that "I intend to return to the United States to reside within two years or when my present work with the International Peace Hospitals permits." In signaling this intent, Ma specifically marks over a section of the official document that indicates he intends to reside "permanently" in the United States. This appears to show an honest presentation of his intentions. He wanted to visit his family, probably for an extended stay, but he had no plan to leave China forever.

In his oath of allegiance, Ma listed two references who could attest to his character and patriotism. One was Lt. Herbert Hitch, the former member of the Dixie Mission who was now an assistant naval attaché in Beijing. The other was Martel Hall, manager of the National City Bank branch in Beijing. If he had it to do over again, Ma might have chosen someone besides Hitch as a reference.

The consular official reviewing Ma's papers wrote an opinion that referred to comments by Hitch.

Although the facts as cited in the applicant's statement on the reverse are believed to constitute the principal reason for his protracted foreign residence, it is understood that much of Dr. Hatem's time in recent months in Yanan has been devoted to matters other than those of a medical character. Lieutenant Commander S. H. Hitch, Assistant Naval Attache, has informed the undersigned that during his stay in Yanan Dr. Hatem appeared to be devoting considerable time to contact work of a propaganda character with members of the American armed forces stationed in Yanan and less time to work in the International Peace Hospital.

Despite this less than enthusiastic reference, consulate officer Fulton Freeman added in his notes that "there has been nothing which would indicate that Dr. Hatem is a member of the Communist Party or that he has ever been disloyal to the United States." The recommendation of the consulate officer was to investigate further the character and movements of Ma over the past several years. John Emerson, head of Japanese affairs in Beijing's American embassy, was recommended as someone to provide more information. An official memorandum was sent to Emerson stating, "I should appreciate it if you would furnish me with a brief statement of your knowledge of Dr. Hatem, and his background. In particular I would like to know whether there has been any indication that Dr. Hatem has engaged in political activities in China."

In a July 2 memo, Emerson responded to this request, explaining that Ma worked primarily with the Bethune International Peace Hospital and as an interpreter for Americans coming to Yan'an. He then added this mixed message:

> So far as I am aware there is, as Mr. Freeman indicates, no evidence to indicate that Dr. Hatem is a member of the Communist Party or that he has ever been disloyal to the United States. He was regarded by all the Chinese in Yanan as an American citizen and had apparently held himself out as such.
>
> There is no doubt that Dr. Hatem was personally sympathetic to the cause of the Chinese Communists and that he supported their viewpoint. With reference to his having engaged in political activities I am not in possession of any information to indicate that he indulged in political activities for the Chinese Communist Party unless his duties as liaison officer with the United States Observers Section could be so interpreted. I have no knowledge of activity by Dr. Hatem which would indicate opposition to or disloyalty to the United States.

Finally, on August 13, the State Department in Washington, D.C., cabled the Beijing Consulate Office with approval for Ma to be issued a new passport, valid for two years. However, there was a catch. The instructions also read:

The applicant's minor child, James Hatem, may not be included in the passport as he is not a citizen under Section 201(g) of the Nationality Act of 1940.

According to Hitch, Ma wanted "desperately" to come back to the United States in 1946, but he was discouraged from returning because of his possible political activities. Years after leaving China, Hitch remembered Ma fondly, but with suspicion. "I thought he was a heroic figure in Yan'an, and I was very fond of him. But I recommended that he not be allowed to return to the States because he was too articulate a spokesman for the Communists, and he might be able to convince others of their cause. We didn't need an intelligent, articulate American communist in our country just then."[9]

So in September, Ma received the formal word that he could return to the United States on his new passport, but Youma could not accompany him. It is not known whether the Party knew of his intention to take his son back to visit the United States, but it is doubtful. When asked about this, Huang Hua says that during their days at the Executive Headquarters he knew that Ma wanted to renew his ties with family and friends in the United States. "But," he states, "he had no interest in returning to the United States."

What did Ma intend to do? He wanted to go home, and he wanted to take his son with him. He knew how desperately his family wanted to see him and his new son. The piggy bank in Grandma's kitchen was filling up, just waiting for the grandchild to arrive. In a 1955 document that passed through the Central Intelligence Agency, Ma's intention to return to the United States appears unquestioned. It states, "he did attempt re-entry in 1946." But there appears no evidence that Ma intended to stay in the United States even if he returned with Youma. The negotiations were still progressing, and he hoped they would create a breakthrough within the next two years that would allow him the opportunity to visit his family. But, despite the fact that his Party membership was never discovered, intelligence reports and State Department evaluations cast just enough doubt on his ultimate allegiance to place roadblocks in his path. The denial of his son's application was a sign of suspicion. He could go back, but he could not take his Chinese family. As Hitch argues, he was just too articulate, and therefore dangerous, to allow him back into the States.

While Ma made plans to return to the United States after the war against Japan, his family in North Carolina decided to contact him directly. After his discharge from the army, Joe Hatem prepared to go to China to visit the brother he had not seen in seventeen years. However, after filling out his travel documents, he received a visit from the Federal Bureau of Investigation (FBI), who told him it would be unwise to make such a journey, especially if he planned to see his brother, a known Communist sympathizer. He might find life difficult after his return. After talking with the family, Joe decided to cancel the trip. The FBI visit dampened the Hatem family's desire to see the wayward Shag. They spoke less and less of him in public and in the family.[10] For years, Ma had delayed returning to his American family, always at his own initiative. Now, when he wanted to see them, the U.S. government prevented it.

The next year's events moved at such a pace that even if Ma had gained permission to take his son on a trip to the United States, he might not have succeeded. Despite his eagerness to visit his American family, Ma's heart was clearly in China's revolution. While the U.S. government investigated, cabled, and discussed his application, Ma continued in his efforts on behalf of the Communist party. At times, this meant returning to Yan'an for consultation and further liaison work with Americans.

Flights to and from Yan'an were frequent, since U.S. military transports made regular runs to the Communist party headquarters. On July 31, 1946, Ma returned on one of these flights in the company of the American radical and writer Anna Louise Strong, already over sixty and desperate to be part of this Chinese revolution. A recent participant in the Soviet Union's experiment, she saw something even greater in China.

Strong's presence in Yan'an was marked by a singular event, the interview she received from Chairman Mao soon after she arrived. In it, Mao laid out the Chinese Communist party's policy for dealing with imperialists, primarily the United States, after the explosion of the nuclear bombs over Japan. Accompanied by Ma and a Chinese interpreter, Strong walked to Mao's cave, where she was introduced to the chairman. The ensuing discussion may have provided Ma with the opportunity to make his most important contribution ever as an interpreter in China, for he helped turn a phrase that gained Chairman Mao international notoriety in the coming struggle between China and the capitalist world.

As they sat on stools outside the entrance to his home, Strong pumped Mao with questions ranging from land reform to imperialism. When she asked him if the United States could not now turn around and use its nuclear weapons on the Soviet Union, Mao answered that of course they could. But he pointed out that the masses of people in the world would oppose such a move and would resist the United States if it tried such a thing. He then added that American reactionaries were merely a—he searched for a word—*chih lao-hu*. The Chinese interpreter told Strong this meant "straw man." Strong asked if he meant "scarecrow." Ma joined the discussion and said, "No, not a *tao ts'ao jen*, but a *chih lao-hu*, a paper tiger." Yes, said Mao, that's it exactly, the United States is like a paper tiger, something that looks like a real and dangerous beast, and scares children, but in fact is harmless. "All reactionaries are paper tigers," Mao said. "Terrible to look at, but melting when the rains come."[11] In years to come, millions of Chinese children would learn to recite the chairman's interview with Anna Louise Strong in which he labels reactionaries paper tigers. And revolutionaries throughout the world recalled the "paper tiger" interview to gain strength in their struggles.

Ma continued to shuttle between Yan'an and Beijing, staying for extended periods in Yan'an when he was needed for liaison work and angling for as much medical support as he could get from international agencies when visiting Beijing. Much of his time in Yan'an was spent with Strong, who grew dependent on his personal and medical attention, a dependency that would last for decades. He accompanied her to evening dances, massaging her old, aching legs after each event. He looked after her social calender, joining her occasionally for a game of cards. The most memorable evening was spent with Zhou Enlai and the newly arrived American, Sydney Rittenberg, when Ma and Zhou defeated the other two Americans in a round of bridge.[12]

Strong was only part of the community Ma associated with during these final days in Yan'an. Wang Guangmei, who had left Beijing in November 1946, moved in next door to Ma and Su Fei when she settled into Yan'an. She remembers how the two of them "took care of me" after her arrival. "I was assigned to the middle level canteen, which was for intellectuals. There was a higher level, which Ma and Su Fei used. They had me over to dinner quite often, and the food was good. Su Fei told me that Ma had the same privileges as Chairman Mao. I was impressed that he was held in such high regard."[13]

Ma continued to associate with the remaining members of the American observation team, who joined Strong, Wang Guangmei, reporter John Roderick, Rittenberg, and others for the films frequently shown at the foreigners' compound. Ma's relationship with Rittenberg, which turned bitter in the years after the Communist victory in China, was at that time cordial. Rittenberg says that on one occasion Su Fei even acted as a go-between for him and Wang Guangmei, inviting them both to dinner one evening with the hope they would strike up a relationship. Nothing came of it, but the meeting would later harm each of them as political movements in post-liberation China took aim at both Rittenberg and Wang, who was by then the wife of Liu Shaoqi. Rittenberg says that when he recounted this episode, including Ma and Su Fei's role, while under interrogation during the Cultural Revolution, he was accused of running a spy ring with the help of Wang Guangmei.[14]

By the fall of 1946 it was clear that the three-sided negotiations were in trouble. As early as June, fighting between the Nationalists and the Communists erupted in the central plains of Jiangsu Province. By August, full-scale fighting was underway in Henan Province, with tens of thousands killed and wounded. Whatever hope the Communists had that Chiang Kai-shek could be held in check while negotiations were under way evaporated by the time Mao granted Strong his "paper tiger" interview. In October, Chiang established a National Assembly to draw up a constitution for the "Republic of China," with Chiang named president. He felt confident, after the millions of dollars in aid and equipment he had received, that the United States would support him. The Communists also drew the same conclusion. By November, Zhou Enlai left the negotiations in Nanjing and returned to Yan'an, telling foreign reporters before he left that the Nationalists and their American supporters would see defeat in the civil war then underway.[15]

By January 1947, General Marshall and President Truman gave up their goal of mediating peace in China. Civil war raged throughout the country, and the United States by this time saw greater security interests in Europe than in Asia. Enough time and money had been spent in China with nothing to show for it. When Marshall left, he attacked both the Nationalists and the Communists for insincerity in negotiations. Despite continued American support for Chiang, the fight in China was just between the Chinese for the first time in over a century. Both parties raced to see who would control the country.[16]

By the end of January, the civil war encroached on Yan'an, with massive numbers of Nationalist troops moving closer by the day. A decision was made to evacuate the area and move into the countryside, where the Communists would continue their fight. As Anna Louise Strong looked on, the move began. Ma, back from Beijing, worked with the hospital staff to move the sick, the wounded, and infants out of Yan'an. It was quite a sight, as a line of donkeys equipped with cribs on either side full of newborn and ill infants headed away from the hospital. Following them were stretcher bearers carrying scores of sick and wounded adults.

In only a few days, the caves that had been full of 180 patients stood empty.[17]

Since the entire Chinese community in Yan'an was being evacuated, the few foreigners living there wanted to move with them. Besides Ma, who was considered part of the Chinese contingent, Strong, Rittenberg, and Sid Engst, another recent arrival, asked to accompany the Party into the hills and countryside. Strong was of particular concern to the leadership. Her health could barely stand up to the harsh winters in Yan'an, where she had certain privileges. She certainly could not handle the hardships of the move. Besides, Mao wanted her to return to Beijing so she could get the word out about the Communist position, especially to expound on his "paper tiger" thesis. But she insisted on staying. They decided to force her to go, but to do it gently, and Ma was assigned the task. One evening in February, Mao, Zhu De, and Zhou Enlai invited the four Americans to dinner. After dinner Zhou and Mao left, leaving Zhu De to tell the Americans what the Party planned for them. He told Rittenberg and Engst they could stay and join the evacuation, while Anna Louise would have to return to Beijing. He told her that Ma had business to attend to in Beijing and would accompany her there. On February 17, 1947, the two of them flew to Beijing, where Ma stayed only for a few days while Strong moved on to Shanghai. He returned before the end of the month with his comrades assigned to the Executive Headquarters. Negotiations had broken down completely, and there was nothing else for them to do in Beijing.[18]

Ironically, after he returned, Ma's old nemesis Kang Sheng placed more damaging material in his Party file, questioning what information the harmful Ma may have purposefully transmitted to his American friends while in Beijing.[19] At the same time the U.S. government was questioning Ma's political leanings and preventing him from reuniting with his family, an influential leader in the Communist party still thought of him as a possible spy for the Americans. It was a predicament he would face throughout the rest of his life.

Back in Yan'an, Ma joined the evacuation effort once again. All of the wounded had not yet left, and he spent most of his time with them. He also found time to take care of a few last-minute liaison matters, but it was obvious this role was drawing to a close. The American observation group was on its way out, and he met with them as they prepared to leave. Only days after he returned he received cigarettes and a letter from Anna Louise Strong and her nephew Robbins. Ma wrote back immediately. It would be his last letter out of the liberated area for some time.

March 5, 1947
Dear Anna Louise,
Dear Robbins,

  Thanks for the trouble of writing me such a nice long letter and the gift you sent, both are highly appreciated. Things are moving fast, Yanan is again in a tense atmosphere and more evacuation is going on. This may be the last batch of letter for some time but all feel that it is temporary. Anna Louise, just the other morning Mrs. Mao came to see us and was talking about you with fondness. She says as soon as things quiet down you must come here again and stay permanently. All the comrades here have you always in mind and constantly mention you.

  Robbins: I know you have the good of the Chinese people at heart and that we both approach the problem from different angles maybe, but I am positive that this side of China—its progressive & Democratic side—i.e. the majority of the Chinese people—are bound to win out in the end and make their contribution to what we like to lightly call Human Civilization.
The best to both of you.
Salute!
Ma Hai Teh[20]

Once, during a break from the activity, Ma and Su Fei took a walk along the river bank and ran into Chairman Mao and his bodyguard, also enjoying time away from the frantic activity of the evacuation. They sat together and talked for a while, with Ma eager to hear Mao's plans. He was especially curious about the movements of Chiang Kai-shek. Mao explained that it was obvious Chiang planned to take over the northeast part of China, especially Harbin and other cities. "If he sends one million soldiers to occupy 100 cities, it makes it easier for us to wipe him out," Mao explained. "Then his other two million troops will be spread out all over China and he won't have a home base. That means he is going to be defeated. He won't have time to save himself."[21]

  In early March, the remaining members of the American observation team flew out of Yan'an, closing that chapter in U.S.–China relations and effectively excluding Ma from any further contact with the United States, including his family, for years to come. As if to mark the event in their minds, Ma, Su Fei, and their comrades in Yan'an looked to the sky on the afternoon the Americans departed and saw U.S.-made bombers flown by Nationalist pilots circling overhead.[22]

  On March 13, Chiang ordered over two hundred thousand troops to attack Shaanxi from the south, the west, and the north. They headed for Yan'an. On March 18, the Party Central Committee decided that all military and Party operations would vacate Yan'an and move to the northern part of the province to continue the fighting. Ma spent his time at the hospital, removing the last of the wounded and packing up as many crates of medical supplies as possible. He and Su Fei were in one of the last groups to leave. Ma marched at the head of the column with the company commander. Su Fei rode a donkey in the middle of the pack. A basket on each side of the donkey carried a child. One held Youma, the other held Yang Xiaoer, son of Yang Shangkun. Their greatest fear was for the safety of the children, especially when Nationalist airplanes dropped bombs on them soon after they crossed the Yellow River.[23]

Their destination was Lin County, in northern Shaanxi. Ma and Su Fei were assigned to live in Shuangta village in Sanjiao township. The Central Committee picked this location as the central headquarters for the reorganization of the foreign ministry. Ye Jianying, Yang Shangkun, Wang Bingnan, Ling Qing, and other leaders relocated there as well. Su Fei was assigned to work with Li Bozhao, wife of Yang Shangkun, implementing land reform in the countryside. Ma found himself doing full-time foreign affairs work while taking care of Youma.[24]

The Party used the evacuation to its advantage by pulling together in one location all who had worked in foreign affairs over the past several years. In this way, they laid the foundation for the future foreign ministry of a liberated China. Ye Jianying headed this new organization, with Wang Bingnan acting as deputy chief. The new foreign ministry set up three sections: the information section, which listened to foreign news broadcasts; the translation section, which spent most of its time translating Chairman Mao's talks into English; and a research section. Ma split his time between the information section, where he listened to foreign news reports, and the translation section, where he polished the English in the translations of Chairman Mao's works. It was a time of intense work and political education. Mao, Zhou Enlai, Zhu De, and other leaders gave frequent talks to this group, stressing the importance of correctly understanding and handling foreign affairs work for the future unified, liberated China. In one talk, Mao told them they should be ready to put into place a new Chinese Foreign Affairs Ministry in 1951, when he predicted they would gain final victory. Ma accepted his new responsibilities as any good Party member would and excelled in his work. Ling Qing remembers fondly the time that he and his Chinese comrades were so impressed with Ma's effort while they lived in Lin County that they voted him the "Model Party Member" of their study group.[25]

By late 1947, the force that was now called the Chinese People's Liberation Army (PLA) had gained victories in several important battles. The most important at the time were victories by the Shaanxi-Hebei-Shandong-Henan Field Army led by Liu Bocheng and Deng Xiaoping. It was decided to move from a defensive to an offensive posture and aggressively take back middle-sized and small cities controlled by the Nationalists. The Communists already held much of the countryside. As this new offensive got underway, and with the optimism stemming from recent Communist victories, Ma, Su Fei and their comrades joined with Ye Jianying's foreign affairs unit and relocated in early 1948 to Xibaipo village in Hebei Province. Mao arrived in May, and the Central Committee here oversaw the final assault to conquer all of China.[26]

Ma was assigned additional duties in Xibaipo. Still assigned to the Foreign Ministry, where he continued to report on foreign radio broadcasts, he now found himself a part-time English teacher preparing young men and women for their future roles as interpreters and officials within the Foreign Ministry. The "Foreign Affairs School" was set up only a few kilometers from Ma's home, and once a week he visited the school to brief the students and staff on foreign affairs. Two who remember his activities well during that period are David and Isabel Crook. They were instructors in this school, which after liberation moved to Beijing and became the Foreign Languages Institute. David hailed from England, whence he had joined the Spanish Civil War and the Communist party, and Isabel was the disillusioned child of Canadian missionaries who rejected her past and now supported the Chinese Communists.

On top of his official work as the school's representative from the Foreign Affairs Ministry, Ma also put to use his influence and expertise as the most experienced foreigner in China's liberation movement. Like other foreigners new to the revolution, the Crooks came to depend on Ma for advice and education. When he first met the pair, Ma was concerned about their poor living condition. While times were tough for everyone, their standard of living was well below what they could have enjoyed if they had merely asked for more help. Even though he worked primarily in foreign affairs, this public health-conscious physician consistently worked to improve hygiene and nutrition. The Crooks seemed to ignore both. The reason was Isabel. She had enjoyed the special privileges of China missionaries her whole life, and rebelled against such treatment when she and David joined the revolution. Ma found her argument "leftist" and told them they could help the revolution more if they took advantage of the few extras offered them, such as a cook and better living quarters. Isabel "carried on quite a struggle" with Ma, and compromised only a little.[27]

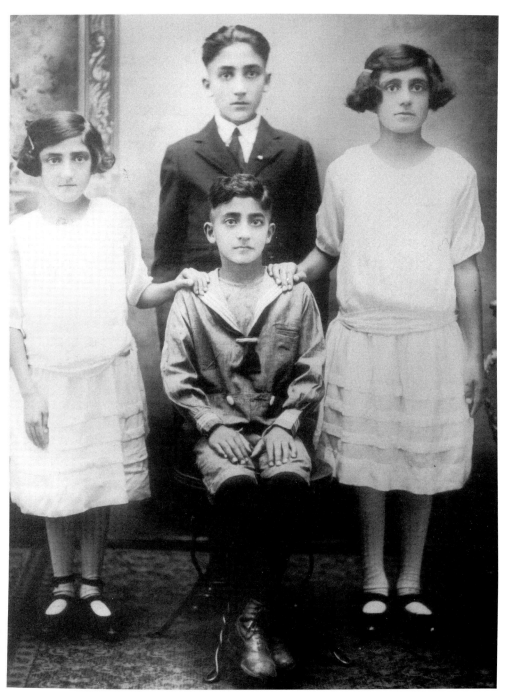

Hatem with his younger brothers and sisters in 1922 (*left to right:* Freda, George, Joseph, and Shafia). (Greg Hatem)

Hatem *(far right, standing)* with classmates at the American University in Beirut, 1930. (Greg Hatem)

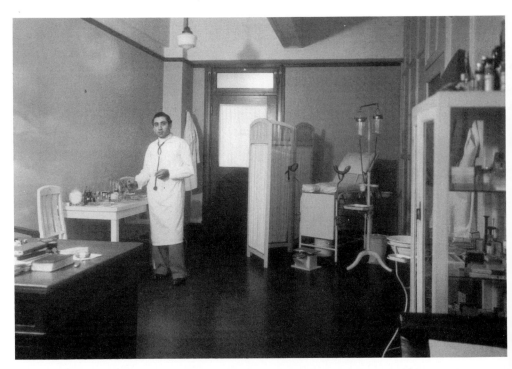

Soon after arriving in Shanghai in 1933, Hatem opened a medical clinic with friends Robert Levinson and Lazer Katz. In addition to practicing medicine here, Hatem offered the clinic a meeting place for the Shanghai Communist underground. He sent this picture to his family in the United States to impress them with his new practice. (Greg Hatem)

Ma stopping by the side of the road to treat a Red Army soldier in China's northwest, 1938. (Edgar Snow Papers, KC: 19/1/9; University of Missouri-Kansas City Archives)

Ma with Chairman Mao in Yan'an, 1945. (Mary Clark Dimond Papers, KC: 19/9/9; University of Missouri-Kansas City Archives)

Wedding picture of Ma and Su Fei, March 1940. The smile from
Su Fei masks the pain she felt from the rejection by her best friends
in Yan'an when she announced she would wed Ma. (Greg Hatem)

Ma greeting Zhou Enlai at the Yan'an airport, 1945. (Mary Clark Dimond
Papers, KC: 19/9/9, UA-KC)

Ma interprets for Ye Jianying at a reception welcoming Col. David Barrett and the Dixie Mission to Yan'an in 1944. Seated around the table are John Colling, Barrett, Zhu De, and Mao Zedong. (Roger Ariyoshi)

Ma Haide with members of the U.S. Army Observers Group (Dixie Mission) in Yan'an, 1945. At far left is Huang Hua, to the right of Ma is Koji Ariyoshi. (Roger Ariyoshi)

In March 1947, Ma Haide helped supervise the evacuation of Yan'an when it was attacked by Nationalist troops following the breakdown of the Marshall talks in Beijing. Here medical supplies are moved by truck and mule on a mountain path east of Yan'an. (China Reconstructs Press)

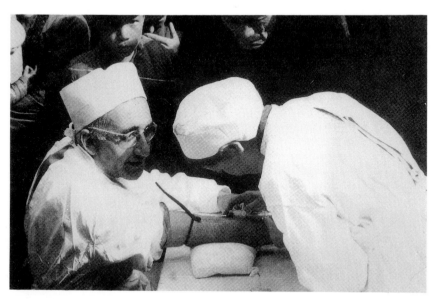

Dr. Ma having blood drawn from his arm in the early 1950s to show skeptical grassland residents that the procedure is harmless. (China Reconstructs Press)

Ma accompanying Edgar Snow to visit Chairman Mao, October 1960.
(Edgar Snow Papers, KC: 19/1/9, UA-KC)

Ma with daughter-in-law Luo Guifu and grandson Ma Jun, 1971.
(Mary Clark Dimond Papers, KC: 19/9/9, UA-KC)

In 1962 Ma traveled to Syria to see his father for the first time in over thirty years. (China Reconstructs Press)

Ma and Anna Louise Strong on vacation at Beidaihe in the early 1960s. In her last years Strong leaned heavily on Ma for both medical and personal support. (Mary Clark Dimond Papers, KC: 19/9/9, UA-KC)

Ma strolling with mentor and best friend Rewi Alley in 1973.
Both men were still under scrutiny at the time by elements in the
Communist party leading the Cultural Revolution. (Mary Clark
Dimond Papers, KC:19/9/9, UA-KC)

Madam Song Qingling hosts Ma to celebrate his sixty-eighth birthday. Also attending are Su Fei and old friend Max Granich. September 1978. (Xinhua News Agency)

Deng Xiaoping toasts Ma in November 1983 at a banquet to celebrate the fiftieth anniversary of Ma's arrival in China. To Ma's right is Deng Yingchao, widow of Zhou Enlai. (Xinhua News Agency)

Ma's family in 1985. At far left is his stepdaughter, Liangbi. To the far right is son, Youma. (Mary Clark Dimond Papers, 19/9/9, UA-KC)

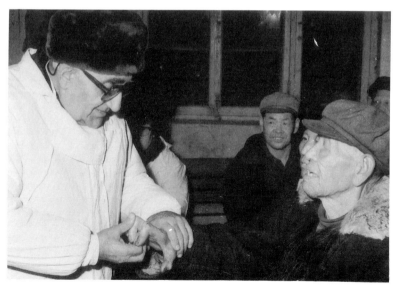

During Spring Festival, 1982, Ma visited the Wangdu Leprosy Hospital in Hebei Province. He made it a point to touch the patients directly, showing other medical workers the limited risk involved. (China Reconstructs Press)

Ma discussing leprosy issues with colleagues at his home shortly before his death in 1988. (China Reconstructs Press)

When the Crooks did manage to ask for special assistance once, Ma was able to help, but not before chastising them once again, this time for failing to understand the revolution they had joined. The struggle focused on a toilet. The Crooks' dining area was only a short distance from the outside toilet, and flies frequented both places. David, impatient with the delay in having the toilet covered, told Ma, "These people take so long to get anything done." Crook then got an earful as Ma lectured him on the history of the Chinese revolution, the hardships it had endured, and the sacrifices that had been required to get to where it was today. "I thought this was completely irrelevant. All I wanted was a covered toilet, not a lecture," Crook recalled. "But then George ended his lecture by saying, 'All of this took 27 years. Is that a long time or a short time?' " These words made an impression on Crook, and he would remember them for a long time. "And we did eventually get a cover for the toilet," he laughed, "probably due to George."[28]

While Ma concentrated on Chinese foreign affairs in Xibaipo, the U.S. intelligence community in China thought it wise to concentrate on him. By now the American government was decidedly opposed to the Communist effort and regarded those who might aid in that cause with growing suspicion. On March 8, 1948, a naval intelligence report on Ma was filed in the American Consulate General's office. Written by the new assistant naval attaché in Beijing who had replaced Ma's friend, Lt. Herbert Hitch, Ma no longer appears as a slightly suspect but friendly American humanitarian. Now he was simply suspect. The report reads in part:

> During the days of the Executive Headquarters in Peiping [Beijing], Dr. Hatem held the position of Medical Advisor to the Communist Branch of that Headquarters. However, personal observation revealed that he was most intimate with the leaders of the Communist Branch and was included in the "official family" of the Communist Commissioner on official parties given by General Yeh Chien-ying. Dr. Hatem was usually careful to avoid political discussions while in Peiping but when the opportunity arose to slip a subtle, favorable word in for the Chinese Communists, he would take advantage of it. It is probable that Dr. Hatem's real job with the Communist Branch, Executive Headquarters, was that of a personal advisor to the Communist Commissioner on relations with Americans.[29]

Although his communication with American officials came to a halt, Ma continued to represent the Communists during the later months of the civil war when the Party sent him, along with Su Fei and Youma, to Shijiazhuang, Hebei Province, to work in the general relief effort on behalf of the liberated areas. In Shijiazhuang, which had recently been taken by the PLA, he served as medical advisor to the Party's office, dealing with U.N. and U.S. Red Cross officials who continued to send food, medicine, bedding, and clothing to the liberated areas. Occasionally, foreign physicians also visited these areas to provide short-term medical assistance. Most of Ma's time was spent trying to get the supplies and personnel around the Nationalist blockade and into the Communist-held areas. Chiang Kai-shek's troops not only threw up roadblocks to the liberated areas, they also threw bullets and attacking airplanes at the Communist relief headquarters. The most frightening episode occurred one day when Ma, away from his living quarters, heard the roar of the planes as they strafed and bombed the area. A young soldier picked up Youma and carried him to an air raid dugout. There the soldier covered the boy with his body, talking to him the whole time to keep him calm. When the attack ended, Ma ran home, only to find a hole in the wall of his apartment house, and an empty room where he had left Youma. He ran to the dugout, where was relieved to find his son unhurt except for a damaged eardrum from the bombing.[30]

Ma returned to Xibaipo. It was now late fall of 1948, and Zhou Enlai gave the foreign affairs staff special instructions to prepare to set up operations on a national scale soon, for they were about to attack and take Tianjin. Beijing would follow soon. Ma was told to assist in the preparation, but he also was told that he would not join the attack on Tianjin.[31] Tianjin fell on January 15, 1949, and within a week the Nationalist army commander in Beijing signed a peace agreement with the PLA. On January 31, PLA troops entered Beijing. By the end of February, Party leaders, surprising even themselves with the swiftness of their victories, entered the outskirts of Beijing and prepared to set up the new government. Ma Haide quickly left Xibaipo with Ye Jianying, accompanying him to his new headquarters in the Summer Palace. He took Youma with him, but Su Fei stayed outside Beijing with her theater group, preparing for their upcoming performances in celebration of China's liberation.[32]

Peiping [Beijing] fell to the Communists today—quietly, politely, and in accordance with her traditions—a feat possible only in China. The Nationalists are bowing their way out while the Communists bow their way in.

New York Times, January 23, 1949

Senator William F. Knowland, Republican of California, charged in a speech in the Senate today that Secretary of State Dean Acheson had "pulled the rug out from under" the Chinese Nationalist Government and demanded an investigation by a joint Congressional Committee of United States foreign policy in the Far East. All of Asia might be brought under Communist control unless the Communists were stopped in China, he declared as he submitted a resolution calling for the inquiry.

New York Times, April 22, 1949

After Beijing was liberated, Ma found himself busier than ever. He was assigned to work with Su Jingguan and Li Dequan to establish new China's Ministry of Public Health. They spent their first few days preparing the takeover and administration of the city's hospitals. It had already been decided that Li would act as minister, with Su assigned deputy minister. But there were celebrations and festivities to enjoy before they settled into their new positions. On February 3, 1949, the PLA held a victory parade, throwing open the gates of the city and marching through Beijing. Ma traveled in from the Summer Palace to watch from the podium of Qianmen Gate. Isabel Crook, pregnant and just entering Beijing by truck, stood below on the street and saw Ma standing on the parapet with Ye Jianying, Nie Rongzhen, Lin Biao, and others, reviewing the soldiers as they passed by. Ma motioned to Isabel to join him, and for six hours they watched the procession. Isabel's clearest memory of that day was the proud contingent of Mongolian horsemen decked out in spectacular colors.[1] Ma's most vivid memory was the PLA's equipment: captured American supplies, uniforms, transport, and weapons. "We were every inch American," he enjoyed telling his fellow countrymen years later.[2]

After the ceremony, those on the review stand withdrew to a restaurant just behind Qianmen Gate well known for its Beijing duck, where they continued the celebration. Isabel sat with Ma. During the dinner this teetotaling pregnant daughter of Methodist missionaries was toasted by General Nie as he rounded the tables. Because she was pregnant, Isabel refused the toast. This was a mistake, and she once again found herself lectured by Ma. "George told me that General Nie and I were both from Sichuan and it was impolite not to return his toast."[3]

On March 25, Mao Zedong, Zhou Enlai, Zhu De, Liu Shaoqi, and other leaders of the Party arrived in Beijing by train. That afternoon Ma accompanied the leaders to a massive ceremony that included another parade, this one led by Mao, Zhou, Zhu De, and others riding in open cars and jeeps through the city. As gongs and drums sounded and flags waved throughout the city, Ma joined in the celebration as a common citizen on the street. He joined in the chants and slogans: "Long live the Chinese Communist party," "Long live the Chinese People's Communist party," and "Long live Chairman Mao." He could do this with ease and conviction, for the slogans summed up his feelings well. The tears that came to his eyes that day also were understandable. He had worked with these men for thirteen years toward a common goal. They now found themselves on the verge of total victory. By May 1950 the victory was complete. Chiang Kai-shek had fled to his island fortress of Taiwan.[4] Now a new task lay before them, building a new China.

In the aftermath of the celebration, Ma moved into temporary quarters with Youma, a bodyguard, and cook. The new home sat on the second floor of a restaurant run by a German family. Within a few weeks the old Ministry of Public Health was taken over by the new masters of China, and Ma found himself assigned to the position of advisor to the ministry. He was allotted a large Japanese-style house that had previously been the home of a senior Nationalist leader. He stayed there for several months, but requested different quarters closer to the Ministry of Public Health. Soon, the ministry purchased him a traditional Qing dynasty home fronting Hohai Lake. Although it needed repair, Ma accepted it gladly. Not only was it just a two-minute walk from the ministry, it also was within walking distance of the home assigned to his old friend and mentor, Madame Song Qingling. With so many people fleeing Beijing, it was a good time to find a home there. Ma would live in this elegant house the rest of his life.[5]

Ma had entered Beijing with the victors. In all matters except ethnicity he felt himself Chinese. But there was one piece missing, and he wanted it put into place. Zhou Enlai had promised him in 1937 that after the country was liberated, Ma would become the first foreigner allowed Chinese citizenship. In September 1949, just days before Chairman Mao's official declaration on October 1 that "the Chinese people have stood up," Zhou, now premier of the country, fulfilled his promise and granted Ma Chinese citizenship. He was the first foreigner to gain this status in the People's Republic.[6]

As he settled into Beijing, Ma occasionally ran into foreigners he had known and worked closely with in Yan'an. Many, including military personnel, remained in China for months after liberation. Now times had changed, and Ma no longer served as the Party's official liaison officer. He had no reason to socialize or converse with them, and, true to his well-established record of keeping far away from political controversy, he avoided most of his old foreign contacts and barely conversed with those he could not avoid. Among these former contacts were journalists he had befriended in Yan'an, some of whom he now walked past without a word, and old Dixie Mission representatives he had practically lived with only a short time before. David Barrett remembers his surprise at Ma's behavior when the two met on the streets of Beijing in 1949. "He was courteous and friendly, but seemed visibly nervous about conversing in public with an American."[7]

Even with foreign friends of the revolution he was not always welcoming. Ruth Weiss, who had known him in the Shanghai underground in the 1930s, returned to China in 1949 to see if she wanted to bring her family back to live there. She was working in New York with the United Nations at the time. When she met Ma, she told him she might bring her children back, but that her Chinese husband had no interest in returning. Weiss recalls that Ma was no longer the gregarious "Shag" she remembered. He was all business, and not at all supportive of her return. "He asked me about my plans, why I wanted to come back with the children alone. Then he told me that he expected I would not come back, that I did not have enough courage to make such a move." Weiss never forgave him for this, she says, even though after she returned with the children in 1951 he explained his remarks as an attempt to "encourage" her.[8] Ma clearly saw his role in post-liberation China as the educator and defender of the Chinese revolution to the foreign community. In some ways this only continued the work he had begun officially in Yan'an when he worked in the liaison office. Now, although he was not officially assigned that role, he relished it. Besides, he could not avoid it. He was a Party member and a Chinese citizen. He felt it his responsibility, or as many Chinese would say, his "duty" to educate and lead the foreign community in China.

On the domestic side of his bicultural life, he threw himself into his work with the Ministry of Public Health and the well-being of his Chinese family. It was obvious early on that his new position would lead him away from his previous work as personal physician to the leadership. One acquaintance from those early years states this reality rather bluntly. "Ma no longer served as personal physician to the leaders. His status changed due to the new bureaucracy. In Beijing one could find Rocke-feller Hospital–trained doctors and other Western-trained doctors who took over for him. Let's be frank, if I'm living up in the hills and sud-denly this doctor from the middle east comes up and there weren't any other doctors there, and I make him my chief physician, then I go to Peking and I've got the pick of doctors in the whole country, am I really going to keep on with this chap?"[9]

It was obvious from the beginning that the medical needs of post-liberation China would be addressed through mass mobilization. While the beginnings of such a strategy had been tested in Yan'an, the stakes were now much higher. But so were the possible rewards, for now the scope of the campaign was the whole country rather than scattered parts of it.

The first activity Ma threw himself into was one he relished, the erad-ication of prostitution in Beijing. On November 21, 1949, Ma attended a meeting of the Beijing People's Congress in Zhongshan Park. Late that afternoon the Congress approved a declaration sponsored by the Munic-ipal Womens' Committee to close down all of Beijing's brothels. A "Committee on Handling Prostitutes" was set up to lead the campaign. This effort began immediately, under the joint leadership of the Munici-pal Public Security Bureau, the Bureau of Civil Administration, the Womens' Association, the Bureau of Public Health, and the People's Court. After the meeting, Ma returned home, had dinner, and told Su Fei that someone would arrive shortly to pick him up, that he had a spe-cial assignment that night. He did not tell her where he was going. He soon left and, with others throughout the city, helped close down 224 Beijing brothels in twelve hours. The prostitutes were assigned to the Women's Production and Education Quarters, where they received edu-cation and medical treatment. Ma and over fifty other physicians from various hospitals and clinics were assigned to treat and study these women. They found that 98 percent carried one or more strains of vene-real disease. It was decided to give them massive doses of penicillin over a period of ten days. In all, over thirteen thousand injections were ordered. The results were encouraging, and within six months most of the women were free of disease. This experience was personally gratifying to Ma, for he now saw that his decision to join with the Communist party in fact allowed him to help rid China of the ills he had witnessed in Shanghai. But it also was gratifying professionally. This method of curing the prostitutes of venereal disease, using enormous amounts of penicillin over a short period, was innovative and held promise for other parts of China.[10] It also showed this American steeped in the tradition of Western ideals how a program of coerced medical treatment carried out for the general good could override concern for individual rights. China, he learned, could attack its medical problems correctly only if done "en masse." Considering the huge problems China faced in the public health arena, this approach appealed to him, and he would defend it for the rest of his life.[11]

The early years of new China were frantic with this kind of activity. Jack Chen, who returned to live in Beijing in 1950, remembers seeing little of Ma during the early 1950s. "He was very busy, like all of us. There was so much to do. A government that had been running a village was now running a country."[12] After such success with the prostitution campaign, Ma, in his capacity as advisor to the Ministry of Public Health, recommended setting up an institute for the study and eradication of skin and venereal diseases. He wanted this institute to concentrate on venereal diseases and leprosy, which he had first encountered in Yan'an. Nothing immediate came of his suggestion, but he continued to advocate it for the next few years. Gerald Tannenbaum, an American Madame Song had recruited as her personal secretary in the newly formed China Welfare Society, often saw Ma in meetings with government officials as they tried to iron out new public health policies. Several of these meetings were led by Zhou Enlai, the new premier to whom all ministers reported. In meetings at this level, Ma knew his role was that of advisor and not leader. "He never acted as a spokesman for the ministry. He was there as an advisor and there were other Chinese officials who were spokesmen for the Health Ministry," Tannenbaum recounts.[13] Within the ministry some confusion arose over exactly how Ma should be treated. When a foreign experts office was established, they raised his salary to match that of other foreigners in China. Ma reacted angrily, telling his Chinese colleagues that just because he had a big nose was no reason to treat him differently from other Chinese citizens. He refused the pay increase.[14]

Ma may have been a Chinese citizen and a tried and tested Party member, but to the Chinese he was still a foreigner. One Canadian Chinese friend who moved next door to Ma in late 1950 says that all of the foreigners were isolated from the mainstream Communist party culture, but Ma was less so than others. This does not mean he was all the way in, however. "Ma was one of the few who was rather fully accepted, but not totally. The average person would not pick up his not being totally accepted unless he knew about China and about the West. It was part of a cultural pattern of the Communist party and the Chinese people to look a bit askance at foreigners [like Ma] even though he contributed a lot and attempted to integrate."[15] And, despite the obvious appreciation high leaders showed for his contributions, unresolved questions remained about his loyalty, questions of the kind that Kang Sheng had placed in his Party file. Advisor was the highest rank he would ever reach in the ministry.

In meetings with Premier Zhou after liberation, it was clear that while Zhou understood Ma's limitations as a foreigner, he also treated Ma as a comrade, not as a foreign guest. At times, in rare informal settings, he relaxed and joked in his discussions with Ma.[16] But usually he was more strict. Zhou was known by his subordinates as a driven taskmaster, impatient with poor work habits, inattention to detail, and lapses in protocol. Unlike his warm and relaxed manner among foreign guests and in the popular perceptions of many Chinese, Zhou often showed his temper, and all who reported to him feared the premier's criticism.[17] It was not unusual in formal settings to see Zhou take aim at Ma. Gerald Tannenbaum, who attended several meetings with the two of them, says, "I couldn't get any feeling of warmth in their relationship at all. In fact, just the opposite. There was a certain chill that grew in the atmosphere when George and Zhou Enlai got close to one another. Zhou, who was known to have a temper to begin with, was not beyond ordering George to do this or do that in front of a whole crowd of people. It was a little embarrassing, to tell you the truth. Here is one example. I went to see Zhou Enlai in 1950, in July, and he gave a banquet for me and several other foreigners, and then after the banquet we were collected outside to have a picture taken, and I being rather the tallest person in the group stood all the way in the back, figuring that is where I should be so I wouldn't get in the way of anybody else. Ma placed himself next to Zhou Enlai, so Zhou turns around and said, 'Where is Tannenbaum?' So I said 'I am back here.' So he said to Ma [and me], 'You go back there, you come here.' Just like that. I was kind of shocked, but I moved. I think that Zhou considered him one of the people, one of the comrades and therefore if he did something wrong, or it was something he had against him he would not hesitate to criticize him openly and directly. That can be an indication of acceptability. . . . If you were not a member of the Party and therefore accepted, Zhou would not have acted that way."[18]

Ma helped set up clinics throughout the city to receive patients suffering from skin diseases. In his clinic at Capital Hospital he split his time between seeing patients and tinkering in the pharmacy, where he experimented with mixing new lotions to treat these illnesses. His foreign looks frightened many of his patients, especially the children, so he began taking small toys to the office to counter their fears. Later he found out he would be better accepted if he passed himself off as a member of the Muslim minority from Xinjiang, an Islamic autonomous region in northwest China. Thereafter he frequently took to wearing the traditional Xinjiang skull cap when traveling on buses or trains. When asked where he was from, he answered he was a Chinese citizen from the Xinjiang region. "It really worked and saved him a lot of trouble," recounts Su Fei.[19]

Once again we see Ma's chameleon nature. He made one of his first major contributions to the revolution by passing himself off as an Arab-speaking follower of Islam. Later, among representatives of the U.S. government, he became a typical American. Now, in order to bridge the gap with common Chinese, he took on the guise of a member of one of China's minorities from the far northwest.

While those who spent years together in caves fighting for the revolution now saw little of each other as they took on their own special roles in constructing a new China, there were occasions in the early 1950s to get together and reminisce about those days. Ma and Su Fei, for example, dined frequently with old friends such as Wang Bingnan and his wife. They also met Chairman Mao from time to time in the years just after liberation. The first time was in mid-1950 when Ma received a phone call at home from the minister of public health. Chairman Mao asked that Ma and his family join him that evening for supper and dancing at Zhongnanhai, the new headquarters of the Party Central Committee adjacent to the Forbidden City. At dusk a large black car arrived to pick up the family and take them to the chairman's home. Meeting them at the door, Mao welcomed Ma as China's newest son-in-law. "Now, since you are a Chinese citizen, you are an absolute Chinese," the chairman told him. Remembering Youma from Yan'an, Mao reached out to hold the young boy, only to see him scurry away, hiding his face in Mao's large sofa. Mao joked with the boy, asking him if he, with his father's big nose, was afraid of Mao with his small nose. The evening ended with a dance, during which Jiang Qing joined the party and Su Fei danced with both the chairman and his son, Mao Anying. The next year, in 1951, Ma and Su Fei were again asked to join Mao for an evening. That would be the last time both would visit socially with Mao, although Ma saw him several other times over the next decades in the company of Edgar Snow and other foreigners.[20]

While Ma's life was exciting and meaningful during the early 1950s, all was not comfortable, either personally or politically. In fact, it was an unbalanced and difficult period in his life as he tried to adjust to the city and all it offered. One thing it offered was frequent and informal contact with foreigners, the first since he had left Shanghai. One old friend relates that Ma was "schizophrenic" during those years. His work and his family were in an almost completely Chinese setting, while his social life was spent almost totally with foreign friends of the revolution. Israel Epstein argues, "He was starved for foreign life at that time and especially enjoyed being with the leftists in town—not with the foreign teachers still at Yenjing."

While he always played the role of senior foreign revolutionary, now he could relax with foreigners who supported and admired the cause he defended. Most of these were American and European Marxists who enjoyed his war stories and knew of his high standing with the leadership. To them he was the closest to an authority on the revolution they could find. Among those he saw regularly during the early 1950s were the British Communist party members Alan Winnington, Nan Green, and Michael Shapiro, and the Americans Sidney Shapiro and Bill Hinton. After Israel Epstein returned from the United States in 1951, he also joined the crowd. Other friends, such as Hans Muller and Rewi Alley, were not yet living in Beijing, although Alley joined the group when he returned in 1953.

Epstein remembers Ma during this period as "a gay lad." He loved to dance and often joined in the parties held at the International Club in the old legation quarters. He also enjoyed going to "the Dump," the irreverent name the foreigners gave to an old run-down beer hall not far from the Beijing Hotel. His frequent companions included Sydney Shapiro, Hinton, and Winnington, all of whom enjoyed not only the beer, but also the Western food served there.[21] Shapiro says, "George did much to broaden my cultural and political base in those enlightening evenings at The Dump, while the beer and steak and potatoes did the same for my waistline."[22] This restaurant and another dubbed "the Mutton Joint" were the traditional gathering spots in those early years where the few English-speaking foreigners capped off political and national celebrations such as May Day, National Day, and Spring Festival. After the parades and speeches, Ma and the other foreigners relished eating what passed for Southern-style barbecue, hot dogs, suckling pig, and potato chips, topped with mustard and ketchup. After the meals, Ma organized songfests of old American favorites such as "Clementine" and "Oh, Susanna." As Rewi Alley commented, Ma was "as American as apple pie" when he was among his fellow Westerners.23

Su Fei rarely, if ever, joined in these gatherings. There were many reasons for this. For one thing, the foreigners spent almost the whole of such evenings speaking entirely in English. Besides, Su Fei now had the opportunity to explore her own career in theater and cinema. She was gone from Beijing for long periods of time working on films, and even in the city she was constantly away from the house working on theatrical or film productions. She naturally socialized with other members of the arts community, many of whom she knew from her days in Yan'an. According to numerous acquaintances, during this period she and Ma went through a period of personal estrangement that lasted for several years, as each gravitated to different social circles and worked in very different and demanding professions that took one or the other out of Beijing for long periods of time. Rumors of their marital problems circulated within the foreign community, and also at the highest government levels. Old stories were dragged up about Ma's relationship with Li Lilian, Otto Braun's wife in Yan'an, as was the story that Su Fei was coerced into marrying Ma and now wanted to be free of him. After liberation there was an upsurge in divorces, as couples moved from the countryside into the cities to begin new lives. Although there is no evidence that Ma and Su Fei seriously contemplated such a move, it is clear that Ma once again discovered a love for Western-style partying. Whether he enjoyed the company of other women is not clear, although many gossiped about it. High Party officials noted with disapproval the rumors about his personal life and his socializing in the foreign community. He was now perhaps a bit too "American as apple pie" for some of his old comrades.

Su Fei also was the target of criticism, as rumors circulated about her spending too much time with the well-known cinema personality Ling Zifeng and his close friends. Whatever the exact nature of the problems between Ma and Su Fei, three conclusions are clear. First, the sweeping accusations fostered by an ever-active Chinese rumor mill must be viewed with some skepticism. The two had problems as they went their separate professional and personal ways, but neither Ma nor Su Fei ever seriously sought divorce. Second, by the early 1960s, and probably before, Ma and Su Fei had reconciled whatever differences they had, enjoying thereafter an enviable relationship until his death. Friends say they reconciled in part at the insistence of Zhou Enlai's wife, Deng Yingchao. One visitor to their home during this period remembers Deng lecturing them on the proper behavior expected of Party members.

Third, the attention their relationship received from Party leaders did little to lessen the suspicion with which some already viewed Ma. In the end, this became the most important consequence of their difficulties.[24]

So, during the early 1950s, Ma encountered two obstacles to his future. One was the lingering, though now unstated, suspicions about his political reliability that dated from the Rectification Campaign. The second was the concern over his personal behavior and his tendency to enjoy the company of foreigners a bit too much while spending too little time at home. He would soon encounter yet another obstacle, a serious political one over which he had no control. Like all foreigners in China at that time, Ma would have to struggle to find a proper place in the growing international socialist movement, a movement led by the Soviet Union and now strongly supported by China. This relationship was solidified after Mao visited the Soviet Union and affirmed that China would "lean to one side" in world events, meaning, of course, it would support the Soviet Union in international affairs.[25] What did this mean for foreigners hailing from countries hostile to the Soviet Union? Where would an American living in China fit into this scheme?

A foretaste of the problems to come arose just as Beijing was liberated. Two Americans close to the Chinese Communist party were arrested on spy charges. Ma knew them both quite well. One was Anna Louise Strong, who was arrested by Soviet authorities as an American spy. The other was Sydney Rittenberg, a friend and confidant of Strong's in Yan'an and, like Ma, a member of the Chinese Communist party. Ironically, he also was Ma's fellow alumnus from the University of North Carolina. Chinese Party officials arrested him only days after the Soviets arrested Strong. Both Strong and Rittenberg became pariahs to the international Communist movement; none dared defend them. Yet all foreigners were tainted by knowing them. One foreigner living in Beijing at the time argues that "when Anna Louise Strong was denounced by Stalin, all members of the foreign community were placed under suspicion."[26]

The second threat to Americans living in China came on June 25, 1950, when the Korean War broke out. American troops flooded into Korea, eventually pushing the invading North Korean troops back across the 38th parallel. China responded by sending several hundred thousand troops into Manchuria to stop the American troops well before they reached the Chinese border. China and the United States, allies only five years before, were now enemies in a brutal war that eventually would kill over a million people before a truce ended it in 1953. One of those killed early in the fighting was Mao Zedong's son, Mao Anying, who had been Su Fei's dance partner only months before during the chairman's dinner party that she and Ma had attended.[27]

The outbreak of war with the United States so soon after the arrests of Strong and Rittenberg cast a pall on the other Americans in China. Ma had the additional stigma of Kang Sheng's spy charges already in his file.[28] His response to these threatening events was predictable: He said little, focused on his work, and supported the Chinese government at every turn. He told his foreign friends, and anyone else who would listen, that his role in China was not political, but medical. He worked with other doctors to plan medical strategy and to organize medical teams and supplies for the troops. During the war there was an international outcry and investigation into the possibility that the United States had used germ warfare on Chinese and North Korean troops. Ma met with the British scholar Joseph Needham to investigate this charge during the latter's visit to Beijing, but he never publicly accused the government of his native country of engaging in such activities.[29] In informal meetings, he never attacked the United States, beyond reiterating China's official position, nor, of course, did he ever defend its actions. His only overt political activity was occasionally to join in demonstrations in which he shouted slogans and carried banners in support of the Chinese troops.[30]

As it closed ranks with the international socialist movement, China invited the Soviets to send experts to help build China into a strong socialist state. Between 1950 and 1956 thousands of Soviet experts helped China push forward in industry, communications, city planning, education, the arts, literature, and health.[31] The Chinese deferred to these Soviet experts, calling them their "big brothers," while those foreigners who had offered their services through the difficult years of the revolution found their own contributions depreciated. This was especially true when it came to Americans. Israel Epstein recalls that all of the old foreigners were "put on the shelf.... The Soviets, thought to be experienced in everything, would not have looked kindly on an American doctor leading anything."[32] Gerald Tannenbaum says that all foreigners, "especially Americans, suffered from being shoved aside temporarily. As for George, the Soviets would come and just elbow him aside."[33] Ma responded by concentrating on his medical assignments. He conducted experiments in his lab at the Ministry of Public Health, treating a roomful of rabbits with experimental drugs to cure skin diseases. He also began an activity that would turn into a lifelong endeavor. "His response to being shoved aside was to go deeper into the countryside to carry out projects that were important to him and the Ministry of Health. . . . That is really the way he avoided confrontation."[34]

While Ma struggled to find his place in a complex new China, the American government sought to place him foursquare in the camp of international communism, its mighty enemy. Intelligence agencies continued to watch him where they could, and former friends and family in the United States felt the heat of that watchful eye. This increased attention came at a time that the U.S. government, after the "loss" of China in 1949, embarked on a widespread search for anyone suspected of supporting communism. A full-fledged Red Scare was on, and it took very little indeed to be suspected of aiding the enemy. It mattered not at all whether one was suspected of aiding the Soviets or the Chinese. To the U.S. government, the two represented equal evils. Besides, many thought China now marched to the orders of its northern neighbor anyway. It was galling that all those years of helping China were rewarded with such evil returns.

Sensational arrests and charges set the tone. In 1949, a former State Department official named Alger Hiss was accused of spying for the Soviet Union. In the summer of 1950, the FBI arrested Julius and Ethel Rosenberg on charges of secretly passing on to the Soviets vital information needed to construct an atomic bomb. Throughout their trial, both the prosecution and the judge commented on how this treason had strengthened both the Soviets and the Chinese. The Rosenbergs were executed three years later.

As hysteria mounted, Senator Joseph McCarthy began a sweeping tirade against supposed Communists and Communist sympathizers working for the U.S. government. Among his targets were the U.S. representatives in China during World War II, especially those who had criticized the corruption of the Nationalists and encouraged the United States to support the Communist war efforts. McCarthy accused them of disloyalty, some even of treason. He labeled them "individuals who are loyal to the ideal and designs of Communism rather than those of the free, God-fearing half of the world. . . . I refer to the Far Eastern Division of the State Department and the Voice of America."[35]

Many of those now under attack were Ma's acquaintances from the Yan'an days. Former members of the Dixie Mission were criticized for "consorting" with known Communists. By 1952, John Service, John Davies, and others staffing the State Department's China desk had been dismissed from the foreign service. David Barrett's military career also was checked by this cloud of suspicion, and he never received the promotion to general that he and others had expected. The hunt for spies and Communist sympathizers lasted for years, poisoning U.S.–China relations until Richard Nixon's visit to China in 1971.[36]

In the spring of 1950, Ma's brother Joe, who had only recently been visited by the FBI, received another scare. His name was brought up at hearings before the Tydings Committee, a congressional investigation of State Department personnel that preceded McCarthy's more famous hearings. During the investigation, John Service's personal address book had been confiscated and admitted in full into the official record. Among the dozens of names listed was "Hatem, Cpl. J.N.: 1385 Service Unit, McGuire General Hospital, Richmond 19, Va." This was the address where Service had found Joe when he brought Ma's letter back to the United States. Ma's earlier worry that his affiliation with China's revolution could hurt his family now bore fruit. Slight as the mention was, Joe and his family came under suspicion. During this period Joe and his family "felt watched," reports Joe's son, Greg.

Ma himself was investigated and labeled during these hearings. His name was first brought forward by John Emmerson, the same John Emmerson who in 1946 had evaluated Ma's potential status as a security risk should he return to the United States. Emmerson was questioned by a congressional investigator.

> *Mr. Sourwine:* Were there any communists from other countries there [in Yanan], as far as you know?
> *Mr. Emmerson:* There was a Russian doctor.
> *Mr. Sourwine:* What was his name, do you know?
> *Mr. Emmerson:* I cannot remember his name.
> *Mr. Sourwine:* Any others?
> *Mr. Emmerson:* I do not believe there were any others. There was a George Hatem. He was there. He is not the one I am speaking of; he is not a Russian.
> *Mr. Sourwine:* Where is he from?
> *Mr. Emmerson:* Mr. Hatem is an American, I believe, who lived many years with the Chinese Communists.[37]

Later during the same testimony, Emmerson received a list of 116 names from Sourwine.

> *Mr. Sourwine:* I will show you, sir, a list of individuals who have been active in the Far East and who have come to the attention of the Internal Security Subcommittee in one way or another. . . . We are

interested in securing as much information as possible regarding the subversive activities, if any, in which any of these individuals may have been involved. And, to you, as an experienced Far Eastern Foreign Service officer, we come for any information you may have.

Emmerson proceeded to acknowledge once again that he knew "Dr. H. Hatem," whose name appears on the list. The testimony then continues with Sourwine reading to Emmerson the names of all those he said he knew. He then tells Emmerson that if he reads the name of someone he "knew to be a Communist or knew as a Communist, . . . or if you think they were pro-communist" stop him and explain. When Sourwine reached Hatem's name, Emmerson responded,

> Well, Hatem was considered a Communist because he had been with the Chinese Communists so long that he dressed like them and was almost identified as one of them.[38]

Ma had now for the first time in public been labeled a Communist, and by implication an enemy, by compatriots in his homeland. And his brother's name appeared alongside others so labeled in John Service's address book. What type of response to these charges and suspicions could this family running a small retail store in rural North Carolina make? It was a painful response, for their oldest son Shafick George had ceased to exist within their community, and even to some degree within the family. Of course, old family friends knew he existed, or at least had existed, but his name was never mentioned. Marie Hatem, who married Joe in 1952, says that as a young girl she remembers the Hatem family having two daughters, but only one son. The first she heard of her brother-in-law was when she visited the Hatem home and saw a high school picture of young Shafick George. "Shag was never talked about," she said, "even though everyone knew he was in China. It was kind of hush-hush. It never was an issue when I went out with Joe. Shag simply did not exist."[39]

Only Joe's mother still mentioned the eldest son, and then only within the family. Marie Hatem remembers, "After I married Joe I'd always go in the kitchen with her and sit and watch her cook. She would tell old stories, and anytime we were alone she would tell me about Shag. She would end *every* conversation with me with, 'I'd like to see my son just one time before I die.' "[40] But that would never happen.

Throughout the early to mid-1950s, U.S. intelligence offices in Tokyo and Hong Kong continued to monitor Ma's activities as much as possible. They did this for the most part by looking for his name in official Chinese publications. Ma's FBI file notes that in 1951 he spoke at a memorial service for two Americans in Beijing. One was Betty Graham, a journalist. The other was his old mentor and sometimes antagonist, Agnes Smedley, who had died in England en route to China. In 1953, the FBI noted that Ma and other foreign residents in Beijing sent a telegram to President Eisenhower urging him to stay the execution of the Rosenbergs. And a memo dated March 3, 1953, from the American consulate general in Hong Kong to the FBI, lists Ma as "an American who might leave China and, because of his pro-communist tendencies, . . . his travel and activities in countries outside the United States might be prejudicial to U.S. interest."[41]

But by 1953, Ma was little concerned with any investigations by any U.S. intelligence agencies. He was more bothered by problems with China's intelligence operatives. Nor did he spend much time thinking about his American family. The best thing he could do for them and for himself during this time of war and mutual recrimination between governments was to ignore them. Just as they ignored him.

During the height of the McCarthy era and the Korean War, there was no communication between the son in China and his family in North Carolina. Not until a photograph showing Ma, Su Fei, and Youma arrived at the Hatem home in 1953 was there even a hint of contact. Even then, the picture was shown only within the family.

An economic offensive against Communism in Asia is the central feature of a Foreign Operations Administration program. . . . The arc of Asia most critical partly encircles Red China.

New York Times, December 1, 1954

On Capitol Hill, Republican Senators Joseph R. McCarthy of Wisconsin and William E. Jenner of Indiana endorse the demand of Senator William F. Knowland, California Republican, for a blockade of Communist China.

New York Times, December 2, 1954

Shag is well, and has had a busy year. . . . Wherever he goes, flocks of babies appear in his trail—his group eliminates so many diseases. A real Father Xmas.

Rewi Alley to Edgar Snow, December 24, 1957

The year 1953 proved a good one for China and for Ma Haide. In July, fighting in Korea ended as all sides signed a truce agreement. The overstretched new government entered a dynamic and stable period. A January 1 editorial in *The People's Daily* declared, "The year of 1953 will be the first year of the country's large-scale construction."[1] The first comprehensive five-year plan was implemented, with optimistic expectations laid out in industry, agriculture, and national defense. One other area earmarked for greater funding and concentration of resources was public health.[2] Ma suddenly found that both personal and medical opportunities opened up for him. Not only did he feel free to contact his American family, but he also got in touch with his old progressive friends from Shanghai now living back in the United States. Among his favorites from that era were Grace and Manny Granich, who in the early 1950s ran a summer camp in Vermont for children of progressive Americans who were under fire during the McCarthy days. Ma wrote them about his purposeful life in new China, and he reminisced about the days in Shanghai. He dwelled only on the positive, which proved easy enough during this period. Grace wrote back in November 1953, envious that their old friend was helping to build a new socialist China. "Manny and I both rejoice in your happiness and good fortune. The 'bitter life' which you so wisely chose back in Shanghai has certainly flowered for you, and we are very glad."[3]

For the first time since moving to Beijing in 1949, Ma ventured out to other parts of China. His first trip was a leisurely one with Rewi Alley to northwest China, where Alley ran a school based on his Gung Ho movement. They reminisced about Ma's early life, about their days in Shanghai, and about the lessons Ma had learned in Yan'an. Ma visited the local hospitals and ancient Silk Road ruins. It was a relaxed visit among old friends, a visit Alley used to his benefit by writing up Ma's tales and putting them in a book published in China years later under the title *Six Americans in China*.[4]

Ma's public health duties took on new life and also got him outside Beijing. In 1951 and again in 1953 the Ministry of Public Health sent teams of physicians to Inner Mongolia, Tibet, and other remote minority regions to investigate health needs in those areas. Ma did not go on these early trips, but when they returned, the teams met with him to report on their findings and plan for future trips.[5] In late 1953 he finally got his chance, however, when he joined newly formed medical teams set up by the Beijing Medical College to evaluate and treat venereal diseases known to exist in epidemic proportions throughout the country. One of the team members, Dr. Wang Hongshen, says her first impressions of Ma were of his big nose, his common clothes, and his serious attention to detail in providing medical services.[6]

In 1954 the fight against venereal diseases and other skin diseases, including leprosy, took a serious step when the State Council issued a twelve-year agricultural development program. It included the decision to eliminate venereal diseases in China and to halt the spread of leprosy during the coming decade. A Dermatology and Venereological Research Institute was set up to lead this effort. It was just the kind of institute Ma had advocated in 1950, and he asked to be assigned to it. Up until that time, he had spent most of his professional time in the laboratory, in various hospital clinics, and in his official capacity as advisor to the Ministry of Public Health. Now Ma found himself assigned as advisor to this new unit. He was joined by Dr. Wang, who had accompanied him to the countryside on previous investigations. The director of the institute was a Soviet physician named Igorov. His official title was also advisor, but the two foreigners shared little more than the same title. Igorov's position and prestige placed him noticeably higher than Ma in the institute's hierarchy. Dr. Dai Zhengqi served as deputy director. This was the same

Dai Zhengqi who, as an army medic finishing the Long March in 1936, was surprised to see Ma and Edgar Snow deliver speeches of international solidarity to him and his fellow Red Army comrades at the front.[7]

On his first visit to the new institute, Ma was taken to Dr. Dai's office and told he would now be Dr. Dai's advisor. Dai knew immediately who Ma was and was noticeably anxious when Ma introduced himself only as a dermatologist come to help. Dai wondered how a man of such stature, this former physician to the Party Central Committee and advisor to the Ministry of Public Health, could be relegated to such a low-level, grass roots institute. Dai asked, "How could a large Buddha like you come to such a small temple?" Ma responded, "Don't say this is a small temple. Its task is so huge we may not fulfill it. If we do we will have achieved a great deal."

Over the next eight months, Ma worked with his new colleagues to set up the institute. Dai, Ma, and Igorov led meetings with experts on venereal disease called in from all over the country. When the time came to implement their program to wipe out venereal diseases, two divergent positions emerged. Ma and his backers advocated massive doses of penicillin administered over a short period of time, based on the experience of closing the Beijing brothels and the preliminary findings from studying outlying areas in 1952. Igorov and his backers, on the other hand, argued that the disease could be cured only over a long period of time using a combination of arsenic, mercury, and penicillin. This disagreement placed Dr. Dai in a quandary. He recalled Chairman Mao's statement that "China leans to one side" in support of the Soviet Union. Here Dai had an American, albeit one he knew to be a Party member and a Chinese citizen, opposing the position of the "big brother" Soviet doctor. Finally, he was saved from having to choose between the two when Ma suggested that they should investigate areas in which the method using massive doses of penicillin had already been implemented, and set up new experimental areas using that treatment. They could then monitor those test cases to see if it proved beneficial. Igorov could then pursue his own interests independent of Ma. This was agreed upon, and Ma prepared for the first of his many trips out to the grass roots. In most cases, Dai says, he and Ma had no choice but to support their Soviet comrade, even though Ma was more popular with his colleagues. "At the clinic level the ordinary doctors asked both foreign advisors to give opinions and support. But most of them trusted Ma more." Igorov left for the Soviet Union in 1955, and no replacement was sent.

Throughout the early days of the institute, Dai could not shake his embarrassment at supervising Ma. He met with the minister of public health, telling him that Ma should be named director of the institute with authority over him and other doctors. He was disturbed by the response. "The answer I received was that Ma was not suitable to be administrative head. Later I found out Kang Sheng had him under suspicion as a spy. Ma seemed to be aware of this, but it did not seem to affect his work."

Dai returned to his office angry at those who had put this stigma on Ma. "Old Ma was wronged by some leaders at that time, and I hoped his case would be cleared up soon. Unfortunately, he was under suspicion until 1976." Dai was helpless to alter Ma's status within the institute. But he knew he could give Ma unofficial help in carrying out his medical work. Generally, those under suspicion are not allowed to move about the country. But because Dai was not told directly about Ma's case, only that Ma was not "suitable" to lead, he allowed Ma to travel whenever and wherever he wanted for the institute. Besides, Dai was an old Long March veteran and he felt protected from any criticism this action might bring.

Su Fei says that after liberation, when Kang Sheng became head of the Party's Central Liaison Department, he continued to suspect Ma. He told others that "Ma Haide cannot work in any important positions, he cannot be granted real power. . . . Ma Haide is bustling about. Keep an eye on what he is doing." For the next two decades, though he was a Party member, Ma was excluded from the activities and meetings that Party members commonly attended. He had to ask friends about pronouncements and decisions made in special Party meetings because no one told him when the meetings would take place. In the safety of his home, or in the homes of others he trusted, Ma's friends encouraged him to write his old comrades, Premier Zhou and Chairman Mao, and tell them of this cloud that Kang Sheng had placed over his head. He refused, but he let them know how he felt about Kang Sheng. "Let Kang Sheng say whatever he wants. I don't care since I did not make revolution for him."[8]

Ma's refusal to seek help from his old Yan'an friends, or to make an issue of his lower status, speaks to his unique and proven ability to survive in a complex and quickly changing China. It also speaks to his understanding of how most Chinese respond to conflict. A typical American response to such unfounded criticism and distrust would have been to make noise about the injustice of it all, and seek remedy from the nearest source. But Ma was by now certainly not first and foremost an American, at least not in his professional and medical life. He was a member of the Chinese Communist party, and he trusted the Party to eventually right this wrong. In the meantime, he would concentrate on his assigned work, and not only refuse to complain, but throw himself fully into the effort. He once again proved himself a model Party member.

From 1953 through the mid 1960s, Ma spent up to half of each year at the grass roots. Except for the disruptions during the ten years of the Cultural Revolution, he continued his trips well into the 1980s. Some friends speculate that Ma spent so much time doing medical work in the field precisely because of the problems he faced in Beijing, in both his personal and political life. Others point to his personality, his love of getting out and mixing with the common people of China, and his dedication to the medical work he relished. As the leader of a medical team in the countryside, he must have enjoyed the freedom of being so far from the political center of Beijing. All these factors probably influenced his desire to take his medicine into China's hinterlands. Whatever the reasons, for the rest of his life Ma found himself in the most remote parts of China, leading the movement to eliminate the twin evils of venereal diseases and leprosy.

Ma, Dai, and Igorov determined that in 1954 venereal disease was most rampant in the border regions of China, where the minority nationalities lived. One of the most serious consequences for these people was the decline in population due to the infertility caused by the disease. In 1952, medical teams had made preliminary investigations into Inner Mongolia and other minority regions. After the institute was set up, Ma was chosen to coordinate and follow up on those earlier visits by leading a new team to Inner Mongolia. He also visited Qinghai Province, and his teams later traveled to Xinjiang Autonomous Region, Hainan Island, Yunnan, Jiangxi, and other remote areas.

The team of physicians, nurses, and technicians who visited inner Mongolia's grasslands were city people unfamiliar with local customs, food, or living conditions. Dr. Wang, who spent years traveling with Ma, remembers him as a stern taskmaster. He told the twelve- to fifteen-member crews that they should try to follow local customs and not offend the Mongolians with superior city attitudes. This sometimes proved difficult for the young men and women not accustomed to the rough ways and diet of the minority people.

There were problems on the Mongolian side as well. In the first place, it was a struggle just to convince them to come together for medical tests. People were scattered throughout the region, following their herds and living in temporary yurts. Even with the assistance of local Party leaders, it took many days to gather them in one place. The team then found that the standard blood test used to check for venereal diseases terrified the Mongolians, who had never seen blood drawn and did not understand its importance. To ease their concern, Ma had several of them stand around and watch a nurse take his own blood. Seeing that he was not harmed, the first of many consented to the test.[9]

After initial tests, the ten-day penicillin treatment was implemented in force, with follow-up visits every year for five years and one final visit after the tenth year. To highlight the success of this program, Ma enjoyed sharing the story of a Mongolian woman married five years, but prevented by syphilis from giving live birth. After receiving treatment during the preliminary visit of 1952, she gave birth to a healthy son. When Ma's medical team arrived in 1955, she demanded another injection, even though tests showed she was cured. She wanted another boy, she told him. She was given the injection and, on the final visit ten years later, she came to tell the team that she now had nine children and, no matter what they said, she would take no more medicine. She had all the children she could handle.[10]

The survey and medical treatment were administered uniformly everywhere, but were adapted to local conditions where necessary. The local authorities first would be notified that a team of physicians was to visit their region. When Ma and his team arrived, he would meet with the leaders to explain the problems of venereal disease, how it should be treated, and what kind of support he needed from them to eradicate it from their homes.

In his presentations to these village leaders, Ma ignored most technical and medical issues. The institute's campaign had a political goal. In villages all over China, Ma and his colleagues attacked the disease first as a social ill to be defeated. "The opening talk," he said, "would be brief and to-the-point and would go something like this: 'Comrades, syphilis is a disease that was bequeathed to us by the rotten society we have thrown out. It's no fault of yours if you have syphilis and no shame should be attached to it. It's only shameful if you cling to your syphilis when you can easily get rid of it. We've got rid of the landlords and the blood-sucking government that looked after their interests and now we have a government that looks after ours. . . . This is our country now and we should all be concerned about the well-being of everyone else. Comrades, we're going forward to Communism and we can't take this rotten disease with us.' "[11]

Ma told them he wanted to survey the entire population under their jurisdiction. He knew that political education would not wipe away the shameful stigma overnight, and in the early days the villagers were told that the health survey was looking for all types of skin diseases, not just sexually transmitted ones. Dr. Yang Lihe, a young doctor who accompanied Ma on several of these outings, says that if other diseases appeared the medical team treated them, but that the primary goal was to find and treat venereal diseases, although they were also on the lookout for cases of leprosy. After Ma and his colleagues first met with village and Party officials, Yang recalls that "the leaders in the village announced to the village through the broadcast system that each person would take a physical examination for skin disease. They then told the people when to meet and where. The next day everyone in the village would begin to line up for the survey. Sometimes this would be as few as 1,000 people, or as many as 10,000. One doctor would see between 200 and 300 people in one day, giving each a physical. After that we ran tests and discovered which ones had the disease. We then made a plan for each one, leaving instructions for the local doctors."[12]

There was little time for sleep. In the evenings Ma and his staff treated all sorts of ailments afflicting the villagers. They also studied test results, and Ma often would order the team to recheck some of the tests he found faulty. "He was very strict with the test checks, and always made us clean the water used in the tests by making a sieve with a bucket and rocks to clean the water before we used it." Ma scolded anyone doing shoddy work. "One time," Dr. Wang recounts, "he grew angry with me because of the way I marked the serum we prepared for those who tested positive. XX marked the bottle with this serum, while XXXX marked another medicine. He criticized me and said it was too easy to give the wrong medicine to someone. I told him this was the way it was always done and it didn't matter, no mistake would be made. He flared up at me, and said this was nothing but bad work."

In rare moments of relaxation, Ma would visit with his medical team and the local populace, telling stories and occasionally organizing a "dance party" on the grasslands. Being away from Beijing so long, he also wanted to keep in touch with his family and the institute. Although his spoken Chinese was excellent, he never learned to write the language, or to read it well, and depended on his colleagues to write down the letters he composed to Su Fei and others.[13]

The appearance of this foreigner leading a team of Chinese medical personnel into remote villages added an extra sense of excitement. The children welcomed him with cries of *waiguoren laile, waiguoren laile*, "a foreigner has come, a foreigner has come." They hovered around him, calling him *da bizi*, "big nose." The adults would stare. Most had never seen anyone quite like him before. His spoken Chinese was good, and he told them he was a Chinese citizen from Xinjiang. But it wasn't until his colleagues took the village leaders aside to show them pictures of Ma in his Red Army uniform that he was fully appreciated. "We told them about his life in Yan'an, how he joined the revolution and how he was a very important person in China and a friend of Chairman Mao, Premier Zhou, and Marshal Zhu De."[14]

After this initial trip to Inner Mongolia, a disturbing trend developed that would follow Ma throughout his life. While he insisted that he and his colleagues adapt to local conditions, these conditions often caused serious medical problems of their own. Sometimes Ma would lead the medical teams while bedridden and feverish. One colleague recounts the hardships he faced in the minority regions. "He experienced different kinds of living conditions, such as living in Mongolian yurts, sleeping on kangs made of mud in shabby inns, and staying in tumbledown temples. Once he even shared an old quilt made of coarse cloth with three other men. When he was bothered by mosquitoes and could hardly fall asleep he would put on a raincoat, tie up both cuffs and bottoms of his trouser legs, and lay down on his work clothes. Sometimes, he had to do this for a month or more. He was reluctant to stop working even when he ran a fever. On one chilly cold day, he and other comrades went to a clinic by horse cart. When they got to the clinic after a day's journey his legs were frozen stiff and could not move. He was unable to get out of the cart until others warmed his feet with warm water."[15] The food, always meager and usually lacking essential nutrients, affected his stomach and gums. "We used to say that Old Ma lost one tooth after each trip," recalls Dr. Wang. "He always came back tired and in need of rest," she adds.

Despite the health risks, Ma found fulfillment in his work. When he returned from Mongolia he spent days writing up his reports, checking test results, and confering with Dr. Dai on future plans. After Igorov's departure, he and Dai called the shots. He also continued to visit the dermatology outpatient clinic in the Capital Hospital every Tuesday and Friday, usually seeing between forty and fifty patients a day.

As for his personal life, Ma continued to socialize with foreign friends while Su Fei spent her time in the arts community. After returning from Mongolia, he took advantage of the declining role of Soviet doctors in Beijing and used his influence to have his physician friend Hans Muller transfered from Shenyang to become vice president of the Beijing Medical College. The two of them then began to meet weekly, sometimes twice weekly, at the home of recent Beijing arrival Rewi Alley. There they talked politics, enjoyed Western food, and listened to the British Broadcasting Corporation and the Voice of America (VOA). They listened to the VOA, Ma said, so they could follow "the hate-mongering against China, some of the things it poured out were both sour and comic." This informal gathering became a tradition among the three well into the 1980s. They and the others that periodically joined them made quite a sight when they congregated at Alley's home in the old legation area of Beijing, just a block from the Beijing Hotel. Sitting around a table set with coffee, English tea, canned meat, cookies, and other rarely seen delicacies, were men dressed in Western clothes, with the serious and proper Muller often in a coat and tie. It was, as one visitor to the weekly session remarked, a Western island in Beijing.[16] One topic rarely discussed, and apparently of little interest to Ma, was their families overseas. The tensions of those times discouraged correspondence, and the less said about foreign contacts the better. Ma heard nothing of his mother's death in 1955, since the family did not contact him. His North Carolina family feared he might be dead and considered declaring him legally dead to free up any legal complications related to family property then being sold.

While Ma and his Western friends tried to follow news from the West, the U.S. government continued to worry itself with this American Communist in China. In February 1955, FBI agents in Washington carried out a review of Ma's activities. They requested additional information from other intelligence operations "concerning subject's activities for use in the event of his return to the United States in considering his eligibility for inclusion on the Security Index." On March 6 and again on March 25, the FBI "Espionage" office received responses outlining Ma's activities in China, with copies sent to intelligence agencies in Tokyo, London, and Washington. In April and May, more information was added, with copies sent to FBI offices in New York and Charlotte, North Carolina, "inasmuch as the subject's parents were last reported residing at Roanoke Rapids, North Carolina. Further, the subject may at a future date return to this community."[17] While nothing new appears in these reports, 1955 was an active period for those American intelligence people who worried about Ma's potential threat to the security of the United States.

Just as the FBI ended its investigation into Ma's family, China began a political movement to "root out hidden counter revolutionaries." One person under suspicion was Ma's next-door neighbor Paul Lind, the Canadian Chinese who recently moved to China where he served for a while as deputy director of the English section of Radio Beijing. Sydney Rittenberg, only recently let out of prison, insists that as a high-ranking Party member with Radio Beijing, he reviewed the Party dossiers of those, like Lind, who were suspected of spying. He says he saw in Lind's file a reference to the Canadian's friendship with Ma, who was himself identified as a suspected spy. The characterization of Ma as a possible spy shocked Rittenberg, who knew Ma was somewhat out of favor, but had no idea how serious the suspicions were.[18] Kang Sheng's charge from a decade before in Yan'an still haunted Ma, even if he was neither questioned nor arrested. While Ma was concerned with little more than eradicating venereal diseases in the villages and grasslands around China, and an occasional Western meal and party, the U.S. and Chinese governments both continued to suspect him of disloyalty.

After the successful trip to Mongolia, Ma next led his team to Qinghai, then in May 1956 to Xinjiang Province, the far northwestern region of China that is home to Muslims related in culture and appearance to the inhabitants of Central Asia. His team consisted of ten doctors, one nurse, and a laboratory technician. They traveled first by train to Gansu Province, where the tracks ended, then joined a military unit traveling by truck to the same destination. The journey took them through the Gobi Desert, with its infrequent oases and camel bones dotting the flat, stony surface. At night they slept in military camps along the road, finally completing the 1,200-mile bumpy trip to the capital city of Urumchi in twelve days. They were then taken to a small town on the Russian border. This was the first medical team ever sent to Xinjiang, and they were greeted there as "Chairman Mao's doctors." Ma and his colleagues spent the next three months working out of yurts and log cabins. They averaged two hundred patients a day. Ma estimated that 99 percent of these people had never received formal medical treatment. They followed the same routine they had established in Mongolia. Ma first met with local leaders, then arranged for mass testing and distribution of surveys. The training of local medics was integrated into the routine as well.[19]

Xinjiang presented the doctors with unique problems. Since Chinese was spoken only by the few trained physicians of the region, interpreters were needed for all interviews and physicals. Also, despite the colorful clothing, music, and dance of the region, many cultural habits made daily life difficult. The food was especially hard to take. Dr. He Daxun remembers, "We all ate the same food as everyone. Strong bitter tea and mutton. Dr. Ma insisted that we all eat like the local residents, and that no one should be treated in a special way. But none of us had ever eaten mutton. Once we were given mutton spread with the fat from a sheep's rear end. It looked like butter. Dr. Ma ate it and said that even though it was awful, we had to eat it."

One of the required customs Ma found distracting, but not altogether distasteful, was the liquor made of fermented horse milk. While many of his staff found the drink repugnant, Ma rather enjoyed it. After returning to Beijing, he recounted that a "frequent distraction would be caused by patients entering with a big leather flask full of koumiss (fermented mare's milk, about as alcoholic as beer), and inviting the doctor to drink with them. This is the custom here, and koumiss is given even to five-month-old babies. When you come into a herdsman's yurt, custom demands that you drink four bowls at once—I mean this literally—you hold two bowls in each hand and are expected to drain all four without putting them down or spilling a drop. At first some of our doctors tried to drink for the sake of politeness. But it made them dizzy, and they would have to rest for 15 minutes after a bowl."[20]

In August the medical team packed up and started on the long journey back home. In an article Ma wrote for a foreign audience, he tells how he reached the decision to escape the constant attention he received as a foreigner in China. He obviously knew his audience well, for his humor is strictly American. He writes

> All the way home I wore the embroidered skull-cap of the Sinkiang (Xinjiang) people, to which I had become accustomed. Being taken for a Uighur, Uzbek or Tarter I met with exceptional courtesy from my fellow-travellers, airline personnel and ordinary people in hotels and stations—the best seat in the aeroplane, concern for my air-sickness, care for my luggage, and first choice food. Everything went swimmingly, except for the fact that they insisted on serving me mutton—thought to be the meat of my people—and as we had eaten little else for three months, I was ready for a change. I felt an impostor, but I'm glad I wore that hat.[21]

Just as Ma set out for Xinjiang, Rewi Alley received a letter from Edgar Snow, now living in New York. Alley and Snow had renewed their correspondence a short while before, and now Snow wanted to contact Shag directly. "It would be good to have some word from Shag, at least for the purpose of dispelling any mystery as to his whereabouts and safety, and to reassure his father, who is still alive," wrote Snow. In an April 24 letter he asked Alley to deliver two letters to Ma. One was from him, the other was a copy of a letter he had received from a reporter for *The Buffalo Evening News*. Alley wrote back some weeks later, telling Snow that Ma was "away on one of his summer trips in the back country of Singkiang [Xinjiang] somewhere eradicating infectious skin diseases of one kind and another. He goes out each summer and we do not see him again until the Autumn as a rule. . . . He never writes to anyone, so if you get a reply you will be luckier than any of us have been." To alleviate any concern Snow might have about Ma's status, he enclosed a photo taken that April. He then added in a postscript, "He leads a very quiet, full and happy life. His main out of office enjoyment is in the skittle alley at the club, or dancing on Saturday nights. He gets most of his fun, however, out of his very fascinating job."

The letter from *The Buffalo Evening News* asked Snow to help trace the whereabouts of "Dr. George Hatem, who spent some time with the Communists in China, and was known as Ma Ha-teh, or more colloquially as 'Doc Ma.' " The letter goes on to say that Snow was known to have traveled with Ma in China, and that the newspaper was also contacting Ma's father in North Carolina.[22] Although Alley delivered the letters when Ma returned, Ma put them aside for a month. He was again exhausted and weak from the trip. Rewi told Snow as much in a letter written in November 1957. "None of us gets any younger, and I spent a month in hospital this year with a bad heart, so cannot now go at the rate I once could. Ma is older too, but his health has picked up a bit this year. Still, the years do take their toll." To regain his strength, Ma took Su Fei and Youma with him on a vacation to the seaside resort of Beidaihe. Ma and his family made such trips to the seashore at least once a year, except for certain periods during the Cultural Revolution. This particular trip provided one unexpected encounter for Ma. He ran into Sydney Rittenberg, whom he had not seen since his release from prison. Ma saw him from a distance, remembered Rittenberg, ran toward him, gave him a hug, and invited him to share ice cream. Ever prudent, Ma never brought up Rittenberg's incarceration. "He was always very discreet," Rittenberg explains. This would be one of the last times that the two North Carolinians would enjoy each other's company. Within a few years they would distrust each other fiercely.

After returning from his vacation refreshed and restored to health, Ma finally returned to his correspondence. Snow's letter expressed his frustration at hearing nothing from Ma for years and also asked Ma to clarify the limits of the promise he extracted from Snow almost twenty years ago to keep his identity secret.

Dear Shag,

The enclosed letter will interest you. This newspaper apparently is preparing to run a story about you. Would you like me to tell them the bare facts as I know them? I have always honored your request that I make no mention of you in my writing, but meanwhile you have seen other Americans

and spoken to them, some of whom have made fragmentary references
to you.

I wrote you some months ago to ask you the same question—i.e., whether
I should now feel free to tell the story of your travels—but I never received a
reply. . . .

The fact that Zavitz [the Buffalo journalist] . . . says that you "spent"
some time in China seems to put it in the past and raises in my mind the
question whether they are not thinking of making you a case of disappearance or foul play. . . .

When I last heard of you I was told you were married and the proud papa
of a number of hai-tzu. I would certainly like to hear from you. When you
write please tell me, also, whether you any longer have any objection to my
writing the story of our experiences—which are really extraordinary now as I
look back upon them—how we happened to meet, and all that?

PS While waiting to hear from you I have replied to the *News'* letter that I
still feel bound by my commitment to you not to discuss your whereabouts
and activities.

On September 16, Ma sat down to write his old friend for the first time
since liberation.

Dear Ed,

Coming back from about four months with a medical team in far-off
Sinkiang. . . . I received your two letters from Rewi. This and my natural las-
situde about writing accounts for the delay in writing to you. . . . Many,
many years and events have gone their way since we last met and no mere
letter is satisfying to chew over such things. With the way things are turning
out in the international field plus the great changes that have taken place in
China it ought to be possible for you to find time to make a trip out here and
look things over. . . . It will definitely be much easier to make this trip than it
was for us to make that trip to Pao-An in '36 with our rubber pillows and
chocolate bars.

Your evaluation of the Zavits letter (Buffalo News) sound reasonable. Such
things have been known to be fabricated, but why should I be picked on.
Anyway, I no longer have any objections to *your* writing the story of our
experiences if you want to. I appreciate greatly your past reticence and the
sending of the letter of Zavitz to me. As for the Buffalo News I am not
thinking of doing anything about it, but I will write my family for once.

While getting back in touch with old friends abroad, Ma took time out
from his busy medical work to influence still other friends of China who

began to come to see for themselves the advances being made. One who would take his message to heart and tell the world of China's successes was Han Suyin, the physician and writer born in China but now living uneasily abroad who became one of China's most combative international supporters. Returning to China for the first time since liberation, she was just coming to grips with the vast changes she found there. Some of what she heard and witnessed was disturbing. From Ma she learned some of the lessons she would later impart through her controversial books. "With Ma Haiteh," she said, "I would spend some hours of one night walking up and down, down and up. To him I revealed all my distress, my trivial and yet important hesitations, and it was he who made my spirit whole and healed me, for after that talk I no longer suffered from suffocation. The tremendous epic of the Revolution now came clearly to me. 'Sister, nothing under Heaven comes easily, and certainly not building a new world,' said Ma Haiteh."[23]

By 1957, and well into the early 1960s, Ma's life followed a routine developed in the early years of the institute. After their Xinjiang trip, his team of experts journeyed south to Yunnan Province, on the border with Myanmar, then known as Burma. Within this one province he found as many as thirty-three national minority groups. During the spring and summer of 1957, his team treated more than 8,000 people and discovered over 2,500 serious cases of venereal diseases. As elsewhere, they treated a variety of diseases at all hours of the night. On several occasions Ma came face to face with local superstitions and the belief that illness comes from evil spirits. Ever careful not to offend the local populace, Ma did not dispute such claims. He did manipulate them, however. Once he treated a young boy suffering from pneumonia. After injections of penicillin and other medicines, the boy slowly recovered. His grandmother, uneasy about the medicine, killed a chicken to appease the evil spirits. Ma and his colleagues convinced the old woman to make the chicken into soup to build the young boy's strength. "The child recovered," Ma said. "We never found out whether the grandmother or her son won the argument as to what had caused the cure."[24]

It was on this trip to Yunnan that Ma was struck by the number of leprosy cases that turned up during mass testing. He helped move some of these cases to the "leprosarium villages" run by the provincial medical services. In years to come, after venereal disease was nearly wiped out, Ma would return to Yunnan to resume treating those leprosy patients he first encountered during this visit.[25]

But no matter how deeply he involved himself in medicine, political campaigns were hard to avoid. What success he had in staying out of them was in large measure due to his extended stays away from politically hot Beijing, as well as his natural tendency to shy away from controversy. His lack of active participation in politics also was due to the Party's reluctance to include him in important discussions. He could not give opinions about issues kept from him. For example, in February, Chairman Mao delivered his speech, "On the Correct Handling of Contradictions Among the People," an important statement outlining how one should "distinguish and correctly handle contradictions between the people and the enemy and contradictions within the ranks of the people." Mao said that the "large-scale, turbulent class struggles of the masses characteristic of times of revolution have in the main come to an end, but class struggle is by no means entirely over."[26] This speech was not made available for public study until June, even though all levels of the Party apparatus carefully studied it during that interval. Ma, however, was still not allowed to attend select local Party meetings when important news was relayed from the Central Committee. He only found out about the content of the speech from a family friend visiting his house.[27]

When the Hundred Flowers Movement heated up in the spring of 1957, Ma had little to say about this campaign to criticize poor work style within the Party. During that period he was out among the villages of Yunnan Province testing the populace for venereal diseases. When Chairman Mao decided the criticism had gone too far, he unleashed the Anti-Rightist Movement, attacking those who had criticized the Party leadership too harshly and who, Mao thought, wanted to overthrow the Party leadership. That movement was in full swing when Ma returned from Yunnan in August, and it continued through the end of the year. He had little time to spend criticizing rightists, however, as he prepared for a survey and testing trip to the northwest during the latter part of the year.[28] It was a good time to be out of Beijing.

By the late 1950s, the results from follow-up visits throughout the country showed remarkable achievements in wiping out venereal diseases. When Ma visited Inner Mongolia in 1955, his investigation showed that as much as 50 percent of the population was infected with syphilis in some villages. During the last follow-up in 1962, however, not one case turned up in random testing. The disappearance of the disease also was signaled by the population explosion in these minority regions, as the story of the Mongolian woman with her nine children attests. In 1950, for example, a study of one group of Mongolian nomads showed that almost 60 percent of the families were childless. Following the anti-venereal disease campaign there, the population increased by 50 percent.

Studies in other areas showed the same results. In sample counties in Gansu Province, a follow-up study five years after mass surveys and treatment began discovered no new cases of syphilis. The same was true of a target village in Jiangsu. In Guangzhou only one new case appeared.[29] Rewi Alley, in one of his frequent letters to Edgar Snow, wrote in December 1957, "Shag is well, and has had a busy year. He is going to Hainan perhaps next year. Wherever he goes, flocks of babies appear in his trail—his group eliminated so many diseases. A real Father Xmas."[30]

Edgar Snow, the writer, has received a passport for travel in Communist China and may already be there, State Department officials said today.

New York Times, July 22, 1960

My son is a very important doctor in China and I want to see him and I want you to get him here.

Nahoum Hatem to Chinese Embassy officials in Syria, 1962

Despite the strides made in practically all areas of China's development during the first five-year plan, Mao Zedong grew impatient. He wanted more, and he wanted it sooner rather than later. In January 1958 he delivered another in a series of important speeches to select Party members, arguing that China must now stress the idea of "uninterrupted revolution." He proposed to "shift the focus of the Party's work to technological revolution."[1] Mao and his supporters knew that the best way to advance technologically in China was to harness the raw power found in the countryside. He said

> Now we must start a technological revolution so that we may overtake Britain in fifteen or more years. . . . After fifteen years, when our foodstuffs and iron and steel become plentiful, we shall take a much greater initiative. Our revolutions are like battles. After a victory, we must at once put forward a new task. In this way, cadres and the masses will forever be filled with revolutionary fervor, instead of conceit.[2]

The movement to take the revolutionary struggle forward during this period came to be known as the Great Leap Forward.

To accomplish the extraordinary goals Mao set for the country, two changes in thinking had to take place. First, everyone had to strive to become both "red and expert," that is, both reliable in politics and knowledgeable at work. Second, the new thrust forward would succeed only if the people put their own private interests aside and worked together in greater harmony. The goal was to join together in a deeper and broader fashion than every before. Mao led with the slogan, "go all out, aim high, and get greater, quicker, better and more economical results to build socialism." For a while it seemed to work.

The landscape throughout China was filled with vast numbers of people digging irrigation ditches, terracing mountainsides, and constructing new factories and buildings. Whole factories were relocated from the cities to the countryside. The rural areas changed most dramatically, as the individual and collective enterprises of the early 1950s gave way to a communal system of farming. These "people's communes" began in earnest in the summer of 1958. Soon 740,000 cooperatives merged into 26,000 communes.

In the cities and in the countryside people felt they were heading toward a new level of development, a step closer to true communism. The whole social structure changed, as people joined communally run kitchens and child care centers. Millions of peasants received simple training in such areas as uranium and petroleum exploration, and villagers around the country learned basic medical techniques to become "barefoot doctors." In the cities, people banded together to build "backyard furnaces" on university sports grounds and other vacant lots so that they might make enough steel for China to surpass Britain in fifteen years. They paid for bus and theater tickets on an honor system. It was assumed that everyone would pay their honest share.[3] In August 1958 the Central Committee issued an enthusiastic statement summing up the achievements of this movement:

> Community dining rooms, kindergartens, nurseries, sewing groups, barber shops, public baths, happy homes for the aged, agricultural middle schools, "red and expert" schools, are leading the peasants toward a happier collective life. . . .
>
> In the present circumstances, the establishment of the people's communes with all-round management of agriculture, forestry, animal husbandry, side occupations, fishery, where industry (the worker), agriculture (the peasant), exchange (the trader), culture and education (the student), and military affairs (the militiaman) merge into one, is the fundamental policy to guide the peasants to accelerate socialist construction, complete the building of socialism ahead of time, and carry out the gradual transition to communism.[4]

In years to come, this Great Leap Forward would be deemed a failure. Inflated figures for agricultural and industrial production were sent to

Beijing to bolster the argument that the Great Leap created unprece-
dented growth in China. But the backyard mills produced only useless
steel, and agricultural production did not meet the needs of the country
for the next few years, in part because the peasants were diverted to
political and industrial duties rather than working their fields. But in
1958, the vast majority of people willingly fell in line to support the radical changes going on all around them. Ma joined right in.

In November 1958, Ma, Dai Zhengqi, and others from the Dermatology and Venereological Research Institute were invited to Jiangxi Province to assist in the control and elimination of syphilis, leprosy, and
ringworm. The Great Leap Forward, then in full swing, presented problems from a public health perspective that the political aims of the movement had not anticipated. It was up to Ma and his colleagues to find a
way to overcome such problems and to produce a political and medical
victory. If ever anyone was challenged to be "both red and expert," it
was this team of doctors.

When they arrived in Ningdu County, Jiangxi Province, Ma, Dai, and
the rest of the team experienced for the first time the dynamics of the
people's communes. Some aspects proved troubling. Ma explained that
"With the development of the people's communes, the Kiangsi (Jiangxi)
health services had run into a new and urgent problem. People who formerly lived and worked in small scattered groups were now concentrated
in large numbers for field and factory work and on the building of large
irrigation projects. They were eating together in public dining rooms,
and the children and old people were also living under new communal
conditions. The dangers of the spread of illness had multiplied and it has
become imperative to eliminate various parasitic and other diseases."

Once the medical problems were identified, the doctors had to implement the correct political solution to solve them, for medical expertise must, like all other skills, be subordinate to correct political analysis.
There was little room for debate on this. Besides, Ma, Dai, and the
others on the team were loyal Party members determined to make their
contribution to the Great Leap. But how? "Our job," said Ma, "was to
translate into concrete terms for preventive medicine the policy of the
General Line—'go all out, aim high, and get greater, quicker, better and
more economical results to build socialism'—and the mass line; to com-
bine the use of modern and traditional Chinese medicine; and to use
bold creative methods in epidemiological work. We accepted our new
task with mixed hesitation and confidence, for we had no clear idea how
the 'General Line' and the 'mass line' could be applied in our work. We

aimed to catch up with the great leap forward that the whole of China was making in other fields."[5]

To attack the problems, the team organized medical work along the lines of a military operation, with "politics in command." The provincial Party secretary was appointed "commander-in-chief" at the "Eliminate Disease and Pests and Propagate Hygiene" headquarters. The chief of the Jiangxi health service office was the deputy. Over one thousand people attended a three-day mass meeting to plan a strategy. People from every spectrum of the community attended, including commune leaders, health chiefs, students, representatives from women's organizations, mid-wives, and traditional Chinese doctors, among others. At the end of the meeting, participants divided into two groups, political and medical. The political group focused primarily on medical propaganda and received a two-day course on how to detect the diseases the health team hoped to attack. Their primary job was to distribute and explain medical question-naires to resident committees found throughout the communes.

Most of the medical personnel had never trained for such work. They were local residents possessing an education equivalent at least to pri-mary school. They received a seven-day course in diagnosing, examining, and treating cases referred to them by the political workers. Each was taught simple skills, such as how to judge skin lesions and how to make blood slides to test for syphilis. Little time was spent on lectures. Practi-cal, on-the-spot training took precedence. After two days of "intern-ship," a test was given to judge who would "graduate" to the level of health worker. China's "barefoot doctors" got their start here. In all, over 2,600 people were trained in the program as either political or health workers.

Ma was encouraged by the initial results and saw them as meeting the "general line" and the "mass line" approach to medicine. Clearly, he told others, they had reduced the time of diagnosis, found a way to run more and quicker tests, and controlled disease more effectively than in the past. "What the mass line in medicine means is that millions of people are getting an elementary understanding of what public health work is all about and the important part every one of them plays in it."[6] This did not mean that a mass medical movement overcame centuries of folk medicine overnight. Superstition still played a part in the peasants' understanding of disease. For many, "spirits" were the main culprit. No peering at blood samples through microscopes could find spirits. But Ma had ways of winning people over. Once he convinced a skeptical old man to look at his own blood smear. "When he looked at his own worms hopping about under the microscope he was flabbergasted. The very next night he brought in six other old grandpas from the commune's 'Happy Home' to be examined."

It was also difficult just to get people to admit to having symptoms. "Of course it was not a simple job," Ma explained. "Nobody wanted to get up at a meeting and say: 'I think I have the symptoms of leprosy.' So special places were designated where people could go to consult and register privately. General doubts were dispelled by presenting the problem in its politico-economic context—you cannot build socialism and achieve prosperity for all with a malaria-ridden population, and children do not grow up healthy and happy if they have worms or hookworm."

The commune system itself was finally utilized to overcome the very problems its original formation had created. The commune organization, with its enormous work teams, brigades, and schools, provided convenient conditions for control. Ma explains, "The usefulness of commune organization and the value of combining Chinese and modern medicine was vividly illustrated in worm (ascaris) eradication. In the Kanchow people's commune the incidence of ascariasis was exceptionally high. To save time and effort a decision was made to treat everybody without examination. While considering the economic aspect, our colleagues of traditional Chinese medicine suggested we use a common local tree root and fruit . . . for medication. . . . Western medicine for worms, though cheap, would still have been quite costly on such a large scale. So we arranged for the public dining rooms to make a brew of the root and fruit, which soon became popularly known as 'health tea', for the whole community. A bowl of the decoction was placed on all tables at each meal for three days running. Toasts were made, the drink taken and, as subsequent tests showed, 85 per cent of those with worms were cleared. A second course of treatment got rid of the remainder."[7]

Summing up his experience in Jiangxi Province only months after leaving, Ma voiced unqualified optimism about the results he and his team witnessed after implementing this new style of "mass line" work. He called the results "miracles" performed through mass participation. He joined others throughout the country reporting astounding success in utilizing the new politics of the Great Leap Forward when he wrote, "Within two months a population of one million people helped to free themselves from malaria, filariasis, ascariasis, hookworm, syphilis, tinea of the scalp (ringworm) and leprosy, all endemic diseases." He argued that this was accomplished with the help of only thirty trained physicians at a cost of only six cents per patient.[8]

At the end of the two-month visit, a national conference was held in

Ningdu to sum up the medical progress so far in the fight against venereal diseases and to discuss what future goals the institute should now set
for itself. Ma served as primary organizer and chair of the meeting. At
this conference, over five hundred physicians from all over the country
came to study how venereal diseases had been eliminated in this one
place, Ningdu. Ma arranged the itinerary for the meeting, which included the testimony of patients, short-term-trained medical workers,
and physicians. It was at this conference that the Dermatology and
Venereological Research Institute first committed itself to shift its emphasis to leprosy and away from venereal diseases, which was well on the
way to being eradicated. From this time until his death, Ma focused his
medical efforts on controlling leprosy.[9]

As the end of the 1950s approached, Ma not only shifted his attention
to leprosy, he also found himself once again playing a limited role in foreign affairs. In September 1958 Anna Louise Strong was invited to China
after having recently been exonerated by the Soviet Union on spy
charges. She arrived expecting a lengthy visit, but instead settled down to
stay, living on the first floor of Rewi Alley's home. She was pleased with
the accommodations, as they had only a few years before been the home
of the Italian ambassador to China. When he was in town, Ma became
her personal physician and kept her company many evenings when he
and Rewi joined her for dinner. Ma also continued to be the teacher,
explaining to a skeptical Anna Louise that the commune system was
responsible for much of the change that amazed her and that the peasants supported it without the drastic measures she had seen Stalin take to
force collectivization on the Soviet peasants in the 1930s. Her biographers argue that it was Ma's gentle persuasion that "converted" her from
a doubter to a believer.[10]

Since the mid 1950s, Rewi Alley had encouraged Edgar Snow to visit
China. After Alley sent a letter in 1956 saying there would be "no great
difficulty" if he wanted to visit the "old camping grounds," Snow began
planning for just such a trip. The problem, he wrote Rewi, was "the difficulties of clearing such a trip with the SD [State Department] here, and
I believe nothing would be gained (except for me personally) if I did not
come there as a fully qualified press representative." The U.S. State
Department refused to allow Chinese journalists to visit the United
States, so the Chinese refused to allow American journalists in, even so
good a friend as Snow. Ma, in a rare letter, wrote and asked him to
arrange another way to come, since many people wanted to see him.
Finally, a compromise was arranged that allowed Snow to maintain his
professional integrity, while not compromising U.S. law and Chinese

diplomatic policies. Rewi Alley issued him a personal invitation to visit China as a fellow writer, not a journalist. He would be Alley's personal guest, without any official involvement by the Chinese Foreign Ministry. Snow accepted the invitation, but insisted on paying all his own expenses. No perception of influence or favoritism would be allowed. Writing commitments required him to postpone the trip several times, but he finally arranged to go in 1960.[11]

In June of that year, Snow arrived at the Beijing airport, not knowing who besides Alley would greet him. He was pleased to see not only Alley, but Huang Hua and Ma, his two traveling companions from 1936. Also present were several Chinese friends and Israel Epstein, an old writing buddy now working for *China Reconstructs*. In the car on the long ride into Beijing, Snow asked Ma to fill him in on details of his life since they had last visited in the early 1940s. "Married a wonderful girl. Two children, nearly grown by now. Bound up the wounds of the revolution. . . . I helped wipe out syphilis in China. That's something. You know it's the dream of every doctor to rid a whole country of at least one disease he knows he can beat."[12]

These accomplishments were later verified when Snow visited the Dermatology and Venereological Research Institute. One of Ma's colleagues told Snow, "Yes, there is practically no venereal problem left. . . . Dr. Ma has done such a good job, professors in medical schools are mad at us. They say that since 1957 they can't find any more active venereal cases even for classroom observations work." Snow was impressed, but skeptical, especially about the training of amateur medical workers and the important role they played. "I think you'll find a lot of skepticism in the West about such claims, Shag." Ma then presented his arguments. And, like Han Suyin and Anna Louise Strong before him, and the Dixie Mission and U.N. representatives before them, Snow found Ma convincing. He says, "Talking to George Hatem was more illuminating than I am able to convey here: he helped me understand the logic of some things that had puzzled me in China. He knew the faults and failures of the regime but he also knew the misery of Old China and the enormity of the problems it presented. Because he was the one American who had for twenty-five years intimately shared the ordeals of the men and women who fought for responsibility to bring China to her feet, his continuing faith in what they were doing merits attention."[13] Ultimately, Snow depended on Ma for the keenest insight possible into modern China, saying later in *Red China Today*, the book that came out of this trip, that he "knows more about Red China and its leaders than any foreigner alive."[14]

After resting in Beijing, Snow took off on a two-month journey around China. Rewi accompanied him for much of that time, as did Ma when he could break away from his work. They also were joined by Yao Wei, a young Foreign Ministry officer assigned to accompany Snow around the country. Just because the Foreign Ministry had not officially invited him was no reason for it not to oversee his visit.

Like the generation before him in Yan'an, the young guide and interpreter Yao was impressed with the way Ma defended China's position to the West. His natural but well-polished presentation stood in stark contrast to the more gruff and direct Rewi Alley. Yao recalls, "I am sure Rewi Alley meant well, but if Ed Snow's ideas were off track Rewi Alley would be there to scold him. There was no diplomacy when Rewi Alley felt Ed Snow had done a wrong thing or said a wrong thing. He was there to snap at him. But Ma Haide was different. He would never do anything like that. Not that he was more colluding in anything he didn't believe in. He was just more sympathetic, more understanding. That is why his relationship with Ed Snow was always one of warmth. He was just more humane, perhaps more knowledgeable to things happening in China. Between Rewi Alley and Ma Haide, Ed Snow always leaned more to Ma Haide in interpretation of things he would not understand. To be fair, I think he had been in the countryside, in poor places more than Rewi. When Rewi went places he had people to help him. Hotels, personal aides. When Ma Haide goes, he would be there just like any other Chinese doctor. I can feel it when he speaks about things, there is warmth to it."[15]

While Ma proved an invaluable resource to Snow, it appears that in the early days of the visit the Chinese government tried to keep him at some distance from Snow. This charge comes from Sydney Rittenberg, who in 1960 held a leadership position with Radio Beijing. As a Party member and a leading foreigner in China, he says he was kept informed of the Snow visit. He insists that when Zhou Enlai organized a welcoming banquet for Snow in the Great Hall of the People, Ma's name was left off the invitation list. Other foreigners were invited, even those like Rittenberg who did not know Snow. The reason for the snub, Rittenberg says, was the Party's continuing displeasure with Ma's personal indiscretions and the charges against him still lingering in his Party file. "I called a friend at the Foreign Ministry," insists Rittenberg, "and told them that Ma is Snow's best friend in China and it was ridiculous not to invite him to the reception. I got a call back and they told me to tell Ma to call the Foreign Ministry. When I told this to George, he said, 'You tell the boys if they want me at the reception they have to call my organization to invite me.' The Foreign Affairs Ministry called and invited him."[16]

It is not just third parties that tell conflicting stories about Ma and Snow in 1960. Ma confused the picture himself. While in Beijing, Snow visited Ma for several days, catching up on more details of his life. Ma told him that he and Su Fei were the parents of two children, including a daughter, Liangbi. Of course Ma was not Liangbi's father, and there is no indication she lived with them, although she did visit often. The second bit of confusing information Ma conveyed to Snow concerned his citizenship. At one point Snow told Ma that he assumed his old friend must now be a Chinese citizen. "Certainly not," Ma responded. "He went to his desk and came back with a fresh green American passport. 'I got it just before I left Peking for Yenan, in 1947,' he said. 'At General Marshall's headquarters. . . . I'm here legally and still an American— unless it's treason to wipe out syphilis.' "[17]

It is difficult to understand why Ma led Snow astray. Ma's friends in Beijing knew that Su Fei showed little interest in discussing her life before she met Ma, and perhaps he decided to claim her daughter as his own merely to keep Snow from digging too deeply into Su Fei's past. On the issue of citizenship, Ma may have used Snow to mislead the U.S. government. He worried about his family, and if everyone thought he still considered himself an American, it might help the family to stay out of harm's way during the anticommunist hysteria of the United States in 1960. On the other hand, Ma might simply have been following his own well-established pattern of staying away from political controversy by keeping his story simple. He wanted to be known as an American doctor who, in the 1930s and 1940s provided humanitarian assistance to the Chinese, and now in the 1950s and 1960s merely continued that work by fighting infectious diseases.[18]

Rittenberg says that with Snow's visit Ma began once more to emerge from the shadows of suspicion and to regain his status in the eyes of the leadership. If there was any doubt about Ma's return to favor, Chairman Mao put it to rest during an interview with Snow just before the reporter left China. At 3:30 in the afternoon of October 22, 1960, Snow was brought to Mao's residence at Zhongnanhai, the Party Central Committee headquarters. In the middle of the interview, Mao decided to turn the visit into a reunion. He told his staff to go fetch Ma, Alley, and Israel Epstein to his home so they might all visit together once again.

Mao had not seen Ma since the chairman's dinner and dance he and Su Fei had enjoyed in 1952. When he arrived, Mao asked him what he had been up to all these years. The chairman knew nothing about Ma's work against venereal diseases and leprosy, so Ma quickly filled him in on the efforts of the Ministry of Public Health. During the dinner and afterwards until almost 10:00 P.M., Ma, Alley, and Epstein listened as Mao explained to Snow his view of China's development and its future. At times Mao asked Ma and the others to give their own views of the current situation, but for most of the evening Snow asked questions and the chairman responded.[19] Although the session was recorded in formal and informal photographs, Snow was asked not to report that he had met with Mao. In *Red China Today,* he remarks only that he met with "a very high official." Within a few days of this visit, Snow was off to Guangzhou and out of China.[20] Ma was thankful for Snow's visit in more ways than one. As he always did with family and friends, he gave Snow a list of things he would enjoy receiving from the West. Within a few months Snow would oblige with cheese for Ma, chocolate for Su Fei, and candies for the children.

Other issues related to foreign relations moved less smoothly for Ma. By 1960, debate raged between the Soviet Union and China on the correct path in developing socialism. The Soviets frowned upon Mao's view of uninterrupted socialism, with Khrushchev comparing him to the despised Trotsky, while China's official press blasted Khrushchev's "revisionist" brand of Marxism. While the debates raged in secret for a while, by 1960 relations had deteriorated to the point that the Soviet Union pulled out its advisors and experts, and China declared its independence from any outside influence. For many in the leftist foreign community in China, especially the Europeans whose domestic Communist parties backed the Soviet Union, the dilemma proved wrenching. They had to choose between loyalty to their own Party or to the Chinese Communist party, which they answered to every day. The community split, and debates raged throughout Beijing as foreigners took sides. Some strongly supported Khrushchev. Two of Ma's friends, the British Gladys Yang and her Chinese husband, who were translators at the Foreign Languages Press, criticized China's Communist party quite openly. Ma's old drinking partner, Alan Winnington, the correspondent for the *London Daily Worker,* followed the orders of his British Communist party and left China. Others soon followed, including friends Nan Green and Janet Springfall.

For Springfall, the decision to side with the Soviets proved especially painful. Unmarried, she had only recently adopted two Chinese children, a young girl and baby boy. She wanted to take them with her to England. This conjured up old wounds, and she was accused of enslaving them. Her request was refused. Desperate that the children be cared for after she left, she called on Ma and asked him to take responsibility for the children. With his contacts and his status, he was her best hope. Breaking from his previous pattern of avoiding political controversy, Ma agreed to help her. He had not taken account of Su Fei, however. When he informed her, she flatly told him that such a commitment was out of the question. It was dangerous to become involved in this issue, even to hint at support for an opponent of the Chinese Communist party. And besides, what would they do with the children? Ma told Springfall that he was forced to break his promise. She then wrote to Zhou Enlai to explain her predicament, and he offered a solution worthy of King Solomon. He allowed her to take the girl with her, but the boy would have to be returned to his parents in the countryside.

Different members of the foreign community who watched this drama unfold reacted differently to Ma's role in it. Gladys Yang felt lasting disappointment in Ma for giving in to Su Fei. Others, such as the Crooks, say that Ma did all he could, and certainly could not have agreed to take in two more children, or look after them, without the support of his wife. Given the political and personal issues at stake, they felt his actions to be courageous.[21]

During the rift between the Soviet Union and China, Ma always supported his own Party without question. But he did so as quietly as ever, and he never completely cut ties with those taking the other side. Israel Epstein observed that Ma's way of showing displeasure with another's action was to refuse to discuss it. Those who disagreed with Ma appreciated this approach. The Yangs say that they had little to do with some of the "sunshiners," like Sydney Shapiro, Israel Epstein, and the Crooks. "We called them 'sunshiners' because they supported China without question on whatever issue arose." "But," Gladys remembers, "even though we were on different sides, we stayed close to Rewi and George, who got along with everybody, no matter which side they were on."[22]

The distractions of Edgar Snow's visit and the Soviet–Chinese rift in Beijing's foreign community interfered little with Ma's efforts to eradicate leprosy. Teams visited outlying areas to survey the population just as they had when attacking venereal diseases, but from the beginning Ma, Dai, and other physicians who had seen such success in eradicating venereal diseases knew that this new campaign would be much more difficult. In the first place, most people who suspected they might have leprosy avoided medical diagnosis for fear that retribution and shame would bedevil not only them, but their families. For centuries the response to leprosy had been exile to isolated areas at best, killing at worst. Suicide was common among those afflicted, and the community, including the medical community, avoided them at all costs. It was obvious that Ma and his colleagues had to deal with a serious social as well as medical problem. Some of the reluctance to mount an attack on leprosy came in part from the local political leaders, who held traditional beliefs about the disease and who refused to allow medical teams in their areas.

In 1960, two pilot programs to study and eradicate leprosy were set up, one in Haian County, Jiangsu Province, the other in Chaoan County, Guangdong Province. Other, smaller projects got underway in other areas, and more than twenty provinces joined the effort within a few years. These operations were coordinated by the newly developed "Leprosy Research Unit" in the Ministry of Public Health. While no one was appointed director of this new unit, everyone looked to Ma to lead the campaign against leprosy.[23]

In order to simply get permission to establish medical teams in the pilot areas, Ma had to use his old revolutionary connections. In Jiangsu, he first visited provincial Party secretary Feng Zichuan, whom he had known in Yan'an. In Guangzhou, he visited Party secretary Tao Zhu, another old comrade. Dai recalls, "He would visit them first, and tell them about our work and how they could use their influence to support the leprosy work in their province. I had no such influence." Following these visits, which Dai says were sessions in "cleaning the brain" of the leaders, Ma took the provincial leaders down to the counties where the work was to take place. He introduced them to those afflicted with the disease, telling them that while leprosy was contagious, it was not "very" contagious. The leaders then "cleaned the brains" of the local leaders, and the teams began their work.[24] "He was a very good 'brainwasher,'" says Dai, "and he used every means necessary to educate people. He could be at dinner, a political meeting, or at a dance. He did propaganda work on leprosy everywhere he went."

The teams entered the two pilot counties and surveyed 95 percent of the population, over seven hundred thousand people. Ma joined in the effort in Chaoan County. When he discovered that only 95 percent participated in the initial survey, he sent the team back to the village level for more study. They finally surveyed 800,000 people—98 percent of the population—and discovered 1,700 people with leprosy.[25]

As on the venereal diseases campaign, Ma expected absolute dedication from his staff. When a suspected case of leprosy was discovered, the team ran four tests on the patient: bacteriological, pathological, immunological, and clinical. One doctor who reported to him during this time remembers what happened if Ma found incomplete test results on his desk. "If someone forgot to run one of these, Ma got quite angry, would criticize the nurse or technician and tell them to run the tests again."[26] On several occasions, he got angry at the poor or unsanitary care given to the patients. He not infrequently brought his assistants to tears, as the wife of Ma's colleague Dr. Yang Lihe discovered one day in Guangdong Province. She was a nurse charged with giving injections to the leprosy patients. Ma examined the needles regularly, since they were reused until they were unserviceable. One night he discovered she was using a damaged needle and criticized her until she burst into tears. "Sometimes," Yang says, "he would check my patient examination and history reports. Even though he could not read Chinese well, he knew medical terms and if one test result was missing he would grow angry. He expected everything to be done carefully, to be done perfectly. He would say, 'Why can't you find the report,' and 'Find it so we can correct the report in time.' But he never got angry with the patients, only the doctors and nurses."[27]

Ma was older now, and prone to ailments stemming in part from his lengthy stays in the countryside. But still he resisted the special treatment offered to both him and his staff. His reputation as an old revolutionary and as a physician had spread far by now, and his appearance in a county was treated as a special event. Dr. Dai says that when they went on their trips the Chinese received 1.50 yuan a day for food, while Ma received 3 yuan, which he always refused. "Old Ma told me that if he accepted this he would feel isolated from the rest of the Chinese." Dai recounts one occasion when Ma's impatience with special treatment boiled over into a provincial incident. It came during the difficult years of the early 1960s after the failures of the Great Leap Forward when starvation was not uncommon throughout the countryside. "Once in 1961 our medical team of seven or eight went to a county to run some tests. The local Party leaders prepared a banquet for thirty people in our honor. Ma was angry at them for wasting so much food, and he refused to go to the dining room. I told him that now it would be a waste *not* to go, and that I would arrange to pay for some of the food and tell them not to do it again. He went, though without enthusiasm. The next day the same thing happened. That time we both refused to go, as did the rest of the team. Later the county leaders came to apologize, saying they had not realized Ma wanted to be treated like a Chinese. They had only acted in a traditional way when a respected foreigner came to their province. Finally, the county leaders were forced to hold a meeting to sum up their poor handling of this, and the whole affair became an example to learn from for everyone in the province."[28]

While Ma was one of several innovators who dedicated his life to the eradication of venereal diseases, it was in the fight against leprosy that he established himself as the dominant pivotal figure in attacking and reducing the spread of a dreaded disease. His ideas, mostly in the realm of social and medical education rather than in research and technology, changed the very nature of how leprosy was understood by those suffering from the disease and by those treating it.

On his initial trips to the pilot programs, Ma distinguished himself by two actions. When he first entered leper villages, he was appalled by the clothing doctors wore to protect themselves from their patients. Covered from head to toe, only their eyes showed to the patients. He lashed out at the physicians, Dr. Wang remembers, when "he saw them covered completely in white. He became angry and said this only frightened the patients, that it made the physicians and nurses look like the Ku Klux Klan." He instructed the doctors to follow his lead, and wear typical physician clothing, without gloves or mask. Of all the actions he took, however, none carried as much weight or represented his view of how to treat this disease as his willingness to touch the patients he met. Most of these people had not felt the touch of another human being in years, some in scores of years, and the impression this made on both patients and doctors was profound. For the patients it often brought tears of joy and release. When Ma greeted new patients he usually shook their hands and hugged them. He took food offered by the patients, and held the diseased parts of the body in his hands during physical examinations. He always washed carefully after these visits, for he knew that leprosy was contagious only if one ignored good hygiene. Such behavior horrified the other doctors and nurses. Their jobs were already at the lowest end of the medical profession. Now were they also expected to risk actually getting the disease through direct contact with patients? Were they required to follow his example? Ma said yes. Most of them said no, and it was only through years of persistent education and a frequent flash of temper that Ma and the few who supported him finally convinced fellow doctors to treat leprosy patients with respect and personal care.[29]

Because China found itself isolated from much of the world, Ma's work went largely unnoticed abroad for many years. It was known only to a few friends like Edgar Snow, who briefly mentioned his work against venereal diseases in *Red China Today*. However, within the international community of leprosy specialists, word circulated that there was a movement afoot in China to deal with the disease. There even was sporadic mention of a mysterious foreigner working on it. One person who heard of this was Dr. Olaf Skinsnes, born to missionaries in China in the early part of the century. After 1949, he found himself locked out of his birth-place, but he still tried to keep up with events there.

In the mid 1960s Skinsnes, who specialized in leprosy prevention and treatment at the University of Hawai'i School of Medicine, visited Hong Kong's leprosy clinics. He went there to see patients and to "get biopsies or . . . feet or something else that had been removed to work on." He visited there often and frequently accompanied Hong Kong colleagues on their rounds. "We started hearing from patients coming down from China that every once in a while an American doctor would visit the lep-rosarium in Guangzhou. . . . I said this was impossible, that there could not be an American doing this work in China. They told me his name was Ma Haide. Nobody knew who Ma Haide was."[30] Not until years later did Skinsnes see a picture of Ma in a Chinese publication, thus veri-fying the stories about this American in China. He eventually contacted the CIA, who paid him periodic visits because he subscribed to several Chinese publications, and asked them to tell him more about Ma. They obliged, providing some background information, including Ma's Amer-ican name. Skinsnes began writing Ma to discuss leprosy work in China and to share information about his own work. It was Ma's first corre-spondence with Americans working on leprosy, and it began a lifelong friendship that culminated in Skinsnes and his wife moving to China after he retired from the University of Hawai'i in the late 1980s to work on leprosy research in Guangzhou. This was arranged by Ma.[31]

In early 1961, Ma returned from Guangzhou, again fighting off fatigue and illness. At first he tried to stave off a newly developed stom-ach ailment by taking a break from his work. He even took to playing tennis at the Friendship Hotel, but ended up with a torn muscle and ruptured blood vessel. While recuperating, he came down with a recur-ring stomach ulcer that was attributed to his long stays in the country-side, especially the diet he endured there. He remained bedridden for over a month. Rewi Alley wrote Edgar Snow of their friend's most recent medical problems, telling him that Ma "has to learn he is 50, not fifteen." By May, however, Ma was back at it, again heading into the countryside with his medical team. As Alley wrote Snow in late spring, "Shag is away for two months in the south with his Lepers."[32] After returning in July, he went to Beidaihe for his annual rest and relaxation. He went back to Beijing in September "very brown and well," according to Rewi.

After Edgar Snow returned to Switzerland and the United States, he continued his regular correspondence with Alley and tried to begin again with Ma. He expected little from Ma, however. On January 10, 1961, he wrote, "Dear Shag, . . . Since I know I won't hear from you more than once in the next twenty years I presume I'll get the . . . news via Rewi, as usual."[33] He had begun writing a book about his trip, and had excerpts printed in international forums such as *Look* magazine. He sent pieces to Ma, including his notes from the talk with Mao.

Red China Today, Snow's account of his trip to China, was published in late 1961, telling for the first time the story of Ma Haide in some detail. Newspapers and magazines picked up part of the story, and by 1962 word of his exploits had reached his American family. Since the Hatem household had heard nothing from China in almost ten years, this news brought them excitement and renewed hope. Nahoum Hatem, healthy and stubborn as ever, told his family that he would see his son before he died. He was eighty-eight years old and had not laid eyes on Shafick for thirty-three years. He told them he would go home to Syria under the pretext of visiting family there, but once he arrived he would contact the Chinese government to tell them who he was. The family still refused to discuss their oldest son in public, and the trip to Syria was passed off to friends as merely a trip to the old homeland. He instructed his daughter Shafia to take five thousand dollars out of the family account and to make arrangements for him to fly to Damascus.

When Nahoum landed in Syria in early August 1962, he set out for what he thought was the Chinese embassy. Instead he wound up talking to representatives of the Taiwan government. He did not know the difference, but when he told them his son was a famous doctor in China and even served as Chairman Mao's physician, they escorted him out. After looking around he finally found the Chinese embassy. He walked in and told the person at the reception desk that he wanted to see the ambassador. Greg Hatem, Ma's nephew, tells how Nahoum approached the Chinese that autumn day. "He went in there kind of wild-eyed and told the people in the embassy that 'my son is a very important doctor in China and I want to see him and I want you to get him here.' They sent a wire back to my uncle in China and said we've got this crazy guy here who says he's your father. Is he your father? He said, 'Yeah, that's my father.' So they told him he had to get to Syria and calm this guy down."[34]

The staff of the Chinese embassy obviously was confused about how to handle this insistent old man. The first time he showed up demanding to see his son they escorted him out. But the next day he returned, as persistent as the day before. When asked who his son was, he said Ma Haide. Familiar with the name, the reception officer passed the information on to the ambassador. Again Ma's revolutionary past came into play. Ambassador Xu Yixin and his wife Lu Hong were old friends of Ma.

While Xu refused to meet directly with the old man, his wife took a stroll into the reception area to get a look at Nahoum. When she looked at him closely she saw a striking resemblance to Ma, and told her husband the man must be Ma's father. Nahoum was then told that the embassy would look into his request and he should return in a few days. In the meantime they cabled Chen Yi, minister of foreign affairs in Beijing, telling him about Nahoum's presence and his demand to visit his son. Su Fei tells what happened next. "We were on vacation at Beidaihe. One day Ma and I were swimming rather far out in the ocean when a hotel attendant came down to shore and shouted at us in the water, 'Dr. Ma, your father is here, Dr. Ma, your father is here.' 'That's ridiculous,' he said, but we went up to shore and to the hotel. There we were given a message, which later we found out was incomplete. It said that his father was looking for him and for the whole family to come to Beijing at once. We rushed back to Beijing, cutting our vacation short, thinking Ma's father was waiting for us. Not until we got to Beijing did we find out about Syria."[35]

Chen Yi, another old friend from Yan'an days, told Ma that he should take his family and travel to Syria to visit his father. Ma balked and said it was not convenient for him to leave now because of his medical work. Chen Yi insisted, and within a week new clothes were tailor-made for Ma, Su Fei, and Youma, and passports and tickets were arranged. Before they left, Chen Yi gave a farewell banquet for Ma and Su Fei. Ma joked that this was quite a send off. Was Chen Yi afraid he might not come back? The minister laughed, saying that after all Ma had been through in the Chinese revolution, he knew his heart was in China and he would return. "I'll give you another dinner when you return," said Chen. "Then you had better make the reservations now," Ma responded. In the back of Ma's mind throughout this bantering was the fear that Kang Sheng would use this opportunity to accuse him of fleeing to the West with his family. Chen Yi's confidence in his allegiance to China meant a lot, and in later years when Chen Yi came under attack during the Cultural Revolution, Ma defended the former foreign minister at some cost to himself.[36]

On the day after the send-off dinner, Ma, Su Fei, and Youma flew to Damascus by way of Moscow and Czechoslovakia. Eastern European Communist party officials were aware of Ma's trip and, when he and his family arrived in Czechoslovakia, Ma was surprised to hear that an old friend wanted to meet him, a friend he had not seen in a quarter of a century and one he probably never anticipated seeing again. It was Otto Braun, the Li De he had shared caves with in Yan'an. Braun lived in East

Germany and had made the trip just to see Ma. Before he would agree to meet Braun, Ma telegraphed the Central Committee in Beijing to ask for approval to visit with Braun. The response was positive, and the two men talked for an entire day, not about politics, but about their personal lives. Ma found a different man than he remembered from the 1930s. The man before him now was reflective and contrite. Braun wanted only to talk about Li Lilian, the woman he had left behind in Yan'an those many years before. He told Ma that he knew he had treated her unfairly, and he wanted to know everything he and Su Fei could tell him about her. Though he had remarried, he thought of her often. They told him that she had not married after he left, and that she was now ill with cancer. He asked them to see her when they returned to China and apologize for him. "But," says Su Fei, "when we got back to Beijing we told Li Lilian nothing of our visit. She was dying of cancer and there was no reason to bring this up with her then."[37]

After a short stay in Prague, Ma and his family left for Damascus. They were met at the airport by embassy officials and taken to a hotel arranged for them. The embassy telephoned Nahoum, who was staying in Lebanon, and told him he should come to Damascus. The next day, it dispatched a car to pick him up and bring him there to visit his long-lost son.

For the next month, Ma shared a room with his father, catching up on decades of family news and marveling at his good health and his curiosity about life in China. Much of this curiosity stemmed from the old man's assumption that Ma must be wealthy due to his contacts with China's top leaders. After a short while together, Nahoum wanted his son to level with him. "It is said that you are good friends with Mao Zedong and Zhou Enlai. So how much property do you have?" Ma replied that he had 9.6 million square kilometers. Nahoum, confused by the answer, then asked him how many houses he owned. "China's houses are all mine," Ma insisted. His father grew impatient with these answers, and told him to quit playing with him. Ma, ever the propagandist, even with the father he had not seen in over thirty years, then went on to explain how socialism worked in China, emphasizing how all the people owned all the land collectively.[38]

His father would have preferred to hear of his son's riches. He was disappointed in his politics, but pleased with other aspects of his son's life. It was obvious that the embassy staff treated his son with special honor, and this made him proud. He adored Su Fei, who cooked and waited on him every hour of the day. He loved being with his grandson, who reminded him of Joe when he was young. Soon after arriving, Ma wrote to the family in North Carolina, telling of his visit with his dad, and asking them to come to Damascus so he could see them too. At times, he sounded remarkably like the oldest son of years past in Geneva and Shanghai. He was still sending them instructions, and still saying he wanted to be with the family. However, he no longer said he was coming home.

> We certainly miss you and dad misses very much the grandchildren. He wants you to write to him and tell him how all of you are, how the children are getting on, what they are doing etc. He would like to know all the news from home. . . . He is very anxious about Shafia's health saying that she works too hard and is highly strung. Dad wants you to relax and take it easy. He wants Joe to take good care of the children. . . .
>
> We are going to stay in Syria for about one month and then return home since we have two months leave and it takes a long time to go back. My son Yu Ma [Youma] has to go back to school soon or he will lose a year and cannot make it up.
>
> Su Fei and I all wish we could see you and the children and be together again.

Ma signed his name in Arabic, with Su Fei and Youma signing their own names.[39]

On September 26, Ma's birthday, Nahoum held a special celebration. More than one hundred people with the surname Hatem showed up. Pictures were taken all around and Ma and other family members used a tape recorder to talk to family back in the United States. The next day Nahoum left for North Carolina, taking with him gifts from Su Fei of silk scarves for all the women in the family. He also brought Ma's most recent list of goods he wanted from the United States.[40]

When Nahoum returned, everyone in the family wanted to know about Shag. Passing around pictures, Nahoum lavished praise on his long-lost son, his son's wife and son, and the Chinese officials he met. But most family members were still skeptical. They wondered what kept him from coming home when he had the chance to leave China. They learned of a daughter who had not come to Syria. Maybe that was the reason. Marie Hatem, Joe's wife, remembers, "That was the first time I found out there was a daughter. We speculated that the daughter was held back to make sure Shag, Su Fei and Youma would return. We didn't know that, but speculated. Then later we found out she was not really Shag's. It was so hush-hush the family didn't know."[41]

Ma and his family left for Beijing via Moscow as soon as his father departed. Arriving back in China on October 10, Ma called Chen Yi to report back, and to remind him of his promise to return. Within days, Chen Yi held a banquet at Beijing's well-known Sichuan restaurant to welcome him back. "Old Ma, I told everyone you would come back, and now I am right," said the foreign minister in his toast. Ma answered briefly. "Of course I came back. I'm Chinese."[42]

While he was settling back into his life in China, U.S. intelligence agencies were trying to find out more about his trip to Syria. The FBI in Washington, obviously alerted to his presence outside China and concerned about his possible threat to U.S. security, asked for an update on his activities from the Tokyo and Hong Kong embassies, which held reports on Americans suspected of aiding the Chinese. Filed on October 30, a month after Ma returned to China, the report, as usual, contained several inaccuracies: "A medical doctor who went to China in 1934 . . . In 1956 he was reported to be holding a position of some responsibility and influence in the Chinese Communist government." The report ends with the promise that "Any further information of interest coming to the attention of this office will immediately be reported to the Bureau."[43]

In 1963 Ma split his time between medical and political work. In July he visited Fujian Province on medical business, then joined his family for their summer vacation at Beidaihe. There he met with Anna Louise Strong and other foreigners.[44] Anna Louise missed the political struggles in the United States, especially the growing opposition to U.S. involvement in Southeast Asia and the civil rights movement sweeping across the American South. While in Beidaihe, she recruited fellow Americans Ma, Talitha Gerlach, Bertha Hinton, and Canadian Dorise Nielsen to join her in issuing a recorded statement of support for the struggle of African Americans. Her talk was played before a rally in Beijing on August 12. In it, Strong identifes Ma by both his American name, George Hatem, and by his Chinese name. While he may have told Chen Yi only months before that he came back from Syria because he was Chinese, it is obvious that for this purpose Ma cared to be seen as an American. Speaking for Ma and the others, Strong said, "As five Americans living and working for considerable time in China, we send our greeting to your rally from Peitaiho [Beidaihe]. We heard by radio the call of chairman Mao Tse-tung to the people of the world to support the American Negros' struggle. We want to bear witness that we, Americans living, working and travelling extensively in China, have seen for ourselves how widely and deeply the Chinese people of all walks of life and of all ages, are interested in the American Negros' struggle for freedom, and give it their full support. . . . We are glad to note that the Negro fighters for freedom now are not being fooled by President Kennedy nor by his brother Bobby. You will be able to pry some rights from them by pressure, but these rights are gained not from their benevolence but by your own struggle and power and not in any other way."[45]

Chairman Mao's concern for the civil rights struggle in the United States, expressed in his "Letter to American Negroes," his first published work in years, was a signal to the Americans in China that they also should publicly support this movement. Anna Louise's taped message was only the first burst of activity from this small group of expatriates. Ma issued the next statement in an article he wrote for the October 1963 edition of *China Reconstructs*. Written from the perspective of a physician familiar with China's improved treatment of its minority peoples, a subject he knew as well as anyone, and of an American having grown up in the South, he presented a four-page diatribe against racism in the United States. The views he expressed in this article seem somewhat out of character for the politically careful Ma, for he rarely used a public forum to openly attack his home country. He had for the past thirty years done all he could to avoid this, preferring to emphasize the positive advances found in China rather than to join in the negative name calling exchanged between the governments of China and the United States. For instance, he never joined in the international peace meetings that his friends Rewi Alley and Anna Louise Strong attended in North Vietnam and other socialist countries. But in this instance he had little choice. The chairman had set the tone, the Party was committed to an important international stand, and he pitched in.

In the article, Ma recalls the "Saturday night beatings of Negroes by the cops, the usual stories of so-called rape followed by real lynchings, of the swindling of the Negro sharecroppers or tenant farmers at the autumn tobacco sales. . . . Naturally there were not hospitals for the Negroes, no guarantees of their right to vote. . . . Though this situation existed 35 years ago when I last lived in Greenville, the description could fit as well today there and in any other southern city. Yet the monopoly-controlled government is trying to make the United States look like the paragon of the 'free world'. What do we see there? Rabid racism, segregation and open discrimination. . . . On the other hand, this same U.S. government has accused China of being 'undemocratic', of 'destroying human rights', 'taking away the freedom of the people', of being 'a police state' and 'not fit to take its place in the community of nations', and of 'crimes' toward her minority peoples ranging from 'bloody massacre' to genocide."[46] To further contrast the two countries, Ma outlined advances in medical care, political power, and education among the minority peoples of China, coming to the unsurprising conclusion that "Mongolians, Hans and members of other minority nationalities possess equal status and enjoy the same rights. . . . Contrast this with United States monopoly capitalism's incited racism, segregation, discrimination and brutal violence against the Negro people."[47]

Ma's repudiation of racism in the United States did not go unnoticed by the FBI or the State Department. In a U.S. Information Agency (USIA) report filed in Hong Kong on October 30 by public affairs officer Earl J. Wilson, Ma is accused of attacking the United States by publishing these comments. At the end of the report Wilson states, "Dr. Hatem was one of four Americans living in Communist China who openly supported Mao Tse-tung's cynical effort to enter the U.S. racial controversy with a statement expressing support for the American negro's struggle against racial discrimination . . . made on August 12, 1963." Wilson also noted that "little is known of Dr. George Hatem, alias Ma Hai-teh." It appears that Wilson failed to review the already substantial file at his disposal, for if he had he would have seen that in fact quite a bit was known about Ma, including his birthplace, which Wilson recorded incorrectly as Greenville, North Carolina.[48]

For the remainder of 1963 and through the next year, Ma weaned himself away from the political fray, leaving the attacks on American racism and imperialism in Vietnam and Laos to his friends, who seemed to thrive on it, while he returned to his medical work. In November 1963 he journeyed south to check on the progress of his medical teams, as usual returning weak and in search of a new set of teeth, which, as Rewi Alley remarked to Snow, made him feel and look "fitter."

On January 15, 1964, Chairman Mao hosted a luncheon for "senior Anglo-Americans" in Beijing. Among those attending were Anna Louise Strong, Israel Epstein, Sydney Rittenberg, Sol Adler, and Frank Coe. Kang Sheng also attended and acted as a second host. Ma was in Beijing at the time, and according to Rewi Alley his health was fine. Why was he not included in this high-powered luncheon with Mao? In the first place, Strong, Epstein, and Rittenberg all had obvious, full-time roles as propagandists for China: Strong as an independent writer, Epstein with *China Reconstructs,* and Rittenberg with Radio Beijing. Adler and Coe had risen to the "top of the pagoda" as nominal political leaders of the American community to whom second-level Chinese leaders such as Kang Sheng gave preferential treatment. It was their job to disseminate formal Party policy to others in the foreign community in China. Ma, on the other hand, was seen by foreigners and Chinese alike as primarily a physician. His understanding of Marxism-Leninism was not taken seriously by the more ideological foreigners, and his presence would not have suited the tenor of the meeting. "Even though he was a Party member, he wasn't into theoretical discussion at all. I doubt if he had ever read a book on Marxism," recalls Rittenberg. Another reason he may not have been invited was the important role Kang Sheng played in the luncheon. He and Ma still distrusted each other.[49]

In the summer of 1964, Ma, Alley, Hans Muller, and others visited Shijiachuang to take part in a ceremony commemorating Norman Bethune. Soon after arriving Ma caught the flu and limped off to recuperate at Beidaihe in an extended stay at his favorite vacation spot with his good friends and family. By late June he had recovered enough to visit a village project in Shandong Province. In October, Edgar Snow returned to interview Mao and Zhou Enlai and to make a documentary film. As in 1960, Ma brought Snow up to date on new events in China and accompanied him on a visit to see the chairman. His own professional demands, however, kept him from seeing as much of Snow this time as he had the last time. In early 1965, Ma spent a cold few weeks in Inner Mongolia, following up on results from earlier testing for venereal disease. In August, he journeyed again to Guangdong Province to check up on "his lepers." Su Fei was away from Beijing at this time, joining in the new "Socialist Education Movement" in which city dwellers were sent to the countryside for long periods to work with the peasants. She and Youma were gone for most of 1965.[50]

All in all, the early 1960s proved productive and fulfilling years for Ma. In fact, despite Kang Sheng's continuing suspicion and the lean years experienced throughout the country following the Great Leap Forward, Ma could look back on some extraordinarily fulfilling events during that period, including solid progress in the fight against venereal diseases and leprosy, an improving relationship with Su Fei, and the reunion with his father and old friend Edgar Snow. What would the next decade hold?

Mao Tse-tung's absence from yesterday's Peking May Day celebration deepens the mystery surrounding his whereabouts and his health. Since he has not been seen publicly for almost half a year, many analysts speculate he may be dead or gravely ill, despite the official assertion last March that he is in good health.

New York Times Editorial, May 2, 1966

The Communists or Communist sympathizers of American origin who are believed to be held under some form of detention in Peking include Sydney Rittenberg, Israel Epstein, and Sidney Shapiro. Information on these men is sketchy.

New York Times, July 11, 1970

On November 24, 1965, Anna Louise Strong celebrated her eightieth birthday at a party hosted by Mao Zedong. In order to show Strong how highly they valued her efforts for China, the Party leadership decided to fly Anna Louise and several of her friends to Shanghai to see the chairman. Mao's presence in Shanghai was unknown to everyone except his inner circle, but his reason for being there would soon be known to all.

Among those chosen to attend the birthday celebration was, of course, Strong's personal physician, Ma. Also attending were Epstein, Rittenberg, Coe, Adler, and Alley, among others. They all were given less than a day's notice to prepare for the November 22 flight on a plane arranged by Anna Louise's host unit, the China Peace Committee. In Shanghai they were housed in the old Jinjiang Hotel. Mao had first told Strong he wanted to dine only with her, but she insisted her friends should also attend. Not many people could insist on anything to the chairman, but he decided to accommodate Anna Louise, and on the morning of November 24 he met with her entourage at 10:30 A.M. for conversation and lunch. Also included were Mao's wife Jiang Qing, who almost never made public appearances, Wu Lengxi, head of the *People's*

Daily, and Yao Zhen, vice chief of propaganda for the Party and an assistant to Beijing mayor Peng Zhen.

In a metaphorical gesture, Mao opened the lunch by pulling out a cigarette, joking that as a smoker he was a member of one faction, while Anna Louise, a nonsmoker, represented another faction. Taken aback by Mao's opening challenge, Anna Louise was saved by Ma, who continued the banter with Mao by offering a challenge of his own. "Are you making this a factional affair?" he asked. "Certainly," replied Mao. Then, zeroing in on his old Yan'an physician, he continued, "The doctors say I should not smoke: I say I do. How many of you people smoke: let the smokers raise their hand with a cigarette." Mao spoke his words in a lighthearted manner, but those who knew him well glanced at one another, questioning the confrontational manner in which this discussion began. Then Mao, seeing that he was outvoted in the smoker poll, laughed and commented: "Well, it seems that in this too I am in the minority." At this, he looked beyond the now bewildered foreign guests and directly at Wu and Yao. "Nevertheless," Mao insisted, "I shall smoke and urge you to also."[1] As David Melton, another American present at the meeting, commented later, "Within six months, we would understand that those remarks, like so many of his apparently informal comments, were fraught with meaning for those who could understand them. Those who could on this occasion were not the American guests, but the Chinese officials who had accompanied us from Peking."[2]

Sydney Rittenberg remembers the moment Chairman Mao acknowledged his minority status. "All of us chuckled politely and the ice was broken. But . . . at that remark I saw Wu Lengxi . . . and Yao Zhen . . . turn chalky white, stop taking notes, and go rigid. Something about what Mao had just said had frightened them. Something about the whole atmosphere was odd."[3]

Mao's banter throughout the day focused on a central theme. The world was changing, and forces of change had shifted in favor of the people, if only the people would actively seek the change. Mao lectured the assembly: "The worst thing in the world is to have dead water. The worst thing in the world is a stagnant pond. When you have a stagnant pool, you have to find some way of stirring things up. Otherwise there is no progress. When you have the right line, you can win so long as you persist in the struggle."[4]

After an hour and a half of talk, Jiang Qing entered the reception room. Mao changed the subject, looked at Ma, and again criticized him. "You health department folks don't look after people's health. See how late it is for eating. My wife has invited us all to lunch." They finished their meal with Mao and returned to their hotel, not fully realizing the extent to which the chairman had used them as a "screen through which his warnings were filtered to his colleagues."[5]

The next evening Premier Zhou, who also was in Shanghai, hosted a second dinner for Anna Louise and her guests. While this dinner was more relaxed, Zhou's behavior caused Ma and the other foreigners to reflect further on Mao's comments. The most telling incident came during a performance by a local singing troupe when they omitted a stanza from "The Long March Cantata," a popular revolutionary musical piece. The stanza had been written by a friend of Zhou's, then under suspicion by some around Mao for counterrevolutionary thinking. Zhou, angry at the omission, led the chorus in singing it himself, and ended the evening by telling everyone that it was important to remember the traditions of old so that the young could learn them.[6]

None yet knew, but for the past two days these American residents of China had witnessed the beginning of what would quickly explode into the Great Proletarian Cultural Revolution. In fact, Mao was in Shanghai to meet with his loyalists and plot the course of this movement. The next ten years would be unlike any in Chinese history. Before the Cultural Revolution was over, many around the table would be imprisoned and their friendships tested, in some cases damaged beyond repair.

It remains a daunting—perhaps impossible—task to quickly and accurately summarize the events of those ten years. They remain too recent, too massive, and too complex to describe succinctly. As historian Jonathan Spence argues, "This movement defies simple classification, for embedded within it were many impulses at once feeding and impeding each other." At a minimum, it can be stated that by early 1966 two factions within the Party, an unofficial one led by Jiang Qing and her Shanghai comrades, and an official one led by Beijing mayor Peng Zhen, developed separate agendas for the Cultural Revolution. Jiang's group argued that there was a sinister faction working within the Party to undermine Chairman Mao's revolutionary policies. So her group focused on the need to wipe out all bastions of bourgeois ideas, especially from the field of art and literature. Peng's group tried to steer the movement in a direction that encouraged academic debate on the issue of art and literature and its place in China's revolution. There was no room for compromise with Jiang and the Shanghai propagandists. The lines were drawn, and by the summer of 1966 Peng Zhen was ousted from power and replaced by Jiang Qing, Kang Sheng, and their supporters. Mao encouraged them, telling China's people that "it is right to rebel against the reactionaries."[7]

For many, it was a time of tremendous enthusiasm and optimism. The younger generation had missed the first revolution, and this was their chance to remold China and keep it on the right track toward establishing true communism, as defined by Chairman Mao. But enthusiasm wore two faces. The idealistic, egalitarian forces of the Cultural Revolution were manipulated by many leaders eager to enhance their own power through the antics of the young revolutionaries. University students and professors put up large-character posters attacking their leaders, and student groups splintered into Red Guard units to show support for the Cultural Revolution and Chairman Mao. Schools closed throughout the country, historic temples and other buildings were destroyed, formerly revered old revolutionaries were now reviled, jailed, tortured, and relegated to common physical labor. Government offices ceased normal operations, and family background dictated political standing. Suspicion lurked around every office and neighborhood. It was not a good time to be a foreigner in China.

By the time Ma and the others returned from Anna Louise's birthday celebration in Shanghai, they found their comrades throughout the capital buzzing about the new movement. For the foreigners who had devoted their lives to the Chinese revolution, the issue had a dimension not faced by their Chinese comrades. Should they participate in the new movement or stay to the side? They split on this question, with Ma in the minority, telling everyone to stay out of it.

During the first several months of the Cultural Revolution, Ma and Su Fei avoided trouble. There was little chance to lead a normal life, however. Ma feared for China when he saw Red Guards beat people only because their parents had been capitalists or landlords. He was furious at those who destroyed the cultural relics of ancient China. To his dismay and distress, his leprosy work came to a halt. A new center in Guangdong Province that was set to open on the eve of the Cultural Revolution was instead shut down. His medical work slowed, although late in 1966 the government called him to escort a group of New Zealand physicians around the country on a trip that took him back to Yan'an for the first time. But even this trip was not free from the political agitation sweeping the country. As he approached the border with Hong Kong to see the group off, the train was commandeered by a group of Red Guards, checking papers and making sure no one attempted to leave China illegally.[8] Ma, like everyone else, was surrounded by chaos. For the time being, he felt safe from personal criticism and political isolation, but all that changed when he returned to Beijing.[9]

Early one morning, only days after his return, Ma found two large, red posters attached to his front door. The posters announced that Ma's house was under the protection of the State Council and that anyone wishing to search the house should call a telephone number listed at the bottom of the paper. Ma knew that he had been targeted, but for now he was protected by old friends in high places. Although shielded from direct criticism, Ma feared that he could be pulled aside for interrogation at any moment. As the movement spread, the Dermatology and Venereological Research Institute was filled with large-character posters criticizing the old physicians and leaders. Ma's close friend Dr. Dai was attacked directly, with some posters saying that Dai had a "high protector," apparently referring to Ma. Other posters criticized the work of the leprosy teams in the countryside, including the research carried out on patients. Ma took this as another attack meant for him. One poster placed outside his office went so far as to criticize—without naming—"the foreigner" working in the ministry.

The newspapers were full of reports promoting revolution in medicine. Doctors all over the country were ordered to study Mao Zedong's writings, to engage in physical labor, and to learn from the peasants and workers how better to practice medicine. The very study of Mao's works by physicians, it was argued, would help cure patients. For example, Xinhua reported the story of a woman worker burned over almost 90 percent of her body. As she was rushed to the hospital, the medical staff was called together to prepare for her arrival. Xinhua states,

A Mao Zedong thought study class was set up. Comrades of the propaganda team, leading members of the hospital's revolutionary committee and the emergency group together studied Chairman Mao's brilliant three constantly read articles. They armed themselves with this teaching of Chairman Mao's "Serve the people whole-heartedly. . . . ." They also criticized the counter-revolutionary revisionist line in medical and health work pushed by the arch renegade Liu Shao-chi. This helped raise their political consciousness. [They] stood facing a portrait of Chairman Mao and vowed: "We'll fight to defend Chairman Mao's revolutionary line!" . . . The political workers reminded the medical group that the greater the difficulty they faced, the more necessary it was for them to put politics to the fore and apply the invincible Mao Zedong thought". . . . The achievement in saving her life fully shows that, tempered in the great proletarian cultural revolution, the revolutionary great unity of the Chinese people has been consolidated and is growing. Guided by Mao Zedong thought, the revolutionary masses in China are constantly creating new wonders.[10]

Ma grew bored and angry. He had no patients and no medical work. Despite his concerns, at the beginning of the Cultural Revolution he pitched in and did his part to encourage the movement. In 1966 he published an article in the journal *China's Medicine* entitled "With Mao Zedong's Thought as the Compass for Action in the Control of Venereal Diseases in China."[11] Quickly, however, he grew disgusted with the ritualism of Mao worship, which he equated to "Westerners reciting the bible," and with the increasing glorification of folk remedies at the expense of scientific medical knowledge. But, like all physicians, he was reluctant to openly criticize these remedies for fear of being branded a counterrevolutionary. Besides, he had endorsed most, if not all, of what Mao Zedong had said and done before all this began. His son Youma and stepdaughter Liangbi joined the Red Guard with his blessings. They all wore Mao pins to show their loyalty to the chairman. It was a wrenching time for Ma. The signals were confusing, and at times he let his anger show.

Once he received a letter from abroad asking his opinion of an article saying that in China doctors thought the injection of chicken blood could cure a multitude of illnesses. Ma exploded and marched over to the office of Liu Xiangping at the Ministry of Public Health. He threw the letter on Liu's desk, asking, "What the hell is this. There is absolutely no scientific basis to this article. How can I answer such a thing? It is blasphemy to China's medical and public health care."[12]

While he seethed at the demise of scientific work in his field, he was assigned responsibility for digging irrigation ditches and monitoring the boilers at the institute. He still could not read Chinese well and asked his colleague and fellow ditchdigger Yang Lihe to translate many of the character posters for him. In one of his lighter moments, he told Su Fei that at least his reading of Chinese had improved slightly as he studied the posters with Dr. Yang.[13]

While Ma spent most of his time at home and at the institute, events in the lives of other foreigners elsewhere in Beijing grew increasingly complex and volatile. Most of the foreigners in China could not identify with Ma's experience dating back to the mid 1930s. Unlike Ma, they had no long-term personal friendship with the old leaders now being criticized, nor did they have the experience of similar events in the past, such as the Rectification Campaign, to put this new movement in broader perspective. They were more recently arrived revolutionaries who saw the Cultural Revolution as their chance to enter full force into the historical stream of world revolution. They saw themselves participating in a movement on the scale of the American Revolution and the Paris Commune. It was their time in history. During the first year of the Cultural Revolution, the central authorities discouraged foreigners from participating. Ma supported this stance, telling all who would listen that this was a Chinese affair, and not one that welcomed foreigners. Many disagreed, especially those who worked as teachers, translators, and farmers, far from the perceived privileged life of the "old hands" like Ma, Alley, and Muller. To make their point, four Americans put up a big-character poster attacking Party authorities in the Foreign Experts Bureau for lavishing special privileges, higher salaries, and better living conditions on foreigners while their Chinese comrades were still poor. This hit a nerve and brought about vigorous debate both in the foreign community and in high Party circles. When Chairman Mao heard of it, he labeled the poster "revolutionary" and, in January 1967, sent foreign minister Chen Yi to meet with all the foreigners in Beijing to share with them Mao's support for their involvement in the movement.[14]

The split in the foreign community came to a head soon afterward. A Red Guard organization, part of the rebel faction, met with foreign experts living in the Friendship Hotel, a large compound housing many of the foreigners in Beijing. They asked these foreigners for their support. Out of this meeting developed the Yan'an-Bethune Regiment, a revolutionary organization made up entirely of foreigners and founded to support the Chinese in reaching the goals of the Cultural Revolution. Ninety people joined the regiment, whose five-person steering committee represented five continents. It was recognized by the Chinese press as a legitimate revolutionary organization equal to others in the country. The members were euphoric. Many of those joining were old friends of Ma, including David and Isabel Crook, Israel Epstein, Joshua Horn, and Sidney Shapiro. Sydney Rittenberg did not join, but was thought by many to be leading it from behind the scenes.

Mao's invitation to foreigners did not change Ma's position. He became even more vehement in his opposition to foreigners playing a role, and he seemed to take it personally when others disagreed. When one medical colleague, Dr. Joshua Horn, decided to accept the chairman's invitation to participate, Ma and Muller went to see him and told him not to join, that it was not his place and that he had no idea of the consequences of his actions. But Horn eagerly went ahead, dismissing Ma and Muller as too conservative.[15] On another occasion Ma saw his old Shanghai co-conspirator Ruth Weiss walking in a shopping district. He stopped her, saying sternly, "I hope you're not part of that crowd in the Yan'an-Bethune group." She was surprised at the sarcasm with which he asked the question and answered that in fact she had not joined. " 'Good,' he said, with a sneer on his face."[16]

Ma was angry and scolded his old friends at every turn. He ridiculed them, saying he had been a member of the true Yan'an Regiment, and they were only adults acting like children in the Red Guards.[17] Once he ran into Rittenberg, Epstein, and others on the sidewalk outside the Friendship Hotel. "I remember," Rittenberg said, "once when I was walking along with a group of the leaders of the Bethune organization and George came along walking past us and he stopped right there . . . and gave me a very loud lecture so that all of them could hear it, saying, 'Sid, you gotta tell these boys to cut this out. They are interfering in China's internal affairs and they have no business making trouble, making waves and this won't do, this won't do at all.' Apparently he thought I was responsible. We all gathered around George and began arguing back with him."[18]

Ma found himself in a distinct minority. Since the founding of the People's Republic he had worn the mantle of senior foreigner in China. His long years in China, his membership in the Party, and his personal relationship with Chairman Mao, Zhu De, Zhou Enlai, and others gave him this status. But now, he found that this enduring status was in jeopardy. Other foreigners, especially Rittenberg and Epstein, were now taking the lead in a new revolution, a revolution Ma wanted no part of. "He felt obligated to be apologetic for those in power," is how one former Yan'an-Bethune Regiment participant remembers Ma.[19] Just as younger Chinese were free to criticize old and revered revolutionaries for becoming soft, so now could junior foreigners criticize Ma, Alley, and the other "conservatives" for the same reasons. "George felt," David Crook argued, "that he was the leader of the foreigners. But he was conservative and Rittenberg took a new look at things. Mao wanted to get rid of the new elite and George was part of that elite. He was loyal to the old timers, and he thought the Bethune-Yan'an Regiment was out to get him."[20]

Now isolated from all his former friends except Alley and Muller, Ma was ridiculed for his privileged life and staid political stance. The three of them forged even tighter bonds, spending time at Ma's house enjoying one of their rare delights, Western-style waffles cooked by Ma's old housekeeper, and at Alley's under the watchful eye of the People's Liberation Army. They knew they had lost their status with other foreigners, but they would not budge in their opposition to the chaos they witnessed around them. They feared for China and themselves. Alley and

Ma took walks around town together, sometimes at the Summer Palace in the dead of winter, so they could talk without fear of being overheard. Even though the foreigners showed little personal animosity toward Ma, most ignored his advice and thought history had passed him by. This break with old friends was shown clearly when Foreign Minister Chen Yi was called before a Red Guard criticism meeting in August 1967. Ma was encouraged to attend by the Yan'an-Bethune Regiment, and forced to attend by the Ministry of Public Health. He agreed to go but said he would not participate in criticizing his old comrade. He was accompanied by Alley and Muller. Once in the meeting hall, he saw big-character posters displayed around the room criticizing Chen Yi. Some members of the Yan'an-Bethune Regiment joined Chen Yi on stage to denounce him. At this point Ma looked at his two friends, and the three of them rose to leave the auditorium in protest. They were stopped by one of the foreign rebels and told they could not leave until the meeting was completed. "I was told this was a 'voluntary' meeting, and choose not to volunteer," Ma responded. They left the hall and returned home, despondent.[21]

One of the few people who could bring the foreign community together under the same roof during this period was Anna Louise Strong. Supportive but naive about the Cultural Revolution, Anna Louise relied on Rittenberg for help in her writing and on Ma for medical care. Rittenberg recalls that "During the Cultural Revolution, George, Rewi and Muller became three depressed individuals who were very unhappy about what was going on and they would talk to Anna Louise about it and not to me. I would be there and overhear some, but they wouldn't challenge me directly. They only talked with Anna Louise about the killings and torturing he saw in his neighborhood. These guys were harping on the negative things to deny the whole revolution, which I thought was wonderful. And I saw them as just a bunch of old fogies who were deep in tradition to the extent where they couldn't understand the new world."[22]

Finally, the Chinese settled the debate between Ma and the Yan'an-Bethune Regiment. After a few months of heightened political activity, some of the more active foreigners began to question their role in the Cultural Revolution. There was a feeling that perhaps they were being manipulated by forces far more powerful than themselves. By the spring of 1967, for example, Chinese who had requested help from these radical foreigners found themselves accused of enlisting the support of "foreign devils." As David Milton recounts, "For those of us who had entered the Cultural Revolution because of its historic and international links with

American, French and Russian revolutions, it was now necessary to face the fact that we had also encroached on the intimate world of a family fight."[23]

The Yan'an-Bethune Regiment split into factions and eventually was taken over by leftists aligned with Rittenberg. Rittenberg was in turn aligned with a faction identified as an enemy of Premier Zhou Enlai. Israel Epstein was named the new leader of the regiment. As the movement progressed down a treacherous path, Rittenberg, Epstein, David and Isabel Crook, and others tried to keep pace with events, all the while convinced their efforts would help China take a revolutionary leap toward true communism. But they were in way over their heads. Ma had been right from the beginning about the role foreigners could play, and for some who joined the fray and got out early enough the consequences were not grave. For Rittenberg, Epstein, the Crooks, and others who stayed in, however, life took a wrenching turn. In December 1967 Rittenberg was placed under house arrest. In February he was taken off to prison, where he would stay for over a decade. Epstein and his wife and the Crooks were arrested shortly after Rittenberg, and they stayed in prison for more than five years. The Yan'an-Bethune Regiment was disbanded.[24] Ma, not known as one to wish anyone ill, forever resented Rittenberg's role in this affair and shed no tears when he left the scene. Over twenty years later, Rittenberg would reflect on that period and the battle he had with Ma. "George took the typical, what was called at the time the Royalist or Conservative position. In retrospect this was wonderful wisdom on his part, though I do think he missed the point of the Cultural Revolution. I guess he was half right and we were half right, but I'm not sure if he wasn't more right than we were."[25]

As 1968 began, Ma still had plenty to worry about. Old comrades were under investigation, some were disappearing. Alley was under constant watch; a soldier was assigned to him whenever he left his house. Ma could not be sure he was safe from the chaos swarming about him. Unbeknown to him at the time, his personal safety was assured by the intercession of Zhou Enlai. In 1967, Zhou telephoned the director of the Dermatology and Venereological Research Institute to inquire into Ma's status. He informed the director that Ma was an old friend of China's revolution and that care should be taken to protect him. There were to be no criticism meetings attacking him. No harm should come to Ma, and if anyone had a problem with him, that person could write to the premier himself expressing his or her opinion. A meeting was immediately called of all members of the institute except Ma. They were informed of the premier's order, and from that day forward no direct criticism of Ma occurred in the institute.[26]

This personal protection did little to protect Ma's Chinese friends, although he himself sometimes stood up to the injustice. Dai Zhengqi, Ma's director before the Cultural Revolution, was one who suffered. Ma was forced to attend a meeting where Dai was criticized by members of the institute for being a "revisionist." Ma interrupted the meeting, saying, "If Old Dai carried out a revisionist line, then so did I. We have been together all along in the institute." The criticism continued, and Dai was accused of plotting with Wang Hongshen, another physician and old friend who worked closely with Ma, and an "unnamed" institute leader of holding secret meetings in this unnamed person's home to plot an overthrow of the rebel leaders of the institute. Everyone knew this third person was Ma, even though they could not say it outright.[27]

On most occasions Ma kept his views to himself and outwardly pretended to support the movement. But when he could, he comforted his old friends under attack. Once Dai was ordered to take coal to Ma's house. When he got to the front door Ma scolded him in front of the Red Guard who accompanied him. Once in the house, however, he forced Dai to sit down and warm himself with coffee and conversation. When he left, Ma scolded him appropriately for all to hear. Wang Hongshen, Ma's other "co-conspirator," was ordered to clean toilets at the institute. She wore a cumbersome placard around her neck identifying her as a "counterrevolutionary," a common punishment for intellectuals at that time. If spoken to at all, she was to be addressed by the "counterrevolutionary" label appearing on the sign. Ma, however, walked by her, inquired of her health, and addressed her as Dr. Wang. "This brought me great comfort during those long days," she recalled in later years.[28]

Aside from his colleagues, Ma worried desperately about himself and his family. Usually outgoing and light in spirit, he grew despondent and fearful of the future. One evening in early 1968 he told Su Fei that it was time to discuss how the Cultural Revolution might affect the family. He told her he was clear in his own heart that he was not an enemy of the people, but he still thought it possible he might be arrested. Israel Epstein, his wife Elsie Chomeley, and the Crooks had just been put in prison. While he had disagreed with their activities, he was appalled that they were arrested. "He thought," said Su Fei, "that if they could be arrested even though they did nothing wrong, so could he. He might be next." He told her that if he was arrested, he would do nothing to harm the family, the Party, or the people of China. She must survive whatever came, take care of Youma, and hope the Cultural Revolution would end soon.[29]

Over the next several months Ma insisted that the family take extra precautions. Su Fei and Youma, now a college student, were not allowed to go to work or to school. Once, when she was shopping close by their house, two Red Guards pointed at Su Fei and denounced her as a traitor for marrying a foreigner. "We were all very nervous and scared, waiting for something to happen," remembers Su Fei.[30] For the next two years the family lived with fear. During part of that time, Youma was sent to Mongolia with other young people to work on a state farm. Ma and Su Fei were visited by friends who encouraged them to leave the country. They could move to Switzerland, where he had friends, or return to his home in the United States. Foreigners throughout Beijing were trying to get out. Their work had been taken away from them and they feared they could wind up in jail like so many others. Even Ma's old friend Hans Muller wanted to return to Germany. But Ma refused to consider it, telling one friend, an overseas Chinese from Britain, that he loved China and now was Chinese. His friend responded, "Well, you may love China, but China does not love you!" Ma exploded, shouting, "Who says China does not love me? The Chinese Communist Party loves me, and the Chinese people love me. That's enough. Why should I expect love from a handful of evil men."[31]

While Ma struggled against anti-foreign sentiment and suspicion of espionage, ironically, his family in the United States faced similar suspicions. In February 1967 the Charlotte, North Carolina, office of the FBI initiated an investigation into Joe Hatem, Ma's brother living in Roanoke Rapids. In a memo to J. Edgar Hoover under the heading "Chinese Communist Activities in the United States," the FBI reviewed Ma's file yet again, in line with Hoover's heightened concern about Communist infiltration into the civil rights and antiwar movements. They were looking for any evidence that Ma might be communicating with Joe in the United States. After the FBI investigated Joe's movements and activities, however, they found nothing. They finally concluded that "no current investigation is recommended." How ironic that in China Ma was suspected of being *anti*-Communist, while in the United States his brother was investigated because Ma was known to be *pro*-Communist.[32]

Rewi Alley, representing as usual both himself and his friend Ma, tried to show a positive face to the international community as he corresponded with friends abroad. Of all the people Alley and Ma wanted to inform and educate about China, Edgar Snow stood paramount. It was not easy under the circumstances, and Alley struggled to find the right words. He wrote to Snow in October 1967.

> Today there is so much change, it is not always easy to catch up. I look forward to the time when it will be possible for you to come again and see us all before we become too hoary and bent. . . . Ma, as full of optimism as ever, was busy carrying in his supply of winter coal when I went to see him the other day. The schools are starting up again, and I do not see Mao Mao for afternoon walks as before. The cultural revolution goes on apace, however, as winter cold begins to blow in over fallen leaves.[33]

During this period Snow tried to arrange a trip to China but found roadblocks at every turn. Some Chinese leaders apparently did not like his portrayal of China after his 1965 visit. Besides, authorities were not keen to show China's current state of chaos to the world. In December 1967, Snow wrote Ma and Su Fei that he wanted to visit them again, "but it seems I'm now persona non grata. How am I to repent if I do not know the nature of my crime?"[34]

By the summer of 1968, Snow grew more than a bit irritated that his status had changed from friend to enemy of China, and he wrote friends to voice his anger. Alley, again writing for himself and Ma, tried to calm Snow's frustration while subtly alerting him to changes in China. He wrote

> Of course you are a real friend to the revolution, and I am sure most top folk believe that. You certainly did come in winter, but now it is spring with stiff gales blowing and dust rising. Yes, you have always worked hard for the Chinese people, to interpret and to clear understanding for them through the international jungle. . . . I hope very much you will be able to come again, stay long and write at your leisure, for there is so much needs writing in this day and age. . . . Someday Shag and I will do what the Chairman said and come to spend a couple of weeks with you. . . . Thanks for the invite to HK. Not possible at this time.[35]

By the fall of 1968, Alley's letters to Snow conveyed more serious news, although still in a subtle way. "A letter sent to the Eps [Israel Epstein and his wife], care of me, came in from you. As I do not know where they are, I have asked the Peace Committee to forward." Israel Epstein and his wife were by then in prison, and Alley of course knew this. Snow must have sensed the gloom in such a comment. Later in the letter Alley sounds more optimistic, telling Snow that "Shag is very well" and Anna

Louise as feisty as ever.[36] Keeping up some sense of normalcy, Ma sent Snow a Christmas card in December 1968 voicing confidence in China's future. Throughout 1969, Alley continued to feed Snow bits of information on the situation in China. In May he told Snow, "Re politics in China, I would not know more than you. Have Hsinhua [Xinhua], *Peking Review,* and that is that. . . . George is happy that Yu Ma [Youma] is away on a state farm in Mongolia, and that he likes it very much. He himself is well, swims every day, and spends most of the rest of his time on meetings."[37]

By late 1969, Snow's impression of China, and of the well-being of Alley and Ma, must have been confused if Alley's letters were his sole firsthand reports. In November Alley told him that, "Here, youth are in the saddle, and we shall see what happens in the way of results." He then informed Snow that Ma is "working harder. Is thinner, by a lot."

In December Alley told Snow that Ma was ill and that he rode to work on a bicycle, fighting "against the wind a bit cold for the 60 years he now comes to." In fact Ma had pneumonia at the time and was hospitalized. Until the Cultural Revolution, Ma had been taken to work by a ministry car if he desired it. Those days were over. In the same December letter, Alley conveyed more of the darker picture to Snow. He told him that if he did come back to China he should not "bring Kodakchrome film, as it cannot be processed here, and film has to be processed before it can be taken out. I had bad luck with the film on my last trip. The negs of the very best shots I put carefully away. But then when I got home found that they were lost."[38]

Despite the problems he faced, Ma never lost confidence in the Communist party, and he and Alley always wanted that positive message to get through to those on the outside. Ma preached perseverance even to their friends who were persecuted daily. When Muller tired of it all and attempted to leave, Ma wrote Zhou Enlai and asked him to personally ask Muller to stay. In the end Muller stayed. Ma told one friend that he was "confident because the Party has led the people in making revolution for decades. How can there be so many traitors and spies? Everything will be straightened out. What is going on is not in line with Party policy and this situation won't last long."[39]

Ma's confidence in the Party was tested to the limit in the fall of 1969. The crisis did not come to him personally, but to Su Fei. One morning at 9:00 A.M. two members of the Military Propaganda Work Team from the Beijing Film Studio, Su Fei's work unit, came to visit her. By that time in the Cultural Revolution the military was active in most units to mediate between various factions. They told her she should accompany them to the studio, but could return soon. Ma objected, but he was powerless to keep her from going. When she arrived at the studio she was taken to a room and told to write a history of her days in Shanghai, especially about her relationship there with Jiang Qing. She said she had nothing to say about her relationship with Jiang, and refused to write anything. Her captors called Ma and told him she was being held indefinitely. Ma called the Military Propaganda Work Team of the Ministry of Public Health to get a car to ride to the studio. Accompanied by Youma, he went to find his wife. When he got to the studio he tried to persuade the officials to let her go, but he and Youma were not even allowed to see her. They left with Su Fei still confined.

In fact, the phone call to Ma was a ruse to begin with. Ma was alerted to Su Fei's detention to get him out of the house. As soon as he and Youma left, forty Red Guards from the Ministry of Public Health stormed into his home. The old housekeeper who had been with Ma since liberation tried to fight the young people off, telling them Ma and Su Fei were good people who gave their life to the revolution. She was pushed aside, but kept screaming at the intruders. Finally they tied her to a chair, stuffed her mouth with a dirty rag, and put her outside in the middle of the courtyard. Ostensibly they were searching for evidence on Su Fei. But they were really looking for any evidence that might incriminate Ma as a spy. The old charges had sprung up again, and the house was emptied of all letters and articles written in English and all pictures with foreigners in them. No documents in Chinese were taken.

When Ma left the film studio, a call was made to the Ministry of Public Health to inform them he was returning. The Red Guards ransacking his home got the message and left before he got back. When he entered the front gate, he saw the housekeeper still tied up in the courtyard and found his home in shambles. Ma wrote to Zhou Enlai telling him of the arrest of Su Fei and the destruction in his home. As a loyal Party member, Ma followed protocol even in this trying time. Rather than send the letter himself, he asked Liu Xinquan, an old friend and at the time head of the military unit at the ministry, to deliver it for him.

For the next several days Ma waited to hear news about Su Fei. Unbeknown to him, she had attempted to escape from custody on the tenth day of captivity during an unguarded moment at breakfast. She took this drastic action after one of her colleagues was beaten to death while in custody. But as she was about to make good her escape by boarding a bus, she was recaptured and placed in solitary confinement. A few days later, word arrived from Premier Zhou that Su Fei should be freed. When told she had not furnished the information they asked for,

Zhou told the studio authorities to let her go anyway, that any problem with Su Fei could be worked out later.

When she returned home, Ma refused to let her out of the house for the next several months. The old housekeeper did all the shopping. Eventually Su Fei and the entire staff of the film studio were sent to the "May 7 Cadre School" outside of Beijing to engage in physical labor and remold their political thinking.[40] While her life was hard and her movements restricted, she was not under confinement. She stayed for more than one year, while Ma stayed in Beijing, struggling against a bout of pneumonia without any family support. The only good news was that he had been allowed to resume medical work, although now at the smaller Fu Wai Hospital as an ordinary doctor of dermatology. While this was a drastic demotion in status, he was happy to practice medicine again, and he eventually used his position to treat old comrades mistreated by the Red Guard. The 1960s had ended badly for Ma and his family, but there were signs that life might improve in the 1970s.[41]

The State Department today described the Chinese invitation to an American table tennis team to visit Communist China as an "encouraging development" and said it would welcome reciprocal visits by Chinese athletic teams to this country.

New York Times, April 8, 1971

As 1970 began, Ma was confined to a bed in his new hospital, Su Fei was working the fields in the countryside, and Youma was still on a state farm in Mongolia. Rewi Alley visited his old friend Ma every afternoon to take him food and share what news he had of friends. After hearing about his illness from Alley, Edgar Snow wrote Ma a note from his own hospital bed, where he said he was fighting a kidney infection he picked up in China when the two of them traveled to Baoan over thirty years before. Snow asked Ma, "Is there such a word for us, living between former oblivion and early death?" Ma, never an avid letter writer and now too weak to respond to Snow, asked Alley to thank Snow for his concern and wish him well in his own recovery.[1]

Two days after Alley sent Snow this letter, Ma was called from his own hospital bed to attend to his old friend Anna Louise Strong, then near death in central Beijing's Fan Di Hospital. Anna Louise distrusted all doctors, but Ma less so than others. She was a difficult patient and had recently reminded Ma of Chairman Mao's statement that people should follow only about half of what doctors suggest. As one of the few who knew how to calm Anna Louise when she grew so obstinate, Ma responded, "Well, why don't you start, then?"

When he arrived at the hospital, the attending physician informed him that she should remain quiet and not speak. When Ma reminded her of this, she said she would not allow the "dictatorship of the proletariat" to be replaced by "the dictatorship of doctors." Ma was there when Zhou Enlai came to visit her. She adored the premier, and his visit raised her spirits. But the end came soon, with Ma nearby.[2] Alley wrote Snow with the news, telling him that "Anna Louise passed away on March 29th, Easter Sunday. . . . George came out from his hospital bed for the last three days and was with her a lot of the time. The first day he came, she was so very pleased to see him. He has since been busy with various things concerning her—meetings etc. going back to bed to the hospital afterwards. He has a heart condition now, following his pneumonia."[3]

Throughout the spring Ma remained confined to his hospital bed while doctors treated his ailments. Su Fei, suffering from inflammation of the knee, returned to Beijing in June to receive medical care and look after her husband. But she could not stay long and returned to the countryside after only a week.[4]

Edgar Snow's appeal to visit China again remained unanswered. In 1969 he had even taken the extraordinary step of writing Mao Zedong directly, asking "would it be harmful if I were to be permitted to renew acquaintance and see for myself the results of the Great Proletarian Cultural Revolution?" The response he hoped for finally came in June 1970, when the Chinese embassy in Paris granted him and his wife permission to enter China. Still weak from his own illness, he delayed the trip until August. On the surface, his arrival was treated much like earlier visits. On hand to meet him were Ma, Alley, Sol Adler, Frank Coe, and his old friend and interpreter, Huang Hua. But the changed circumstances quickly became apparent. Huang Hua had been allowed out of a May 7 Cadre School for the occasion, Alley's home was encircled by People's Liberation Army soldiers, and Israel Epstein, who usually greeted Snow, was in prison.[5]

During his five-month stay, Snow saw less of Ma than during the 1960 and 1965 visit. What he did see sent conflicting messages. Although she was allowed home in order to help entertain Snow, Su Fei lived most of the time at a May 7 Cadre School when not visiting Beijing. On the one hand, Snow found it an "explorable mystery" how Ma could afford the comfortable lifestyle he seemed to enjoy during what was obviously a difficult period in China. He noted that Ma had a full-time housekeeper, beautiful antiques, and furniture and that he lived in a home that included "a maid's quarters, dining room, kitchen, bath, living room, guest room and large master bedroom, courtyard, garden, entrance court and front gate."[6] On the other hand, even though he received verbal assurances from Ma that his family was fine, he also heard stories of the harsh conditions Su Fei and others of the older generation endured at the May 7 schools. He noted that life for his old friends was "bleak" and that Ma was clearly concerned for his family's health and safety.[7]

Snow pressed Ma, Alley, and Huang Hua to explain what the Cultural Revolution meant for China. Why was their good friend Israel Epstein in prison, and how could someone as loyal as Liu Shaoqi be branded an enemy of the people? In one conversation, Huang Hua tried to explain the "crimes" Liu had committed, only to leave Snow unconvinced. Finally, speaking more sharply than usual, Ma interrupted to remind Snow that the Chinese Communist party runs the affairs of China, and that it has the right to dismiss or expel anyone it wants from posts both inside and outside the Party.[8]

It was soon obvious to Snow why he was allowed to visit China. It had little or nothing to do with the Cultural Revolution. He was to carry a message to the U.S. government that the leaders of the People's Republic wished to discuss upgrading relations between the two countries. Snow was in China for show. Zhou Enlai told him as much, saying he wanted diplomats in Beijing to notice Snow's attendance at functions with high officials. The most important event he attended was the October 1 celebration at Tiananmen Square commemorating the twenty-ninth anniversary of the founding of the People's Republic. To his surprise, Zhou Enlai escorted Snow and his wife to a position on the review stand next to Chairman Mao. The picture of an American standing by the chairman sent an unmistakable message around the world. Later Mao told Snow that President Nixon would be welcome to visit China. He reported this as soon as he left China.

Unlike previous visits, in 1970 Ma attended few of the meetings between Snow and China's leaders. While Snow visited locations outside Beijing, agonizing over the plight of old friends and trying to grasp the meaning of the Cultural Revolution, Ma stayed in Beijing until almost the end of Snow's trip. One of Ma's primary tasks was to act as social coordinator, showing Snow's wife Lois around the streets of Beijing while Snow visited leaders. In October he also accompanied the Snows to visit Madame Song Qingling, whose palatial home was only steps away from Ma's own courtyard.[9]

Once Huang Hua brought Snow to Fu Wai Hospital to visit Ma. It was awkward for them all, since Ma's status had dropped to the point that Huang Hua felt embarrassed to show him at his current duties.[10] Snow's book *The Long Revolution,* published after this trip, makes almost no mention of Ma. This stands in stark contrast to the the glowing references to Ma and his medical work that appear in *Red China Today,* written after Snow's 1960 trip.[11]

Throughout his visit, Snow was constantly beset by the recurring illness he had written Ma about months before. In January 1971 he grew so ill that he coughed up blood and had trouble urinating. Ma told him to remain for a while in China for medical treatment. Zhou Enlai, supported by Ma and Alley, encouraged Snow to take an extended rest at Beidaihe, but Snow resisted. He was ready to leave China. Short of patience with the many incomprehensible changes he found, and short of the cash that only his writing about this trip could generate, he finally left for Switzerland in February 1971. He was accompanied to the Hong Kong border by Ma, Alley, and Huang Hua.[12]

Although Ma saw less of Snow during this visit than either of them might have wanted, the international repercussions that followed would lead to unimaginable changes in Ma's life, both personal and professional. China was ready to crack open its door to the West. Snow's visit was the first sign. In April the Chinese invited the U.S. table tennis team, then playing in Japan, to visit China on a goodwill mission. Almost without hesitation the U.S. government approved the trip, beginning a stage of "Ping-Pong diplomacy."[13] Emerging from the shadows of political isolation, and on the verge of once again playing the role of cultural go-between, Ma was invited to attend the banquet welcoming this group of Americans to China.[14]

China also began to emerge from isolation. Ma's old friends Max and Grace Granich from his Shanghai days and John Service and Koji Ariyoshi from the Dixie Mission paid visits to Ma before the year was over. Occasionally he accompanied some of them to Madame Song's home for tea, where they talked of old times and of China's prospects. Because political developments remained volatile, these early visitors were sometimes frustrated with the dearth of "inside" information they received from Ma, Alley, and other old friends. Ma and Alley never shared the downside of China with outsiders, no matter how close the old ties.

Ma saw his role in 1971 the same as he had in 1944: Defend the Communist party, trust in the Party, support China by highlighting the positive advances. Ma was at it again, playing the role of China defender and Party faithful to foreigners anxious to understand new China. In 1944 Ma never mentioned the abuses of the Rectification Campaign to foreigners visiting Yan'an, even though he had been targeted for criticism. The same held true now. The Cultural Revolution was not an event Ma felt the need to glorify. But no foreigner in China would hear direct criticism of it from him, only a defense of its successes. One visitor in 1971 argued that Ma was the perfect person to introduce China to Americans. He said that Ma's way was to soft sell China's policies. "He uses his attributes to lead the neophyte gently through the Hegelian use of contradictions and dialectic materialism until—voila! the recent skeptic finds himself led to an endorsement of all things Mao."[15] Snow was one of the few who understood this, telling Service in December 1971, "It is not surprising that you did not learn more about 'what was going on' from friends in China. They are very close-mouthed about such things."

In the fall of 1971 an American medical delegation arrived, the first such delegation invited by the government since 1949. Others soon followed, all hoping to meet with Ma. After these visits, Ma's stature in the West grew, as visitors left China with stories of his work against venereal diseases and leprosy. Snow, back in Europe working on his new book, wrote Ma that "everything seems to be moving along splendidly" and that he wanted to arrange for Ma to visit Europe and the United States on a speaking tour. "You are world famous now," Snow wrote him.[16]

While the opening signaled by the Ping-Pong team's visit allowed Ma to see old friends and make new ones, it also would give him the chance to finally reunite with his American family and, eventually, American culture. When word of the table tennis trip hit the airwaves, one of the most surprised and delighted Americans to hear the news was Joe Hatem in Roanoke Rapids, North Carolina. He had heard almost nothing from his brother since the mid 1960s. The minute he heard that the Ping-Pong team was going to China, he looked at his wife Marie and said, "I'm going." Shocked at the idea, she responded that he certainly was not going off to China. "Here I was with four children, I'd never been anything but a housewife, and he wanted to go traipsing off to the four corners of the world leaving me to run the clothing store. I was mad, but he said he was going. First he got his passport, then flew up to Ottawa to get a visa. I didn't know if he'd come back alive or dead. He wrote Shag and said he was coming. He told me he would be gone for two weeks."[17]

Before 1971, Joe Hatem's children had no idea they had an uncle. His name was never mentioned, and although a few pictures of him could be found in his parents' home, his identity was never revealed to them. Joe's oldest son, Joe Pat, remembers thinking the pictures in his grandparents' house were of his own father as a child. To Marie, Joe's brother in China had never been a part of their lives at all. But now the curtain was about to be raised on the family secret. On the eve of Joe's departure, he sat his children down and told them of their Uncle Shag, of his life in China as he understood it, and of his plan to visit China. They were to tell no one about their uncle, or of their father's impending trip. The family told people that he was going to Lebanon for a visit.[18]

In July 1971 Joe left for China. When he arrived at the Beijing airport he was met by Ma and by Su Fei, who had been reassigned to Beijing from the May 7 Cadre School just for the occasion. The brothers had not seen each other for forty-two years, and neither knew what to expect.

The first shocker came from Joe, who wanted everyone to know where he stood on the question of national loyalty. President Nixon had just announced his intention to visit China in the coming year, and Joe wanted to wave the flag in this new era of openness. Into this land of drab blue and gray clothing, off stepped Joe in red polyester pants and a red, white, and blue shirt. "Joe said he wanted them to know he was an American," laughed Marie. Seeing him walk down the plane steps, Ma broke the ice first, laughing and shielding his eyes from the glare of the pants. They embraced and from the beginning showed affection and a closeness undiminished over forty-two years. While Joe expected to stay two weeks, the Chinese government had made other plans. They told him that because he and his brother had not seen each other for forty-two years, he would be their guest for forty-two days so the two could reunite properly.

Joe stayed at the Beijing Hotel, where he was treated royally. He enjoyed walking the streets in his colorful clothing—red was his favorite—and did not mind the constant stares of people fascinated by this colorful foreigner. Su Fei was delighted with Joe and greatly amused by his manner. If anyone ever fit the American stereotype, Joe was the one. She remembers, "When Joe came he liked to show his money sticking out of his back pocket as he walked down Wangfujing Street in his colorful clothes. When he visited famous places he would write on the walls, 'Joe Hatem was here.' And he always wanted to test how honest people were. He brought food from Hong Kong and every time he got off an airplane he would leave a box of crackers on the seat to see if anyone would steal it. It was always returned."

Instead of showing disapproval, Ma found his brother's antics refreshing. They delighted in each other's company, with Joe slowly growing accustomed to Ma's status in China and the respect many held for him. They visited oil fields in the north, the beach at Beidaihe, and finally Yan'an. It was during a walk there that Joe finally grasped how highly respected his brother was in China. Mistaking Joe for Ma, an old man approached him and grabbed his hand to thank him for treating an injury years ago during the war. "See how I can use my hand," he told Joe. "That made Joe feel so good about Shag and his life in China," recalled Marie.

While Joe received the royal treatment in China, his wife and four children heard nothing from him. Two weeks went by and Joe had not returned. Then one day, while Marie was working in the clothing store, the radio flashed a report about her husband. She says that she "dropped whatever I was holding and listened as the announcer told of Joe's trip to

China to be with his brother for the first time in forty-two years. It said that Shag was in good health. It identified Joe as a businessman from Roanoke Rapids. Of course we had told everybody that he was in Lebanon." By the end of Joe's stay he and Ma had reunited the family separated for so long. Joe would return to China annually for the next several years.[19]

While Ma welcomed the reunion with his American family, he also worried about the physical deterioration of his old friend Edgar Snow. Finally healthy again himself, Ma knew that Snow was seriously ill when he left China in February. By mail, he kept up with the visits and diagnoses of the various doctors. On December 6 Snow wrote Ma that he felt constantly fatigued and was awaiting final results on a series of tests to determine what ailed him. He told Ma that he had been asked to cover the Nixon trip for *Life* magazine but doubted if his health would allow it.

Snow thought he might have hepatitis, but the tests showed cancer of the pancreas, and he underwent surgery within days of writing Ma. His condition was terminal, he was told, and he would be in pain for the time he had remaining. He left the hospital over the Christmas holidays. His wife Lois decided to pursue every possible medical alternative, however, and wrote letters to friends in Missouri, New York, Paris, and London. She also wrote Ma and, over her husband's signature, Mao Zedong and Zhou Enlai in Beijing. The letters to Mao and Zhou did not convey the gravity of Snow's illness, only his apology for not being able to cover Nixon's visit.

Lois' news shocked Ma, and he felt he had to do something. In comments to a mutual friend, Ma said, "[I] Just received a sad tragic letter from Lois Snow telling me that Ed has been operated on. A fatal cancer involving the pancreas and liver was found. Letter came in the late afternoon mail. It has terribly shaken Su Fei and myself and we are feeling numb. The letter was written at Ed's bedside on Dec. 15th. In a letter to her I hoped that both would find it feasible to come and live in China. Whatever treatment can be given abroad China can do it as well plus a warm 'serve the people' spirit that Ed will appreciate and need."[20]

Responses from around the world offered sympathy and encouragement, but no cure or promise of hope. Finally, the letter from Ma arrived, encouraging Lois to bring Snow to Beijing "where every attention would be paid, every comfort administered, every bit of scientific knowledge applied." Letters followed from Zhou Enlai, Mao Zedong, and Song Qingling. On January 19, 1972, Snow responded to Zhou that he was too weak to travel, but that he would send Ma the details of his illness.

When this news reached Beijing, Zhou Enlai called the minister of public health and told him to have Ma come see him at once to discuss Snow's condition. Zhou told Ma to travel to Switzerland to bring Snow back to Beijing for treatment. A hospital suite in Beijing was readied to accommodate Snow, Lois, and their two children, and a Chinese airplane was especially fitted for the trip. Ma was told to take one other doctor and two nurses from Beijing, and that two additional nurses from the Algerian embassy would meet him when he arrived. A telegram informed Lois Snow of the plans.

The day before he left Ma once again went to see Zhou. As the meeting came to an end, Zhou asked him what he was going to wear to Switzerland. Ma, wearing his usual padded jacket, told Zhou he would take the coat he was wearing. "You will *not!*" said the premier. "You'll disgrace us all in that." So he had someone call a tailor, who made Ma a new tweed suit, complete with beret and trousers, that very day.

On January 24, Ma and his medical team arrived at Snow's home riding limousines provided by the Chinese embassy. Lois relaxed for the first time in over a month. "Shag (as I learned to call him from Ed) was there smiling, with grief in his soft brown eyes. I closed my own and felt skyborne with relief." Ma immediately went to see Snow, held his hand and talked quietly for a short while. By the next evening he knew the gravity of the situation, and told Lois, "We had made a home out of a hospital for you in Peking [Beijing]; now we'll stay here and make a hospital out of your home." Ma and the other Chinese paid full attention to Snow, Lois recalls, and made him again a person rather than a case. "They were able not only to release him from the worst of his physical misery," she recounted, "but to bring him a tranquillity, a dignity in dying that made it more bearable—not only for him but for me, for our two children, and for our families and friends. They were to affect everyone they met."

When the Swiss doctors came, Ma acted as interpreter for French, English, and Chinese, as well as senior physician. In Chinese medical style, all parties were included in the discussions about Snow's treatment, from the lowest-ranking nurse to all members of the Snow family. Ma spent much of the time with Snow, reminiscing about old times and figuring out ways to make him more comfortable. As word got around Geneva that he was in town, requests from the community poured in. He talked on the phone with a few old friends from medical school days. One evening he agreed to address a meeting of medical personnel at a local hospital to discuss medicine in China. But mostly he stayed at Snow's bedside.

During the last week of Snow's life, Huang Hua arrived from his post as Chinese ambassador to the United Nations in New York. He spent two days with Snow and Ma, reuniting for the last time the trio that had gathered secretly in Xi'an in 1937 to begin a journey that would alter all their lives. Now Huang, with Ma at this side, read Snow a message from Chairman Mao. After finishing, Snow looked up and commented weakly, "Well, we three old bandits."

On February 15, Snow died after slipping into a coma. Joe Hatem flew to Switzerland as soon as the death was announced and stayed with his brother through the funeral. After delivering the eulogy for Snow at a memorial service in Geneva, Ma accompanied Lois and her children on a two-week vacation in the Swiss Alps. While there, they watched television reports of Nixon stepping off the plane to shake hands with Zhou Enlai. Ma returned to Beijing in late March.[21]

Back in China, Ma sensed the great change taking place after Nixon's visit. There was no way to avoid it, as Western delegations and individuals seemed to all want time with him. Helen Foster Snow, Edgar Snow's first wife who had spent time with Ma in Yan'an in 1937, visited China and found Ma a warm and gracious host. She acknowledged this, she said, despite the fact that he was "completely sinicized" and prone to evading the truth.[22]

By summer Ma was back at work in his hospital, but he found little time to practice medicine because of the "visitors from all over, Switzerland, Italy, Australia, Holland, etc. Doctors galore."[23] He spent as much of his time discussing China's political situation as he did medicine, especially the sudden disappearance and downfall of Lin Biao, recognized until that time as Chairman Mao's successor, and the ongoing struggles of the Cultural Revolution. Ma explained these events through an elementary introduction to Marxism–Leninism–Mao Zedong Thought. Lin Biao's fall could be explained, he told visitors, if they could grasp the difference between "internal contradictions," where differences are worked out peacefully by majority vote or consensus, and "external contradictions," where the minority tries to go behind the backs of the majority to create dissention. It is at this point that traitors come to the fore, he emphasized. It was that way with Liu Shaoqi, Ma said, and it was that way with Lin Biao. The Cultural Revolution, he insisted to foreign friends, was a good thing because it raised the political awareness of every Chinese citizen and sharpened people's ability to analyze not only China's activities, but "imperialist actions" abroad.[24]

But Ma's time was not spent only with inquisitive foreigners. In the summer he welcomed the birth of his first grandson, Ma Jun, born to

Youma and his wife of two years, Luo Guifu. He started regular correspondence with his American family and looked forward to more China visits by relatives from North Carolina and Buffalo. The forty-year absence of contact did not seem to diminish Ma's place as the older brother in the family. In some ways he picked up where he had left off in Shanghai. He still felt it his duty to advise the family on matters of importance. It seemed natural to him and welcome on the other end. His cousin Theresa in Buffalo had written to him, for example, lamenting the nonconformist, rebellious nature of her son Tod, then much out of favor with his parents. Ma, the original rebel in the family, used the occasion to defend not only young Tod, but perhaps himself too, when he wrote to tell Theresa that "Tod will mature on his way of finding what and where and when he wants to change the world. It is also good that one does not get into a rut too early but struggles on to make a better place for the future people to live in. The mess that now exists in many countries shows the need for more struggle, revolution and creativeness. Show him this from me, please."[25]

A few months after this exchange, Theresa and Ma's sister Shafia flew to Beijing at the invitation of the Ministry of Public Health. Early in the visit, sister Shafia let decades of resentment loose when she reminded Ma of the sacrifices she and others made for him all the years he was away. But after releasing emotions pent up for forty years, Theresa and Shafia took to Ma and his family as if no time had passed. "Our relationship with Shag did not change from our early, pre-teen day. We were very comfortable with each other," said Theresa. And Ma was equally relaxed and playful as ever with them. Every morning he called them at their Beijing Hotel room and identified himself as the "Diaper Service," referring to the newly born grandson in his own home. Correspondence continued on a regular basis after the two returned to the United States, with Theresa sending ten dollars to each member of the Ma family who had a birthday. This included Su Fei's daughter Liangbi, along with her husband and two children. Rewi Alley had told her privately, to her great surprise, that the daughter was not actually Ma's child, but she knew that Ma treated her like a daughter, and that he would have been upset if Liangbi were treated differently.[26]

The year 1973 proved to be an auspicious one for foreigners living in China, and for Ma in particular. On March 8, Premier Zhou Enlai hosted a dinner at the Great Hall of the People for internationalists who had suffered during the Cultural Revolution. Also attending were Jiang Qing and her supporters, who would later be labeled the "Gang of Four." Ma was invited and was relieved to see his old friends Israel Epstein and his wife Elsie, Gladys Yang, and David and Isabel Crook, all recently released from prison. Zhou apologized to those who had been falsely accused of crimes, and to those who had been made to feel unwelcome during the recent past. The way was cleared for foreigners to regain their reputations and to continue contributing to the Chinese revolution. Most of them stayed in China for the rest of their lives, despite the harshness of prison and the isolation they felt during the Cultural Revolution. Of special significance to Ma was the the premier's added announcement that Sydney Rittenberg was staying behind bars. Ma blamed him most for the trouble foreigners encountered during the Cultural Revolution. Zhou insisted that Rittenberg had indeed committed crimes. After dinner, Ma told Alley that Rittenberg's continued imprisonment "couldn't have happened to a better man."[27]

In 1973 Ma became the most visible foreign resident in China. Foreign journalists interviewed him, though he rarely met with any that were not introduced by friends from abroad, and his picture appeared all over the United States. The articles elevated him to international standing with titles such as "An Evening in Peking with One of the Heroes of China" and "Dr. George Hatem—He's the Most Famous American in the People's Republic of China." One story in the *Honolulu Star-Bulletin* on June 28 opened with, "We met a 63 year old hero of the Revolution when we were in China—and he is an American."[28] Ma also was interviewed on ABC television.

Ma's celebrity status accelerated when, on August 12, his picture adorned the cover of *Parade* magazine, the Sunday newspaper supplement with a readership of millions. The story introduced Ma to the American public as "a legend in his own time." The author described him as "A short, stocky, charming, informal man, profound, philosophical, and well read." It was a sympathetic account of a man who asked to "discuss his work rather than himself." Most of the story dealt with China's campaign against venereal diseases, a triumph the American public found moving, told by a modest man attractive in his commitment and simplicity. A photograph of Ma and his family also appeared in the story. With the publication of this article Ma no longer "belonged" to a small number of China hands and physicians already familiar with him. He was a figure of historical proportions whom the American public could be proud of, even if he was a Communist. As always, Ma presented himself and his adopted country in a light that allowed foreigners to appreciate China's accomplishments without delving into ideology. As the author pointed out at the end of the story, Ma was one of China's great friends.[29] Once again he proved his worthiness, his "friendship," to those leaders who trusted him as far back as the mid 1930s.

Ma's response to all this attention was predictably humorous and self-deprecating. While recuperating in Beidaihe from another bout with his heart in October, he wrote a friend that he had seen the *Parade* article and had given other interviews. "The cult of the personality seems to grow apace and the head will be so enlarged and swollen that you will be able to cut half of it off when you visit."[30] Lloyd Shearer, the author of the *Parade* story, forwarded offers from fifteen publishers wanting to commission biographies. Ma answered with a quick note, "Too busy treating the sick to toot my horn."[31] At the same time, he quite obviously enjoyed the attention and wanted those now meeting him for the first time to understand his contribution and his place in history. Once, while dining in 1973 with a small group of American and Canadian journalists, he was asked how long he had lived in China. The question did not please him, and he responded sharply, "I helped liberate Beijing."[32]

In 1974 Ma tried to pay more attention to his medical practice at Fu Wai Hospital. This proved difficult, however, as his heart condition plagued him to the point that he required regular plasma transfusions. He spent a great deal of time meeting with foreigners in China and writing letters to friends, a practice he spent more and more time on as the years progressed. He asked trusted friends like Manny Granich "not to quote us friends when you write. It does not help when news makes a circle back to here." Unbeknown to those outside China, the political situation inside the country was far from stable, as Mao's health deteriorated and his wife's power increased. Ma was now living a life far removed from the stress of only a few years before, but he could take nothing for granted. What he said and how it was reported was a serious concern.

Besides requesting discretion, he enthusiastically pushed the current political agenda. He wrote letters to friends abroad, both new and old, detailing and defending political swings in China. The movement in 1974 to tie the "traitor" Lin Biao to feudal, Confucian thinking was, he said, "a political education movement of keeping a proper orientation to a world outlook going on towards socialism and then communism." Comments like this embarrassed some friends, who thought he must be writing such things because his mail was read. "He was too intelligent a man to really think some of those things," said reporter and friend Hobart Duncan.[33] He blasted U.S. policies, arguing that there seemed "no end to the inflation, pollution, unemployment and stink of capitalism." China, on the other hand, had "no energy crisis, no unemployment, no inflation."[34] As usual, he never wavered from the Party line with anyone outside his close circle of trusted foreign friends in Beijing.

In November, Ma took a much anticipated trip to Lebanon. Su Fei accompanied him on this triumphant return to his ancestral homeland and to his old school. While there, he met with medical colleagues and lectured at the American University on the role of the "barefoot" doctors in the countryside. He glowed in the spotlight, noting that the "auditorium (where I sat below many a time) was full and the revenge was sweet, they had to listen for a change." He visited relatives, about "one million," he said, since "half of Lebanon seemed to be Hatems or related to them" and toured the country as an honored guest of the Lebanese government.[35]

During 1975 the struggle within the Communist party took on added intensity. Jiang Qing and her followers, planning to take over the government upon Mao's death, directed subtle attacks on Zhou Enlai, who was by then fighting cancer, and Deng Xiaoping, whom Chairman Mao had only recently rehabilitated. Despite improving relations with Western countries, including the United States, official attacks on the West increased. "Wholesale Westernization," the Chinese press declared, meant loss of national identity and the Chinese spirit. It meant turning China's socialist economy toward a capitalist one.[36] With arguments like this, and with the impending demise of the old revolutionaries like Mao and Zhou, no one could predict what would happen in China from day to day. Certainly Ma remained cautious, as he was still prohibited from engaging in leprosy work and was concerned that his tainted official Party file could be called up at any time.

Despite this uncertainty, two events at the end of the year brought Ma personal satisfaction. One was President Gerald Ford's visit to China in December. Ma's diplomatic skills were still in demand, and he attended the state banquet for the president in the Great Hall of the People.[37] The other event must have brought Ma even greater satisfaction, for in December his old nemesis Kang Sheng died—the man whom he described to select foreign friends in Beijing as an "ignorant, bigoted son-of-a-bitch who thought everyone was as selfish as he was."[38] Of course, to all but those few, he maintained Party discipline and never criticized Kang. Only weeks afterward, in a letter to Manny Granich, Ma referred to Kang respectfully as the "warrior comrade," a phrase used in official Chinese obituaries.[39]

Ma no doubt would have been amused to discover that as he fretted about his future in China, FBI offices in Boston and Charlotte opened a five-month investigation into his activities and relationships with people in those areas. The reports, blacked out to hide names of those Americans investigated, end with the comment that "future information regarding captioned subjects will be made available to Charlotte and other interested parties. Information copies are being designated to New York . . . in view of their past and possible future investigative interest in captioned subjects."[40]

The year 1976 was one of extremes for Ma, his family, and his adopted country. In January, Zhou Enlai died. Ma told friends in the United States that words were not adequate to express his sorrow. Instead, he sent them a poem by Alley written in honor of Zhou. Madame Song, "shattered" by the news of Zhou's death, grew frailer by the day. Ma turned much of his attention to her during this period, visiting her when he could and exchanging letters often when she was in Shanghai or in seclusion. Su Fei developed an illness diagnosed as heart trouble, and Alley continued to fight shingles and other ailments. In North Carolina, Joe suffered from congestive heart problems, and the family asked Ma to come visit. He told them it was inconvenient to leave China.

In March, Ma underwent surgery to check on a possible malignancy in his prostate gland. Although it was diagnosed as benign, he was weak for several months afterward. Despite the distractions, Ma continued to make himself available to visitors from abroad, defending the goals and methods of the Cultural Revolution at every turn. In one conversation with American physician Grey Dimond, Ma discussed a mutual friend who suffered during the most chaotic period of the Cultural Revolution. He argued that the friend "came out of it with a new socialist class consciousness. He freely admits that previously he was still 'thinking like a mandarin.' " To Dimond, Ma staunchly defended Chairman Mao's role in starting the Cultural Revolution, especially his ability at age seventy-three to "rebel against his old comrades whom he thought had forgotten the objectives of the revolution." Of course privately Ma supported many of these old comrades, some of whom were his personal friends.[41]

Several tragedies followed that summer. Zhu De died—the old warhorse of the Red Army and one of the most revered men in China. An earthquake wracked north China, killing hundreds of thousands and destroying towns and villages in its wake. Ma's home was damaged, and his family was forced to move to alternative quarters while repairs were made. Then, in August, his son Youma, now working as a reporter for the magazine *China Reconstructs,* suffered a near-fatal fall while covering a story. Known in Beijing as a dashing figure who could light up any party, Youma also was known as one of the most daring photojournalists in Beijing. One day he climbed up the ladder of a fire truck to get a better angle on a photo, then slipped, falling to the ground. Several bones were broken, including his jaw, and most of his teeth were knocked out. Already taking care of Su Fei, Ma now spent most of his waking hours looking after his son.[42]

On September 9, 1976, Mao Zedong died, starting a scramble for power in China's highest circles. On October 6 the old revolutionaries still in power orchestrated the arrest of Mao's wife Jiang Qing and three others who made up the Gang of Four. Ma joined in the celebration of this dramatic turn of events, telling friends in uncharacteristic exuberance, "Like a boil that has reached its ripe time, the knife was used and the pus of the GANG OF FOUR . . . was eliminated from the body politic and the system. [Without their elimination] we would have seen a tragedy of massacres and coup, the taking over of the glorious Chinese Party and we would have sunk into the hell of revisionism."[43]

The year that had begun with the death of Premier Zhou and continued to be dominated by death and despair, now ended on a positive note for Ma. The Cultural Revolution that Ma publicly hailed but privately abhorred came to an end. Su Fei recovered from her heart problem and Youma's cast came off at the end of November. When not home tending to his family, Ma was in Fu Wai Hospital "mending the crocked and decrepit." Even Alley felt better, traveling in the south, and Madame Song, elated with recent events, appeared to be as healthy as she had been in some time.[44] Invigorated, Ma now looked to the final stage of his life, one that would take him back into his work against leprosy and deeper into his effort to bring his two cultures still closer together.

President Carter announced a "historic agreement" tonight under which the United States and China will establish diplomatic relations on January 1. . . . Mr. Carter said . . . "In recognizing the Government of the People's Republic of China, we are recognizing a simple reality."

New York Times, December 16, 1978

What does [Dr. Ma] feel, he who has devoted his life to eradicate VD, seeing it return? He smiles gently. "I can only say: we did our best."

Han Suyin in *Wind in My Sleeve*, recalling a conversation with Ma Haide in the mid 1980s

The year 1977 ushered in a period of rebirth for Ma. Though his health was declining, he found strength in the Party's renewed confidence in him. Early in the year he was appointed senior advisor to the Ministry of Public Health. Prior to the Cultural Revolution he had been advisor to the Dermatology and Venereological Research Institute, a subsection of the ministry. This new appointment offered him substantially more influence than before the Cultural Revolution, and a stronger platform on which to advocate his programs and positions. The Chinese Academy of Medical Science also appointed him senior dermatologist at the prestigious Capital Hospital. But most important for Ma, he could finally return to his leprosy work. Ten years had passed since he had been able to work on eradicating leprosy, and he relished the work ahead despite the daunting task of rebuilding the program. Friends and colleagues congratulated him on his "return." Madame Song wrote on July 1 to tell him that "This was due long ago, I should say, but at last you are being recognized for what you are."[1]

Ma spent the summer of 1977 at Beidaihe trying to regain his health. While there he welcomed foreign friends for long discussions on China's current situation. Always optimistic, he searched carefully for the right words to convince Americans that China was doing well. He told them that the arrest of the Gang of Four was something akin to running for office and losing in the United States. The Chinese people celebrated the change, he said, and throughout the country they rejoiced in the streets when they heard in April that Deng Xiaoping had returned to power. The "contradictions here have ended" with the downfall of the Gang of Four, he said. He wanted Americans to know China was strong and united.[2]

On September 9, still weak but energized by the changes taking place in China, Ma attended the opening ceremony of the Chairman Mao Memorial Hall. The invitation signified great prestige, for only those with long-standing ties to the Party and Chairman Mao gathered to honor Mao that day. Standing with "all the Long Marchers of the Red Army who could attend," Ma became one of the first of millions to enter the hall and file past the bier. He told friends that it was "an atmosphere of great homage, respect and love for Mao Zedong the great architect of our present."[3]

Although eager to return to work, Ma could not take up his new duties because of his continuing illness. In late September he experienced acute jaundice and "massive" internal bleeding. Exploratory surgery discovered possible pancreatic cancer. Additional surgery was ruled out due to the "advanced" stage of the illness, and radiation treatments commenced. Ma understood the seriousness of the diagnosis, and told family and friends he thought he might live another six months.[4]

In early 1978, with everyone thinking he was on his deathbed, the Party finally gave formal recognition to Ma's contribution to China's revolution. After years of living under the shadow of suspicion orchestrated by Kang Sheng, Ma requested that the Ministry of Public Health review his Party file and exonerate him of any trumped-up charges. After his file was reviewed at the Party's central headquarters, an official delegation visited Ma to tell him that his Communist party record was now wiped clean. All suspicion of being a "foreign spy" was dismissed, and from that day forward he would be privy to all Party documents and information others of his rank enjoyed. After four decades of service to the Communist party, Ma finally gained its unqualified confidence.[5]

Almost immediately, Ma was appointed a member of the Chinese People's Political Consultative Council, a legislative body comprised of representatives from the Communist party and smaller "democratic" parties allowed to exist in China. Its function is to advise the government on a broad spectrum of issues, including medical concerns. Although he was only able to contribute in a limited way at first, he did attend meetings while convalescing in the hospital and at home. Later, after he felt better, he became a permanent member of the Standing Committee, where he argued for laws that would allow more humane treatment of those with leprosy. Wang Guangmei, chair of the council at the time, remembers that once "we were discussing the proposed Second Marriage Law. Some members wanted to have lepers declared unable to marry. Dr. Ma resisted this motion, argued his case, and won the day. I then passed his comments along to the Women's Confederation and others on his behalf."[6]

While Ma was undergoing medical treatment, his family in the United States heard of the seriousness of his condition. Desperate to help his brother, Joe called Leonard Woodcock, then head of the American liaison office in Beijing. He asked Woodcock to visit Ma and let him know how his brother was doing. Woodcock inquired into Ma's condition and asked to visit with him, but his request was denied. Infuriated, Joe asked Woodcock to try again, but the attempt again proved futile. Finally, after he was confident of the diagnosis, Ma discussed his condition with Joe and agreed to come to the United States for both a long-overdue reunion and a farewell visit. In March he inquired of the American liaison office about the status of his citizenship, but was told that he would need to come to the office to fill out a questionnaire before it could be determined.[7] He decided not to persue the issue, and in April he and Su Fei flew to the United States on Chinese passports. They carried twenty thousand provided by the Chinese government for expenses. He was about to see his home country for the first time in almost 50 years.[8]

Ma's return to the United States was triumphant. When he and Su Fei landed at Dulles Airport near Washington, D.C., Han Xu, an old comrade from the 1940s who was now deputy chief of China's liaison office, greeted him. Joe, fearing the worst, met him with a wheelchair to take him on to North Carolina. Although he had lost forty pounds, Ma insisted he was still strong enough to walk. In North Carolina, he visited Duke University Medical Center, where they found no sign of cancer but showed concern for the massive doses of radiation he had received in China. His strength slowly returned, and many noted his hearty appetite and his disdain for the new American trend toward low-fat meals. He had little trouble downing fair-sized servings of steak, hot dogs, or fried chicken at one sitting. He also asked for the Lebanese foods he remembered from his childhood. In some cases he was the only one who remembered the recipes, and everyone pitched in to fix the family dishes of fifty years before. Much to his family's amusement, Su Fei had even brought along a large bib she had made for him to use when he ate.

He visited the University of North Carolina, which proudly claimed him as an alumnus now "venerated" in China. As he passed through the school, he reminisced about classes he had taken and clubs he had belonged to. Before leaving he presented the university with a woodblock portrait of himself treating a young child. He later was asked to update his biography for the alumni yearbook and to add comments if he wished. He concluded his sketch with a challenge to his former classmates:

> Fifty years after leaving university confers the right to share with classmates some thoughts, pontificate (if you feel like it) and summarize a little the wisdom we are supposed to acquire. I hope all of us will be able to do this for our reunion in another decade. In the meantime I hope all of us can look back on a productive half century in which we made the world a better place to live in for our children and grandchildren. History had demanded this of us.[9]

A few months later, the University of North Carolina School of Medicine honored Ma with its highest honor, the Distinguished Service Award. The award was in recognition of the fact that Ma "played a major role in virtually eliminating venereal diseases and prostitution in the People's Republic of China."[10]

Ma also attended the fifty-first class reunion at his high school in Greenville, which he seemed to enjoy despite having little or nothing in common with those he left in the small southern town in the mid 1920s. Newspapers from around the state interviewed him and published accounts of his exploits. He assured the press that conditions in China were good and that he hoped for more U.S.-China exchanges. This was the message he pushed the hardest, telling one reporter in Greenville, "I hope that I, and each of you, my old friends, will try to establish a deep understanding between over 1 billion people who live in China and America."[11]

Joe's wife and children did not know what to expect from Ma. What they found was a jovial sage, full of advice and encouragement. He fit right in as the older brother and uncle, "just as though he had never left," recalled his sister-in-law Marie. The biggest impression he made on Marie was the constant challenge he issued to everyone he met. Over coffee one morning he asked her "What have you done for the people of the world?" Well, she argued, she had raised four children, not a small contribution. "No, he said, what have *you* done for the people of the world." "That's the kind of person he was," remembers Marie, "always forcing you to think of others."[12]

The trip lasted six months. After several weeks in North Carolina, he embarked on a whirlwind tour of the country, traveling first to Washington, D.C., where he stayed at the Chinese government's quarters at the invitation of Han Xu. He then went to New York, where he reunited with Robert Levinson, fellow medical student and sojourner in China in 1933. He stayed with Dr. and Mrs. Sam Rosen, friends from Rosen's first visit to China in 1971. While in New York, he also appeared on national television, comparing the state of health care in China and the United States. Although he was impressed with the technology he saw in hospitals, he said he was concerned about the patient, who seemed to be lost in the high-tech world of medical care. Before leaving the city, he was approached by a publishing representative from Little, Brown, who asked him to write his autobiography, and, according to Greg Hatem, offered up to one million dollars for the account. He refused. "I haven't done anything that interesting," he told the publisher.[13]

From there he headed to a reunion with his Buffalo relatives. Soon after arriving he visited the Roswell Park Memorial Institute to undergo further medical evaluation. The physicians there concurred that he might have cancer, but the exact location was not clear. He appeared strong, and no additional problems could be found.[14]

The visits in Buffalo were hectic affairs. Whatever he needed, or wanted, he got. "He would have three or four of us at one time on various errands," his cousin Theresa recalls. Theresa's garage was converted into a new bedroom especially for Ma, and the family tried to protect him from the barrage of requests coming from all quarters. His youngest cousin Ernie, the same cousin sent off to North Carolina in the 1930s to soothe the pain Ma's mother felt when her son failed to return from China, delighted in looking after Ma. "We used to screen his calls, with people like Ted Koppel and other famous people calling to get some of his time." Theresa's husband, unaccustomed to such activity, moved out of the house during this and subsequent visits.[15]

After leaving Buffalo, Ma and Su Fei visited with his old friend Max Granich in his Cape Cod summer home. There he was visited by Walter Cronkite, Barbara Walters, and other journalists, who engaged him in conversation for hours. Finally, on the last leg of his trip, he traveled to the West Coast, where he spoke on the promise of U.S.–China relations at the national convention of the U.S.–China People's Friendship Association. The FBI monitored his activities in California, along with those of his hosts. Before leaving the United States, he visited Grey Dimond and his wife in Kansas City, Missouri. There he toured the newly opened Edgar Snow Memorial Collection at the University of Missouri.[16]

During the trip Ma's health improved dramatically. He ate as much as he wanted—which was a lot—and gained weight. He assumed the cancer was in remission. Because of his good health, he and Su Fei continued on to Europe, where they toured England and France and visited for two weeks with Lois Snow in Switzerland. In November they returned to China.[17] Commenting later on the trip, he said he was asked many times if he experienced culture shock in the United States. "I didn't, and felt pretty stupid about it, as I was plainly expected to answer 'Yes'." He adjusted so easily, he said, because he had been familiar with American culture before, and "I'd come to understand its basics through Marxism."[18]

After his return to Beijing, Ma was exhausted and bothered by pain in his stomach, but anxious to resume his work with the Ministry of Public Health and to see his friends. The Cultural Revolution had strained his relations with many foreign friends in China. He was cordial with Israel Epstein and other former members of the Yan'an–Bethune Regiment, but not warm as before. And he remained as contemptuous as ever of Sydney Rittenberg, refusing to speak to him the first time they met after Rittenberg was released from prison in November 1977. The friends he most wanted to see, of course, were Madame Song, Rewi Alley, and Hans Muller. On December 2, he attended Alley's eighty-first birthday party and wrote Madame Song about his trip.[19]

He submitted the formal report on his trip to the ministry, then addressed colleagues about his impressions of Western medical practices. In the talk he defended China's advances and the importance of sticking to a socialist approach to medicine. He told them, "Everyone realizes by now that China has a fairly well developed public health system. When we say we'll wipe out leprosy, we're believed—we have a scientific reputation." He told them that China could learn modern medical practices from abroad, but "We must develop along lines suitable to China. We can't just copy from abroad, though some people here and there find that hard to understand . . . can you imagine a block of apartment houses in America where you could get anyone with symptoms [of V.D.] to sign up on the board? Theirs is a highly individualist society. We can work the way we do here because ours is a different, cooperative type."[20]

Despite his return to activity in Beijing, friends still worried about his health. Song Qingling wrote, "It was so good of you to write despite your tummy ache, which I hope will vanish soon after medical attention. I am afraid the long exhausting trip was the cause of it. . . . Do keep up the medical care! We cannot afford to be in jitters again about your health!"[21] But the "tummy ache" Madame Song worried about persisted. By March Ma was in severe pain. He vomited blood and fainted. Attending physicians told him the cancer had come back in full force. Wu Weiran, China's most noted surgeon and physician to members of the Party Central Committee, said they should operate to repair the damage. Other doctors said it was too late to operate, that the cancer was in the last stages and nothing could be done to save him. Wu, backed by Hans Muller and Su Fei, wanted to operate anyway, "even if there's only one chance in a hundred." Ma, with his family gathered at his bedside, was asked to make the final decision. He told them to operate, but that if he died he wanted no autopsy or memorial meeting, only a simple funeral. The operation began immediately, with Wu performing the surgery and Hans Muller in attendance. What Dr. Wu discovered surprised everyone. No evidence of cancer was evident, but a "big, deep ulcer with active bleeding" had developed. Ma also suffered from gallstones. The 1977 diagnosis had been wrong. The original pain was due to gallstones left untreated and the ulcer developed from the intensive radiation he underwent when it was thought he had cancer of the pancreas. The misdiagnosis embarassed his colleagues, and, while he never berated or publically criticized his physicians, Ma trusted no one with his health except Wu Weiran for the rest of his life.

The operation took nine hours, with Wu taking out the gallbladder, part of the small intestine, and other parts of the stomach damaged beyond repair. Wu reports that Ma's condition remained critical for several weeks and that he almost died following the surgery. Finally, after several months of additional surgery and treatment, he recovered. He now suffered only from a hernia due to the removal of parts of his stomach. After regaining his strength, Ma joked with Wu that the protruding hernia made him look seven months pregnant.[22]

By the summer of 1979 Ma felt strong enough to accept Leonard Woodcock's invitation to a July 4 celebration at the American liaison office, and then to vacation at Beidaihe. Staying in the special compound set aside for foreigners living in China, he showed off his huge scar at the beach, danced with his wife and others during the evening parties held outside, and visited Alley in his cottage a short distance from the compound. He also took time to talk with some of the young American "foreign experts" recently arrived in China as teachers and editors. He and Alley invited small groups of them to Alley's cottage for tea, encouragement, and conversation. Fully recovered, Ma felt better than he had in years and looked forward to the future.[23]

Once back in Beijing, he came to the aid of Madame Song, protecting her from unwanted visitors and obligations. She wrote him in September,

> Dear Shag:
>
> Please answer [John] Service that "I am too much occupied with duties to have anyone write my biography" (confidentially, I am against such attempts and have refused several *friends already*. Ego dictates all biographies—I prefer my work to tell what I've done. Definitely, please make it known to Service et al. As for Han Suyin's film, I heard unfavorable comments about it already. Please *don't* let anyone approach me to see her for I am too busy and tired to attend to her![24]

A week later Madame Song invited Ma and several close friends to her home to celebrate his sixty-ninth birthday.

Now that he knew he had some years left, Ma once again put his energy into the cause of leprosy control. In November he traveled with Su Fei to Canada where he attended a memorial meeting in honor of Norman Bethune. He also visited the United States again. Although he visited friends and family, he concentrated on gathering financial and technical support in the West to fight leprosy in China. While visiting New York, he presented a formal report on his activities to Ling Qing, China's permanent representative to the United Nations. Ling, impressed and a bit humored by the seriousness with which Ma took his responsibilities, remarked to others that Ma seemed to follow Party discipline no matter where he was![25]

In February 1980, Ma, Hans Muller, and Richard Frey were honored at a reception by the Ministry of Public Health to commemorate forty years of service to China. During this period he continued to treat patients twice a week in the outpatient clinic at Capital Hospital. The rest of the time he spent visiting leprosy patients. He discovered that while leprosy work had not stopped completely during the Cultural Revolution, treatment had reverted to traditional isolationist methods of dealing with the disease. He met with old colleagues such as Dai Zhengqi, Yang Lihe, and Wang Hongshen to formulate plans to eradicate the disease. He arranged for international leprosy experts to visit China and read the latest journals on the disease. He found that the treatment of leprosy had been improved by the use of drugs that easily could be obtained from abroad and manufactured in China. This thrilled him, because Ma had never enjoyed the research involved in eradicating a disease as much as he did the delivery of education and medicine to the people. American leprosy expert Dr. Olaf Skinsnes remembers sitting in Ma's home one evening in 1980 discussing their common passion. Ma, he said, was most concerned with the total eradication of the disease through mass education and treatment rather than working in a clinic studying the disease. "For any kind of research problem, mechanisms, or immunities he was sort of left out in the cold. He wasn't enthusiastic about it. But as soon as you offered him some way of eradicating leprosy he lit up."[26]

In early 1981 Ma toured the country, meeting patients and physicians. His work was cut short in June, however, when he turned his attention to an increasingly frail Song Qingling. Madame Song, who had been in ill health for years, took a sudden turn for the worse, and Ma was called to her bedside. With other doctors, he tried in vain to revive her. She died May 29. Writing their mutual friend Manny Granich after her death, Ma said, "We are all sad and bereaved, just as you are, at the great loss suffered by China and friends around the world with the passing of that great woman of our era, Soong Chingling [Song Qingling]. The end came suddenly and there was no pain or suffering. Su Fei, Rewi and I were at her bedside. . . . Rewi and I went to Shanghai with the ashes and Urn for the burial at her family burial place."[27] Standing by her grave with Alley, Ma thought of the struggles he had gone through with Madame Song and the other revolutionaries from the 1930s.[28] Smedley, Snow, Strong, and now Song Qingling were dead. Of the old gang, only he and Alley remained.

During June, July, and August, Ma and Su Fei visited Australia and New Zealand. He spoke at the International Leprosy Congress in Darwin, and his paper was published in the international journal *Leprosy Review* in 1982. Summing up his visit, he said that he "gave 45 radio, TV and press interviews and talks. All this in addition to the 13 public lectures and 14 talks on scientific subjects to post-graduates."[29] "Our travels covered the equivalent of three Long Marches and an extra 5000 kilometers." When he returned to China, Ma continued at the same torrid pace. In August, he dined with President Jimmy Carter at the Great Hall of the People, then traveled to Jiangsu Province to investigate leprosy control. Once back in Beijing, he focused on an upcoming national conference on leprosy to be held in Guangzhou.[30]

At the Guangzhou conference, minister of public health Cui Yuli announced Ma's appointment as leader in the movement to control and eradicate leprosy in China. Ma chaired the meeting and challenged everyone attending to "rid China of leprosy by the year 2000." He told them that leprosy could now be cured by short-term chemotherapy, and that it was not contagious forty-eight hours after the patient had taken medication. What everyone had to do now was find all those infected and treat them, using the same mass-education methods of the venereal diseases campaigns in earlier years. Properly treated, patients could be cured in one or two years, he insisted. He told his colleagues that "leprosy is preventable, curable, and not to be feared." Then, he said, they would have to attack the social stigma of the disease, and integrate patients as contributing members of society. This became his life's goal, and a call to arms to those involved in the movement.[31]

The next year began the way 1981 had ended, with Ma busy fostering international goodwill and attacking leprosy. In February, he spoke at a memorial meeting in Beijing to mark the tenth anniversary of the death of Edgar Snow. During Chinese New Year, Ma inaugurated a public education effort that came to be called the "Leprosy Festival." To kick off the movement, he visited patients at the Wangdu Leprosy Hospital in Hebei Province, accompanied by provincial government leaders and national television and print journalists. There he made national news when he took the hand of a patient to inspect his sores. The patient was as shocked as the leaders and journalists, and cried as he told Ma that he had suffered from leprosy for twenty-five years and this was the first time anyone had touched him with his bare hands in all that time. Ma made it a point to shake hands with the patients he visited, to share tea and food, and to inspect with his own hands the festering sores on hands and feet. He insisted that his wife and son accompany him on trips, just to show people how safe he considered the disease if it was treated properly.[32]

In May, Ma and two Chinese colleagues left Beijing for a stopover in Japan and a month-long visit to the United States. This was followed by visits to Canada, England, Switzerland, India, and Thailand. This sixty-eight-day tour, funded by Belgium's Damien-Dutton Society, was primarily a fact-finding and fund-raising mission.

As on previous trips, he gave numerous interviews and took time to visit family and friends. But this was primarily a business trip. In the United States he visited well-known leprosariums in Hawai'i and Louisiana, as well as experts at the Center for Disease Control in Atlanta and federal officials in Washington, D.C. Still considered a potential threat to the U.S. government, he again was closely monitored by the FBI, whose offices in Washington, Charlotte, and Honolulu were alerted to his presence in their jurisdictions.[33]

In India, Ma saw leprosy cases similar to those found in China, but in economic conditions far removed from his experience. India had one million leprosy patients in 1982, and his hosts told him it would take one hundred years to rid the country of the disease. Ma, who hoped to accomplish the feat in two decades in China, was later asked by the prime minister, Indira Gandhi, at a reception held in his honor to advise her on better ways to fight leprosy. Ma asked her permission to speak frankly, then said, "Your leprosy work is not effective. Your people are too poor, some of them can't even afford to buy a cake of soap to wash with. Many are malnourished and live with parasites. While your physicians are better trained and your technology more advanced, the living conditions of your people do not allow for resistance to disease, and curing them becomes difficult."[34]

In Thailand, Ma visited Dr. David Scollard, a leprosy expert affiliated with a small privately funded clinic. Scollard found Ma jovial and pleasant, but not interested in small talk. He impressed upon Scollard his conviction that the best way to rid a country of leprosy was the way it was done in China, through a public health system that emphasized mass education and mass treatment. "For Ma," said Scollard, "the medical tool was public policy—for some it's a stethoscope, some a scalpel and for some a microscope. But for Ma it was mass campaigns through public policy. This was his tool, and he was never apologetic about using it to change the masses. He was forward in affirming the Communist Party line, and seemed to care little about political rights. He cared for the right to be healthy."

Scollard recalls that Ma "was always searching for answers on how to deal with the stigma of leprosy. He said research was no longer necessary. What patients needed now was job training and social rehabilitation. When the talk turned to research Ma became impatient, saying that preventive medicine was the best medicine in the long run. He was very emphatic on this point." As for his relationship with patients, Scollard believes that if Ma had stayed in the United States "he would have been great with bedside manner." Combining his personal touch with his confidence in mass education and use of public policy, Scollard said Ma could have played a role similar to that of former surgeon general C. Everett Koop.[35]

When Ma returned home that summer he was convinced that, given China's social, political, and economic structure, it was the most likely place in the world to eradicate leprosy. Based on his findings from the trip and his already well-formed opinions, he moved to make drastic changes, always with the intent to diminish the social stigma of the disease. Among the changes were the downsizing of special leprosy villages and the return of cured patients to their homes. He also advocated relocating patients who still suffered from the disease to villages closer to urban centers, where more expert care would be available.[36]

As 1983 began, Ma's health once again took a downward turn. In October of the previous year, he underwent surgery to repair a hernia. At that time Wu Weiran wove a mesh net around the hernia, then sewed him up. In December, during a routine X-ray analysis, "a small dense shadow of less than one centimeter in diameter was noted at the left upper lung field." A CT scan revealed an enlarged prostate gland. On January 4, 1983, exploratory surgery discovered cancer in both the lung and prostate gland. On January 20, Ma's prostate, testicles, and part of one lung were removed.[37]

To everyone's surprise, Ma recovered quickly from the surgery, confident that the cancer had been removed but anxious about how many times a man of his age could undergo this trauma and still get work done. He told Youma after this latest surgery that "While the operations on me have been successful, nobody can live longer than a few years after so many. I've got to hurry with my work and make the best of my time."[38]

In April, Ma's international reputation began to garner him the first of several awards he would receive during the final few years of his life. He received the Leprosy Award of the Damien-Dutton Society of Belgium, a prize first instituted in 1953 and given annually for service in the cause of leprosy prevention and eradication. Since Ma was too weak to travel to Europe, U.S. ambassador Arthur W. Hummell presented the award in Beijing.[39]

By May, Ma had recovered his strength well enough to make another trip to the United States. As before, the FBI prepared for his arrival, this time sending a profile of his personal history to San Francisco and Kansas City, two of his expected stops. The purpose of the trip was threefold. First, he attended the commencement exercises of the University of Missouri at Kansas City, where Edgar Snow received a posthumous degree. He also spoke at a symposium held to discuss Snow's life. Huang Hua traveled with him. After this stop, Ma went to Duke University in North Carolina and to Roswell Park Memorial Institute in Buffalo for follow-up medical visits. At both medical centers he received good news, confirming Wu Weiran's diagnosis that, while his health demanded close scrutiny, there appeared to be no need for further surgery at the time.[40]

Before leaving the United States he visited his family in Buffalo and North Carolina, where his brother was just recovering from heart surgery. While in North Carolina he attended the graduation from medical school of his nephew, Joe Pat. The first relative since Ma to enter the medical profession, Joe Pat insists that his "Uncle Shag" was the reason he went into medicine and eventually received a degree in public health. For Marie, the fondest memory of that visit was when Ma agreed to attend mass with the family to celebrate Joe Pat's graduation. She knew that he had left the church long ago, but she requested that the family be together that day. "I felt privileged he would go to that service," she said.[41]

After leaving his family, Ma visited Washington, D.C., attending National Day celebrations at the Chinese embassy on October 1 and meeting with officials at the National Institute of Health. Ambassador Zhang Wenjin noted that during his visit to the embassy Ma "became the center of attention," telling Henry Kissinger and other visitors lively stories of his life in China. On his way out of the country he delivered a speech at a meeting of the U.S.–China People's Friendship Association and visited with former ambassador Leonard Woodcock. Woodcock's memory of that meeting sheds light on Ma's culinary biases. Woodcock recalls that they were invited to dine at the Pritikin Institute, known for its low-cholesterol, low-fat diet. Ma was not impressed. He remarked upon receiving his meal, "That's hardly worth getting my bib out for. Good god, if people actually eat this food, they deserve to live a long time."[42]

On November 22, soon after arriving back in China, over two hundred people gathered for a reception at the Great Hall of the People to honor Ma on the fiftieth anniversary of his arrival. The affair was hosted by China's paramount leader, Deng Xiaoping, and attended by Huang Hua, Yang Shangkun, and Deng Yingchao, widow of Zhou Enlai, and others. Many of his old friends from Yan'an days joined him, as did his family, Rewi Alley, and colleagues from the Ministry of Public Health. The following day the English-language *China Daily* ran a front-page story and photo of Deng Xiaoping toasting Ma, with Su Fei looking on. That same day *People's Daily*, the official organ of the Communist party, ran a lengthy article written by Huang Hua entitled "The Chinese Revolution Is His Life-long Undertaking—50th Anniversary of Comrade Ma Haide's Work in China." Huang Hua ended his summary of Ma's contributions by saying, "it is necessary for us to learn from Comrade Ma Haide, carry forward his revolutionary spirit of devoting his whole life to the struggle for the cause of communism, . . . Health and longevity to Comrade Ma Haide!"[43]

By early 1984 the burdens of old age and sickness in both him and his closest friends occasionally brought out the melancholy in Ma. Writing

Manny Granich, he confided that Alley had "a number of ailments that will have to be solved one by one. . . . He is 87 this year and many parts of the circulatory system are running into trouble or running down." He added, "When you reach this present era and age, many happenings among our friends make us sad." He told Manny that Harrison Salisbury was in China with John Service, each trying to get him and Alley to retrace the Long March with them, "but we old crocks are no longer able to indulge in such shenanigans."[44]

Back in North Carolina, brother Joe had been diagnosed with cancer in January. Ma planned to go back to the United States to spend time with him. He wrote friends that he planned neither to travel around nor entertain many visitors so he could focus on his brother. In April he arrived in North Carolina, where he spent long hours with Joe at his bedside reminiscing about their childhood and talking about their families. He stayed for two months; Joe died in July, not long after Ma returned to Beijing.[45]

Despite the distractions of old age and illness, Ma pushed forward his agenda in medicine and politics. Always explaining, educating, and pounding home the message, he took every opportunity to emphasize the positive aspects of China's growth, and to play down the new Chinese fascination with foreign technology. China had to follow its own path, he reminded everyone. "We must never forget," he insisted, that this means a socialist path. In 1984 he said, "Many of our people go the United States or elsewhere and are dazzled by the big medical centres they see. They begin to look doubtful when we talk about traditional medicine. . . . A medical centre in the United States is impressive, and some of our people come back and say, 'The first thing to do in modernizing medicine is to build a medical centre.' But . . . this is not what we need and we can't deal with it. A modern American style medical centre would use up one quarter of Beijing's electricity. Modernization has to be Chinese style."[46]

On the question of socialism and its future in China, Ma remained upbeat and confident. Explaining his view to a foreign friend disturbed by reports of creeping capitalism in China, Ma wrote in late 1984, "The strange outcry about China going capitalist has no foundation in reality. . . . The socialism in China has deeply anchored roots, so don't worry. You have to see it to believe it."[47]

That same year was the first of several in which he avoided surgery. Acting in his periodic role of diplomat, he attended a banquet that spring honoring President Ronald Reagan. After the banquet he traveled extensively in China's countryside investigating leprosy programs and also went abroad to attend international symposiums and raise funds for his own work. During 1984 and 1985, he attended international meetings in Japan, India, Hungary, and the Philippines.

Awards continued to pile up. In July 1985, while on another fund-raising trip to the United States, he received an award from the W. K. Kellogg Foundation for "outstanding international contributions to the field of public health." In September, California's state senate awarded him a Certificate of Recognition for his work in international public health. In October, he was elected a Distinguished Member in the Lyman A. Brewer III International Surgical Society.

He did not spend all of this trip in formal settings. In late July he again visited Leonard Woodcock, this time at his home in Ann Arbor. He spent some of his time raising money, but the rest relaxing with the former ambassador. Reflecting on that visit, Woodcock says, "I remember Hatem as the kind of guy you got to know quite well very quickly. Very outgoing person. I remember it was a lovely morning, and we were out on our deck and he said, telling me of the things he wanted to do, 'I don't have much time left.' I'm sure he knew his days were numbered, although looking at him even then you would have believed there was absolutely nothing wrong with him."[48]

Of all his activities during this period, however, the most important happened after he returned to China. He spearheaded the opening of the China Leprosy Control and Research Center in Guangzhou, a project he had proposed since before the Cultural Revolution. In November 1984 it took in its first patients, although the official opening came a year later.

Ma spent much of 1985 laying the groundwork for operations at the center. The Leprosy Control and Research Center officially opened in November, with Ma as director and his old colleague Dai Zhengqi as assistant director. Ma presented the keynote address. To commemorate the event, China held its first international conference on leprosy control, with over one hundred specialists from nineteen countries attending. The China Leprosy Foundation and the China Leprosy Association also were established at that time, and Ma was named president of both organizations. The organizations were formed for the purpose of raising money for China's efforts against leprosy.[49]

Over the next three years, Ma's travels and contacts brought in over ten million dollars from contributors in Italy, Japan, the United States, Holland, Belgium, Germany, and Canada. The assistance came in the form of money, scholarships for medical students, medical supplies, and vehicles. Ma raised funds any way he could, and—displaying the same brashness he used when sending his family his lists of needs—he wrote friends with requests. To one old Dixie Mission friend he wrote, "things are moving and we hope that we can eradicate leprosy by the year 2000 in the main. If there are funds around your way they can be sent to CHINA LEPROSY FOUNDATION, c/o Dr. Ma Haide . . . checks, money orders, etc."⁵⁰

In 1986 Ma found himself the recipient of more international citations and awards. It seems that everyone who shared a history with China's most famous foreigner wanted to claim him as their own. In March, Lebanese president Amin Gemayel, represented by his country's ambassador to China, Frida Suhama, presented Ma with the Ordre de Cedre-Commander. In April, Ma went back to the United States, this time without Su Fei, to attend the annual Conference of American Physicians. Then he traveled to Edgar Snow's hometown of Kansas City, Missouri, where on April 25 he received an honorary doctorate from the University of Missouri at Kansas City. Ma's take on this award was summed up in letters to Grey Dimond, chancellor of the university's medical school and a friend of Snow and Ma. "I will be in Kansas City . . . on April 25 for that honorary degree that you engineered for me and for which I am the last of the three red bandits [Edgar Snow, Huang Hua and Ma] thank you for it. . . . I realize that this is a degree that belongs to Snow and to China and to the American people. I receive it in that spirit."⁵¹

From Kansas City, Ma traveled to Buffalo, where the mayor named him an honorary citizen of the city and decreed May 16 as "Doctor George Hatem Day." The State University of New York in Buffalo named him honorary lecturer of the medical school, and articles on his life appeared in local newspapers and university publications.⁵² He sat for another interview with *Parade* magazine, where he was "credited for playing the major role in eradicating venereal disease and prostitution" in China and "is now occupied with eradicating leprosy in China."⁵³ He then traveled to Belgium, Germany, Switzerland, and other European countries, seeking funds for his leprosy work and further strengthening contacts with leprosy experts.

In the United States, Ma also raised some funds for a new project initiated by Su Fei that was unrelated to leprosy. Before arriving, Ma informed select friends in the United States that Su Fei had written a movie script chronicling the journey he and Snow had made to Baoan together in 1936. She planned to direct the film when production began. Ma asked Grey Dimond in Kansas City to help him raise $150,000 for the project. "An immediate sum of $50,000" was needed to begin this international production. He hoped the Edgar Snow Memorial Fund that Dimond directed would spearhead this effort. Ma seemed particularly keen to see the movie made, stressing, "It would be a pity if the present production team ready to go would be held up for another year for financial reasons. The opportunity is at hand for a historical project to be completed and quickly. The foreign exchange sum is not that enormous for a film. . . . There is an immediate and urgent requirement about this I feel."[54]

At first glance, Ma's insistence that friends in the United States raise money for a film glorifying his place in history appears out of character for a man who shunned the spotlight for so long. Publishers, journalists, and friends had tried for years to entice him either to write his memoirs or to consent to interviews for a full biography. He always refused. After all, none of the senior Party leaders with which he identified had written their stories or allowed such accounts to be written. Madame Song's appeal to Ma to keep biographers away from her door represented this position well. But it is clear that in his later years he wanted to step out of the shadows and get the credit he deserved. Perhaps the American individualism he had long suppressed surfaced again. He was not totally "sinicized."

Some suggest that this change had been taking place for some time. In an earlier visit to the Edgar Snow Collection in Kansas City in the late 1970s, Ma insisted that without the assistance he provided Snow, *Red Star Over China* may not have been written. Snow's first wife, Helen Foster Snow (Nym Wales), was furious when she learned that Ma took such credit, and friends were surprised to hear Ma laying claim to Snow's efforts.

While he spent little effort documenting his own importance to China's revolution, Ma rarely discouraged others from telling his story as long as he was not directly involved in the telling. In 1983 Grey Dimond published *Inside China Today,* a book primarily recounting discussions he had with Ma over a two-year period in the late 1970s. It also offered bits of his life story and observations on his role in China. While family members on both sides of the Pacific say that Ma was displeased by the book, one Chinese acquaintance admits that he asked her to translate parts of it for publication in China.[55]

While in Kansas City to receive his honorary degree, Ma found that Dimond had raised "a few thousand" dollars for the film project. Su Fei was excited to hear the news and wrote Dimond to thank him for his help and to stress the importance of more financial assistance. Writing with the help of Ma's personal secretary, Sun Yizhi, she said, "Since you are a man of influence and the Snow Memorial Fund, Inc. is very well-known in the United States, we . . . believe that you may be able to raise a satisfactory amount of fund[ing] for our film."[56] After he returned to China, Ma wrote Dimond to thank him for his efforts on behalf of Su Fei. He said he hoped that "the Edgar Snow Memorial Foundation will still work on this educational project as one of its own." Over the next year Ma wrote other friends throughout the United States asking them to help raise money for the film project. It became evident, however, that the project needed far more money than could be raised. The film that Ma considered of "historical" importance never got off the ground.[57]

Ma returned from his latest trip exhausted. He had visited seven countries and made presentations at sixteen leprosy organizations in his effort to raise money for his own work in China. During his absence, Alley had suffered a heart attack and Muller, already suffering from Parkinson's disease, had broken his hip. To regain his strength and escape the stifling heat of Beijing's summer, Ma and his family again vacationed at Beidaihe. Once rested, he attended an eleven-province conference on leprosy eradication, this time stating that China could now be free of the disease by 1990 rather than 2000. After the conference, he visited Guangzhou to lead training sessions in leprosy rehabilitation and escort a delegation of Japanese health officials through several provinces.[58]

While preparing for these conferences and trips, Ma was informed that he would receive yet another honor later in the year. The prestigious Albert Lasker Medical Research Award was presented to Ma and five other physicians in late November in New York. In announcing the award, the *New York Times* stated that Lasker Award winners often go on to win the Nobel Prize for medicine. This had happened to forty-two winners since it was first given in 1944. Su Fei accompanied Ma to receive the fifteen thousand dollars that came with the award. Sharing recognition with three physicians in the new field of AIDS research and two in cell growth, Ma stood out as a public health official rather than a researcher. The citation states that Ma made "legendary contributions to the conquest of venereal disease and the eradication of leprosy in China." His contributions "made medical history and improved the health and well-being of 800 million people."[59] The award must have been especially sweet for Ma, who was never one to spend much time in the lab. Now his public health efforts in mass education and treatment were recognized at the highest international level as equal to the more prestigious field of medical research.

Such international acclaim elevated Ma's public standing even higher. Before leaving New York, he was approached by Jacqueline Kennedy Onassis at Doubleday to write his autobiography. Again he refused.[60] He also was asked by medical officials in other parts of the world to assist them in fighting leprosy. In answer to one request from Missouri, Ma said, "As for leprosy in Missouri, when I get through the eradication of leprosy basically in China, I would like to take up the problem of eradication of leprosy from Missouri. In the meantime, use the Multidrug Therapy and wait for my next visit!"[61]

While China's opening to the West provided the opportunity for Ma to tell the world about its progress in public health, and for his own reputation to grow, the rapid changes came at a price he found troubling. As usual, he shared his private opinions with only a few friends in China and expressed only optimism to the outside world. In 1986 he was asked in the United States about the return of prostitution to China. He said that it had risen "a relatively small amount in a country of more than a billion people. . . . You can't open up a country to a Western culture, to hundreds of thousands of tourists and foreigners per year, without altering some of its social ethics and values. Compared to what it was 50 years ago, prostitution in China today is less than a drop in a very large bucket."[62] In the summer of 1987, just after returning from a medical conference in Moscow, he wrote, "China is on a good track and I think that it has made another breakthrough on how to build socialism in this stage of history. . . . When I was . . . in Moscow we heard envious remarks about China's reforms and its progress."[63]

In the privacy of his home, and especially during visits with Alley, Ma's optimism sometimes faltered. Sidney Shapiro, a frequent guest during the evening sessions at Alley's home in the mid and late 1980s, recalls the frustration all of them felt at the changes in China. Then entering his nintieth year, Alley voiced his concerns more bluntly, and more often, than Ma. What, he asked, could be done about graft in government, the return of prostitution and venereal disease to China, child-labor abuses, and the lack of a legal system to deal with the growing tide of lawlessness. Students were not taught to think for themselves, Alley said, and teachers were paid only to get students through the entrance examination, not to learn anything. "Is it any wonder China has fallen behind little places like Hong Kong, Taiwan, Singapore, and even south Korea," he grumbled.[64]

Of primary concern to Ma was the rapid decline in the prestige of the Communist party, the institution that had sustained him for fifty years. He acknowledged that dishonesty, greed, and corruption existed within the Party, and he feared for the Party's future. But, even with his old friends, Ma stayed upbeat. He insisted that China had changed much for the better since 1949. The problem, he argued, was that China had just not changed enough. A feudal economic structure was abolished, but feudal customs and habits in personal relationships had never been cleaned away. The Party was not free of this influence, and Mao Zedong was partly to blame, he said. "For the most part, when we followed his advice, the country progressed. But somewhere along the line—I'm talking about after Liberation—he stopped taking his own advice, and began slipping back into feudal, autocratic ways. No one could disagree with him. . . . We still haven't entirely recovered. There's still a lot of confusion in people's minds." Ma told Alley and Shapiro that the problems did not have to take China away from socialism and deeper into feudalism or capitalism. "The Party," he said, "made mistakes before—terrible mistakes that brought terrible losses. But it always came back, recognized its mistakes, corrected them and went on to new achievements. . . . Our Communist Party has the will and the determination and the ability to come through. We've done it before, and we'll do it again," he insisted.[65]

In 1987 Ma suffered a new ailment in the form of diabetes. Dr. Wu Weiran put him on daily medication and a special diet, which he ignored. He continued to request funds from abroad for Su Fei's film, sending copies of the script to old and new friends. In April he joined dignitaries from around China to honor Rewi Alley at a banquet in the Great Hall of the People to commemorate his sixtieth year in China.

More academic honors came to Ma. The University of North Carolina, at the urging of its alumnus and Ma's nephew, Joe Pat Hatem, awarded Ma a diploma for the work he began in 1927. Waiving three credits of English, the university awarded him a bachelor's degree as a member of the class of 1987. Ma, concerned only that his degree be "with honors," gladly accepted the gesture but did not travel to Chapel Hill that spring. He accepted the degree from an official delegation to Beijing later in the year. In September he also received an honorary doctor of science degree from the State University of New York at Buffalo. Held in Beijing, the ceremony was attended by his old Yan'an comrade who was soon to be president of China, Yang Shangkun.[66]

Though Ma weakened noticeably in 1987, losing weight at an alarming rate, he insisted on traveling into the countryside. In July he visited Shandong to inspect leprosy work, and in October he went south to Hunan Province to "look over the leprosy situation among the minorities on the mountain valleys."[67] During these inspections he tired easily and rested often. "When he came in a room he looked very tired," remembered one friend, "but when he saw people who wanted to talk about leprosy, he straightened up, looked proper and went to work."[68]

When Ma returned to Beijing he turned his attention to Alley, who had spent the past several months at Beijing Union Medical Hospital under the care of Dr. Wu. Alley was strong enough to attend his nintieth birthday party in November, but he was growing weaker every day. On December 26, after returning from an inspection tour of Kunming Province, Ma shared breakfast with Alley in the hospital. They reminisced about Chairman Mao, who would have been ninety-four that day, and Ma left him in good spirits. Later that evening Alley suffered a cerebral embolism and heart attack. Wu called Ma and a team of physicians to Alley's side, but he died shortly after midnight.

The year ended on this sad note for Ma. His and Alley's relationship had begun in the early 1930s and never wavered over the next half century. Now, except for a seriously ill Hans Muller, Ma's friends were all gone. In a letter to Grey Dimond he said, "With the passing of Rewi, another step of history has passed on. I have lost a dear, valued and irreplaceable comrade, mentor and friend. The world and China has lost one of its great sons."[69] Ma faced the coming year with one remaining goal—to wipe out leprosy in China in the next two years.[70]

In January 1988 Ma received his final international honor when the government of India presented him with the Gandhi International Leprosy Award. With Youma by his side, Ma went to New Delhi to receive the award. Afterward they flew to Hong Kong, where John Colling, an international businessman and Ma's friend from Dixie Mission days, hosted a formal reception for him. By the time they returned to Beijing, Chinese New Year had begun, and Ma attended a celebration at the Great Hall of the People as the guest of Party secretary Hu Yaobang, Prime Minister Zhao Ziyang, and President Yang Shangkun.[71]

Ma grew weaker by the day. Wu says that by early 1988 Ma had lost his appetite, although an examination showed "nothing." Wu placed him in the hospital and explored further, suspecting cancer. In April Ma left his hospital bed to speak at a memorial service honoring Alley. In May he wrote Theresa in Buffalo, telling her of his affliction. "Today is my 67th day in the hospital—Beijing Hospital, Room 315. My usual hospital and my usual life saving doctor Wu Weiran M.D., the one with the feather hands and golden scalpel." He also told Theresa that he would make one more trip to the United States. At the encouragement of Wu and Su Fei, Ma agreed to attend the World Congress of the International Conference of Physicians for the Prevention of Nuclear War in Canada. He then planned to visit Buffalo and North Carolina. Su Fei told Wu she knew this would be Ma's last time to visit with his American family, and she wanted him to go. Wu accompanied Ma, acting as companion and physician.[72]

After delivering his speech at the conference in Canada, Ma visited Theresa and Martha in Buffalo, then stopped off at Rosewell Park Memorial Institute for further tests. While the physicians examining him agreed something was terribly wrong, the cause remained unclear. In Buffalo, Theresa remembers, "He could no longer eat, forcing himself to consume a few mouthfuls. He no longer had us running about fulfilling his errands. We had long conversations."[73] From Buffalo, Ma and Wu went to North Carolina, where Marie Hatem and her family were shocked at his appearance. "We couldn't believe how he looked. All his clothes were so big on him that Greg had to go buy new ones to fit him. He was real quiet, laying on the sofa mostly."[74]

Before returning to Beijing, Wu and Ma visited friends in Kansas City and San Francisco. By the time he landed in Beijing he needed assistance just to walk. His family took him to Beidaihe at his insistence, even though Wu advised against the trip. Ma insisted the beach and ocean air would revive him. In a few days Wu went to Beidaihe to check up on him. When he arrived he found that Ma, against doctor's orders, had attended a conference on the utilization of foreign funds in China's leprosy work. "I'm going if I have to crawl," he had insisted. Finally, after three weeks at Beidaihe, Ma grew so weak he could not drink water without assistance. He had no strength to resist Wu's insistence that he return to Beijing and enter the hospital. When the train arrived in Beijing, Youma carried his father to a waiting car, then took him to Beijing Union Medical Hospital where Wu could look after him. He began intravenous feeding and medication, and by September he had rallied enough to dictate letters and make inquiries into leprosy work and the political situation in China.[75]

Ma did not mind dying, he told several family members and friends, except that he wanted to live just two more years to see his goal of wiping out leprosy in 1990. Ma insisted that he receive regular reports from Hu Daxun, recently appointed at Ma's insistence as general secretary of the China Leprosy Association. "Following my reports, Dr. Ma would give me instructions," remembers Hu. Ma also received regular visits from his old colleague Dai Zhengyi. In September the nineteenth International Leprosy meeting took place in The Hague. On September 2 Ma met for one hour with Hu, Dai, and Zhang Yifang, the three who would represent China at the conference. Within days of this meeting, he began drifting in and out of consciousness. When the three delegates arrived back in Beijing, they were told at the airport that Ma was gravely ill. They went straight to the hospital to report on their trip, only to find him in a deep coma.[76] On October 3 Ma died at the age of seventy-eight.

An autopsy determined the cause was "seedlike" cancer spread throughout the body. Within hours his body was placed under the crimson hammer and sickle, and aging revolutionaries poured into the hospital to honor an old comrade. They had first met him in the dusty hills of Shaanxi, a young American humanitarian who asked little else except to serve China's revolution. They knew him now as the internationally known Ma Haide, famous throughout the world for helping China rid itself of venereal disease and leprosy, and to the end a loyal member of their Chinese Communist party.

When word of Ma's death reached Buffalo, Theresa visited her priest and requested a traditional forty-day mass for her cousin. The priest told her that would be impossible because Ma was a Communist. Shocked and angry, she fired back, "I don't care what you call him, he was a humanitarian and he deserves it." The mass commenced immediately.[77] As the Communist Ma Haide lay in state under his Party's flag in Beijing, Shafick George Hatem had the prayers of his family's church in New York speeding him to heaven. Even in death he answered with ease to different names and crossed between cultures without missing a step.

On the morning of August 27, 1993, three black limousines filed through Holy Cross Cemetery outside Buffalo, New York. Hundreds of small Chinese and American flags and scores of placards announcing "Hatem —Ma Haide Nativity" lined the route to the gravesite. Those inside the limousines could see the large red banner of the People's Republic of China standing alone beneath a shade tree, marking their destination. As a crowd of people gathered, the limousines stopped next to the Hatem family plot, and the Chinese and American families of George Hatem, known throughout the world as Ma Haide, walked toward the freshly dug grave. They were followed by Chinese government officials and surrounded by over two hundred friends, colleagues, and admirers. Some in attendance spoke Chinese, but no English. Others spoke English, but not a word of Chinese. Several spoke both. Ma's widow, Su Fei, headed the line of mourners, accompanied by her grandson, Ma Jun, carrying the ashes of his grandfather. China's ambassador to the United States, Li Daoyu, and its minister of public health, Chen Minzhang, followed closely behind. Dr. Wu Weiran, personal physician to Ma, Deng Xiaoping, and the late premier Zhou Enlai also joined the group.

Following remarks by the Reverend Monsignor Joseph Joseph, pastor of the St. John Maron Roman Catholic Maronite Church, Ma Jun placed the urn in the ground, and Su Fei, followed by members of both Chinese and American families, took turns filling the grave with small shovelfuls of dirt. At the memorial service that followed, Ambassador Li opened with remarks on the life and contributions to China made by his friend Ma Haide. Mayor James D. Griffin of Buffalo spoke on the pride his city felt for George Hatem, one of its most renowned sons. John Colling, an American friend since the days of the Dixie Mission, spoke of his friend the humanitarian and cultural go-between. The last speaker was Zhou Youma, Ma's only child.

The Buffalo service marked the third funeral and fifth memorial tribute held for Ma Haide. The first ceremony honoring him was organized in Beijing just after his death on October 3, 1988. Among those attending were President Yang Shangkun, Premier Li Peng, and Deng Yingchao, widow of Zhou Enlai. Ma's body lay in state, covered by the crimson hammer and sickle banner of the Chinese Communist party. The next service took place almost a year later, in September 1989, at the Great Hall of the People. Over four hundred representatives from around the world attended, with the ashes later interred next to old comrades at the Cemetery for Revolutionaries outside Beijing. The inscription on the tombstone was written in the hand of President Yang Shangkun. Su Fei, Youma, nephew Greg Hatem, and others later traveled to Yan'an, where, in accordance with Ma's wishes, ashes were scattered in the Yanhe River. Now, also at his request, the city of his birth and the church of his ancestors welcomed home this prodigal son one final time.

I: FAMILY AND CHURCH

1. *The Catholic Encyclopedia,* vol. IV (New York: The Encyclopedic Press, Inc., 1910).

2. Interview with Greg Hatem, Raleigh, North Carolina, July 10, 1992. Greg Hatem retains Nahoum's original discharge papers.

3. Su Ping and Su Fei, *Ma Haide* (Shenyang: Liaoning Renmin Chuban She, 1990), p. 3.

4. Ibid., p. 4; interview with Greg Hatem, July 10, 1992; notes on the early life of George Hatem written by Theresa Hatem Ode in 1989 from personal papers of Ma Haide now in the possession of Su Fei.

5. Jonathan D. Spence, *In Search of Modern China* (New York: W. W. Norton and Company, 1990), pp. 265–268.

6. Interview with Marie Hatem, Raleigh, North Carolina, July 11, 1992.

7. Rewi Alley, *Six Americans in China* (Beijing: International Culture Publishing Corp., 1985), p. 4.

8. Ibid., p. 5.

9. Israel Epstein, *Woman in World History: Life and Times of Soong Ching Ling (Madam Sun Yatsen)* (Beijing: New World Press, 1993), pp. 1–4.

10. Interview with Theresa Hatem Ode, Buffalo, New York, August 29, 1993.

11. Su Ping and Su Fei, p. 5.

12. Interview with Theresa Hatem Ode, August 29, 1993.

13. George Hatem, "American Childhood, Chinese Maturing," *China Reconstructs,* October 1984, pp. 26–27.

14. Spence, pp. 322–323.

15. Su Ping and Su Fei, p. 11.

16. Hatem, "American Childhood," p. 27.

17. Spence, pp. 337–339, and Edgar Snow, *Red Star Over China* (New York: Grove Press, 1978), p. 149.

18. Ma Hai-Teh, "Contrast in Equality, U.S. Negroes and China's Minorities," *China Reconstructs,* October 1963, p. 6.

19. Hatem, "American Childhood," p. 27.

20. Johanna Grimes, "Most Famous American in China Is a North Carolinian," press release, University of North Carolina at Chapel Hill, September 12, 1973.

21. Elmer Bendiner, "Virtue from Beyond the Seas," *Hospital Practice,* January 15, 1985, p. 130.

2: THREE SCHOOLS, THREE COUNTRIES

1. Bendiner, pp. 130–131; interview with Greg Hatem, July 10, 1992.

2. Lloyd E. Eastman, "Nationalist China in the Nanking Decade, 1927–1937," in *The Nationalist Era in China, 1927–1949,* ed. Eastman, Ch'en, Pepper, and Van Slyke (New York: Cambridge University Press, 1991), pp. 1–2; Spence, pp. 353–372. For a description of Rewi Alley's life in China, see Geoff Chapple, *Rewi Alley of China* (Sydney: Hodder and Stoughton, 1980).

3. Telephone interview with Salvitere Turchielli, November 27, 1992.

4. Edgar Snow, *Red China Today* (New York: Random House, 1970) p. 263.

5. Hatem, "American Childhood," p. 27.

6. Grimes.

7. Ibid.

8. Interview with Salvitere Turchielli, November 27, 1992.

9. Summary of personal data on Shafick George Hatem, University of North Carolina Alumni Files.

10. Roger N. Kirkman, "An Account of My Meeting with Dr. George Hatem (Ma Hai-Teh), May 17, 1978," University of North Carolina Alumni Files.

11. E. Grey Dimond, *Ed Snow Before Paoan: The Shanghai Years* (Kansas City, Missouri: The Edgar Snow Memorial Fund, University of Missouri-Kansas City University Archives, undated), pp. 8–9.

12. Interview with Salviteri Turchielli, November 27, 1992.

13. The university's report of its investigation prior to awarding the degree outlines Hatem's academic record: "The UNC–CH record shows that he was enrolled from Fall Quarter 1927 through Spring Quarter 1929 as a candidate for the Bachelor of Science degree in Medicine, which at that time was offered through the School of Applied Science. That degree program required a total of 27 prescribed courses and electives, normally over a 3-year period, and—unlike our present B.S. Medicine degree program—did not require satisfactory completion of the first year of medical school here or elsewhere. Of those 27 courses, Dr. Hatem passed 26 (with no grade lower than C) during his two years here and lacked only credit for a fourth English course in order to qualify for his degree."

14. Freedom of Information Act (FOIA) search, Hatem's passport application, 1929.

15. Interview with Theresa Hatem Ode, August 29, 1993.

16. Hatem, "American Childhood," p. 27.

17. Su Ping and Su Fei, p. 12.

18. E. Grey Dimond, *Inside China Today: A Western View* (New York: W. W. Norton, 1983), p. 27.

19. Telephone interview with Herbert Hitch, August 10, 1991.

20. David Perlmutt interview with Herbert Hitch in *The Charlotte Observer*, July 5, 1992.

21. Unlike other government agencies that released documents, the CIA completely denied access to George Hatem's file for the purposes of this biography.

22. Interview with Greg Hatem, July 10, 1992.

23. Hatem, "American Childhood," p. 26.

24. Chapple, p. 46; Janice R. MacKinnon and Stephen R. MacKinnon, *Agnes Smedley: The Life and Times of an American Radical* (Berkeley, California: University of California Press, 1988), pp. 144–145; Edgar Snow, *Journey to the Beginning: A Personal View of Contemporary History* (New York: Vintage Books, 1972), pp. 8–9.

25. May Ahdab-Yehia, "The Lebanese Maronites," in *Arabs in the New World: Studies on Arab-American Communities,* ed. Sameer Y. Abraham and Nabeel Abraham (Detroit, Michigan: Wayne State University, Center for Urban Studies, 1983), p. 153.

26. American University in Beirut transcripts of Shafick G. Hatem, recorded December 16, 1931, on file with the medical school of the University of Geneva.

27. Hatem, "American Childhood," p.28.

28. Interview with Marie Hatem, Raleigh, North Carolina, July 11, 1992.

29. Su Ping and Su Fei, p. 14.

30. Interview with Theresa Hatem Ode, August 29, 1993.

31. Eastman, pp. 9, 23; Spence, pp. 389–392.

3: COMING HOME—SOON

1. Hatem, "American Childhood," p. 28.

2. Bendiner, p. 131. Several commentators on Hatem's life have written that it was during the bicycle trip taken in the summer of 1930 that he enrolled in the medical college in Geneva. As letters to his family show, this was incorrect. See Su Ping and Su Fei; Dimond, *Inside China Today;* Snow, *Red China Today.*

3. Bendiner, pp. 131–132; interview with Greg Hatem, July 10, 1992.

4. Bendiner, p. 131.

5. Jacques Guillermaz, *A History of the Chinese Communist Party, 1921–1949* (New York: Random House, 1972) pp. 234–239.

6. George Hatem, "The Irreducible Wassermann," Medical College of Geneva University thesis, 1933.

7. FOIA search, passport renewal application, 1931.

8. Snow, *Red China Today,* p. 263.

9. Bendiner, p. 132.

10. Otto Braun, *A Comintern Agent in China, 1932–1939* (London: C. Hurst, 1975), p. 253.

11. Hatem, "American Childhood," p. 28.

12. Dimond, *Inside China Today,* p. 28.

13. Interview with Todd Ode, Buffalo, New York, August 26, 1993.

14. Su Ping and Su Fei, p. 16.

15. Interview with Theresa Hatem Ode, August 29, 1993.

4: SHANGHAI MARXISTS

1. Snow, *Red China Today,* p. 263. On his passport application Hatem states that he entered Syria in 1921 rather than the actual date of 1929. It is a mistake that neither the State Department nor Hatem corrected when reviewing the application.

2. Bendiner, p. 132.

3. Ma Haide, "Fifty Years of Medicine," *Beijing Review,* November 17, 1984, p. 16.

4. Wilfred Burchett, with Rewi Alley, *China: The Quality of Life* (New York: Penguin, 1976), p. 227.

5. Alley, pp. 5–6.

6. Hatem, "American Childhood," p. 27.

7. Snow, *Red China Today,* p. 263.

8. Ma Haide, "Fifty Years of Medicine," pp. 16–17.

9. Su Ping and Su Fei, p. 19.

10. Snow, *Red China Today,* pp. 263–264.

11. Ma Haide, "Fifty Years of Medicine," p. 17.

12. Burchett, p. 228.

13. Hatem, "American Childhood," p. 27.

14. Interview with Su Fei, Beijing, February 9, 1993.

15. Su Ping and Su Fei, p. 19.

16. Adalbert T. Grunfeld, "Friends of the Revolution: American Supporters of China's Communists, 1926–1939," doctoral dissertation, 1985, New York University, University Microfilms International, 8603879, p. 73.

17. Interview with Ruth Weiss, Beijing, February 11, 1993.

18. Interview with Su Fei, February 9, 1993.

19. Letter from George Hatem to Rewi Alley, December 15, 1956; Ma Haide personal papers, Beijing.

20. Ma Haide, "Working for Soong Ching Ling in Yanan," *Beijing Review,* October 31, 1988, p. 34.

21. Grunfeld, pp. 64–73.

22. Burchett, pp. 55–56.

23. Chapple, p. 63; Grunfeld, p. 75.

24. Rewi Alley, "The Ma Haide I Know," *China Pictorial,* December 1980, p. 24.

25. Ma Haide, "Fifty Years in Medicine," p. 17; Su Ping and Su Fei, pp. 23–24; Burchett, p. 56.

26. Ma Haide, "Fifty Years in Medicine," p. 17.

27. Ibid., pp. 17–18.

28. The claim that Shippe was a Comintern agent comes from Helen Foster Snow (Nym Wales) in an interview of May 13, 1991.

29. Interview with Ruth Weiss, Beijing, July 16, 1991.

30. Ibid.

31. Ma Haide, "She Sent Me to Shaanxi," *Beijing Review,* June 15, 1981, p. 18.

32. Su Ping and Su Fei, p. 35.

33. Epstein, p. 276.

34. Su Ping and Su Fei, pp. 24–28; Grunfeld, p. 168.

35. Letter from George Hatem to Lazer Katz, Ma Haide personal papers, Beijing.

36. *History of the Chinese Communist Party, A Chronology of Events, 1919–1990* (Beijing: Foreign Languages Press, 1991), pp. 93–96; Spence, pp. 404–409.

37. Alley, "The Ma Haide I Know," p. 24.

38. Bernard E. Read, S. G. Hatem, Yu Bao Dju, and Wei Yung Lee, *Industrial Health in Shanghai China,* vol. 2: *A Study of the Chromium Plating and Polishing Trade* (Shanghai: Chinese Medical Association, 1936).

39. Ibid., p. 15.

40. Ibid., p. 9.

41. Ibid., pp. 23–24.

42. Hatem, "American Childhood," p. 29.

43. Ma Haide, "Notes of Dr. Ma Haide's Early Life," Ma Haide's personal papers, Beijing.

44. Interview with Theresa Hatem Ode, August 29, 1993.

5: THE RED ARMY CALLS

1. Ma Haide, "Fifty Years of Medicine," p. 18.

2. Grunfeld, p. 171.

3. Burchett, p. 229.

4. MacKinnon and MacKinnon, p. 167.

5. Snow, *Red China Today,* p. 264.

6. Lloyd Shearer, "Dr. George Hatem—He's the Most Famous American in the People's Republic of China," *Parade,* August 12, 1973, p. 4.

7. Quoted in Judie Telfer, "George Hatem, American Doctor in China," *Beijing Review,* October 31–November 6, 1988, p. 33.

8. Interview with Ruth Weiss, July 16, 1991.

9. Hatem, "American Childhood," p. 29; George Hatem, "Notes of Dr. Ma Haide's Early Life," unpublished manuscript from Ma Haide's personal papers, p. 7.

10. Alley, *Six Americans in China,* p. 9.

11. Ma Haide, "Fifty Years of Medicine," p. 18.

12. Su Ping and Su Fei, pp. 38–39.

13. Hatem, "Notes of Dr. Ma Haide's Early Life," p. 7.

14. George Hatem, "Working for Soong Ching Ling in Yanan," *Beijing Review*, October 31, 1988, p. 34.

15. Su Ping and Su Fei, p. 40; Su Fei, *Travels to the West* (unpublished screenplay), pp. 15–19; Hatem, "American Childhood," p. 29.

16. Hatem, "Working for Soong Ching Ling in Yanan," p. 34.

17. Snow, *Journey to the Beginning*, p. 152.

18. Ibid.

19. John Maxwell Hamilton, *Edgar Snow* (Bloomington, Indiana: Indiana University Press, 1988), pp. 67–68; Snow, *Journey to the Beginning*, p. 152.

20. Interview with John Roderick, Honolulu, April 14, 1992.

21. Snow, *Red China Today*, p. 261; Alley, *Six Americans in China*, p. 44; Huang Hua, *Renmin Ribao*, November 23, 1983, p. 3. All place the meeting in Xi'an rather than Zhengzhou.

22. Interview with Huang Hua, Beijing, August 17, 1992.

23. Telephone interview with Helen Foster Snow, May 13, 1991.

24. Snow, *Red China Today*, p. 261.

25. Dimond, *Inside China Today*, p. 136; interview with Helen Foster Snow, May 13, 1991.

26. Quoted in Dimond, *Inside China Today*, p. 136.

27. Ibid. This attempt by Hatem to portray himself as the protector of Snow as they entered China does not sit well with friends of Snow, especially his former wife Helen Foster Snow. She insists that Hatem's description of himself as Snow's protecter and leader of the trek to Baoan are untrue, and that he lies about them for the same reason she accuses many Chinese Communists of lying, namely, to make history serve a political purpose. Grey Dimond, a friend of both Snow and Hatem, tries to reconcile the differences in his book, *Inside China Today*, though his attempt is unsuccessful. There is obvious disagreement on the issue, and either Snow altered his story to make the saga of his trip more personal to the reader, or Hatem does the same for his own ends. After reading through the diaries and notes of Snow, I believe Snow's account of his own contacts but trust that Hatem truly believed he was the more anointed of the two as they entered the Red Army region.

6: TWO BANDITS IN SEARCH OF CHAIRMAN MAO

1. Hatem, "American Childhood," p. 29.

2. Su Fei, *Travels to the West*, pp. 26–28.

3. Helen Foster Snow, *The Chinese Communists* (Westport, Connecticut: Greenwood, 1972), pp. 314–315. This book was originally published in 1952 under the title *Red Dust*.

4. Interview with Huang Hua, August 17, 1992.

5. Su Fei, *Travels to the West,* pp. 26–32.

6. Interview with Huang Hua, August 17, 1992.

7. Snow, *Red China Today,* p. 262.

8. Snow, *Red Star Over China,* pp. 11–13, 557–558; Su Fei, *Travels to the West,* p. 35; Dimond, *Inside China Today,* pp. 257–258 fn.

9. Hatem, "Notes of Dr. Ma Haide's Early Life," p. 8.

10. Interview with Huang Hua, August 17, 1992.

11. Epstein, p. 309.

12. Su Fei, *Travels to the West,* p. 40.

13. Ibid., p. 40–41; Su Ping and Su Fei, p. 41.

14. Snow, *Red Star Over China,* p. 24.

15. Su Fei, *Travels to the West,* pp. 42–44.

16. Interview with Huang Hua, August 17, 1992.

17. Su Fei, *Travels to the West,* pp. 44–46.

18. Ibid., pp. 47–53; Su Ping and Su Fei, p. 43; Snow, *Red Star Over China,* p. 26.

19. Su Fei, *Travels to the West,* pp. 58–59; Su Ping and Su Fei, p. 43.

20. Ibid., p. 29.

21. Quoted in Snow, *Red China Today,* p. 265.

22. Snow, *Red Star Over China,* p. 37.

23. Ibid., p. 41. While Snow speaks of his trip in the singular, Hatem was with him every step of the way until they reached Baoan.

24. Ibid., p. 42.

25. Su Fei, *Travels to the West,* p. 80; Su Ping and Su Fei, p. 52. Much of the story of the journey taken by Snow and Hatem is presented in different, even contradictory, retellings by Su Fei and Edgar Snow. I have studied the various presentations and reconstructed the story as accurately as possible. Keep in mind that Snow admits to shading his story to protect sources, and Su Fei, as a screenwriter, takes poetic license with certain events.

26. Ibid., p. 82.

27. Snow, *Red Star Over China,* p. 44.

28. Ibid.

29. Su Ping and Su Fei, p. 53; Snow, *Red Star Over China,* p. 44.

30. Su Ping and Su Fei, p. 54; Snow, *Red Star Over China,* pp. 45–46.

31. Su Fei, *Travels to the West,* pp. 85–87.

32. Snow, *Journey to the Beginning,* p. 158. The comments Zhou made about Chiang did not find their way into print until 1957. Soon after the interview, a united front was arranged between the Communists and the Nationalists, and Zhou asked Snow not to print his "frank and disparaging opinions" about Chiang because the two parties would be working together again, this time against the Japanese.

33. Snow, *Red Star Over China,* p. 59.

34. Ibid., p. 62.

35. Su Ping and Su Fei, p. 55.

7: A NEW NAME, A NEW LIFE

1. Snow, *Journey to the Beginning*, pp. 159–160; Su Fei, *Travels to the West*, p. 86; Hamilton, p. 71.

2. Snow, *Journey to the Beginning*, p. 167.

3. Tracy B. Strong and Helene Keyssar, *Right in Her Soul: The Life of Anna Louise Strong* (New York: Random House, 1983), p. 292; Su Fei, *Travels to the West*, pp. 87, 88.

4. Interview with Huang Hua, August 17, 1992.

5. Snow, *Journey to the Beginning*, p. 160; Hamilton, p. 78.

6. George Hatem, "New Life in China," *China Reconstructs*, February 1985, p. 44.

7. Hatem, "Notes of Dr. Ma Haide's Early Life," p. 9.

8. Su Ping and Su Fei, pp. 58–59; Su Fei, *Travels to the West*, pp. 91–92; Snow, *Journey to the Beginning*, p. 160.

9. Su Fei, *Travels to the West*, p. 93. In modern Chinese politics, "putting a cap" on someone holds a special, sometimes terrifying meaning. To have a cap placed on your head, be it symbolic or real, is to be labeled with a particular political designation, usually negative, such as counterrevolutionary, rightist, or capitalist-roader. This was especially true during the anti-rightist movement of 1957 and the Cultural Revolution of 1966–1976. It should be noted that Snow told this story somewhat differently in *Red China Today* (p. 266), where he insists that Hatem reminded him in 1960 that it was Snow who removed his cap and placed it on Mao's head. As with other discrepancies, such as the invisible letter versus the torn five-pound note, the facts are difficult to discern. Each case appears to be an effort to show that one is more intimate than the other with the Party leadership. In the case of the hat, I tend to believe Hatem's story as told to his wife. His relaxed manner and effusive personality would certainly have allowed him to act in this manner.

10. Ma Haide, "Fifty Years of Medicine," p. 18.

11. Snow, *Red Star Over China*, p. 98.

12. Ibid., p. 66. In the 1938 edition of the book, the text stood alone as seen here. In the 1978 edition a footnote tells who the physician was and presents a brief biographical note on Hatem.

13. Interview with Huang Hua, August 17, 1992; Su Ping and Su Fei, pp. 58–59.

14. Snow, *Red China Today*, p. 266.

15. Interview with Huang Hua, August 17, 1992.

16. Ibid.

17. Snow, *Red Star Over China*, p. 257.

18. Interview with Dr. Dai Zhengqi, Beijing, February 6, 1993.

19. Snow, *Red Star Over China*, p. 290.

20. Ma Haide, "Fifty Years of Medicine," p. 20.

21. Interview with Huang Hua, August 17, 1992.

22. Hatem, "New Life in China," p. 45.

23. Alley, "The Ma Haide I Know," p. 25.

24. Interview with Huang Hua, August 17, 1992. Huang disputes the fact that Hatem originally called himself Ma Hande, and only remembers calling him Ma Haide. Evidence of the original name Hande comes from letters that Hatem signed in both pinyin and Chinese characters in the weeks following the visit to the mosque. The letters come from the Edgar Snow Papers.

25. Hatem, "American Childhood," p. 29.

26. Ibid.

27. Hatem, "Notes of Dr. Ma Haide's Early Life," p. 10.

28. Hatem, "American Childhood," p. 9.

29. Quoted in Alley, *Six Americans in China*, p. 11.

30. Ibid.

31. Agnes Smedley, *The Great Road: The Life and Times of Chu Teh* (New York: Monthly Review Press, 1956), p. 344.

32. Harrison E. Salisbury, *The Long March: The Untold Story* (New York: McGraw-Hill, 1985), pp. 322–323.

33. Su Ping and Su Fei, p. 65.

34. Interview with Huang Hua, August 17, 1992.

35. Alley, *Six Americans in China*, p. 10.

36. Hatem, "New Life in China," p. 44.

37. A reference to Agnes Smedley. Later references to M and G are Max (Manny) and Grace Granich.

38. Letter from Ma Haide to Edgar Snow, KC: 19/1/9 Edgar Snow Papers, University of Missouri, Kansas City Archives.

39. Letter from Ma Haide to Edgar Snow, Edgar Snow Papers. Throughout this text I quote Hatem exactly as he wrote, with no changes in spelling or use in punctuation with the exception of a dash (—) inserted infrequently to show a break in sentence structure.

40. To my knowledge this account of the Red Army has never been published in its entirety, although isolated bits of it have been paraphrased by Smedley, Snow, and perhaps others.

41. Letter from Ma Haide to Edgar Snow, December 3, 1936, Edgar Snow Papers. Snow was first an "honest journalist" and second an admirer of the Chinese Communist party. He was not persuaded by this letter to delete Mao's comments on class struggle, and he continued to quote them in later versions of the interview.

42. Ma Haide, "Fifty Years of Medicine," p. 19.

43. Ibid., p. 18.

44. Su Ping and Su Fei, p. 63.

45. Spence, p. 422.

46. Huang Hua, *Renmin Ribao*, p. 3.

47. Hamilton, p. 82.
48. Snow, *Red Star Over China*, pp. 412–413.
49. *New York Times,* January 8, 1937, p. 8.

8: STAYING OUT OF MESSES

1. By early 1937, the adopted name Ma Hande had been changed to Ma Haide.
2. Braun, p. 190.
3. Ibid., p. 253.
4. Ibid., p. 217.
5. Interview with Su Fei, February 9, 1993.
6. Braun, p. 249.
7. Ibid., pp. 217–219.
8. Hatem, "New Life in China," p. 44. Information on joining the Party comes from Su Ping and Su Fei, pp. 67–68, and Huang Hua, *Renmin Ribao.*
9. Hatem, "New Life in China," p. 44.
10. Interview with Huang Hua, August 17, 1992.
11. Ibid.
12. Hatem, "New Life in China," pp. 44–45; Alley, *Six Americans in China,* p. 14.
13. Alley, *Six Americans in China,* p. 12.
14. MacKinnon and MacKinnon, p. 187.
15. Ibid., p. 186–187.
16. Helen Foster Snow, *My China Years* (New York: William Morrow, 1984), p. 262.
17. Letter from Agnes Smedley to Edgar Snow, April 19, 1937, Edgar Snow Papers.
18. Helen Foster Snow, *The Chinese Communists,* pp. 250–251.
19. Agnes Smedley, *Battle Hymn of China* (London: Victor Gollancz, 1944), p. 123; letter from Agnes Smedley to Edgar Snow, April 17, 1937, Edgar Snow Papers.
20. Agnes Smedley to Edgar Snow, April 19, 1937, Edgar Snow Papers, UMKC.
21. Quoted in MacKinnon and MacKinnon, pp. 188–189.
22. Smedley, *Battle Hymn of China,* pp. 122–123.
23. Braun, p. 249.
24. Quoted in MacKinnon and MacKinnon, pp. 190–191.
25. Roger Faligot and Remi Kauffer, *The Chinese Secret Service* (London: Headline Publishers, 1989), p. 126.
26. Ibid., p. 191.
27. Interview with Helen Foster Snow, May 13, 1991.

28. Foster Snow, *My China Years,* p. 262; interview with Helen Foster Snow, May 13, 1991.

29. Interview with Helen Foster Snow, May 13, 1991.

30. Foster Snow, *My China Years,* p. 262.

31. Interview with Huang Hua, August 17, 1992.

32. Interview with Greg Hatem, July 10, 1992.

33. MacKinnon and MacKinnon, p. 337.

34. Interview with Su Fei, February 9, 1993.

35. Ibid.

36. Smedley, *Battle Hymn of China,* p. 118.

37. Ibid., p. 341.

9: THE ETERNAL OPTIMIST

1. Evans F. Carlson, *Twin Stars of China* (New York: Dodd, Meade and Company, 1940), p. 171–172.

2. Ted Allen and Sydney Gordon, *The Scalpel, the Sword: The Story of Dr. Norman Bethune* (New York: Monthly Review Press, 1973), pp. 22–23.

3. Ibid., p. 75.

4. Ibid., p. 120.

5. Quoted in Allen and Gordon, p. 164.

6. Ibid., p. 167.

7. Letter from James Bertram to Edgar Snow, April 9, 1938, Edgar Snow Papers.

8. Jean Ewen, *China Nurse, 1932–1939* (Toronto: McClelland and Stewart Limited, 1981), pp. 49–52.

9. Ibid., p. 85.

10. Quoted in Allen and Gordon, p. 186.

11. Ibid., pp. 186–187.

12. Quoted in Ewen, p. 90.

13. Ibid, pp. 90–91.

14. Allen and Gordon, p. 192.

15. Quoted in Allen and Gordon, p. 194.

16. Letter from Ma Haide to Edgar Snow, December 5, 1939, Edgar Snow Papers.

17. Report from Norman Bethune to China Defense League, China Aid Council, July 1, 1939, Edgar Snow Papers.

18. Quoted in Allen and Gordon, pp. 200–201.

19. Ibid., p. 282.

20. Ibid., p. 298.

21. Ibid., pp. 261–262.

22. Ibid., p. 225.

23. Ibid., pp. 300–316.

24. Letter from Ma Haide to Edgar Snow, December 5, 1939. Edgar Snow Papers.

25. This note is in the possession of Mrs. Arlene Duncan of Honolulu, Hawai'i.

26. Ma Hai-teh, "Ashes of Revolutionaries Mingle Together," *Chinese Literature,* 1978, vol. 2, p. 112.

10: YAN'AN'S MOST BEAUTIFUL COMMUNIST

1. Epstein, p. 351.

2. Chapple, pp. 117–118.

3. Ibid., p. 119.

4. Braun, p. 255.

5. Ross Terrill, *The White Boned Demon* (New York: William Morrow, 1984), pp. 125–126.

6. Interview with Su Fei, February 9, 1993.

7. Interview with Jack Chen, Honolulu, May 9, 1990.

8. Braun, p. 249.

9. Terrill, pp. 137–154.

10. Interview with Su Fei, February 9, 1993.

11. Zhou Yongnan, "Ma Hai-de and Su Fei Visit Her Family," *Zhejiang Daily,* May 23, 1987; interview with anonymous source, Beijing, 1993; Su Ping and Su Fei, pp. 104–105.

12. Su Fei, "I Took Up the Challenge," *Women of China,* February 1982, p. 37.

13. Interview with anonymous source, February 8, 1993.

14. Interview with Su Fei, February 10, 1993.

15. Ibid.

16. Snow, *Red China Today,* p. 267.

17. Interview with Su Fei, February 10, 1993.

18. Su Ping and Su Fei, p. 105.

19. Interview with Su Fei, February 10, 1993.

20. Two anonymous interviews, Beijing, February 8, 1993, and February 10, 1993.

21. Interview with Su Fei, February 10, 1993.

22. Ibid.

23. Ibid.

24. Ibid.

25. Ibid., Su Ping and Su Fei, pp. 107–108.

26. Ibid.

27. Ibid.

28. Burchett, p. 230.

29. Su Ping and Su Fei, p. 110.

30. Ibid.

31. Su Fei, "Dr. Ma Haide: A Wife's Memories," *Beijing Review*, October 16–22, 1989, p. 39.

32. Interview with Su Fei, February 10, 1993.

33. Su Fei, "I Took Up the Challenge," p. 38.

34. Ibid.

35. Su Ping and Su Fei, p. 111.

36. Su Fei, "Dr. Ma Haide: A Wife's Memories," p. 39.

37. Su Fei, "I Took Up the Challenge," p. 38.

11: A SUSPECTED SPY

1. Terrill, p. 166; Su Ping and Su Fei, p. 80.

2. Interview with Israel Epstein, Beijing, February 9, 1993.

3. Letter from Edgar Snow to Jim Bertram, December 13, 1939. Edgar Snow Papers.

4. Harrison Forman, *Report from Red China* (New York: H. Holt, 1945), p. 50.

5. Letter from Ma Haide to Edgar Snow, December 5, 1939. Edgar Snow Papers.

6. Ibid.

7. Ibid.

8. Su Ping and Su Fei, p. 112.

9. Ibid., pp. 112–115.

10. *History of the Chinese Communist Party, 1919–1990*, pp. 136–139.

11. Ma Hai-teh, China Defense League Newsletter, August 15, 1940 (copies in the possession of Israel Epstein).

12. Hatem, "New Life in China," p. 45.

13. FOIA Search, State Department Document.

14. Interview with Greg Hatem, July 10, 1992.

15. Interview with Ling Qing, Beijing, February 5, 1993.

16. Su Ping and Su Fei, pp. 114–115; *History of the Chinese Communist Party, 1919–1990*, p. 142.

17. *History of the Chinese Communist Party, 1919–1990*, p. 147.

18. Guillermaz, p. 364.

19. Ibid.

20. Spence, pp. 472–473.

21. Quoted in Mark Selden, *The Yenan Way in Revolutionary China* (Cambridge: Harvard University Press, 1971), pp. 191–192.

22. Ibid., pp. 188–191.

23. *History of the Chinese Communist Party, 1919–1990*, p. 147.

24. Interview with Han Xu, Beijing, February 3, 1993.

25. *History of the Chinese Communist Party, 1919–1990*, p. 149.

26. Interview with Su Fei, February 10, 1993.

27. Spence, p. 599.

28. *History of the Chinese Communist Party, 1919–1990*, p. 150.

29. Ibid., pp. 152–153.

30. Interview with Su Fei, February 10, 1993.

31. Ibid.

32. Su Ping and Su Fei, p. 163.

33. Ibid., pp. 163–164; interview with Richard Frey, Beijing, February 5, 1993. The case of Wang Ming's suspected poisoning is also told by Wang Ming in his memoirs, *Mao's Betrayal* (Moscow: Progress Publishers, 1975). In this recounting Wang Ming says that Dr. Qin Maoyao, on orders from Chairman Mao, intentionally poisoned him with mercury. He blames Ma Haide for agreeing with Qin's prescription. He also accuses Ma of refusing to try the medicine himself to prove it was not poison. He never places ultimate blame on Ma for the poisoning episode, and he recounts that Dr. Qin was imprisoned during the Rectification Campaign because he confessed to poisoning him. He also says that at the conclusion of the Rectification Campaign, Qin was released and allowed to recant his confession, altering it to say he had merely made an error in judgment and had not intended to harm Wang Ming. Wang, pp. 41–43 and p. 151. P. P. Vladimirov, argues that in fact it was Kang Sheng, cooperating with Mao, who orchestrated the attempted poisoning of Wang Ming (Vladimirov, *China's Special Area, 1942–1945* [Bombay: Allied Publishers, 1974], p. 95). Exactly what happened in this intriguing episode is difficult to decipher. It is clear, however, that Kang Sheng stuck Ma Haide with charges of incompetency and perhaps attempted murder and held this over his head for the next several decades.

34. Interview with Richard Frey, February 5, 1993.

35. Interview with Sydney Rittenberg, Honolulu, November 15, 1990.

36. Interview with Israel Epstein, February 9, 1993; interview with Huang Hua, August 17, 1992; and interview with Su Fei, February 10, 1993.

37. *History of the Chinese Communist Party, 1919–1990*, pp. 154–155.

38. Guillermaz, p. 367; interviews with a number of Party members in China.

39. Su Ping and Su Fei, pp. 117–119.

40. Ibid., p. 73.

41. Ibid., p. 75.

42. Ibid., pp. 83–84.

43. Ibid., p. 87.

44. Ibid., pp. 76–78.

12: WITH AMERICANS AGAIN

1. Vladimirov, p. 499.

2. Ibid., p. 18.

3. Ibid., pp. 37, 130. These remarks by Vladimirov were picked up by Faligot and Kauffer, who claim Ma and Su Fei were in the service of Kang Sheng from their Yan'an days until after 1949. As interviews with friends and relatives attest,

Ma was always suspicious of Kang Sheng, and the feeling undoubtedly was mutual.

4. Interview with Jack Chen, May 9, 1990.

5. Interview with Huang Hua, August 17, 1992.

6. Foreman, p. 47.

7. Hatem, "New Life in China," p. 45.

8. John Colling, *The Spirit of Yenan* (Hong Kong: API Press, 1991), pp. 4–5.

9. Spence, p. 478; Colonel W. J. Peterkin, *Inside China, 1943–1945* (Baltimore, Maryland: Gateway Press, 1992), pp. 17–18; Colling, pp. 1–4; interview with John Colling, Hong Kong, May 19, 1992; David D. Barrett, *Dixie Mission: The United States Army Observer Group in Yenan, 1944* (Berkeley: University of California, Center for Chinese Studies, China Research Monographs, 1970), pp. 22–26; Michael Schaller, *The United States and China in the Twentieth Century* (New York: Oxford University Press, 1990), pp. 97–100; interview with Clifford Young, Honolulu, November 11, 1991.

10. Peterkin, p. 87.

11. Interview with Herbert Hitch, March 22, 1991.

12. Colling, pp. 21–22; Vladimirov, pp. 211–212.

13. Barrett, p. 29.

14. Interview with Ling Qing, February 5, 1993.

15. Ibid.

16. Ibid.; interview with Clifford Young, November 11, 1991.

17. Ibid.

18. Barrett, p. 53.

19. Ibid.

20. Vladimirov, p. 252.

21. Ibid., pp. 216, 493.

22. Telephone interview with Wilbur J. Peterkin, December 4, 1992; William P. Head, *Colonel Wilbur Peterkin and the American Military Mission to the Chinese Communists, 1944–1945* (Chapel Hill, North Carolina: Documentary Publications, 1987), p. 129.

23. Interview with Peterkin, December 4, 1992.

24. Interview with John Service, September 30, 1990.

25. Joseph W. Esherick (ed.), *Lost Chance in China: The World War II Dispatches of John Service* (New York: Random House, 1974), p. 101.

26. Interview with John Colling, May 19, 1992.

27. Head, p. 54; Koji Ariyoshi, "Huang Hua: World War II Liaison Officer Assigned to the U.S. Mission," *Honolulu Star-Bulletin*, November 17, 1971, p. A-23.

28. Interview with John Service, September 30, 1990.

29. Interview with John Colling, May 19, 1992.

30. Interview with Peterkin, December 4, 1992.

31. Interview with Huang Hua, August 17, 1992.

32. Ariyoshi.

33. Peterkin, pp. 20, 22, 25, 85, 90.

34. Interview with John Roderick, April 14, 1992.

35. Letter written by Shoso Nomura to Gertrude Noyes, February 5, 1990, E. Grey Dimond Papers, KC: 11/1/1, University of Missouri–Kansas City Archives.

36. Interview with Ling Qing, February 5, 1993.

37 Peterkin, pp. 97–98.

38. Schaller, pp. 91, 103–104; Barrett, pp. 55–65.

39. Peterkin, pp. 117–118.

40. Perlmutt interview with Herbert Hitch, July 5, 1992; Schaller, pp. 104–105.

41. Schaller, pp. 108–109.

42. Ariyoshi.

43. Interview with former Dixie Mission member who requested anonymity.

44. Hatem, "Notes of Dr. Ma Haide's Early Life."

45. Head, p. 95; Paul Domke's report to Colonel Peterkin, May 22, 1945, from the personal papers of Paul Domke, shown to the author by Mrs. Paul Domke.

46. Domke, report to Peterkin.

47. Interview with John Service, September 30, 1990.

48. Interview with Herbert Hitch, March 22, 1991.

49. Su Ping and Su Fei, p. 117.

50. Interview with John Roderick, April 14, 1992.

51. Peterkin, pp. 100, 118.

52. Head, p. 22.

53. Schaller, pp. 111–114.

54. Interview with Clifford Young, November 11, 1991.

13: ON TO BEIJING

1. Interview with Huang Hua, August 17, 1992; interview with Han Xu, February 3, 1993.

2. Interview with Wang Guangmei, Beijing, February 11, 1993.

3. Hatem, "New Life in China," p. 45.

4. Interview with Wang Guangmei, February 11, 1993. Before the interview, Wang Guangmei told me that she rarely grants interviews, though she is inundated with requests from both foreigners and Chinese. This, of course, is not surprising, given her high profile in China since the early 1950s and the nature of the controversy surrounding her husband's vilification during the Cultural Revolution and her own imprisonment and hardships during and after that period. However, her memories of Ma Haide were strong, and she wants his story told.

5. Ibid.

6. Interview with Betty Chandler, Beijing, February 2, 1993.

7. Telephone interview with Robbins Strong, May 7, 1991.

8. The following information and quotes, unless otherwise noted, are gathered from State Department documents gained through an FOIA search.

9. Interview with Herbert Hitch, March 22, 1991.

10. Interview with Greg Hatem, July 10, 1992.

11. Quoted in Strong and Keyssar, pp. 218–219.

12. Strong and Keyssar, pp. 225, 228.

13. Interview with Wang Guangmei, February 11, 1993.

14. Sydney Rittenberg and Amanda Bennett, *The Man Who Stayed Behind* (New York: Simon and Schuster, 1993), pp. 100, 406–407.

15. *History of the Chinese Communist Party, 1919–1990*, pp. 178–181; Schaller, p. 116.

16. Schaller, p. 116.

17. Strong and Keyssar, p. 227.

18. Ibid., pp. 228–229; Su Ping and Su Fei, p. 127.

19. Sidney Shapiro, *Ma Haide, The Saga of American Doctor George Hatem in China* (San Francisco: Cypress Press, 1993), p. 154.

20. Letter from Ma Haide to Anna Louise Strong and Robbins Strong, March 5, 1947, Anna Louise Strong Papers, University of Washington Library, Seattle.

21. Yan Changlin, *Jinwu Mao Zedong Jishi* (Changchuen: Jilin Renmin Chubanshe, 1992), pp. 340–341. It is noteworthy that Ma Haide would be identified in this official remembrance of Mao Zedong as a close comrade of the chairman's. In the book this section is introduced with, "Mao was taking a walk along the bank of the Yan River. He happened to see the American friend Ma Haide and his wife Su Fei. Since they knew each other very well, they sat on the rocks by the river and talked."

22. Su Ping and Su Fei, pp. 127–128.

23. Ibid., p. 128; *History of the Chinese Communist Party, 1919–1990*, pp. 182–183.

24. Su Ping and Su Fei, p. 131.

25. Interview with Ling Qing, February 5, 1993.

26. Su Ping and Su Fei, pp. 132, 133; *History of the Chinese Communist Party, 1919–1990*, p. 185.

27. Interview with David and Isabel Crook, Beijing, February 6, 1993.

28. Ibid.

29. Naval Intelligence Report, March 9, 1948. FOIA.

30. Su Ping and Su Fei, pp. 134–136.

31. Interview with Ling Qing, February 5, 1993.

32. Su Ping and Su Fei, p. 136; Spence, p. 508; interview with Su Fei, February 10, 1993.

14: CLOSING THE BROTHELS

1. Interview with David and Isabel Crook, February 6, 1993.

2. Quoted in Harrison Salisbury, *The New Emperors* (New York: Little Brown, 1992), p. 480 f.

3. Interview with David and Isabel Crook, February 6, 1993.

4. John K. Fairbank and Edwin O. Reischauer, *China: Tradition and Transformation* (Boston: Houghton Mifflin, 1978), p. 482; Su Ping and Su Fei, pp. 136–137.

5. Su Ping and Su Fei, pp. 137–138.

6. Ibid., p. 138.

7. Interview with John Roderick, April 14, 1992; Barrett, p. 52.

8. Interview with Ruth Weiss, Beijing, July 16, 1991.

9. Interview with Jack Chen, May 9, 1990.

10. Su Ping and Su Fei, pp. 145–149.

11. Hatem, "New Life in China," p. 72.

12. Interview with Jack Chen, May 9, 1990.

13. Interview with Gerald Tannenbaum, Santa Barbara, April 14, 1991.

14. Su Ping and Su Fei, p. 141.

15. Anonymous interview.

16. Interview with Sydney Rittenberg, November 15, 1990.

17. This view of Zhou Enlai was given to me by several Chinese who worked under him in the foreign ministry during the 1950s, 1960s, and 1970s.

18. Interview with Gerald Tannenbaum, April 14, 1991.

19. Su Ping and Su Fei, pp. 140, 149, 164.

20. Interview with Su Fei, February 10, 1993.

21. Interview with Israel Epstein, February 9, 1993.

22. Sidney Shapiro, *An American in China* (Beijing: New World Press, 1979), p. 69.

23. Alley, *Six Americans in China*, pp. 31–32.

24. Information on the relationship between Ma and Su Fei in the early to mid 1950s was gathered from interviews with several Chinese and foreign acquaintances living in China and abroad. I respect their requests that these comments remain anonymous.

25. Spence, p. 524.

26. Anonymous interview.

27. Schaller, pp. 140–141.

28. Strong and Keyssar, p. 246; Rittenberg and Bennett, p. 136.

29. Interview with Gladys Yang, Beijing, February 4, 1993.

30. Interview with Su Fei, February 10, 1993.

31. Spence, p. 584.

32. Interview with Israel Epstein, February 9, 1993.

33. Interview with Gerald Tannenbaum, April 14, 1991.

34. Ibid.

35. Quoted in Schaller, p. 133. Previous paragraphs outlining the U.S. government's response to the defeat in China also are from Schaller, pp. 125–133.

36. Ibid., pp. 133–134.

37. *The Amerasia Papers: A Clue to the Catastrophe of China*, vol. 2, prepared by the Subcommittee to Investigate the Administration of the International

Security Act and Other Internal Security Laws of the Committee on the Judiciary, United States Senate, January 26, 1970 (Washington D.C.: U.S. Government Printing Office, 1970).

38. Ibid., pp. 1759–1760. Inaccurate information presented during these hearings can be seen in the erroneous initial "H," given as Hatem's first initial, and in the following testimony that lists Rewi Alley as an American interested in agriculture. Of course, in one respect Emmerson's information was correct. Hatem was a Communist.

39. Interview with Greg Hatem, July 10, 1992; interview with Marie Hatem, July 11, 1992.

40. Interview with Marie Hatem, July 11, 1992.

41. FOIA search. Betty Graham's death is remembered well in the Beijing foreign community. She committed suicide in response to a failed attempt at romance with British Communist party member Alan Winnington.

15: MEDICINE TO THE MASSES

1. *History of the Chinese Communist Party, 1919–1990,* p. 235.

2. Spence, p. 546.

3. Letter from Grace Granich to Ma Haide (Shag), November 12, 1953, Ma Haide personal papers.

4. Alley, *Six Americans in China,* p. 25.

5. Ye Ganyun, "We Esteem Highly His Moral Integrity and Intellectual Achievements," *China Leprosy Journal,* July 1989 (Special Issue in Memory of Dr. Ma Haide), p. 14.

6. Interview with Dr. Wang Hungshen, Beijing, February 6, 1993.

7. Unless otherwise noted, the information on Ma's medical work from 1953 through the end of his career in China comes from interviews with Dr. Dai Zhengqi and Dr. Wang Hungshen, Beijing, February 6 and February 12, 1993.

8. Su Ping and Su Fei, p. 164.

9. Ibid.

10. Josh Horn, *Away with All Pests* (New York: Monthly Review Press, 1969), p. 87; interview with David and Isabel Crook, February 6, 1993.

11. Horn, p. 91.

12. Interview with Dr. Yang Lihe, Guangzhou, May 20, 1991.

13. "Our Profound Memory of Senior Advisor Ma Haide, Institute of Dermatology, CAMS," *China Leprosy Journal,* July 1989, p. 21.

14. Interview with Yang Lihe, May 20, 1991.

15. "Our Profound Memory of Senior Advisor Ma Haide," p. 21.

16. Interview with Israel Epstein, February 9, 1993; interview with Chen Hui, Beijing, February 13, 1993; Dimond, *Inside China Today,* pp. 47–49; Hatem, "New Life in China," p. 44.

17. FBI documents obtained through FOIA search.

18. Interview with Sydney Rittenberg, November 15, 1990.

19. Ma Haide, "On the Sinkiang Road," *China Reconstructs,* February 1957, pp. 22–25; Ma Haide, "Clinic for the Kazakhs," *China Reconstructs,* March 1957, pp. 12–15; Interview with Hu Daxun, Beijing, February 10, 1993.

20. Ma Haide, "Clinic for the Kazakhs," p. 13.

21. Ibid., p. 15.

22. Letters from the Edgar Snow Papers. The following letter citations in this section also are from that collection.

23. Han Suyin, *My House Has Two Doors* (New York: G. P. Putnam's Sons, 1980), p. 169.

24. Ma Haide, "Health for the Ahsi People," *China Reconstructs,* December 1957, p. 24.

25. Ibid., p. 25.

26. *History of the Chinese Communist Party, 1919–1990,* p. 262.

27. Su Ping and Su Fei, pp. 165–166.

28. Letter from Rewi Alley to Edgar Snow, March 19, 1957, Edgar Snow Papers.

29. Horn, pp. 86–87.

30. Letter from Rewi Alley to Edgar Snow, December 27, 1957, Edgar Snow Papers.

16: SHAG AND HIS LEPERS

1. *History of the Chinese Communist Party, 1919–1990,* pp. 268–269.

2. Quoted in Spence, p. 577.

3. Interviews with a number of Chinese residents who joined in these efforts.

4. Quoted in Spence, p. 579.

5. Ma Haide, "Wiping Out Disease by Mass Action," *China Reconstructs,* August 1959, pp. 9–11.

6. Snow, *Red China Today,* p. 276.

7. Ma Haide, "Wiping Out Disease by Mass Action," pp. 9–11.

8. Ibid.

9. Interview with Dai Zhengqi, February 12, 1993.

10. Strong and Keyssar, p. 297.

11. Interview with Yao Wei, Hong Kong, May 18, 1991; letters from Rewi Alley to Edgar Snow and from Ma Haide to Edgar Snow, Edgar Snow Papers.

12. Snow, *Red China Today,* p. 49.

13. Ibid., pp. 276–277.

14. Ibid., p. 261.

15. Interview with Yao Wei, May 18, 1991.

16. Interview with Sydney Rittenberg, November 15, 1990. The charge by Rittenberg that Ma was about to be shut out of important gatherings with Snow cannot be verified, but it again shows the conflicting stories that abound concerning Ma and the difficulty in either proving or disproving many of them. Yao Wei, who was with Snow throughout the four-month trip, says that Ma was

included in Snow's trip from the beginning. "I am sure that Zhou Enlai would know that Ma Haide and Ed Snow were friends before. I don't want to sound contradictory to anybody, but to organize a reception at the Great Hall of the People, the organizers would not include Sydney Rittenberg."

17. Snow, *Red China Today*, p. 269.

18. It is also possible that Snow knew the truth and presented it this way to continue covering his friend. This, however, is unlikely, given Snow's reputation for reporting with integrity. It is more likely he would have left the mention of the passport out of his book had this been the motive.

19. Interview with Chen Hui, February 13, 1993 (Chen Hui served as an interpreter for this session); Hamilton, p. 224.

20. Letter from Rewi Alley to Edgar Snow, November 8, 1960, Edgar Snow Papers. Snow, *Red China Today*, p. 43.

21. Interview with Gladys Yang, February 4, 1993; interview with David and Isabel Crook, February 6, 1993.

22. Interview with Gladys Yang, February 4, 1993.

23. Interview with Hu Daxun, Beijing, February 10, 1993.

24. Ibid.

25. Interview with Yang Lihe, Guangzhou, May 20, 1991.

26. Interview with He Daxun, February 10, 1993.

27. Interview with Yang Lihe, May 20, 1991.

28. Interview with Dai Zhengqi, February 12, 1993.

29. Su Ping and Su Fei, pp. 179–180; interview with He Daxun, February 10, 1993.

30. Interview with Olaf Skinsnes, Guangzhou, May 19, 1991.

31. Ibid.

32. Letter from Rewi Alley to Edgar Snow, May 2, 1961, Edgar Snow Papers.

33. Letter from Edgar Snow to Ma Haide, January 10, 1961, Edgar Snow Papers.

34. Interview with Greg Hatem, July 10, 1992.

35. Interview with Su Fei, February 10, 1993.

36. Su Ping and Su Fei, pp. 141–143.

37. Interview with Su Fei, February 10, 1993. According to Sidney Shapiro (*Ma Haide*, p. 53), Li Lilian returned to her husband after Braun left Yan'an.

38. Su Ping and Su Fei, p. 144.

39. Letter from Ma Haide (Shag) to Shafia and Joseph Hatem, August 25, 1962, now in the possession of Greg Hatem.

40. Su Ping and Su Fei, pp. 144–145; interview with Greg Hatem, July 10, 1992; interview with Marie Hatem, July 11, 1992.

41. Interview with Marie Hatem, July 11, 1992.

42. Su Ping and Su Fei, p. 145.

43. FBI document received through FOIA search.

44. Letter from Anna Louise Strong to Edgar Snow, July 1, 1963, Edgar Snow Papers.

45. State Department document, August 14, 1963, received through the FOIA.

46. Ma Hai-Teh, "Contrast in Equality," p. 7.

47. Ibid., p. 8.

48. USIA document, FOIA search.

49. Strong and Keyssar, p. 320; interview with Sydney Rittenberg, November 15, 1990.

50. Letters from Rewi Alley to Edgar Snow, April 10, August 6, and October 9, 1965, Edgar Snow Papers.

17: THE CULTURAL REVOLUTION—NOT OUR AFFAIR

1. Strong and Keyssar, p. 330.

2. David Milton and Nancy Dall Milton, *The Wind Will Not Subside: Years in Revolutionary China, 1964–1969* (New York: Pantheon Books, 1976), p. 104.

3. Rittenberg and Bennett, p. 288.

4. Ibid,. p. 289.

5. Milton and Milton, p. 104.

6. Ibid., p. 292; Strong and Keyssar, p. 331.

7. *History of the Chinese Communist Party, 1919–1990,* pp. 324, 329; Spence, pp. 603–604.

8. Dimond, *Inside China Today,* p. 137; letter from Rewi Alley to Edgar Snow, November 22, 1966, Edgar Snow Papers.

9. Interview with Su Fei, February 12, 1993; interview with Yang Lihe, May 20, 1991.

10. Foreign Broadcast Information Service (FBIS) vol. 1, no. 114, June 13, 1969.

11. From unpublished "Biographical Note on Dr. Ma Haide (George Hatem)," Ma Haide personal papers.

12. Su Fei and Su Ping, p. 176.

13. Ibid.

14. Milton and Milton, p. 214.

15. Interview with Sydney Rittenberg, November 15, 1990.

16. Interview with Ruth Weiss, July 16, 1991.

17. Interview with Su Fei, February 12, 1993.

18. Interview with Sydney Rittenberg, November 15, 1990. In post-liberation China Ma was known to many new foreign friends as George, rather than Shag, which was reserved for old friends and family.

19. Telephone interview with David Milton, August 4, 1991.

20. Interview with David and Isabel Crook, February 6, 1993.

21. Su Fei and Su Ping, p. 175; letter from Rewi Alley to Edgar Snow, December 8, 1969, Edgar Snow Papers.

22. Interview with Sydney Rittenberg, November 15, 1990.

23. Milton and Milton, p. 235.

24. Ibid., pp. 235, 257, 283, 302–304.

25. Interview with Sydney Rittenberg, November 15, 1990.

26. Interview with Yang Lihe, May 20, 1991.

27. Interview with Dai Zhengqi, February 6, 1993; Su Fei and Su Ping, pp. 167–168.

28. Interview with Wang Hongshen, February 6, 1993.

29. Interview with Su Fei, February 10, 1993.

30. Ibid.

31. Su Fei and Su Ping, p. 172.

32. FBI document, FOIA search. As is customary, much of this document is blacked out. However, it is obvious that the investigation focused on a member of Ma's family living in North Carolina in 1967. Due to Joe's earlier meetings with friends of Ma, who were accused of being friendly to the Communist movement, and the fact that Ma's father was by then dead, it is assumed Joe was the one under investigation.

33. Letter from Rewi Alley to Edgar Snow, October 27, 1967, Edgar Snow Papers.

34. Letter from Edgar Snow to "Shag and Su Fei," December 10, 1967, Edgar Snow Papers.

35. Letter from Rewi Alley to Edgar Snow, June 12, 1968, Edgar Snow Papers.

36. Ibid., September 23, 1968.

37. Ibid., May 27, 1969.

38. Ibid., December 8, 1969.

39. Su Fei and Su Ping, p. 169.

40. The May 7 Cadre School, named after a directive issued on that day by Mao Zedong, set up to remold the thinking of intellectuals through physical labor and study sessions called "criticism–self criticism" meetings, where they were to evaluate their deductions on Mao Zedong Thought and socialism.

41. Su Fei and Su Ping, pp. 166–170; interview with Su Fei, February 12, 1993; letter from Rewi Alley to Edgar Snow, January 31, 1970, Edgar Snow Papers.

18: JOE COMES TO CHINA

1. Letter from Edgar Snow to "Shag," March 10, 1970; letter from Rewi Alley to Edgar Snow, March 25, 1970, Edgar Snow Papers.

2. Strong and Keyssar, p. 345.

3. Letter to Edgar Snow from Rewi Alley, April 2, 1970, Edgar Snow Papers.

4. Ibid., April 7 and June 19, 1970.

5. Hamilton, pp. 267–269; notes from Edgar Snow Diary no. 1 from 1970 visit, Edgar Snow Papers.

6. Edgar Snow Diary no. 1, from 1970 trip, Edgar Snow Papers.

7. Hamilton, p. 261.

8. Edgar Snow Diary no. 2 from 1970 trip, Edgar Snow Papers.

9. Letter from Edgar Snow to Shag, June 3, 1971; Edgar Snow Diary no. 2, Edgar Snow Papers.

10. Interview with Huang Hua, August 17, 1992.

11. Edgar Snow, *The Long Revolution* (New York: Random House, 1971).

12. Hamilton, p. 273; Edgar Snow Diary no. 3, from 1970 trip, Edgar Snow Papers.

13. Spence, p. 629.

14. Interview with John Roderick, April 14, 1992.

15. E. Grey Dimond, *More Than Herbs and Acupuncture* (New York: W. W. Norton, 1975), p. 172.

16. Letter from Edgar Snow to Shag, June 3, 1971; letter from Edgar Snow to George, September 11, 1971; letter from Edgar Snow to Jack [Service], December 6, 1971, Edgar Snow Papers.

17. Interview with Marie Hatem, July 11, 1992.

18. Ibid.

19. Interview with Su Fei, Beijing, February 12, 1993; interview with Marie Hatem, July 11, 1992.

20. Letter to Grace and Manny Granich, December 24, 1971, Ma Haide personal papers.

21. Information on Ma Haide's trip to Geneva in 1972 comes from interviews with Su Fei; from Lois Wheeler Snow's accounting of that event in her book *A Death with Dignity: When the Chinese Came* (New York: Random House, 1974); and from Shapiro, *Ma Haide*.

22. Interview with Helen Foster Snow, May 13, 1991.

23. Letter to Manny Granich, August 31, 1972, Ma Haide personal papers.

24. Dimond, *Inside China Today*, pp. 83–84.

25. Letter from Ma Haide to Theresa Hatem Ode, October 11, 1972. Tod Ode keeps this letter close and says that the comments by his Uncle Shag eased the pressure he felt at home and confirmed for him the stand he had taken in striking out on his own as a musician and rebel. To this day, he says, his uncle is his role model.

26. George (Shafick) Hatem, *Early Background*. Unpublished notes from Ma Haide papers and interview with Theresa Hatem Ode, August 29, 1993.

27. Milton and Milton, pp. 371–372; Shapiro, pp. 160–161.

28. Hobart Duncan, "An Evening in Peking with One of the Heroes of China," *Honolulu Star-Bulletin*, June 28, 1973.

29. Shearer, "Dr. George Hatem."

30. Letter to Manny Granich, October 10, 1973, Ma Haide personal papers.

31. *Parade*, January 18, 1987, p. 21.

32. Interview with Mrs. Arelene Duncan, Honolulu, February 22, 1990.

33. Ibid.

34. Letters to Manny Granich, April 6, 1974, January 5, 1975, Ma Haide personal papers.

35. Letter to Manny Granich, January 5, 1975, Ma Haide personal papers.

36. Spence, pp. 642–643.

37. Interview with John Roderick, April 14, 1992.

38. Shapiro, p. 154.

39. Letter to Manny Granich, January 13, 1976, Ma Haide personal papers.

40. FBI documents dated December 23, 1975; January 26, 1976; February 23, 1976; and April 29, 1976, obtained during FOIA search.

41. Su Fei and Su Ping, p. 176; unpublished "Summary of Ma Haide's Medical History" obtained from Dr. Wu Weiran; Dimond, *Inside China Today,* pp. 75–76; interview with Marie Hatem, July 11, 1992.

42. Letter from Song Qingling (Suzi) to Ma Haide (Shag), August 16, 1976, Ma Haide personal papers; interview with Lynette Shi, Honolulu, April 18, 1991.

43. Letter to Manny Granich, November 8, 1976, Ma Haide personal papers.

44. Ibid.

19: SURROUNDED BY COMRADES

1. Letter from Song Qingling to Ma Haide, July 1, 1977, Ma Haide personal papers.

2. Dimond, *Inside China Today,* pp. 99–102.

3. Letter to Manny Granich, September 12, 1977, Ma Haide personal papers.

4. Interview with Dr. Wu Weiran, Shanghai, February 2, 1993; Shapiro, p. 173.

5. Su Fei and Su Ping, p. 177; Shapiro, p. 154.

6. Letter from Song Qingling to Ma Haide, March 9, 1978, Ma Haide personal papers; interview with Wang Guangmei, February 11, 1993.

7. U.S. State Department files, March 31, 1978, obtained through FOIA search.

8. Telephone interview with Leonard Woodcock, October 18, 1990; Shapiro, p. 173.

9. University of North Carolina Alumni "Dope Sheet" for class of 1932, Alumni Office, University of North Carolina, Chapel Hill.

10. University of North Carolina, Chapel Hill, School of Medicine press release, February 9, 1979.

11. Monte Basgall, "Life Spent in China Changing the World," *The News and Observer,* Raleigh, North Carolina, May 10, 1978; Roger Kirkman, "An Account of My Meeting with Dr. George Hatem (Ma Hai-Teh)," unpublished report, May 17, 1978, University of North Carolina Alumni Association files.

12. Interview with Marie Hatem, July 11, 1992.

13. Interview with Greg Hatem, July 10, 1992.

14. Shapiro, p. 181.

15. Interview with Ernie Hatem and Tod Ode, Buffalo, New York, August 27, 1993; Theresa Hatem Ode, unpublished notes, Ma Haide personal papers.

16. Shapiro, p. 174–175; FBI document, January 15, 1980, obtained through FOIA search.

17. Shapiro, p. 181.

18. Hatem, "New Life in China," p. 46.

19. Interview with Israel Epstein, February 8, 1993; interview with Sydney Rittenberg, November 14, 1990.

20. Shapiro, pp. 180–181.

21. Letter from Song Qingling to Ma Haide, December 5, 1978, Ma Haide personal papers.

22. Interview with Wu Weiran, February 2, 1993; unpublished medical record of Dr. Ma Haide, obtained from Wu Weiran; Shapiro, pp. 181–182.

23. Observations and discussion with Ma Haide, from my visit to Beidaihe, summer 1979.

24. Letter from Song Qingling to Ma Haide, October 20, 1979, Ma Haide personal papers.

25. Interview with Ling Qing, February 5, 1993.

26. Interview with Olaf Skinsnes, May 19, 1991.

27. Letter to Manny Granich, June 8, 1981, Ma Haide personal papers.

28. Ibid.

29. Letter to Paul C. Domke, September 2, 1981, Ma Haide personal papers.

30. Ibid.; letter to Manny Granich, September 23, 1981, Ma Haide personal papers.

31. Interview with Dai Zhengqi, February 12, 1993; Su Fei and Su Ping, p. 178.

32. Su Fei and Su Ping, pp. 180–181; Dr. Ma Haide (George Hatem) (Beijing: China Reconstructs Press, 1989), p. 75.

33. FBI document, June 4, 1982, obtained through FOIA search.

34. Su Fei and Su Ping, p. 20; interview with Dr. David Scollard, Honolulu, November 5, 1992.

35. Interview with David Scollard, November 5, 1992.

36. Interview with Dai Zhengqi, February 12, 1993.

37. Interview with Wu Weiran, February 2, 1993; unpublished medical record of Ma Haide, obtained from Wu Weiran.

38. Su Fei and Su Ping, p. 184.

39. "Leprosy Aid Award Goes to Ma Haide," *China Daily,* April 16, 1983.

40. Interview with Wu Weiran, February 2, 1993; interview with Leonard Woodcock, October 18, 1990; FBI document, May 18, 1983, obtained through FOIA search.

41. Interview with Marie Hatem, July 11, 1992.

42. Interview with Leonard Woodcock, October 18, 1990; Shapiro, p. 193.

43. Huang Hua, "The Chinese Revolution Is His Life-long Undertaking: 50th Anniversary of Comrade Ma Haide's Work in China," *People's Daily,* November 23, 1983, p. 3.

44. Letter to Manny Granich, March 17, 1984, Ma Haide personal papers.

45. Ibid.; interview with Marie Hatem, July 11, 1992.

46. Ma Haide, "Fifty Years of Medicine," p. 34; Hatem, "New Life in China," p. 72.

47. Letter to Manny Granich, December 30, 1984, Ma Haide personal papers.

48. Interview with Leonard Woodcock, October 18, 1990.

49. Interview with Dai Zhengqi, February 12, 1993; letter to Paul Domke, October 25, 1985, Ma Haide personal papers.

50. Letter to Paul Domke, October 25, 1985, Ma Haide personal papers.

51. Letter to Grey Dimond, February 22, 1986; letter to Grey Dimond, March 10, 1986, Ma Haide personal papers.

52. City of Buffalo, Executive Chamber Proclamation, May 16, 1986; George Hatem (Ma Haide), *China Reconstructs Press,* p. 97.

53. Lloyd Shearer, "George Hatem and Prostitution in China," *Parade,* June 22, 1986, p. 14.

54. Letter to Grey Dimond, March 11, 1986, Ma Haide personal papers.

55. Dimond, *Inside China Today,* p. 137; interview with Helen Foster Snow, May 13, 1991. Ma was displeased in part, he told one of his nephews, because Dimond had secretly taped their conversation. Information on the request for translation of the book comes from an anonymous interview in Beijing.

56. Letter from Su Fei to Grey Dimond, May 17, 1986, E. Grey Dimond Papers.

57. Letter to Grey Dimond, August 12, 1986; letter to Hobart Duncan, November 3, 1986, Ma Haide personal papers.

58. Letter to Grey Dimond, August 12, 1986; letter to Grey Dimond, September 19, 1986, Ma Haide personal papers.

59. Harold M. Schmeck, "AIDS Research Rivals Share a Major Award," *New York Times,* September 23, 1986, pp. C1, C3.

60. Shearer, "George Hatem and Prostitution in China," p. 14.

61. Letter to Grey Dimond, December 26, 1987, Ma Haide personal papers.

62. Shearer, "George Hatem and Prostitution in China," p. 14.

63. Letter to Max Entell, August 10, 1987, Ma Haide personal papers.

64. Shapiro, pp. 202–203.

65. Ibid., pp. 205–209.

66. Letter from Associate Dean Frederick W. Vogler to Dean Gillian T. Cell, College of Arts and Sciences, University of North Carolina, Chapel Hill, October 6, 1986; letter from Joe Pat Hatem to Associate Dean Vogler, January 26, 1987, Alumni Office, University of North Carolina, Chapel Hill.

67. Letter to Grey Dimond, September 30, 1987, Ma Haide personal papers.

68. Interview with Mrs. Olaf Skinsnes, Guangzhou, May 20, 1991.

69. Letter to Grey Dimond, January 3, 1988, Ma Haide personal papers.

70. Ibid.; letter from Wu Weiran to Grey Dimond, December 29, 1987, Edgar Snow Papers.

71. *Dr. Ma Haide (George Hatem),* China Reconstructs Press, Beijing, 1989, pp. 102, 129, 153.

72. Letter to Theresa Hatem Ode, March 25, 1988; Theresa Hatem Ode

unpublished Family History, Ma Haide personal papers; interview with Wu Weiran, February 2, 1993.

73. Theresa Hatem Ode Family History, Ma Haide personal papers.

74. Interview with Wu Weiran, February 2, 1993; interview with Marie Hatem, July 11, 1992.

75. Interview with Wu Weiran, February 2, 1993; Shapiro, pp. 210–211.

76. Interview with Hu Daxun, February 10, 1993; interview with Wu Weiran, February 2, 1993.

77. Interview with Theresa Hatem Ode, August 29, 1993.

EDGAR A. PORTER first visited China in 1976 as a young American intrigued by the accomplishments of China's revolution. He visited again in 1978, and in 1979 he began a two-year residency in Henan Province, where he taught in a provincial college and experienced the day-to-day adventures of a foreigner in modern China. He was particularly drawn to those few aging foreigners who had thrown in their lot with China and its Communist party in the heady days of the revolution and who chose to stay despite hardships and disappointments.

Today Edgar A. Porter is acting associate dean of the School of Hawaiian, Asian and Pacific Studies at the University of Hawai'i and holds an appointment to the graduate faculty in Asian Studies. He is the author of numerous articles and two previous books on China: *Foreign Teachers in China, Old Problems for a New Generation* and *Journalism from Tiananmen* (ed.). Porter received his bachelor's degree from St. Andrews Presbyterian College and his doctorate from Vanderbilt University.